PREFACE

A perusal of the literature written, speeches given, workshops held and university courses offered that address the changing family indicates by the sheer quantity of production an accelerated interest in what is happening to some of our cherished images of what a family ought to be and to do. Much of what has been written, from our perspective, has centered on the examination of those images by focusing on the main characters without giving attention to the supporting cast. That is, the tendency has been for the main characters within family units to be investigated with less emphasis on the impact that elements outside families have on those units.

However one chooses to define a family—as nuclear, extended, a group of individuals related by blood line, a single individual in a household, a group of individuals related by purpose, and the list goes on and on—no one family unit exists by itself or acts out its life stages by itself. The reality of the family life drama is played on a stage where the scenery is not stationary, the roles are not well defined, and the audience expectation is high. It is our intent to explore that scenery, those roles and expectations—the issues of what families are like today and what the impacts on families are from outside sources. The pain and frustration felt by individuals within families, the stress and strain of divorce, crime, poverty, poor health and a number of other social ills are great. To us these are compounded by and, perhaps, founded on a lack of insight into and understanding of several areas of the environment which have impacts on families.

It is out of this concern that the articles which follow were chosen. The pieces are ordered in such a fashion as to allow one who reads the collection in its entirety to see the relationships between the many selected supporting environments and families who live within those environments. The exploration included in this reader encompasses both positive and negative relationships between individuals, families and the environment.

The first section, entitled "Universal Environmental Elements," is a collection of readings chosen to speak to the point of where we are now, the "givens" that families now work with—in essence, an exploration of the reality of the present environment. From this base, these givens, the other two sections explore selected areas of the environment. It is within these two sections that aspects of the environment currently being questioned are discussed.

The focus of the second section, "Human Needs, Family and Community," is an examination of present views of families and an interface of those views with three selected impacts on families. In addition to the exploration of change and the family model, the discussion

includes concerns about our changing sense of community, the paradox of life support and leisure, and our increased awareness of troubled families. The criterion for selecting these three
impacts was that they were to include those areas of family life over which families can still have
control.

"Government-Family Interlock," the third section, contains articles in which the authors
explore part of the multiple impact of social policy on family life. It is not a discussion of
present social programs; such a discussion will be obsolete as soon as it is published. It is
an analysis of the many kinds of ongoing policies that exist in our social policy structure and
the ways in which the reader can interpret the impacts of those policies. Included because of
the expanse of their impact are discussions of housing, child care and health care and the
aspects of those policies that are supportive of or in conflict with family and individual welfare.
The underlying concern of this section is the extent to which individuals within families are
controlled by persons outside of those families.

In our search for supportive materials for these concerns, we found several articles that
could have been placed in any one of the several sections. We affirm the reader who selects
to rearrange the articles into different categories or to shift readings from one section to
another. The introductions to each section are explanatory of our decisions; we have made no
attempt to cross-reference our choices.

Within the editorial commentaries, we have refrained from speaking of "the family" and
wish the readers to do the same—so that all of us concerned with the study of families can begin
to address ourselves to many kinds of families as the foci of our discussions.

Every attempt has been made to give appropriate credit to authors whose works are presented here; any errors have been unintentional.

We thank our colleagues, friends and families who found references, who shared with us
articles in which they found meaning, and with whose consultation we made the choices of
the readings presented. We acknowledge all those persons whose support and helpfulness have
engendered much in the formation of the book you are reading.

Evelyn Eldridge
Nancy Meredith

Environmental Issues:
Family Impact

Edited by

Evelyn Eldridge
Nancy Meredith

Iowa State University
Ames, Iowa

Burgess Publishing Company
Minneapolis, Minnesota

Consulting Editor to the Publisher

Norma H. Compton
Purdue University
West Lafayette, Indiana

Cover photo by Bruce Buck

Copyright © 1976 by Burgess Publishing Company
Printed in the United States of America
Library of Congress Catalog Card Number
ISBN 0-8087-0518-0

10 9 8 7 6 5 4 3 2 1

CONTENTS

SECTION 3 GOVERNMENT-FAMILY INTERLOCK

UNIVERSAL ENVIRONMENTAL ELEMENTS

Introduction

Introduction

Among the environmental factors that influence the way in which individuals and families work out their lifestyles and life goals, there are four that seem omnipresent. The first of these is the pace of change and the resultant cultural uncertainties in our sense of direction. The industrial revolution, the post-industrial revolution and the age of cybernetics have created some problems in the balance of technology and people. Where the pace of modern life is such that it conflicts with the peace of one's existence, there arises a question of what priorities should be of the first order.

Secondly, an economic reality exists for every individual and collectively for every family. It has a private dimension in one's attitude about the goods and services considered necessary for survival and satisfaction. It has a public dimension in the distribution of those goods and services and in the fact that the "times" directly affect what can be done both in the private domain and on the national scene.

Population growth, an exponential yet unpredictable phenomenon, is the third pervasive influence regarded as a universal "given" in this section. It must be considered in every prediction and policy, whether in a family decision to procreate or a policy decision on use of resources or distribution of goods and services. It is there and it must be dealt with.

The fourth suggested variable affecting all human activity is resource allocation and use. With finite resources, increasing population and growing social needs, we may well have reached a new level of need—recognition of universal interdependence. Let us hope that with a creative citizenry we can recognize priorities and fashion breakthroughs that will give us relief from some of our more vexing environmental problems, rather than adding to the ecological impact of those that we already have.

Commentary—Evelyn Eldridge, ed.

IA SOCIAL CHANGE

Reshaping the American Dream

by Thomas Griffith

Not long ago a handful of middle-level executives, talking informally around a luncheon table in Manhattan, found themselves all agreeing with one of their number who said, "I think children born fifty years ago could look forward to a better future than my children can." On the face of it, that's a pretty shocking observation, for a basic ingredient of the American dream is that the members of each succeeding generation shall be further advanced than their parents in the pursuit of happiness.

These executives were themselves middle class, and probably understood that not every son in Scarsdale, Scottsdale, or Grosse Pointe should be able to do better and live better than his father. When taking off from a fairly high starting point, some will fall instead of rise. But the executives meant more than incomes or titles; they were also talking about the kind of world, the kind of America, their sons and daughters would inhabit. They were not speaking in the put-down vocabulary of our times in which a phrase like "the American dream" can be used only in irony, but from the despair about these times felt by those who are not themselves cynical.

PROMISES FULFILLED

Yet the despair seems, at the least, to be premature. A persuasive case can be made that if the American dream is dead, or dormant, it is because the dream of the fathers has been mostly realized, while the dream of the sons has not yet been successfully formulated. Like all dreams, the American dream has never been easy to describe in the cold light of day. In its traditional form, it included both our purpose as a nation, embodied in such propositions as "liberty and justice for all," as well as the personal goals that echo in the familiar phrase, the land of prom-ise. To all but the most cynical, it will be seen that liberty does extend from sea to shining sea (the cynical are often the best exemplars of it); that justice is now more evenly shared, even by minorities, than at any time in our history; and that the land of promise has proved to be so, not universally, but for successive generations in the millions.

Reprinted with permission from *Fortune,* April 1975, pp. 88, 90, 91, 204.
Thomas Griffith, former editor of *Life,* author of *The Waist High Culture* (1959) and *How True* (1974) is presently a columnist for *Time, The Atlantic,* and *Fortune* magazines.

But dreams achieved become mundane. The achievements bring new problems. Justice more evenly shared has been accompanied by higher crime rates. The great improvements in material well-being often do not satisfy. To have all the dreams that money can buy seems not enough; in the words of Peggy Lee's song: "Is That All There Is?"

Not many Americans are so naive as to think that money automatically brings happiness. They are not experiencing the hedonist's hangover. What seems to be bothering them are some of the practical trade-offs that mass affluence has required. People feel that the vast and impersonal technology that brings them their comforts and satisfies their needs has somehow diminished them as individuals. Most Americans are "better off" than they once were, but are less singular for being so, and feel less individually attended to. They take the wonders of their possessions for granted, and the failures (so different from the TV commercial's glamorous promise) resignedly.

They can be well fed, well clothed, and well sheltered, but live in a pattern indistinguishable from their neighbors: they crowd the same highways, watch the same television shows, queue up at the same supermarket checkout counters. They can afford to travel more and farther because of economies of scale; they fly in jumbo jets to places where hospitality is calibrated, rooms are standardized, and service is chain-management functional. "Getting away from everybody" gets harder and harder as more and more people can afford to try.

The newest dent in the American dream of affluence comes from the discovery that our resources (and the world's) are more finite than we thought. This challenges that delicious American freedom, the right to be prodigal and uncaring—that open, generous, spontaneous attitude sometimes so envied, sometimes so deplored, by more parsimonious and tradition-confined foreigners. Americans have always believed that "there's plenty more where that came from"; you don't divide the wealth, you multiply it. And thus every man's ambitions—to make, to sell, to buy—somehow can be felt to serve the common good.

If rapid growth is no longer the easy answer to our problems, the alternatives to it are difficult for a nation with an economy so attuned to growth. Adding this to so many other matters they worry about, many Americans have lost confidence in what they once regarded as their natural ally, the future.

YEAR TEN OF THE TRANSITION

The contemporary fear of the future might be lessened if it were realized that we are now well into a period of drastic change, rather than just at the beginning edge of it.

The frame of mind that sighs nostalgically for a more assured past seems to regard each current new year as a darkening, and finds confirmation of this belief in some event that is new and horrendous—hijackings, Watergate, Arab oil—which colors the times, but does not really define them. The transitional period we are now in has been going on for at least a decade. It has been five years since the worst campus eruptions; seven since the worst ghetto disorders. The postwar 1945-65 years are now a recognizable historical era, and a radical change in attitudes has taken place since then. In the tenth year of the transition we can be said to be coming to better terms with the way we actually live. We are gaining on disorder, yet without having found an agreed direction.

THE PATIENT YOUNG

But if the future shape of society is far from clear, one prediction is already possible: those parents who fear for the future may find that their children are better prepared to live in it than the parents are.

The young generally seem able to take or leave alone the goodies that society turns out for them; they don't use dress, for example, to mark their place in the pecking order. When a computer fouls up the father's charge accounts, the result may be splenetic rage, and a rush to straighten things out; his son is more apt to toss the bill in the wastebasket and wait for the computer to unsnarl itself. In their casual, slouching patience, the young have adapted creatively to crowded situations.

Their loyalties are internalized, and not given to institutions. Their rejection of hierarchy in society is deep-seated; their scorn of institutions is often cited as proof of honesty and freedom from cant, which it often is, but it also sanctions in some of them the right to "rip off" institutions. To judge by the books they favor and the films they see, they feel empathy only toward the rootless, whom they do not so much admire as sympathize with. Open to new ideas and experiences, they remain opaquely unopen to established values.

Since the young, in their numbers, will be the survivors, their continuing attitudes will inevitably set the tone of the American future. So far, having rejected, ignored, or satirized most of the old values, they have been largely content to rely on the purity of their own intentions as a substitute. They have managed to discredit, in some measure, the country's leadership elites in many fields, but are not yet in position to become leaders themselves, and besides have an in-built resistance to the exercise of authority by anyone, including one another. Their most charitable assumption about anyone in power is that he has been compromised, where he has not been corrupted; and his role is seen to be, in one of their favorite words, manipulative.

The victims of this attack have included anyone—business executives, union leaders, editors, politicians—who had a powerful voice or sat in a powerful chair. And when "the Establishment" came under attack in the violent Sixties, it proved more vulnerable than anyone expected—perhaps because (contrary to the image conjured up by the young) it never really had all that much authority, or never existed as a common body of views.

In any event, successful men in the prime of life found both their authority and their motives challenged. The challenging still goes on. "I can stand the arguments," says the president of a large midwestern university, "if only they didn't question my integrity."

THE ELASTIC INSTITUTIONS

The leadership elite is back in control of day-to-day affairs, even in the universities, but what they have lost, in terms of both self-confidence and a mandate, will not be easy to replace. It can be said of a number of American institutions—as the British political scientist Harold Laski said of the American presidency—that they are surprisingly elastic. These institutions can expand quickly to meet new challenges, but they can also shrink, particularly when there is no broad agreement about what they should be leading us toward. The shrinkage of leadership is both the best evidence and worst symptom of disagreement about a national purpose.

When in trouble the familiar response of most perplexed citizens is to look to the White House for leadership. But the control that presidential leadership often exerts over competing ambitions in our society has been damaged by an unprecedented dozen years that began with John F. Kennedy's assassination and ended with an interim President operating from a fragile political base as the first Chief Executive not elected to national office. Restoration of vigor and trust to the White House is indeed essential if the American dream is to be restored as a working model, but as Laski has said, truly strong presidencies grow not so much from magnetic leadership as from a strong sense in the citizenry of urgent and shared goals.

A case can be made that business leaders have been the real energizers of this materialistic society. Turning its back on Europe's luxuries and privileges, America from the beginning set out to be a working place. With so much to be done, culture was scorned as effete. And thus developed a nation of great egalitarian vigor, crudeness, impulsiveness, hard work, and ambition. Even today, and even among the young, criticisms directed against materialism come up against a stronger demand for goods and services, a stronger need for jobs.

As for the business leadership itself in these uneasy ten years of transition, it has done much to shore up its defenses. It has met, deflected, blunted, or accepted some of the charges that critics have brought against it; it has to a degree changed its way of thinking on many subjects, including pollution, consumerism and minority rights. But in general, it has moved in a manner--giving ground bit by bit--and in a direction it doesn't want to go. Even more unsettling, it is not even clear about the direction, and is thus in no position to lead the way.

POLEMICS IS A GROWTH INDUSTRY

All of which suggests that the country is in for constant hassles between contending claimants for public support, for coalition politics instead of strong leadership. And it suggests a new growth industry of lawyers, lobbyists, and polemicists, all engaged not so much in public relations as in relations between publics. This situation might be celebrated more, as the happy disorder of freedom, if it did not so often lead to an anarchy of powerlessness, in the absence of that most essential ingredient of democracy, common consent.

An absence of common consent in present-day society is in fact what the transition is about. If the Establishment had all the power it was assumed to have, and even if it were prepared to turn over power or leadership to someone else, it could find no one to give the baton to. We have lived with multiple and contending interests before, but never have those interests been so articulate and skilled at getting attention. Those who assault the citadels of the Establishment flaunt the banner of "accountability," demanding a kind of democratic plebiscite on all institutions. They rarely assume responsibility for restoring what they tear down; like the slothful waiter, they shrug: "That's not my table."

"HELL NO, I WON'T GO"

Yet out of this near-anarchic wrangling of the transition years, a new set of attitudes seems likely to emerge. The process can be seen at work in the case of one value—patriotism—that has traditionally been regarded as the very symbol of America's faith in itself.

There has been a decided decline in Americans' sense of their own uniqueness and superiority as a nation. Those who see this as a decline in patriotism (though it is really not that) find abundant evidence in the "Hell No, I Won't Go" attitudes about Vietnam, and the ways in skits, songs, and clothes that the once untouchable American flag has come to be derided. (A genius for the offensive gesture is one of the skills of the television generation.)

But now there is fairly broad agreement that Vietnam was a regrettable overextension of American power, and attitudes about Vietnam seem less an index of patriotism than they did. "Hell No" brings memories of the Oxford Union resolution in 1933 not to fight for King and Country. Seven years later, when Britain's survival was really at issue, those young "I Won't Go's" fought the Battle of Britain.

The kind of patriotism many still sigh for, and want overtly demonstrated by others was really at its most intense a century ago, in another unsettling time. Patriotism then was proud but suspicious, excluding and parochial. The immigrants of many tongues and cultures had to be quickly immersed in a melting pot if America was to survive in its own identity. New York City's school superintendent in 1896 considered it his duty to "fuse and weld" immigrant children into "one homogeneous mass, obliterating from the earliest moment" any trace of the "obstructive, warring, and irritating elements" they brought with them.

The promise of America to the immigrant millions was that their sons could be what they themselves could not. The achievement is that so many have come here, and so few have left. But a more secure and sophisticated America no longer tries so hard to root out what was alien in a person's past. He is free to take pride in that past, and latter-day patriots feel enriched by their country's diverse strains.

AT HOME ABROAD

Any contemporary American holds three memberships. He inhabits a nation, gives obedience to a government, and belongs to a culture. The governmental part—thanks to the constitutional fear of too powerful a state—is often the least consequential part of his activities. His culture is no longer bounded by the Atlantic and Pacific, but gives and takes from everywhere. An American might even concede that in smaller and more homogeneous democratic nations such as the Netherlands and Denmark, the public's affairs are often tended to with more civility and stability than here. If he works abroad, he often finds such societies more congenial to live in, while remaining resolutely American.

Contemporary patriots must also come to terms with the fact that the U.S., while still widely respected abroad, is also the target of a great deal of criticism. One reason for this change is that where once the practical idealism of Jefferson, Thoreau, and Lincoln was our most familiar export, now Americans are a conspicuous economic presence in other countries.

What a pity, too, that at the moment after World War II when the U.S. belatedly accepted its responsibility as a great power, it should have to concentrate its energies on building global alliances in contention with the U.S.S.R. In the process, the American signal to the rest of the world, and to itself, became somewhat less clear.

THE BEACON BECOMES A SHIELD

American foreign policy has always combined idealism and self-interest in a semi-stable mixture. That mixture worked marvelously in the Marshall plan. But as foreign policy came to be defined by the Cold War, foreign aid was soon allocated not to the most needy but to the most exposed of our client states. Occasional attempts to align ourselves with forces of change were failures.

American policymakers came more and more to value order in other countries and allied themselves with those who provided it. The policymakers shut their ears to those whose cries of freedom we would once have responded to. A lot of Americans felt the good name of this nation had thus been damaged. Even among its allies the U.S. seems now less of a beacon and more of a shield.

Carrying the shield was an unpleasant task reluctantly taken up and on the whole successful; times have now sufficiently changed so that the harder edges of that policy are now less called for. A very basic reason for wishing success to detente with the Soviet Union is not just that it will decrease the cost of armaments, or make nuclear war less likely, but that it will bring about a condition in the world where America may once more be true to itself abroad. This is to be on the side of free people, but favoring trade and travel and exchange with all, acting justly itself and concerned with justice everywhere. That still seems a legitimate part of the American dream.

America today appears at a point of intersecting complexities, but this is not the same as describing an America in decline. In fact, the supply of earnest preoccupation with America's direction seems as large as it ever was, though conclusions are more various and less optimistically expressed. Voters are too diverse and prickly in their attitudes to be easily assembled into obedient political machines, which is the way democracy once got its work done. To some degree they reflect that other field of expansion in which America has been so prodigal—education—which develops talents and expands horizons in such numbers as to produce a sense of frustrated possibilities—an educated discontent.

THE LATENT ORDER

The result is not a society gone soft, unpatriotic, or indifferent, but thwarted and baffled. Its members may feel powerless to achieve but can be quite forceful in denying, and they now demand, in a thousand little forays, that all institutions—government and business particularly—pay them heed. They do so in an often sour spirit of scorning piecemeal victories over what they cannot on the whole change.

The bold constitutional decision to place all sovereignty in the people can lead to a great deal of aimlessness when the people are of many minds. And the awareness that so many problems are interlocked, and that even the experts, with all their information, are not agreed on the solutions, makes it harder for any leader to put forward a program with confidence and to amass support for it. These conditions reinforce a general feeling of powerlessness. Sometimes it seems as though the best that can be said for our present circumstances is that all the disputing elements in our society are being thoroughly canvassed.

Yet it is not romantic to insist that, though no politician has lately been able to summon it up, there exists beneath all the apparent divisions in this country a latent order, a wish to reach common decisions, an epoxy of spirit that is well called patriotism. The proof of this spirit, in the midst of uneasy transition, lies in the directions that—despite considerable provocations—the U.S. has not taken. It has recoiled from, rather than responded to, those who would incite the nation to violence; it has been angered by official abuses of power.

Americans uneasily sense some permanent change in their condition, and see more change required of them, even if they are sometimes daunted by the lengthy agenda of what needs doing. In the doing of these things, however, there may yet return a pride in accomplishing them together. The merit of freedom, so instinctive to the American character and not lightly to be surrendered, has always depended on the unforeseen uses that can be made of it. The direction that this nation is now taking is certainly not clear, but then ages like that of the Holy Roman Empire and the Renaissance found their identity, and their names, only long afterward. It may be that for a long time we will be unable to define the new kind of society we are making, but will simply discover ourselves living in it.

IB THE ECONOMIC CLIMATE

Economics in Conflict

by Eber Eldridge

When J. F. Kennedy became President of the United States an almost ritualistic optimism pervaded popular thought. There was abundant faith in our values, in our systems and our ability to achieve our goals. In the 1960s a dramatic change occurred with a growing sense of concern about the future and an increasing skepticism of the inevitability of world-wide material progress. The 1960s will probably be recorded in history as the decade of rebellion. Actions and reactions, both physical and verbal, were commonplace in registering objection to the operation of both the economic and political mechanisms. There was a significant erosion in confidence in our ability to shape the future. During the 1970s this lack of confidence continued, although it became more calm, and contained more reflective thought.

Leonard Silk, a contemporary commentator on the economic scene, has voiced this question. "The soaring prices of oil and other world commodities, the shortage of food, the heightened tension between the developed and the developing countries, the new disease of stagflation—are all these manifestations of a trenchant crisis of something far deeper and more enduring—the approaching end of the world's explosive population and economic growth?" [1]

Similar concerns are emerging as basic issues beneath the day-to-day politics and economics of all nations. The world's cardinal objective seems to be shifting from growth to survival.

The notion of some ultimate limit to economic growth should not be viewed as surprising in an environment of finite resources and infinite wants. Yet the problem did not fully emerge until the publication of *Limits to Growth* in 1972 with its grim prediction that the world could not sustain economic growth forever. That question is still being debated and is followed by a second question challenging the wisdom of pursuing economic growth, even though it might be attainable.

A plethora of writers and commentators have advanced such pronouncements as: (1) economic growth has caused all of society's present problems, (2) economic growth wastes our natural resources and will be an eventual threat to our survival, and (3) economic growth has caused the disintegration of our values, our integrity and our sense of perspective. Many similar accusations implicate the villain, "economic growth."

[1] Leonard Silk, "From Growth to Survival," *New York Times*, November 19, 1974.

Presented by Dr. Eber Eldridge, Professor of Economics, Iowa State University, at the Dean Helen LeBaron Hilton Business and Industry Seminar, College of Home Economics, Iowa State University, 1974.

Dr. Eber Eldridge is Professor of Economics at Iowa State University, Ames, Iowa.

Some of the accusations are true; some are true sometimes; some are completely false.

It is my purpose to sort through the existing confusion surrounding the question of economic growth and add to rational thought. In this article the focus will be on the economic system. But the economic system will be considered within the perspective of these three systems—the economic system, the political system, and the ethics system. All human activity in the world uses these three systems. Appearance, objectives and functions will vary from one nation to another but some form of all three will be used by every nation to carry out its social and economic affairs.

MEASURING ECONOMIC GROWTH

Economic growth or economic progress is usually measured by the gross national product (GNP). The gross national product is the total value of the goods and services produced in the nation in a period of time, usually one year. It is one of the indicators of our economy and has been climbing almost steadily in the past 30 years, exceeding one trillion dollars for the first time in 1971.

GNP, however, is an oversimplified measure of economic progress. It is possible for GNP to increase because of inflation. In that case, we have no additional goods and services, just more costly ones, and we may have more income but no greater purchasing power. Usually, however, the GNP figure is adjusted for increases due to inflation thus giving a purchasing power measure.

In addition to adjusting for inflation, GNP needs to be adjusted for population. The population has been growing in this country and, with more people, you would expect that there would be more goods and services. When GNP is figured on a per person basis, the GNP per person has increased over the past 30 years. In 1958 the GNP per capita was $2,538. In 1973 it was nearly $4,000 measured in 1958 dollars (adjusted for inflation). Thus by any measure the GNP in the United States has been increasing constantly, and each of us on the average has had more goods and services.

Economic growth and population growth should not be confused when measuring progress. The history of the United States shows that economic growth has been associated with population growth—but the two types of growth need not have a positive correlation. For instance, if there is a fixed amount of resources and these resources are the source of most GNP, the GNP per capita might decline with increased population. Many economists have pointed out that the large population base and the rapidly increasing population of China, India, Africa, and Bangladesh (and many other countries) are the primary reasons for the lack of economic growth. The rapidly increasing population makes it nearly impossible to achieve a per capita increase. By the same token it is perfectly possible for a nation to have economic growth and economic progress with a stable or declining population.

ECONOMIC GROWTH VS. QUALITY OF LIVING

Many who have become disenchanted with economic growth in the 1960s and 1970s maintain that economic growth is in conflict with improvement in the quality of living. This statement represents the first of three challenges to the economic system that I would like to examine with you. The proponents of the "no growth" course sincerely believe that pursuing such a course would reduce congestion, eliminate pollution, stop the waste of natural resources, avoid destruction of natural beauty and reduce the hurry, tension, frustration from competition. These are all desirable objectives with which it would be difficult to disagree. But there is certainly no guarantee that a no-growth course will produce these results. Those insisting that such results would automatically follow are promoting an illusion of an "impossible dream" primarily because they are ignoring the potential consequences of a no-growth policy. Perhaps the ignoring of consequences is not deliberate; perhaps a failure to recognize consequences is the result of a lack of understanding of the process of economic growth and the association with quality of living.

In order to make this point more explicit I will use a hypothetical example.

Imagine a nation or economy where no tools exist, technology is absent, productivity is at a very low level and specialization has not occurred. In such a society it would be imperative for everyone to produce his own necessities—food, shelter, and clothing. In Table 1, Stage I, 100 percent of available work time would be required as an input simply for survival. In this agrarian society let's assume that one man has an idea—an invention. Whatever the invention, assume the output of this individual is doubled. Soon the tool will be used by everyone—we have the beginning of technology and specialization. Three very important facts should be noted: (1) tools bring productivity, (2) tools are technology, and (3) technology plus productivity gives us economic growth. The result of this new invention causes the society to move into Stage II, Table 1.

The technology was effective; therefore, only 70 percent of the people are now needed to produce food, shelter, and clothing. Thirty percent are released to do other things. What other things? Twenty percent will produce other new tools to support the agrarian production. Five percent will be used to transport and distribute the materials to the population not involved in producing necessities. The remaining 5 percent in Stage II are not needed for necessities, support or transport.

They begin providing activities to improve the society. Perhaps education, or a form of health care, or a form of recreation, or some other activities emerge. These are activities that are associated with "quality of living." It is important to note that "quality of living activities" did not begin to appear in this society until people were released from producing the necessities by the process known as economic growth.

TABLE 1. ECONOMIC DEVELOPMENT

PERCENTAGE EMPLOYMENT BY SECTOR

Stage	Food, Shelter, Clothing	Support	Transport	Other
I	100	0	0	0
II	70	20	5	5
III	50	15	10	25
IV	20	10	10	60
V	5	5	5	85

We can carry this story further by examining Stages III, IV and V in Table 1. The productivity process continues and the number of people needed to produce food, shelter and clothing for the entire population is steadily reduced by technology, productivity and economic growth. In addition, technology and productivity begin to appear under the support column—the activities which are known as industrialization, manufacturing, etc. show productivity increases. The transport problem becomes larger in Stages III and IV, and more people are employed—but productivity again appears in transportation from Stage IV to V through new methods, new ideas and the use of technology.

The message to be learned from Table 1 is in the final column called "other" which depicts the emergence of social services. Services continue to grow until this employment sector contains 85 percent of the entire work force. The "other" column includes those activities that are often associated with improvement in the quality of living—health care, education, recreation, culture and aesthetics. The principal point in Table 1 is that services emerge after economic growth has released workers from other pursuits.

Although Table 1 is a hypothetical example, it does have a relationship to the real world. In the United States less than 5 percent of the work force produces food. Table 2 shows the change in the work force which has occurred between 1920 and 1970 in the United States. The first grouping, called primary employment, is comparable to the first column used in Table 1. The primary employment was reduced by 72 percent in this period (1920-1970) through the application of technology, the improvement of productivity associated with economic growth. The secondary employment is comparable to the second and third columns in Table 1. This shows an increase of 73 percent in employment.

TABLE 2. EMPLOYMENT CHANGE BY SECTOR IN THE
U.S., 1920-1970

Employment Sector	Percent Change 1920-70
Total Primary	-72.1%
Agriculture Forestry, Fishery Mining	
Total Secondary	+73.1%
Manufacturing Construction Trans. - Util.	
Total Tertiary	+288.9%
Whole - Ret. Trade Finance, Ins., R.E. Bus., Pers. Service Ent., Rec. Services Prof. and Gov. Services	
Total Employment	+87.8%

The tertiary employment is comparable to the final column in Table 1 and is associated with the services. This sector increased by nearly 300 percent in the same period of time.

Economic growth through productivity released workers from other forms of employment and made possible the addition of many services to the society. Economic growth made this possible in two ways—the physical labor was made available for use in the services, and income from increasing productivity made it possible for society to support these additional services.

Therefore, activities such as education, social services, health services, recreational services and cultural activities become possible through the process of economic growth.

Consequences of No-Growth

Now, let us examine the position of the advocates of no economic growth. It has been well demonstrated that it is impossible to "fine tune" the economy to a point of absolute stability. Economic activity will either be advancing or regressing. Therefore, the advocates of no-growth are in effect prescribing a downward turn in the production of goods and services. A no-growth policy might occur for one or more of the following reasons: (1) a reduction in available energy; (2) a reduction in available resources of production; (3) a rapidly increasing population; (4) a change in people's values (referring to a decrease in the desire of the population to purchase goods and services or to pursue economic profits).

The first observable results of a no-growth policy would be a decline in the per capita income. The level of living would decline and unemployment would rise. Most of the service employment occurs in the public sector and is supported by taxes. A casual observance of the political history of the United States tells us what will happen to political thought when incomes decline and unemployment rises. The first demand is to cut public spending. The alternative to reducing public spending would be an increase in payments to the public sector through taxation. If the policy makers listen to popular political demands, spending will be reduced—which means reduced employment in the service sector and reduced services offered to the society.

A political decision of this nature could trigger a chain of events causing a regression from Stage V to Stage IV, and toward the types of economic activities more closely associated with necessity as illustrated in Table 1.

First Conclusion

Therefore, the conclusion from examining the first issue is as follows: continued growth and economic activity is necessary—unless we wish to lower our level of living and reduce the number of services performed.

Advocates of the no-growth policy do not fully recognize the consequences of such a policy. Therefore, it is quite possible that the desire to have no economic growth in order to improve the quality of living could have the converse result—a reduction in the quality of living.

Resource Waste Curtailed

The no-growth advocates have one valid point which should be under-lined, emphasized, and publicized for national policy attention. Historically our economic growth has been associated with the waste, the exploitation and the misuse of resources—especially irreplaceable natural resources. It would be difficult to argue that the waste of resources can continue for any length of time. The controversial and debatable publication, *The Limits to Growth* published in 1972, served one commendable purpose. It focused the world's attention on resource depletion, generating the following conclusion: "If the present growth trends in the world population, industrialization, pollution, food production and resource depletion continue unchanged, the limits to growth on this planet will be reached sometime within the next 100 years. The most probable result will be rather sudden and uncontrollable decline in both population and industrial capacity."

This grim report has been effectively challenged, both in terms of the assumptions used and the accuracy of the procedure. Nevertheless, the basic issue of resource waste and depletion cannot be argued.

However, those who argue that all growth must be stopped because of resource waste ignore the possibility of achieving economic growth in another manner. Economic growth through productivity increase is not necessarily wasteful of resources. It is productivity increase that I have been discussing under the first point in this paper. Economic growth through productivity increase is not well understood by the general public. The GNP can be increased by getting more out of our present resources. This is achieved primarily through the use of new technology and management practices. Economists say that productivity cannot be realized without the use of some new resources. However, if energy were not a problem a large proportion of our materials could be recycled. We would approach a situation where there is a bank of available recycled resources. This would provide economic growth and greatly extend the time that our resources could be used. Therefore, stopping waste, eliminating resource misuse, implementing practices of conservation and recycling does not necessarily mean that economic growth through productivity increase needs to be de-emphasized.

IS OUR ECONOMIC SYSTEM WORKING?

The second issue that I wish to examine is the assertion that our economic system is not working effectively. The proponents of this claim use statistics to show that we have had a tremendous increase in material consumption but not in human happiness. We have not achieved the "good life." They say that many people are richer but less happy. It is true that we can document a rising tide of social discontent. Not all the evidence is conclusive but it does appear that people are either less satisfied or more willing to express their dissatisfaction than in the past decades.

If we were to grant the possibility of some degree of truth in these assertions, one must ask this question: If we are not happy—if we are not finding the good life—is the economic system responsible for this condition? There is justification for posing this question. In order to understand the justification we must realize that all human activity takes place under the influence of three major systems. The first is the ethics system.

The Ethics System

The ethics system is difficult to explain because of its intangibility. Economists have referred to the "moral climate." In simple terms, it refers to basic honesty, the trust and confidence we have in each other and our institutions. The ethics system gives the climate of stability to all human activity. It embraces an understanding that we live by the rules of the system. Without this ethic, without this agreement, paper money would be useless. We would have no credit. Credit cards would be unacceptable. It would be impossible to write a personal check or draw a contract. We would have no confidence in anything without absolute physical value.

Some current commentators on the political scene maintain that the social discontent at the present time is due to the fact that the level of the ethics system seems to be eroding. They point to the Watergate incident, the Lockheed scandal, the problems in the CIA and the FBI. Whether or not our level of ethics is eroding it must be recognized that unless our ethics system gives us a climate of trust, confidence, and stability neither our political nor economic system can operate effectively.

The Political System

Our political system is a mechanism through which our nation express its wants, its goals, its objectives. Our political system is a representative democracy based on the principle of majority rule.

One weakness of the political system is that decisions are made by the voters, yet, the low percentage of voters indicates that decisions are not made by the majority of the populace. In addition, we seldom vote directly on a specific issue. We vote on candidates in accordance to their expressed position on various issues.

As with most systems, there are imperfections and criticisms. Nevertheless, the political system under which we operate is the system through which we express our goals and objectives for the present and for the future.

The Economic System

The third system is our economic system. This is a mechanism through which we produce and distribute our goods and services, and distribute the economic rewards. The economic system is a tool, or a machine, designed to accomplish these purposes. In one sense we could liken this to another machine, the automobile. The automobile can be a very useful, very constructive, very desirable tool to accomplish our business or recreational goals. This same tool, the automobile, can be destructive, it can kill, it can be costly to individuals and society. How the automobile is used (for good and for evil) is not the fault of the automobile, the machine, but rather the responsibility of the driver. As a machine the economic system can be used for good, or it can be used for evil. It is not the fault of the machine (the system) but the responsibility of the driver (the people). Therefore, if we, as a society, are not happy, if we have not achieved the "good life," if competition is ruthless, if economic justice is missing, if we place material things above all else, does the fault belong with the economic system, the machine, or with the driver, the people who operate the economic system?

If the driver (the people) abuses the economic system, if there are victims or consequences, such as poverty, unemployment, monopoly force, political payoffs, these can be corrected. They can be corrected by recognizing and accepting our societal responsibilities. The political legal system gives us the opportunity to express our conscience and correct some of the ills or consequences generated by the individuals in the economic system.

In the past we have used the political system to bring more economic justice into the operation of the economic system. There are three ways in which this has been done. The first is to place more restraints on the people (the driver) who participate in the economic system. These are laws, regulations, penalties for abuses. Secondly, we can modify the machine so it becomes more difficult for individuals to abuse it. This includes such things as anti-trust laws, minimum wage laws, fair practice laws, higher inheritance tax, consumer protection. Thirdly, we can practice more economic justice by assisting the victims of the misuse of the economic system. This is done by unemployment compensation, welfare and special social services.

Second Conclusion

The conclusion is this: There are abuses and there are victims but our three systems operating together can eliminate or correct these abuses if we (the people using these systems) really desire that such abuses be alleviated.

OUR IMPORTANT PROBLEMS ARE NON—ECONOMIC?

The third issue that I would like to examine is the assertion that most of the important problems facing society are non-economic in nature.

It is true that we have many major problems facing us—potential energy shortage, environmental pollution, excess population growth, inefficient population distribution, dwindling natural resources, wasteful and disorganized land use, concentration of wealth and power, increasing poverty, continuing prejudice, growing world-wide cartels.

Some of the above problems are consequences of the operation of our economic machine. Some are consequences of increasing congestion. It is true that they cannot be solved directly by our economic system although a technological breakthrough could be of tremendous assistance.

Need an Economic Base

In the final analysis these are political questions to be dealt with and solved through the political process but—we do need an economic base. Perhaps environmental pollution is a good example to illustrate the need for an economic base.

To a very significant degree, excess pollution occurs because of the absence of any clearcut property rights to the environment. Because the environment is owned by all of us in common this valuable resource has gone unpriced and has been generally regarded as a free good—thus the dumping of waste into the environment carrying no explicit monetary costs for the polluters. Their economic activities were priced at less than full cost. But growing concern over environmental pollution has initiated action by society to remedy the problem. Such devices as direct controls regulating the discharge of waste into the environment are being used with growing frequency. In addition there are many examples of internalizing or including pollution abatement costs in the cost of production. In these instances, pollution intensive goods are made more expensive and consumption of them is thereby reduced, and pollution intensive methods of production are made more costly as well as providing incentives to producers to seek methods of pollution abatement. So we are in the process of making adjustments for reducing environmental pollution.

To those who would argue that the cost of a healthy environment is prohibitive Solow suggests, "The annual cost that would be necessary to meet decent pollution abatement standards by the end of the century is large but not staggering. One estimate says that in 1970 we spent about $8½ billion (in 1967 prices) or about one percent of GNP for pollution abatement. An active pollution abatement policy would cost perhaps $50 billion a year by 2000 which would be about two percent of GNP by then. That is a small investment of resources. You can see how small it is when you consider that GNP grows by four percent per year on the average. Cleaning up the air and water would entail a cost that would be like losing one-half of one year's growth between now and the year 2000. What stands between us and a decent environment is not the curse of industrialization, not the unbearable burden of cost, but just the need to organize ourselves consciously to do some simple and knowable things. Compared with the possibility of an active abatement policy, the policy of stopping economic growth in order to stop pollution would be incredibly inefficient."[2]

Perhaps a hypothetical illustration would help clarify the need of an economic base for pollution control. Let's assume that our level of living is $100. In order to clean up all air and water pollution, let's assume there would be a pollution abatement cost of $10.

In this situation we have three alternative courses of action: (1) ignore pollution; use GNP as we always have; (2) reduce the level of living to $90 and spend $10 for pollution abatement; (3) conserve natural resources, improve productivity, increase level of living to $111. Pollution control would increase slightly to $11. This would leave our level of living at $100, unchanged compared to what it was before pollution abatement control.

This simple example illustrates how an economic base and economic growth would be necessary in order to correct pollution without lowering our level of living. We needed an economic base in Table 1 (the efficient production of food, shelter, and clothing); we needed increasing growth in that base through productivity in order to provide services and amenities, "the good life."

---

[2]Robert M. Solow, "Is the End of the World at Hand?" in *The Economic Growth Controversy*, ed. Andrew Weintraub et al. (White Plains, N.Y.: International Arts and Sciences Press, 1973).

Third Conclusion

Similarly, we need an income base and improving growth (via productivity) if we are to deal with our future problems without reducing our level of living—even though those future problems are largely non-economic in nature.

IC POPULATION DYNAMICS

Population and the American Future:
The Commission's Final Report

by Richard Lincoln

*Our immediate goal is to modernize demographic behavior in this country;
to encourage the American people to make population choices, both in the
individual family and society at large, on the basis of greater rationality
rather than tradition or custom, ignorance or chance. This country has already moved some distance down this road; it should now complete the
journey. The time has come to challenge the tradition that population
growth is desirable: What was unintended may turn out to be unwanted,
in the society as in the family.* – Population and the American Future,
Chapter 1.*

A conscious government policy to help "improve the quality of life" by gradually slowing
and eventually halting U.S. population growth was recommended by the Commission on Population Growth and the American Future. The Commission's final report was delivered to the
President and the Congress in March after two years of deliberation. The 24-member panel
pointed out that "at a minimum, we will probably add 50 million more Americans by the end
of the century" as an echo-effect of the post-World War II 'baby boom'. Beyond that, the
Commission held, continued growth would confer no possible benefit to the nation or its
people, while it would aggravate some of our most pressing social and economic problems..
Slower growth, the Commission stated, will not eliminate these problems, "but it will reduce the urgency, the 'crash program' character of much that we do. It will buy time for the
development of sensible solutions."

The Commission members emphasized that while slower growth "provides opportunities,
it does not guarantee that they will be well used. It simply opens up a range of choices we
would not have otherwise .... Successfully addressing population requires that we also address our problems of poverty, of minority and sex discrimination, of careless exploitation of
resources, of environmental deterioration, and of spreading suburbs, decaying cities, and
wasted countrysides."

* New American Library, New York, 1972

Reprinted with permission from *Family Planning Perspectives,* Vol. 4, No. 2, 1972.

The Commission pointed out that the country could "cope with rapid population growth for the next 30 to 50 years. But doing so will become an increasingly unpleasant and risky business . . . adopting solutions we don't like . . . before we understand them."

The Commission, therefore, called upon the nation to "welcome and plan for a stabilized population," emphasizing that "achievement of population stabilization would be primarily the result of measures aimed at creating conditions in which individuals, regardless of sex, age, or minority status, can exercise genuine free choice. This means that we must strive to eliminate those social barriers, laws, and cultural pressures that interfere with the exercise of free choice and that governmental programs in the future must be sensitized to demographic effects."

While advocating an eventual average two-child family, the panel stated that this average could — and ought only — be obtained by voluntary means with "respect for human freedom, human dignity, and individual fulfillment; and concern for social justice and social welfare. To 'solve' population problems at the cost of such values would be a Pyrrhic victory . . . ."

DIVERSITY ENCOURAGED

The Commission indicated that an average two-child family may be achieved "by varying combinations of nonmarriage or childlessness" combined with "substantial percentages of couples who have more than two children." The Commission found it "desirable" that stabilization be attained "in a way which encourages variety and choice rather than uniformity."

In the long run, average zero population growth, the panel pointed out, "can only be achieved . . . with fluctuations in both directions." If, through individual informed free choice, the population grows at less than the replacement level for a period of time "we should prepare ourselves not to react with alarm, as some other countries have done recently (e.g., Japan and Rumania) when the distant possibility of population decline appears." Indeed, the Commissioners found, "there might be no reason to fear a decline in population once we are past the period of growth that is in store," and, "in any event it is naive to expect that we can fine-tune such trends." Certainly, we should not withhold the means to prevent or terminate unwanted pregnancies since "a nation's growth should not depend on the ignorance or misfortune of its citizenry."

Of the many possible paths to achievement of population stabilization, the Commission stated its preference for a gradual course "which minimizes fluctuations in the number of births; minimizes further growth of population; minimizes the change required in reproductive habits and provides adequate time for such changes to be adopted; and maximizes variety and choice in life styles, while minimizing pressures for conformity." Population stabilization could not be reached quickly, the panel pointed out, without social and economic disruption caused by an "accordion-like continuous expansion and contraction" of average family size over the next several decades.

One such "optimal path," which could achieve replacement fertility in 20 years and population stabilization at 278 million in 50 years (excluding the effect of immigration), would involve:
- a decline in the proportion of women becoming mothers from 88 to 80 percent,
- a decline in the proportion of parents with three or more children from 50 to 41 percent,
- an increase in the proportion of parents with one or two children from 50 to 59 percent,
- an increase of two years in the average age at which a mother bears her first child,
- an increase of less than six months in the average interva between births.

ACT NOW TO BUILD ON CURRENT TRENDS

The Commission found cause for belief that "something close to an optimal path can be realized" providing that deliberate action which can encourage desirable trends is taken quickly. Favorable developments cited by the panel include: a historic long-term decline in average family size (temporarily interrupted by the post-World War II baby boom); continued birthrate declines over the last decade despite the coming to reproductive age of the baby-boom babies; improvements in the employment and social status of women; mounting public concern over the negative effects of population growth; a decline in the number of youthful marriages; preferences by younger couples for smaller families than their elders desired; improved effectiveness of contraceptives; increased access to legal abortions; the experience of at least 10 other countries which have, in the last half-century, experienced periods of replacement fertility.

The panel warned, however, that if its recommendations were not adopted quickly, instead of encouraging a desirable trend "we may find ourselves in a position of trying to reverse an undesirable trend."

The Commission cited several "unfavorable elements which threaten the achievement of stabilization," including the potential for a repeat baby boom; our "ideological addiction to growth"; "pronatalist" laws and social institutions, including mass media projections of stereotypical women's roles; restrictions on availability of contraception, sex education and abortion; reawakened fear of 'race suicide', such as occurred during the Depression.

Action now is also important, the report stated, because the 1970s are probably a "critical . . . decade in the demographic transition . . . involving changes in family life and the role of women, dynamics of the metropolitan process, the depopulation of rural areas, the movement and the needs of disadvantaged minorities, the era of the young adults produced by the baby boom, and the attendant question of what their own fertility will be—baby boom or baby bust."

POLICY RECOMMENDATIONS

The Commission indicated that it sought to make policy recommendations which were technically, politically and economically feasible; recommendations which, while speaking to population issues, embodied goals "either intrinsically desirable or worthwhile for reasons other than demographic objectives."

To move the nation toward realization of these goals, the Commission assessed a broad range of current policies and programs and recommended a comprehensive set of changes in existing policies or adoption of new policies. The Commission's principal recommendations called for:

• elimination of involuntary childbearing by substantially improving the access of all Americans (regardless of marital or socioeconomic status) to effective means of fertility control;

• the improvement of the status of women;

• more education about population, parenthood, sex, nutrition, environment and heredity;

• maintenance of foreign immigration levels, and more rational guidance of internal migration to metropolitan areas;

• increased biomedical research in human reproduction and contraceptive development;

• more and better demographic research, including social and behavioral research, and census reporting, and statistical reporting and evaluation of family planning services; and

• organizational changes in government necessary to attain the recommended objectives.

INVOLUNTARY CHILDBEARING

Some dozen of the Commission's major recommendations were designed to enable "all Americans, regardless of age, marital status, or income . . . to avoid unwanted births." The panel pointed out that while most couples plan to have between two and three children, because of "youthful marriage, far-from-perfect means of fertility control, and varying motivation, many of these couples will have children before they want them and a significant fraction will ultimately exceed the number they want." Citing the 1970 National Fertility

Study, the panel pointed out that of all births to currently married women between 1966 and 1970, "15 percent were reported by the parents as having never been wanted." An additional 29 percent were reported as having been born before the parents wanted them. Thus, a total of 44 percent of all births to married couples in those five years were unplanned (see Table 1). The Commission made a "conservative" estimate from these findings that "2.65 million births occurring in that five-year period would never have occurred had the complete availability of perfect fertility control permitted couples to realize their preferences." The panel pointed out that the incidence of unwanted fertility, with its "enormous" financial, social, health and psychological costs, remained highest for the poor and the poorly educated. "Mainly because of differences in education and income — and a general exclusion from the socio-economic mainstream — unwanted fertility weighs most heavily on certain minority groups," such as blacks and, "probably," Puerto Ricans, Mexican Americans and Indians, as well. (Thus, the panel reported, "if blacks could have the number of children they want and no more, their fertility and that of the majority white population would be very similar.")

TABLE 1. UNWANTED FERTILITY IN THE UNITED STATES, 1970*

Race and Education	Most Likely Number of Births per Woman	Percent of Births 1966-1970 Unwanted	Percent of Births 1966-1970 Unplanned (including unwanted)	Theoretical Births per Woman without Unwanted Births
All Women	3.0	15	44	2.7
College 4+	2.5	7	32	2.4
College 1-3	2.8	11	39	2.6
High school 4	2.8	14	44	2.6
High school 1-3	3.4	20	48	2.9
Less	3.9	31	56	3.0
White Women	2.9	13	42	2.6
College 4+	2.5	7	32	2.4
College 1-3	2.8	10	39	2.6
High school 4	2.8	13	42	2.6
High school 1-3	3.2	18	44	2.8
Less	3.5	25	53	2.9
Black Women	3.7	27	61	2.9
College 4+	2.3	3	21	2.2
College 1-3	2.6	21	46	2.3
High school 4	3.3	19	62	2.8
High school 1-3	4.2	31	66	3.2
Less	5.2	55	68	3.1

* Based on data from the 1970 National Fertility Study for currently married women under 45 years of age. Source: Population and the American Future, p. 164.

While only one percent of the first births were reported by their parents as having never been wanted, nearly two-thirds of sixth and higher order births were so reported; these births were concentrated in the later years of childbearing, the Commission found, where mother and child are at greatest risk of death or damage. Eliminating unwanted births in the older ages would also sharply reduce the incidence of such hereditary diseases as mongolism. Similarly, the Commission pointed out, 17 percent of all births occur to teenagers at a time when the likelihood of adverse health and social consequences for mother and infant is much greater than if the birth were postponed to the years between 20 and 35. The postponement of these early mistimed births to later ages could result in a "distinct improvement in the survival, health, and ability" of the children born.

So "that only wanted children are brought into the world," the Commission adopted a series of recommendations to:

- provide full financing of all health services related to fertility,
- enact affirmative state statutes providing for abortion on request,
- extend the family planning project grant programs,
- eliminate legal restrictions on access to contraceptive information and services,
- increase investment in reproductive research and contraceptive development,
- eliminate administrative restrictions on voluntary contraceptive sterilization,
- develop programs to train required medical and paramedical personnel to deliver fertility-related health services,
- develop programs of family planning education.

LEGAL RESTRICTIONS

Twenty-two states have laws restricting or regulating the sale, distribution, advertising or display of contraceptives, and six more have restrictions on selling or advertising prophylactics. These laws range from prohibition of contraceptive sales to the unmarried in Massachusetts and Wisconsin (recently declared unconstitutional by the U.S. Supreme Court) to laws prohibiting sale of contraceptives or prophylactics through vending machines, advertising them on outdoor billboards or even displaying them in drugstores. The Commission held that such laws "inhibit family planning education as well as family planning programs, and/or impinge on the ready availability of methods of contraception to the public. By prohibiting commercial sales, advertising displays, and the use of vending machines for nonprescription contraceptives, they sacrifice accessibility, education, and individual rights . . . ."

The Commission recommended that states not only "eliminate existing legal inhibitions and restrictions on access to contraceptive information, procedures, and supplies," but "develop statutes affirming the desirability that all persons have ready and practicable access" to them.

The Commission pointed out that some three million couples in the childbearing years had, by 1970, elected contraceptive sterilization; this comprised nearly one in five couples able to bear children who did not want to have any more. Despite the great — and increasing — popularity of this method of family limitation, the Commission pointed out that many physicians would not perform such operations because of fear that they might be sued or prosecuted, and many hospitals imposed requirements limiting the operation to persons of specified age or previous parity. The Commission recommended that all such requirements be eliminated so that the decision for contraceptive sterilization "be made solely by the physician and patient."

The Commission found that "the various prohibitions against abortion throughout the United States stand as obstacles to the exercise of individual freedom: the freedom of women to make difficult moral choices based on their personal values, the freedom of women to control their own fertility, and finally, freedom from the burdens of unwanted childbearing." The Commission also held that such prohibitions "violate social justice," forcing women to bear unwanted children, or to undergo dangerous and illegal abortions to avert unwanted births, with less burden on the rich woman — who has had access to medically safe, and expensive, abortions—than the poor woman, "forced to risk her life and health with folk remedies and disreputable practitioners."

The Commission stated that "abortion on request" in New York, California and eastern European countries brought the procedure "from the backrooms to the hospitals and clinics" with consequent reductions in illegal abortions and resultant maternal mortality. (Thus, in New York City, maternal mortality rates "dropped by two-thirds the year after abortion became available on request . . . [and] there is no reason to suspect that the maternal death ratio will continue to decline.") The Commission also pointed to evidence that New York's abortion law had sharply reversed illegitimacy rates, which had been rising since first recorded in 1954. (There were nearly 10 percent fewer out-of-wedlock births for the first nine months of 1971 in New York City as compared to the same months in 1970.)

Legalizing abortion would also "exert a downward influence on the United States birthrate," the Commission predicted, based on the evidence in New York City. (New York showed a 12 percent decline in births in 1971 over 1970 — three times the national decline.) The panel warned that "abortion should not be considered a substitute for birth control, but rather as one element in a comprehensive system of maternal and infant health care." It affirmed that "contraception is the method of choice for preventing an unwanted birth," and predicted that "with the increasing availability of contraceptives and improvements in contraceptive technology, the need for abortion will diminish." At the present time, however, the more than half-million legal abortions and "an unknown number of illegal abortions" performed in the year ending June 30, 1971 indicate that there is still a widespread "social and personal failure in the provision and use of birth control," and many Americans still "must resort to abortion to prevent an unwanted birth."

For these reasons, the majority of the Commissioners affirmed that "women should be free to determine their own fertility, that the matter of abortion should be left to the conscience of the individual concerned, in consultation with her physician and that states should be encouraged to enact affirmative statutes creating a clear and positive framework for the practice of abortion on request."

The Commission recommended that "with the admonition that abortion not be considered a primary means of fertility control . . . present state laws restricting abortion be liberalized along the lines of the New York State Statute, such abortions to be performed on request by duly licensed physicians under conditions of medical safety."

The Commission also recommended that "federal, state, and local governments make funds available to support abortion services in states with liberalized statutes [and] that abortion be specifically included in comprehensive health insurance benefits, both public and private."

Dissents from the majority recommendation on abortion—on various grounds*—were registered by five of the 24-member panel: Alan Cranston, John N. Erlenborn, Paul B. Cornely, Grace Olivarez and Marilyn Brant Chandler.

---

* Mrs. Chandler advocated reform of abortion laws which restrict abortion to conditions which threaten the pregnant woman's life; she favored abortion requested by a woman and approved by her physician and a hospital committee, performed in a hospital or clinic, when the gestation period does not exceed 18 weeks. Congressman Erlenborn, Dr. Cornely and Miss Olivarez opposed abortion as "destruction of human life." Senator Cranston decried the "inconsistencies and inequities" in existing state abortion laws, but said he could not join in the Commission's recommendation because of the "social and ethical implications of such action now."

REPRODUCTIVE, CONTRACEPTIVE RESEARCH

Unwanted pregnancies will continue to occur, the Commission declared, until methods of fertility control are made universally available which are "safe and free of any adverse reactions; effective, acceptable, coitus-independent, and accessible commercially rather than medically; and inexpensive, easy to use, and reversible. This goal will be reached only if research efforts equal the magnitude of the task." The report stated that while the pill and the IUD "represented significant breakthroughs in a field which has been largely neglected by science for most of human history," in terms of the potential technology which should be feasible, these methods remain "fairly primitive." This, the Commission said, is because "our knowledge of basic reproductive biology is inadequate." We do not yet know "the role and functioning of the ovary and the testes, of the egg and the sperm, of the process of fertilization itself, and the normal course of gestation." In addition to such basic investigation, far more effort than is currently being expended must be devoted to development of new contraceptive methods and evaluation of the safety and effectiveness of existing ones. The Commission found the $75 million for 1973 research expenditures projected by DHEW's Five-Year Plan "modest" in terms of the need, but "far above the total amounts requested" for this purpose by DHEW – only $44.8 million for FY 1973. "This amount is far too small," the panel declared, "for a task which is crucial both in dealing with the population problem and in improving the outcome of pregnancy for women and children." The Commission projected that at least $250 million annually would be needed for population-related research: $100 million (in federal funds) for basic biomedical research in human reproduction, $100 million (mostly in federal funds) for developmental work on methods of fertility control, and at least $50 million (in federal funds) for behavioral and operational research.

The Commission recommended that "this nation give the highest priority to research in reproductive biology and to the search for improved methods by which individuals can control their own fertility." The panel called for the appropriation and allocation in FY 1973 of the full $93 million authorized for this purpose," rising to "a minimum of $150 million by 1975; and that private organizations continue and expand their work in this field."

UNWANTED BIRTHS AND THE POOR

The 1965 and 1970 National Fertility Studies showed that while all socioeconomic groups experience unwanted pregnancies, "they occur most often and have the most serious consequences among low-income couples." Since 1967, the Commission report pointed out, the federal government has sought to increase the availability of family planning to low-income couples, largely through project grant programs carried out by DHEW's National Center for Family Planning Services and by the Office of Economic Opportunity. "With a relatively modest federal investment, organized family planning programs have succeeded in introducing modern family planning services to nearly 40 percent of low-income persons in need." To reach the majority of those in need who remain unserved, the Commission reported, "will clearly require additional federal authorizations and appropriations as well as increased support for these programs from state and local governments, and from private philanthropy." The Commission estimated that perhaps $50 million annually might be forthcoming for family planning services from state and local governments and private sources and urged more financial support from these sources; the bulk of the funds, however, will have to come from the DHEW and OEO project grant programs. Specifically, the Commission recommended new legislation to extend the current family planning project grant program under Title X of the Public Health Service Act from FY 1973 to FY 1978, and provide "additional authorizations to reach a federal funding level of $225 million in fiscal year 1973, $275 million in fiscal year

1974, $325 million in fiscal year 1975, and $400 million thereafter . . . ." It also recommended maintenance of the project grant authority under Title V of the Social Security Act beyond 1972 at the current level of funding (about $30 million annually), and continuation of OEO family planning programs "at current levels of authorization" (about $21.5 million annually).

The Commission urged that "no means test be applied in the administration of these programs. Their purpose must be to enlarge personal freedom for all, not to restrict its benefits only to the poorest of the poor." The Commission pointed out that "there are many nonpoor individuals who need but who do not receive adequate fertility control services" who may become poor through unwanted childbearing if they are denied services.

The panel considered and rejected proposals to revise tax policies, or provide financial incentives — or disincentives — to encourage couples to have small families, or to discourage them from having large families. "Clearly, no proposal to penalize childbearing or reward nonchildbearing can be acceptable in a situation in which fertility control is not completely reliable and large numbers of unwanted births occur." The Commission pointed out that, in practice, proposed bonus payments for not bearing children, and withdrawal of public benefits from those who bear too many, have been directed toward the poor, and "almost without exception . . . toward one group — welfare recipients."

What is more, all proposals to penalize childbearing — even those not specifically directed at the poor — "have the effect of penalizing the child and his siblings."

In addition to dismissing such proposals on the grounds of social equity, the Commission dismissed the frequently asserted claim that "Because assistance payments are based upon the number of children in the family, welfare mothers have more children in order to increase their monthly payment." The panel added that there is no "evidence that present tax policies and public expenditures promote the birth of additional children in any social class." Rather, the Commission found, "the reverse might be true." As an example, the panel cites the fact that births to welfare mothers in New York City declined from 18.9 percent in 1959, when payments were low, to 11.3 percent in 1970 when the payments were much higher; and for the nation as a whole the average family size of welfare recipients declined between 1967 and 1969, a period when welfare payments were increasing.

The Commission also reviewed — and rejected — various proposals to require parents to assume all or a greater proportion of the costs of their children by withdrawing subsidies for education, health and social services; levying a fee for childbearing or providing a bonus for not having children; or relieving nonparents of some or all of the tax costs of education, health, and other services for children. "The only reason to alter present policies which are supportive of children," the panel said, "would be if an even higher good were to be served. We cannot foresee any goal with a higher priority than insuring the welfare of future generations."

FERTILITY—RELATED HEALTH SERVICES

In order that "future generations of Americans . . . be born wanted by their parents, brought into the world with the best skills that modern medicine can offer, and provided with the love and care necessary for a healthy and productive life," the Commission recommended "a national policy and voluntary program to reduce unwanted fertility, to improve the outcome of pregnancy, and to improve the health of children." To implement this program, the Commission urged that public and private health financing mechanisms pay the full cost of all fertility-related health services, including prenatal delivery and postpartum services, pediatric care for the first year of life, contraception, voluntary sterilization, safe termination of unwanted pregnancy and medical treatment of infertility.

The Commission estimated the total cost for such a program to range from $6.7 to $8.1 billion annually in the next five years, but pointed out that all but about $1 billion of this total cost is already being financed (although these critical services are distributed unevenly, with many persons receiving only some of them or receiving services of poor quality).

The Commission added that the "costs . . . would, in all probability, be more than offset by the benefits to individuals and society of the delivery of healthy children and the prevention of unwanted pregnancies." The panel held that the financing of these services "could easily be integrated into current publicly administered health financing systems, and made part of a new comprehensive national health insurance system. Congress should include this coverage in any health insurance system it adopts."

Covering the costs of such a program would not guarantee the delivery of these services to those in need of them, the Commission pointed out, declaring that "systematic attention" must also be given "to the organization and delivery" of the services. To accomplish this, the Commission recommended that programs be created to train doctors, nurses and paraprofessionals in the provision of all fertility-related health services, develop new patterns for the use of such personnel, evaluate improved methods of organizing service delivery, and establish the capacity to provide services in areas which have few health resources.

TEENAGE SERVICES AND EDUCATION

A number of the recommendations in the Commission report were addressed to meeting the health and social problems leading to and resulting from adolescent pregnancy.

The Commission cited a recent national study by Drs. John Kantner and Melvin Zelnick of Johns Hopkins University, which showed that 27 percent of unwed girls 15-19 years of age had already experienced some sexual intercourse. This rose from 14 percent of 15 year-old girls to 44 percent of 19-year-olds. Only 20 percent of sexually active teenage girls used contraceptives regularly, with the majority using them not at all or seldom (although almost all of them had heard about the pill). "Such a low incidence of contraceptive use," the report stated, "is particularly significant when less than half of these girls knew when during the monthly cycle a girl can become pregnant." Significant rates of sexual activity and little use of contraception among teenagers have led to rising rates of adolescent pregnancy, venereal disease, illegitimacy, forced (and unstable) marriage and recourse to abortion, the report stated.

The Commission pointed to the fact that out-of-wedlock adolescent birthrates had increased as much as threefold between 1940 and 1968 and venereal disease had become "epidemic." In 1968 more than 600,000 infants — 17 percent of all births — were born to teenagers; and one-fourth of girls who recently reached their twentieth birthday had already borne a child. At best, the Commission pointed out, adolescent pregnancy — especially in the early teens — involves serious health and social consequences — far more severe than for women over 20. The infants of these young mothers "are subject to higher risks of prematurity, mortality, and serious physical and intellectual impairments than are children of mothers 20 to 25." Those girls who bear a first child at an early age — inside or outside of marriage — tend to bear subsequent children at a rapid rate. ("Sixty percent of girls who had a child before the age of 16 had another baby while still of school age.") Education and employment opportunities of these girls are likely to be seriously impaired. ("Pregnancy is the number one cause for school drop-out among females in the United States.") The psychological effects, the report states, "are indicated by a recent study that estimated that teenage mothers have a suicide rate 10 times that of the general population."

The Commission attributed much of the recent rise in adolescent pregnancy — with all its attendant social and health problems — to the denial of accurate information about sexuality, parenthood and birth control and the inaccessibility of effective birth control services.

The Commission was highly critical of those "well-organized and vocal" opponents of sex education who, to the panel members' "regret," had "successfully forestalled sex education in

13 states." Keeping youngsters in ignorance, the Commission members stated, "does not serve to prevent sexual activity, but rather promotes the undesirable consequences of sexual behavior — unwanted pregnancy, unwanted maternity, and venereal disease."

The Commission urged that "funds be made available to the National Institute of Mental Health to support the development of a variety of model programs in human sexuality" based both in schools and the community. The panel recommended that "sex education be made available to all, and that it be presented in a responsible manner through community organizations, the media and especially the schools." Because of the "serious social and health consequences involved in teenage pregnancy and the high rates of teenage out-of-wedlock pregnancy and venereal disease," the Commission also urged "the elimination of legal restrictions on access to contraceptive and prophylactic information and services by young people." It recommended that "states adopt affirmative legislation" permitting minors to receive such information and services "in appropriate settings sensitive to their needs and concerns." It asked that organizations such as the American Law Institute, the American Bar Association and the Council on State Governments "formulate appropriate model statutes."

The Commission urged that not only should "birth control services and information be made available to teenagers . . . regardless of age, marital status, or number of children," but that there be implemented "an adequately financed program to develop appropriate family planning materials, to conduct training courses for teachers and school administrators, and to assist states and local communities in integrating information about family planning into school courses such as hygiene and sex education."

While stressing "the necessity of minimizing adolescent pregnancy by making contraceptive information and services available" to sexually active youth, the Commission urged that adolescents who do become pregnant "not be stigmatized and removed from society." It urged that "school systems . . . make certain that pregnant adolescents have the opportunity to continue their education, and that they are aided in gaining access to adequate health, nutritional, and counseling services." It also held that the "word 'illegitimate' and the stigma attached to it have no place in our society." The panel recommended that "all children, regardless of the circumstances of their birth, be accorded fair and equal status, socially, morally, and legally." It called for "revision of those laws and practices which result in discrimination against out-of-wedlock children."

EDUCATION IN POPULATION, FAMILY LIFE AND HUMAN REPRODUCTION

In addition to sex and birth control education, the Commission made numerous other recommendations in the educational field to help young people "make rational, informed decisions about their own and their descendants' future . . . ."

The Commission called for a program of population education to provide young people with "knowledge about population processes, population characteristics, the causes of population change, and the consequences of such change for the individual and for the society." The Commission could find "no evidence that anything approaching an adequate population program now exists in our schools. Very few teachers are trained in the subject and textual materials are scant and inadequate." Citing evidence that "federal funds amounting to $25 million over the next three years are needed in this field," the panel pointed out that no appropriations have been made under authorization which has existed for the past two years, and that DHEW has requested only $170,000 for population education in FY 1973.

The Commission recommended the enactment of a Population Education Act "to assist school systems in establishing well-planned population education programs so that present and future generations will be better prepared to meet the challenges arising from population change." It asked that federal funds be appropriated for teacher training, curriculum development, materials preparation, research and evaluation, support of "model programs," and for assisting state departments of education to "develop competence and leadership in population education."

At the college level, the Commission urged that population study be included in all introductory social science courses.

The panel advocated education for parenthood, encompassing "a diversity of styles of family life in America today," including acceptance "without stigma" of those individuals who choose to remain childless. It urged that young people be made aware of the real costs of raising children, both emotional and financial (the latter estimated to average $60,000 from birth through college for a first child): "With some idea of the financial demands of children, parents can plan ahead and be better prepared to provide the kind of life they want for their children."

The Commission chided the mass media for depicting family life in a way that "bears little resemblance to that experienced by most of the population," and urged the media ("a potent educational force . . . American children and adults spend an estimated average of 27 hours a week watching television") to "assume more responsibility in presenting information and education for family living to the public." The Commission also called on community agencies, "especially the school," to assume a more active and more sensitive role in education for parenthood, and that financial support be provided for such programs by DHEW.

The panel, citing estimates that one in 15 children may be born with "some form of genetic defect," also called for increased support of research to identify genetically related disorders; development of better screening techniques, and better ways to provide genetic counseling services; improved care of those suffering from genetic disorders; and "exploration of the ethical and moral implications of genetic technology." To this end, increased private and public funding was urged "to develop facilities and train personnel to implement programs in genetic screening and counseling."

The Commission stated its belief that "genetic education is an important component in any program of education for parenthood." The panel also urged that such material be included in school curricula, and that professional education of medical and health workers be expanded so that they learn to "recognize genetically related problems and . . . refer them to available genetic counseling services."

THE STATUS OF WOMEN

The report pointed out that women today "marry earlier, have smaller families earlier, and live longer than they did 50 years ago." With less and less of their lives spent in maternal functions, women more and more are beginning to work, seek higher education and "choose roles supplementary to or in place of motherhood." While this trend is likely to continue, and even intensify, with more women foregoing motherhood entirely, the Commission found that our society has "not yet fully accommodated these changes in our social, legal, and economic structures." The panel remarked that "it would seem good social policy to recognize and facilitate the trend toward smaller families by making it possible for women to choose attractive roles in place of or supplementary to motherhood." This change, the report stated, should not be sought on demographic grounds alone, but as a means of offering "a greater range of choice" so that men and women can "be free to develop as individuals rather than being molded to fit some sexual stereotype." The Commission stated that it would be "particularly helpful if marriage, childbearing, and childrearing could come to be viewed as more deliberate and serious commitments rather than as traditional, almost compulsory behavior."

The panel expressed doubt that jobs usually open to women, of low pay and status, have much effect in reducing fertility. It indicated, however, its belief that "attractive work may effectively compete with childbearing and have the effect of lowering fertility . . . ." The Commission also found "abundant evidence" that higher education is associated with smaller families, and urged that "institutional discrimination against women in education should be abolished."

Despite improvements in the legal status of women over the past century, the Commission stated that "equal rights and responsibilities are still denied women in our legal system." It urged that the proposed Equal Rights Amendment to the U.S. Constitution (approved in March by the Congress) be ratified by the states, and that "federal, state, and local governments undertake positive programs to ensure freedom from discrimination based on sex."

CHILD CARE

The Commission found that the child-care arrangements made by working mothers — especially those with limited incomes — "are frequently inadequate." The Commission pointed to the "critical significance of the first three years of life for the emotional, and intellectual, as well as the physical, development of children." Adequate full-time developmental child-care programs, the Commission held, could tap the enormous learning potential of pre-school children, and might also work to reduce fertility by offering women who want to work the opportunity to enter or reenter the labor force much sooner than they would be able to otherwise. While such programs are expensive (the Commission cited one estimate of $20 billion per year for the "best kind" of program for the 18 million children from families with incomes under $7,000), the panel indicated that those who could afford to pay should do so, and the union and industry programs should be expanded to help defray the costs. The Commission stated, however, that public funds would still be necessary to "stimulate innovative programs and research, and to subsidize services for lower-income families."

The Commission recommended that "public and private forces join together to assure that adequate child-care programs, including health, nutritional, and educational components, be available to families who wish to make use of them." It also urged continuing research and evaluation of the benefits and costs to children, parents and the public of various child-care arrangements.

ADOPTION

The Commission found that "the demographic impact of adoption on the birthrate in the United States is minimal." Nevertheless, "the symbolic value of adoption as a mode of responsible parenthood ["adopt after two"] may come to outweigh its direct demographic impact." The Commission urged "changes in attitudes and practices to encourage adoption thereby benefiting children, prospective parents, and society"; such changes might include more subsidizing of poorer families qualified to adopt, and a review by appropriate bodies of "current laws, practices, procedures, and regulations which govern the adoptive process." Such a review, the Commission urged, should examine legal eligibility requirements, such as age, race, marital status, religion, socioeconomic status and labor-force status of prospective mothers.

IMMIGRATION

The Commission pointed out that immigrants are now entering the United States at the rate of almost 400,000 a year, and that net immigration accounted for about 16 percent of total population growth between 1960 and 1970. If immigration were to continue at the present rate, and each immigrant family were to have an average of two children, then immigrants arriving between 1970 and the year 2000 and their descendants would account for almost a quarter of the population increase during that period. To achieve population stabilization and continue immigration at the present rate would require an average of 2.0 children per woman, rather than the 2.1 children needed for stabilization if there were no immigration. Such stabilization would occur at a later date and imply an eventual population about eight percent larger than if there were no international migration.

Immigrants not only contribute to the growth of the population, but affect its distribution. Immigrants tend to prefer metropolitan areas and are concentrated in a few of the largest cities; two-thirds of recent immigrants indicated their intention to settle in six states. The Commission urged that the flow of immigrants "be closely regulated until this country can provide adequate social and economic opportunities for all its present members, particularly those traditionally discriminated against because of race, ethnicity, or sex." Despite the problems associated with immigration, the Commission majority felt that the present level of immigration should be maintained because of "the compassionate nature of our immigration policy" and in recognition of "the contribution which immigrants have made and continue to make to our society." The Commission recommended, however, that "immigration levels not be increased and that immigration policy be reviewed periodically to reflect demographic conditions and considerations."

While urging a freeze on the level of legal immigration, the Commission called for a crackdown on illegal entry — which, it said, "exacerbated" many of our economic problems. The panel called for Congressional legislation imposing "civil and criminal sanctions on employers of illegal border-crossers or aliens in an immigration status in which employment is not authorized."

MIGRATION AND METROPOLITAN GROWTH

With ever-increasing rapidity, the United States has been transformed in this century from a rural to a metropolitan society. At the beginning of the century, the Commission pointed out, six in 10 Americans lived on farms or in villages. Today, nearly seven in 10 live in cities of 50,000 or more, or in their suburbs; this proportion is likely, the Commission predicted, to grow to 85 percent before the century's end. Such metropolitan growth is the inevitable consequence, the report stated, of "the social and economic transformation of the United States . . . from an agrarian, to an industrial, and now to a service-oriented economy." Migration has been from low-income rural areas and from abroad to metropolitan areas, from one metropolitan area to another, and from central cities to suburbs. This pattern of growth has left in its wake such well-publicized problems as congestion in central cities, air and noise pollution, aesthetically unattractive suburban growth, and emergence of the "two societies" — poor blacks in the central cities, affluent whites in the suburbs.

"Population growth is metropolitan growth," the report declared. The Commission pointed out, however, that while past migration to big-city areas lies at the root of present concentrations, natural increase is now "the dominant source of metropolitan growth" (three-fourths of such growth over the past decade). The trend toward bigness of metropolitan areas cannot be checked substantially unless national population growth is slowed or stopped. Thus, the Commission reported, "the most effective long-term strategy for stabilizing local (metropolitan) growth is through national stabilization, not redistribution."

Nevertheless, the Commission held, there is a need to do something now about the problems brought about by population maldistribution; and there will still be problems of "congestion, pollution, and severe racial separation" in large metropolitan areas, even after stabilization is attained. The Commission called for "attenuating and simultaneously better accommodating" present trends in population distribution through a "dual strategy":

• "encouraging the growth of selected urban centers in economically depressed regions," and
• seeking "to enhance choices of living environments for all members of society . . . ."

The Commission recommended that the federal government "develop goals, objectives, and criteria for shaping national population distribution guidelines" as a basis for regional, state and local plans and development. Other federal action urged by the Commission included:

• anticipation, monitoring and evaluation of the demographic effects of such governmental activities as defense procurement, housing and transportation programs, zoning and tax laws,

• development of a national policy to establish criteria for the use of land "consistent with national population distribution objectives and guidelines,"

• provision of technical and financial assistance to regional, state, metropolitan and local governmental planning and development agencies,

• coordination and implementation of a "growth center strategy."

The Commission advocated such a "growth center strategy" (encouraging migration to cities in the 25,000-350,000 population range with "a demonstrated potential for future growth" to 50,000-500,000 people) "as an alternative to the traditional paths to big cities," since in some chronically depressed areas "the most prudent course is to make the process of decline more orderly and less costly . . . ."

Such a strategy, the Commission stated, should emphasize "human resource development"— namely, quality education, training and other vital services needed to "improve the quality and mobility potential of individuals . . . ." It should also be coupled with worker relocation counseling and assistance to enable individuals "to relocate with a minimum of risk and disruption."

On the state or regional level, the Commission called for the establishment of state or regional development corporations which would have the responsibility and the necessary power to implement more comprehensive development plans—either themselves acting as the developers, or as "catalysts" for private development.

RACIAL POLARIZATION

The Commission deplored the increase in racial polarization which has occurred in the wake of metropolitan growth; it urged that "action be taken to increase freedom in choice of residential location through the elimination of current patterns of racial and economic segregation and their attendant injustices." This, the panel said, will require "vigorous and concerted steps" to promote bias-free housing within metropolitan areas and, specifically, assurance by federal and state governments that more suburban housing for low- and moderate-income families is built.

The Commission also called for more programs "to equip black and other deprived minorities for fuller participation in economic life," including coordinated programs of education, health, vocational development and job counseling.

While calling for a "long-run national policy of eliminating the ghetto," the Commission pointed to the "short-run need to make the ghetto a more satisfactory place to live." The panel urged that "actions be taken to reduce the dependence of local jurisdictions on locally collected property taxes" as one way of promoting a "more racially and economically integrated society." The Commission found that "given the heavy reliance of local jurisdictions on locally collected property taxes, the very structure of local government in metropolitan areas . . . provides incentives for people and activities to segregate themselves, which produces disparities between local resources, requirements, and levels of service, which in turn invite further segregation." The Commission called for a more "progressive" tax program, through which revenues are "raised on the basis of fiscal capacity and distributed on the basis of expenditure needs."

The Commission also advocated "restructuring of local governments" to reduce "overlapping jurisdictions with limited functions and the fragmentation of multipurpose jurisdictions. . . ." The Commission suggested that metropolitan-wide government might be appropriate for some areas, and a "two-tier system" like Toronto's for others.

VITAL STATISTICS, SOCIAL RESEARCH

The Commission emphasized that increased research into population-related social and economic problems was needed as much as more biomedical research. The panel pointed out that in FY 1972 only $6.7 million of the $39.3 million spent on population research was devoted to behavioral aspects. It indicated that federal support for social and behavioral research in population needed to be increased over the next several years to a total of $50 million annually.

The panel made a number of other specific recommendations, among them:

• more rapid development by the National Center for Health Statistics of comprehensive statistics on family planning services, including all patients to whom family planning services are provided, with uniform statistical definitions and standards, in a coordinated federal-state local system,

• adequate financial support for the biennial national Family Growth Survey to be commenced by the National Center for Health Statistics late this year, as a continuation (with a substantially enlarged household sample) of the Growth of American Families and National Fertility Studies previously undertaken by private organizations, exemption from the general freeze on training funds to support programs to train scientists specializing in social and behavioral research in population.

A NEW RESEARCH INSTITUTE

The Commission found that the Center for Population Research (CPR), created within the National Institute of Child Health and Human Development (NICHD) in 1968 has become "inadequate" to carry on the needed biomedical, social and behavioral population research. The panel pointed out that if all of the population research funds recommended by it for FY 1973 were approved, the CPR component of NICHD research would be greater than all other components combined.

The Commission called for moving the population research program from NICHD to a new National Institute of Population Sciences "to provide an adequate institutional framework for implementing a greatly expanded program of population research." The panel held that creation of a separate institute would provide a "stronger base" from which to carry on expanded biomedical, social and behavioral population research; could attract better scientists; would facilitate acquisition of laboratory and clinical space needed for a diversified research program as well as . . . help in commanding the level of funding that . . . is necessary but which had not been forthcoming."

The Commission also called for:

• substantial enlargement of the capacity of DHEW in the population field by "strengthening the Office of Population Affairs and expanding its staff,"

• creation of an Office of Population Growth and Distribution within the Executive Office of the President to "establish objectives and criteria for shaping national growth and distribution policies; monitor, anticipate and appraise the effects on population of all governmental activities . . . and the effect that population growth and distribution will have on the implementation of all governmental programs . . ."

THE ECONOMY AND THE ENVIRONMENT

Before making its recommendations, the Commission carefully investigated — and finally rejected — the opposing claims that, on the one hand, slowing population growth could hurt business or threaten workers' jobs, or, on the other hand, that we must take drastic measures to reach zero population growth quickly, lest we ravage all of our resources and irreversibly pollute the ecosphere.

On the economic side, the Commission stated that it had "looked for and . . . not found, any convincing economic argument for continued national population growth," in terms of the economy as a whole, of business or of "the welfare of the average person." Indeed, the Commission found, "the average person will be markedly better off" economically if we move toward replacement fertility than if families are larger.

As to ecological damage, the Commission found that population growth exacerbates but is not the "sole culprit" causing such problems. "To believe that it is," the report states, "is to confuse how things are done with how many people are doing them."

In the long run, the Commission said, the solutions to our ecological problems will require "conservation of water resources, restrictions on pollution emissions, limitations on fertilizers and pesticides, preservation of wilderness areas, and protection of animal life threatened by man." It will require "development of clean sources of energy production" such as nuclear fusion, and adequate "pricing of public facilities and common property resources . . . such as rivers and air." (The report remarked that "at present, most monetary incentives work the wrong way, inducing waste and pollution rather than the opposite.")

Gradually slowing population growth, the Commission pointed out, will not solve any of these ecological problems, but it will help us "buy time" to find sensible solutions. However, the Commission found no merit to "the emergency crisis response." Zero population growth could not be attained rapidly "without considerable disruption to society," including serious dislocations in employment, education and business as families' average childbearing was forced to shrink and expand, contract and enlarge again over several decades. In addition, the authoritarian means which would be necessary to attain these undesirable ends would probably be unenforceable, and certainly would be repugnant in a democratic society.

About the commission report

The 24-member Commission* was established by Congress in March 1970, at the suggestion of the President, to examine:
* the probable course of population growth, internal migration and related demographic developments between now and the year 2000,
* the resources in the public sector of the economy that will be required to deal with anticipated population growth,
* ways in which population growth may affect the activities of federal, state and local governments,
* the impact of population growth on environmental pollution and on the depletion of natural resources,

* The members of the Commission are: John D. Rockefeller 3rd, Chairman; Grace Olivarez, Executive Director, Food for All, Inc., Vice Chairman; Christian N. Ramsey, Jr., M.D., President, The Institute for the Study of Health and Society, Vice Chairman; Joseph D. Beasley, M.D., The Edward Wisner Professor of Public Health, Tulane University Medical Center; David E. Bell, Executive Vice President, The Ford Foundation; Bernard Berelson, President, The Population Council; Arnita Young Boswell, Associate Field Work Professor, School of Social Service Administration, University of Chicago; Margaret Bright, Professor, Department of Behavioral Sciences, and Professor, Department of Epidemiology, School of Hygiene and Public Health, the Johns Hopkins University; Marilyn Brant Chandler, Housewife, Volunteer, Student; Paul B. Cornely, M.D., Professor, Department of Community Health Practice, College of Medicine, Howard University, and Assistant to the Executive Medical Officer, Welfare and Retirement Fund, United Mine Workers of America; Alan Cranston, United States Senator, California; Lawrence A. Davis, President, Arkansas Agricultural, Mechanical and Normal College; Otis Dudley Duncan, Professor of Sociology, University of Michigan; John N. Erlenborn, United States Representative, 14th C. District of Illinois; Joan F. Flint, Housewife, Volunteer; R. V. Hansberger, Chairman and President, Boise Cascade Corporation; D. Gale Johnson, Chairman, Department of Economics, University of Chicago; John R. Meyer, President, National Bureau of Economic Research, Professor of Economics, Yale University; Bob Packwood, United States Senator, Oregon; James S. Rummonds, Student, Stanford School of Law; Stephen L. Salyer, Student, Davidson College; Howard D. Samuel, Vice President, Amalgamated Clothing Workers of America; James H. Scheuer, United States Representative, 22nd C. District of New York; George D. Woods, Director and Consultant, The First Boston Corporation.
Executive Director of the Commission is Charles F. Westoff; Robert Parke, Jr., is Deputy Director.

• the various means appropriate to the ethical values and principles of this society by which the nation may achieve a population level properly suited to its environmental, natural resource and other needs.

More than 100 experts on economic, environmental, governmental and social problems prepared research papers for the Commission and an additional 100 witnesses submitted testimony at public hearings in Washington, D.C., Los Angeles, Little Rock, Chicago and New York.

Both the scholarly papers and the sometimes heated testimony posed many issues, reflecting different value frameworks and social priorities. The Commission was required to sort and moderate these, and then make recommendations which were: based upon verifiable fact; economically, technically and politically feasible to implement; consistent with the Commission's basic finding that a goal of eventual population stabilization is desirable; and consistent also with what the Commission described as "the fundamental values of American life."

The research papers, to be published by the Government Printing Office for the Commission this summer, include: Judith Blake, "Coercive Pronatalism and American Population Policy"; Phillips Cutright, "Illegitimacy in the United States: 1920-1968"; Frederick S. Jaffe, "Family Planning Services in the United States"; John F. Kantner and Melvin Zelnik, "Sexuality, Contraception, and Pregnancy Among Pre-Adult Females in the United States"; Suzanne Keller, "The Future Status of Women in America"; Jane A. Menken, "Teenage Childbearing: Its Medical Aspects and Implications for the United States Population"; Harriet F. Pilpel and Peter Ames, "Legal Obstacles to Freedom of Choice in the Areas of Contraception, Abortion, and Voluntary Sterilization in the United States"; Harriet B. Presser and Larry Bumpass, "Demographic and Social Aspects of Contraceptive Sterilization in the United States: 1965-1970"; Jeanne Clare Ridley, "On the Consequences of Demographic Change for the Roles and Status of Women"; Ronald R. Rindfuss, "Recent Trends in Population Attitudes"; Norman B. Ryder and Charles F. Westoff, "Unwanted Childbearing in the United States: 1970"; Sheldon Segal, "Possible Means of Fertility Control: Distant or Near"; Christopher Tietze, "The Potential Impact of Legal Abortion on Population Growth in the United States"; and Stephen Viederman, "Population Education in the Elementary and Secondary Schools of the United States."

ID ENVIRONMENTAL CONCERNS

The Crisis of Man in His Environment

by René Dubos

The general worry about the environment has resulted in a distortion of the meaning conveyed by the phrase "human ecology." At present, this phrase is exclusively identified with the social and biological dangers that man faces in the modern world. But there is more to human ecology than this one-sided view of man's relation to his environment. In the long run, the most important aspect of human ecology is that all environmental factors exert a direct effect on the development of human characteristics, in health as well as in disease. In fact, it can be said that the body and the mind are shaped by the adaptive responses that man makes to the physicochemical, social, behavioral, and even historical stimuli that impinge on him from the time of conception to the time of death. Genetically and phenotypically, man is being constantly transformed by the environment in which he lives.

Human ecology therefore involves both the pathological and the formative effects of the total environment. I shall first illustrate by a few examples these two aspects of the problem, then attempt to formulate a general approach to the study of the interplay between man and environmental forces.

The general state of public health has greatly improved during the past century, but therapeutic procedures have played a relatively small role in this achievement. Advances in health and in the expectancy of life have come chiefly from higher standards of living, and from the application of natural sciences to the prevention of infectious and nutritional diseases.

Although the early sanitarians did not use the phrase "human ecology" their slogan "pure air, pure water, pure food" implied sound ecological concepts. Their awareness of the effects that environmental factors exert on biological health was furthermore supplemented by a shrewd understanding of man's emotional needs. For example, they advocated that urban areas be ornamented with trees and flowers and that city dwellers be given ready access to country lanes.

Thanks to their efforts, we have gone far toward solving the problems of infectious and nutritional disease generated by the first Industrial Revolution. Unfortunately, the new revolution in the ways of life and in the environment that is now occurring in technological

Ekistics, March 1969, Vol. 27, No. 160, pp. 151-154. Reprinted with permission.
Dr. René Dubos is Professor Emeritus of Rockefeller University in New York City and is the first recipient of the Institut de la Vie prize for his work with environmental problems.

societies is bringing about profound changes in the pattern of diseases, causing in particular alarming increases in various types of chronic and degenerative disorders.

Whereas the 19th century was concerned with malnutrition, overwork, filth, and microbial contamination, the diseases most characteristic of our times result in large part from economic affluence, chemical pollution, and high population densities. The medical problems are still largely environmental in origin, but they have different ecologic determinants.

The average expectancy of life has increased all over the world and especially in prosperous countries as a result of the prevention of early deaths that used to be caused by acute infections and malnutrition. But, contrary to general belief, life expectancy past the age of 45 has not increased significantly anywhere in the world, not even in the social groups that can afford the most elaborate medical care. It is no longer permissible to take comfort in the belief that various types of vascular diseases, of cancers, of chronic ailments of the respiratory tract, have become more prevalent simply because people live longer in affluent societies. The increase in chronic and degenerative diseases is due in part at least, and probably in a very large part, to the environmental and behavioral changes that have resulted from industrialization and urbanization.

The so-called diseases of civilization are certainly the results of man's failure to respond successfully to the stresses of the modern environment. But, there is as yet no convincing knowledge of the mechanisms relating the environment and the ways of life to the increased incidence of chronic and degenerative diseases among adults. Granted the deficiencies in etiological understanding, it is obvious nevertheless that man feels threatened and is threatened by the constant and unavoidable exposure to the stimuli of urban and industrial civilization; by the varied aspects of environmental pollution; by the physiological disturbances associated with sudden changes in the ways of life; by his estrangement from the conditions and natural cycles under which human evolution took place; by the emotional trauma and the paradoxical solitude in congested cities; by the monotony, the boredom, indeed the compulsory leisure ensuing from automated work. These are the very influences which are now at the origin of most medical problems in affluent societies. They affect all human beings, irrespective of genetic constitution. They are not inherent in man's nature but the products of the interplay between his genetic environment and the new world created by social and technological innovations. To a very large extent the disorders of the body and mind are but the expression of inadequate adaptive responses to environmental influences which differ drastically from the conditions under which man evolved.

As already mentioned, hardly anything is known concerning the natural history of the diseases characteristic of modern civilization—let alone concerning methods for their treatment. It is urgent therefore to develop a new science of human ecology focused on the conditions prevailing in the technological environment.

One can take it for granted that medical science will continue to develop useful techniques for treating cancers, vascular diseases, and other degenerative disorders; methods for organ transplants and for the use of artificial prostheses will certainly be improved during the forthcoming decades. But most of the conditions that will thus be treated need not have occurred in the first place. Greater knowledge of the environmental determinants of disease would certainly constitute the most important factor in helping biomedical sciences to improve human health. Prevention is always better than cure, and also much less expensive.

As presently managed, the technological urban civilization subjects all human beings to endless and dangerous stresses. Yet men of all ethnic groups elect to live in huge megalopolises, and indeed manage to function effectively in this traumatic environment. Most of them seem to develop tolerance to environmental pollutants, intense stimuli, and high population density, just as they develop herd immunity to microbial pathogens that are ubiquitous.

The acquisition of tolerance, however, is not an unmixed blessing. Air pollution provides tragic evidence of the fact that many of the physiological, mental, and social processes which make it possible to live in a hostile environment commonly express themselves at a later date in overt disease and in economic loss. During the past two centuries, for instance, the inhabitants of the industrial areas of Northern Europe have been exposed to large concentrations of many types of air pollutants produced by incomplete combustion of coal, and released in the fumes from chemical plants. Such exposure is rendered even more objectionable by the inclemency of the Atlantic climate. However, long experience with pollution and with bad weather results in the development of physiological reactions and living habits that obviously have adaptive value, since Northern Europeans seem to accept almost cheerfully conditions which appear unbearable to a non-experienced person.

Unfortunately, adaptation to the stresses of the present often has to be paid in the form of physiological misery at some future date. Even among persons who seem to be unaware of the smogs surrounding them, the respiratory tract registers the insult of the various air pollutants. Eventually, the cumulative effects of irritation result in chronic bronchitis and other forms of irreversible pulmonary disease. Generally, however, this does not happen until several years later.

Chronic pulmonary disease now constitutes the greatest single medical problem in Northern Europe, as well as the most costly. It is increasing in prevalence at an alarming rate also in North America and it will undoubtedly spread to all areas undergoing industrialization. There is good evidence, furthermore, that air pollution contributes to the incidence of various cancers—not only pulmonary carcinoma. It also increases the number of fatalities among persons suffering from vascular disorders. The delayed effects of air pollutants thus constitute a model for the kind of medical problems likely to arise in the future from the various forms of environmental pollution.

Noise levels that are accepted almost as a matter of course bring about a progressive impairment of hearing; pathogens that do not cause destructive epidemics because they are ubiquitous and have therefore elicited herd immunity can generate endogenous infections when resistance to them is decreased by physiological or mental stress; crowding, regimentation, or intense stimuli that become acceptable through habituation indirectly elicit physiological or behavioral disorders. In brief, most adaptive adjustments to deleterious influences are achieved at the price of bodily or mental disturbances later in life. Some at least of these disturbances contribute to the diseases of civilization.

From the point of view of the general biologist, an environment is suitable if it enables the species to reproduce itself and increase its population; but this concept is not applicable to man. An environment allowing man to produce a family and to be economically effective during his adult years should be regarded an unacceptable one if it generates disease later in life. This of course is the case for many modern technological and urban environments, which rarely destroy human life but frequently spoil its later years.

Human ecology thus differs from orthodox biomedical sciences in the much greater emphasis that it should put on the indirect and delayed effects of environmental forces, even when these do not appear to cause significant damage at the time of exposure.

Man's responses to the environmental forces that impinge on him determine to a very large extent how his genetic potentialities are converted into existential, phenotypic reality.

Contrary to what is commonly assumed, genes do not determine the traits by which we know a person; they only govern the responses he makes to environmental stimuli. Such responses become incorporated, usually in an irreversible manner in the person's whole being and thus mold his individuality. This is true not only for emotional characteristics, but also for most other physical, physiological, and mental characteristics. Man makes himself in the very act of responding to his environment through an uninterrupted series of feedback processes. Since each person continues to respond to environmental stimuli throughout his life and to be lastingly modified by such responses, individuality can be defined as the continuously evolving phenotype.

Many of the most striking differences in size, shape, attitudes, and mental abilities between ethnic groups are not innate; they are expressions of environmental influences. In other words, men are as much the products of their environment as of their genetic endowment. This is what Winston Churchill had in mind when he asserted "We shape our buildings, and afterwards our buildings shape us."

The influences experienced very early in life during the formative phases of development deserve emphasis, because they exert profound, and lasting effects on the anatomical, physiological, and behavioral characteristics of the adult. Experimentation in animals and observations in man have revealed that the fetus and the newborn can be so profoundly affected by environmental conditions acting indirectly through the mother, or directly after birth, that the adult reflects throughout his life the consequences of this early experience. Early influences are of particular importance because man's body and brain are incompletely developed at the time of birth. Hence, the need for precise observations and searching experimental studies concerning the conditions of prenatal and early postnatal life.

Biological and social deprivation are well known to have deleterious effects on development. For example, there is now overwhelming evidence that various types of deprivation early in life exert irreversible damage on learning ability—a fact of obvious importance in all underprivileged populations. On the other hand, it is also possible that some of the conditions prevailing in affluent societies have undesirable consequences.

It is known that injection into newborn mice of particulate materials separated from urban air greatly increases the frequency of various types of tumors during the adult life of these animals. If this observation can be extrapolated to human beings, the worst effects of environmental pollution are yet to come, since it is only during the past decade that large numbers of babies have been exposed to high levels of pollutants in urban areas.

It is known also that animals offered a rich and abundant regimen early in life thereby become conditioned to large nutritional demands as adults and tend to become obese. This may explain why the bigger baby does not necessarily become a healthy adult.

By acting on the child during his formative stages, the environment thus shapes him physically and mentally, thereby influencing what he will become and how he will function as an adult. For this reason, environmental planning plays a key role in enabling human beings to actualize their potentialities.

Children who are denied the opportunity to experience early in life the kind of stimuli required for mental development, do not acquire the mental resources that would be necessary for the full utilization of their free will. It is not right to say that lack of culture is responsible for the behavior of slum children or for their failure to be successful in our society. The more painful truth is that these children acquire early in life a slum culture from which escape is almost impossible. Their early surroundings and ways of life at a critical period of their development limit the range of manifestations of their innate endowment and thus destroy much of their potential freedom.

It would be unethical and in any case futile to try creating one particular type of environment optimum for all mankind. Such a course would impose a common pattern of development on all human beings and thus would be tantamount to suppressing their freedom. Society should instead provide as wide a range of environmental conditions as practically and safely possible so that each human being can select the experiences most suitable to the development of his attributes and to the prosecution of his goals.

Human potentialities, whether physical or mental, can be realized only to the extent that circumstances are favorable to their existential manifestation. For this reason, diversity within a given society is an essential component of true functionalism; the latent potentialities of human beings have a better chance to emerge when the social environment is sufficiently diversified to provide a variety of stimulating experiences, especially for the young. As more and more persons find it possible to express their biologic endowments under a variety of conditions, society becomes richer and civilizations continue to unfold. In contrast, if the surroundings and ways of life are highly stereotyped, the only components of man's nature that flourish are those adapted to the narrow range of prevailing conditions.

Thus, one of the most important problems of human ecology is to study the effects of environmental forces not only in the here and now, but also with regard to their future consequences.

Living with Interdependence:
The Decades Ahead in America

by Abraham M. Sirkin

For at least a century, ever since the vast American continent was opened up for development, Americans have had a comfortable sense of self-sufficiency and independence. Now, in the mid-1970s, this sense is being severely eroded by a new reality and by new perceptions.

The new reality is the altered relationship of the United States to the rest of the world. It is reflected in these import-export figures: The percentage of U.S. domestic consumption of petroleum derived from oil imports rose from 15% in 1960 to about 40% in 1974. The U.S. may become completely dependent on other countries for six of the 16 important non-fuel minerals needed for domestic industry, according to one estimate. It may become partially dependent on non-U.S. sources for six others.

In 1972-1973 American farmers depended on foreign markets to absorb 72% of their wheat as compared to 58% during the 1963-1967 period. U.S. oil seed exports rose in the same period from 40 to 52% of American output.

The new perceptions concern world population explosion, economic growth, and environmental considerations.

Whereas U.S. population is expected to grow from 213 million today to about 260 million in the year 2000, world population is likely to multiply from about four billion to six billion or more by the end of the century. World industrial output has expanded from about one trillion dollars' worth in a little over two decades. In the face of these soaring numbers we are discovering that the fossil fuels we need can be drained to exhaustion; that the minerals we use are nonrenewable resources which sooner or later will run out; that the world's food output—dependent on such unreliable factors as weather, farmers' decisions and governmental policies—may be inadequate to feed the world's hungry and undernourished; and that present patterns of economic growth may be doing irreversible damage to the life-sustaining biosphere.

These new realities and perceptions are making Americans increasingly aware of interdependence in its two different aspects. One is the interdependence of nations. All nations, even superpowers, rely to some extent on other nations for essential ingredients in their economies, living standards, or security. The other aspect of interdependence is the complex interaction among the issues of population, energy, resources, pollution, food, money supply, economic growth and development. A problem in one sphere aggravates problems in others. Population, for instance, affects all the other factors, as does the availability of energy. The more we use mineral resources, the more we pollute the biosphere. It is these inter-connected problems that have given rise to the current worldwide debate over "The Limits to Growth."

Both aspects of interdependence will impose new requirements on individual nations as well as on the international community. Adjustments will be needed in the workings of national institutions and in the life-styles and work habits of ordinary citizens.

Recent public discussions have focussed on the national policies related to interdependence and on whether the American public does or does not approve of them.

This article is an edited version of a paper prepared for the National Commission on Coping with Interdependence. It was originally published by the Aspen Institute for Humanistic Studies, Program in International Affairs, Princeton, New Jersey.

The Futurist, published by the World Future Society, 4916 St. Elmo Avenue, Washington, D.C. 20014. Abraham M. Sirkin, a Washington consultant on foreign affairs, is currently a consultant to the State Department and the National Academy of Sciences.

The future relevance and effectiveness of national policies will depend on the way Americans respond to the impact of interdependence in their daily lives. What material and psychological impact will interdependence have on Americans in the next five, 10, or 25 years? In particular, what will this impact be in the three important areas of energy, environment, and food?

ENERGY ADJUSTMENTS

In one way or another, Americans will be adjusting to the worldwide energy bind for the rest of this century. Petroleum is exhaustible. Temporary gluts and new discoveries may obscure this fact for some years or even decades, but cannot alter it. The price will never be what it was. Every possible substitute for oil is beset with technical, financial, or environmental problems.

The forecasters disagree with each other. Some are certain that the worst will be over by 1985 when coal, offshore oil, and nuclear plants will once again meet all our energy requirements. Others expect the energy crunch to be with us well into the next century when we may learn to tame the heat of nuclear fusion or to tap the energy we need from sun, wind, and wave. In either case, we cannot escape a tough and demanding conservation program for the coming decade or longer. Americans will have to make changes in the way they travel, where they live, and how they use energy in homes, factories, and offices. Changes may be brought about by controls, high prices, or both.

Transportation

Cars are going to be smaller, lighter, and more efficient. Detroit has already agreed to improve mileage per gallon in 1980 models by 40% over current products. If prices of both cars and gasoline remain high, consumers will also have to make numerous adjustments in their automotive expectations and habits.

● Americans will keep cars longer, especially if the manufacturers are encouraged to build for endurance as well as efficiency.

● The percentage of families having second cars will not rise as it has in the past and may even decline.

● More factory and office workers will join car pools to go to and from work.

● If gasoline is rationed or restricted or becomes more expensive, Americans will use their cars less frequently. They will eliminate less essential trips altogether or use other means of transportation.

● The auto industry will be geared to a lower output of cars and to a higher production of buses and other "people movers." Thousands of auto workers will need to be retrained and relocated.

With reduced emphasis on the automobile as a primary force in the nation's economy, alternate means of transportation will receive more attention from both the public and the private sectors.

● City-dwellers and suburbanites will shift increasingly to taxis and dial-a-ride systems as well as to buses and subways. Transit systems will extend their services substantially if they prove to be really efficient and energy-saving.

● The federal government and the carriers will begin restoring the nation's railroads to move larger numbers of interurban passengers and a greater volume of long-haul freight.

● If the railroads are rehabilitated, truck, barge, and rail freight movement will become more integrated. Short-haul trucks, for example, will deposit loaded or empty trailers on flat-bed rail cars to be "piggy-backed" for long hauls to central freight depots for redistribution by trucks at the other end.

• More Americans will switch to bicycles as a means of going to work and doing household errands.

Residences

If fuel for personal transportation continues to be costly or becomes scarce, Americans will have to make different choices about where they live. It will be too expensive or too inconvenient to live far from civic centers or public transit. Rising population and the force of inertia will contribute to further "urban sprawl" but the tendency will be slowed. New suburban developments will tend to be clustered. The return to central cities will swell beyond the present trickle.

Wherever Americans live, they will be watching their electricity meters more closely. As during the oil embargo of 1973, they will keep their thermostats up in summer and down in winter, and turn off unnecessary lights. They will study the thermal efficiency labels on furnaces, air conditioners, hot water heaters, washers, dryers, freezers and ovens before purchase and will be more sparing in their use.

Good insulation will be a nationwide concern. Local authorities and home buyers will insist on compliance with new standards of insulation in construction. For owners of existing buildings the new watchword will be "retrofit." Many will take advantage of tax concessions to insulate their homes in order to reduce heating and cooling charges.

Industry

Industry today accounts for more than 41% of the nation's total energy consumption. According to one calculation, about one-third of the energy is wasted. In a vigorous conservation effort, management will be expected to alter designs, rearrange processes, recover waste heat, improve insulation, use more recycled materials, and effect better maintenance. Managers and workers together will have to develop an energy-saving discipline. They will turn off idle machines and be alert to needless use of light, heat, and cooling facilities. Many factories will introduce late shifts to help level electrical loads. Thousands of workers will be learning for the first time what it means to turn day into night and night into day.

The key to conservation of electrical energy may be an essential change in the rate structure. Today, the more energy we use, the cheaper the rate. Tomorrow, individuals and firms who "over-use" energy beyond certain standards may face price and tax penalties.

Energy Supply

As small-scale solar energy systems become less costly, more Americans will choose to install solar devices for heating and cooling purposes. As conscientious citizens, Americans will need to understand the trade-offs between energy requirements and environmental restraint. Energy/environmental conflicts exist in the areas of offshore drilling, strip-mining, converting coal into gas, and extracting oil from shale.

Supporters of environmental causes have had considerable success in keeping power plants, refineries, and offshore oil rigs away from certain communities or regions. Now that the energy problem is impinging on all citizens, communities are likely to be more favorable to nearby sitings of equipment capable of producing needed gasoline and power.

When local ecological concerns merge with regional and national considerations, however, the environmental factor may become a serious obstacle to the easy solution of energy problems. The strip-mining of coal involves the costs of restoring the landscape to something like its former state. Political see-sawing on the trade-offs involved is bound to continue for a good many years. Extraction of oil from shale requires the massive use of water, which may not be available in the needed volume, and pollutes water emanating from the process. Water may also prove to be the ultimate restraint on the widespread use of synthetic processing to convert coal into gas.

Nuclear Options

Americans will continue to agonize about nuclear energy decisions. The bulk of our research and most of our forward planning in energy have been geared to nuclear energy, with the objective of saving oil for non-electricity purposes. The government and the utilities have been counting on hundreds of atomic fission plants to provide relatively cheap, clean and plentiful electricity in the decades ahead. Now doubts are developing on each score.

The net energy gain in nuclear power development is in dispute. Technological problems have not been solved and reactors are sometimes inoperable for lengthy periods. The short-term cleanliness of the energy produced is countered by growing fears of the diversion or theft of nuclear materials. Still unresolved is the method of disposing of nuclear wastes with half-lives of 24,000 years. Americans will be faced with at least three choices:

1. Stop all nuclear power development. Shift either to fossil fuel plants, with their attendant environmental problems and costs, or prepare for a period of greater sacrifice in comforts and living standards.

2. Go full speed ahead with atomic development, including the fast breeder reactor, and learn to "live with the atom."

3. Continue with the present type of nuclear reactor but stop short of the breeder and hold off recycling highly toxic plutonium in a compromise effort to tide us over the worst of the shortage. In the meantime, we could expand the use of coal and solar energy and wait for the less hazardous atomic "fusion" process to be developed.

The choice will not be an easy one, and it does not belong only to a few experts and decision-makers in government and industry. The debate over nuclear power is likely to be one of the most participatory decision-making processes of our time.

ADAPTING TO ENVIRONMENTAL LIMITS

We are constantly reminded that all metals and minerals, as well as fossil fuels, have "outer limits." Experts do not agree as to exactly what this means or what we should be doing about it. For any nonrenewable resource, such as a mineral, it is true that in some metaphysical sense there is a limit to what exists in or under the earth (including the seabed). But for the most part: (1) no one knows how much that is; (2) man can and does invent new technologies for exploration, extraction, and processing; (3) man can change the quantity by changing his ideas about the acceptable price and quality; and (4) man can change the length of time a mineral resource will last by using it more carefully and substituting other materials for it. The concept of "outer limits" is a moving target, and to a very large extent man controls the rate at which the target moves.

Nevertheless, we can still begin to see what could be the bottom of the barrel for some minerals in terms of present techniques of exploration, predicted rates of use, possible substitutions, known technologies, and a currently acceptable range of prices. Mercury, chromium, and tin are on the "threatened" list of the National Academy of Sciences Committee on Mineral Resources and the Environment. We may also be running out of tungsten (needed in jet engines, light bulbs, and certain machine tools) by the end of the century.

Quite apart from the complex issue of "outer limits," certain facts are clear about the impact of resource interdependence.

• The mineral-producing countries, even if they do not succeed in forming an OPEC-like cartel, will generally be getting higher prices for nonrenewable commodities.

• The processing of virgin metals consumes far more energy and produces more pollution than the processing of recycled materials.

• The United States is now highly dependent on foreign sources for many of its essential minerals. Spokesmen for the less-developed countries point out that Americans—representing only 6% of the world's population—consume about 30% of the earth's resources. Even though this latter percentage is constantly declining, U.S. consumption is still regarded as excessive.

When we add all these points together, the only reasonable answer is a vigorous national program of conservation. Such a program would save energy, improve the balance of payments, reduce pollution and push further away whatever the outer limits for materials may be.

To accomplish these objectives Americans will have to alter their throw-away habits and do more recycling. The slogan of consumers will have to be "fix it" rather than "junk it and get a new one." Americans may even have to take their beer bottles back to the store, if the current controversy over the relative merits of disposable containers culminates in restrictive legislation.

Americans will also have to press for the revision of freight rates which now charge less per pound for virgin ore than for scrap metal enroute to be recycled. As demand for wood pulp begins to strain the limits of even a renewable resource, Americans will be bundling up their newspapers separately from the rest of their household wastes for recycling purposes.

Taxpayers will need to finance new technology capable of salvaging usable materials from processed solid waste. In St. Louis, for example, solid wastes are put through a hammermill shredder which separates out the ferrous metal to be sold for scrap; processes three-quarters of the waste as a cleaner-than-coal fuel for the local electric power company; and leaves only a tenth of the city's residential wastes to be buried as landfill.

Most irksome may be the need to conserve water, which may be in short supply for agriculture, mining, manufacturing, and the impressively wasteful American bathroom.

Some Americans have reacted sharply to a society they consider unduly oriented to material concerns and have moved away from urban technological influences to a more simplified existence in the country. Most individuals, however, are not yet prepared for a complete reversal in life-styles. Neither is there agreement as to where a rational and sensible conservation policy may lie between the extremes offered by "euphorians" and "catastrophists." Nevertheless, the future welfare of the United States may well depend on a far-reaching attack on wasteful practices by this generation of Americans.

COPING WITH POLLUTION

The immediate environment has long been the subject of concern and action for many Americans. Now we are also becoming aware of a whole variety of twentieth century activities which may have harmful effects on people in other countries and on the entire biosphere. The consequences of atmospheric pollution and unclean oceans extend beyond national boundaries.

The impact of man-made pollution on the normal chemical and biological ecosystem has been marginal until this century. In the past 100 years, however, industrial and agricultural revolutions coupled with the life-styles of exploding populations have introduced massive doses of matter into the biosphere with still undetermined consequences.

The growing literature on potential damage to the environment is producing a lengthening roster of man-made pollutants and disturbing possible consequences. Phosphates from pesticides, detergents, and factory sewage destroy the offshore spawning grounds of fish. Nitrogen from fertilizers kills fish in lakes and rivers. Mercury from factories flows out to sea and poisons the human food chain. Sulfur dioxide from fossil fuels and nitrogen oxides from car exhausts contribute acidity to rainfall. Fluorocarbons from coolers and aerosol cans may be eroding the ozone layer that protects the entire globe from the cancerous effects of ultraviolet rays. Carbon dioxide from the combustion of fossil fuels in vehicles and power plants may seriously affect the earth's climate and food supply. In the view of some climatologists, carbon dioxide may even heat the earth's environment enough to melt glaciers, leading to the inundation of land areas.

As the foremost industrial power and the user of a substantial portion of the world's resources, the United States has created a poor image by generating more than its per capita share of pollutants. A 1970 estimate published in the environmental journal of the Royal Swedish Academy of Science linked the United States to serious global pollution problems. The United States was held to be responsible for one-third of the carbon monoxide, three-eighths the sulfur oxides, one-fourth the hydrocarbons, one-sixth the nitrogen oxides, and one-half the particulates found in the atmosphere.

Many atmospheric pollutants come from fossil fuels burned in U.S. automobiles and power plants. Thus, federal, state, and local measures to eliminate the harmful domestic impacts of air pollution will have a beneficial effect globally.

In this respect, the current controversy over the best means to stop emissions of sulfur dioxide from electric power plants using fossil fuels is symbolic. Environmentalists are urging the federal government to require the installation of gas "scrubbers" in coal-burning power plants.

The scrubbers would remove the sulfur before it could be emitted from the stacks. Many companies say the scrubbers are too costly and would result in higher electricity rates. They propose building higher stacks which would remove the sulfur danger from the immediate vicinity.

The sulfur dioxide problem is obviously one of domestic vs. global priorities. Scientific opinion is apparently unanimous in the view that tall stacks merely cast the sulfur further afield, even beyond national borders. According to a National Academy of Sciences committee, tall stacks "may be said to provide a lesser risk to nearby populations and a greater risk to populations of distant, wider areas." Growing interdependence will require Americans to alter activities and habits which endanger not only themselves but other countries and the entire globe.

The United States is not unaware of its global responsibilities. It has joined in an international agreement to prevent and to clear up oil spills at sea. It has entered into cooperative environmental arrangements with individual countries and participates in the environmental programs of NATO, the Organization for Economic Cooperation and Development (OECD), and the United Nations. Most significant of the activities of the U.N. Environment Program (UNEP) may be "Earthwatch," a fledgling monitoring operation, which is now developing a series of diagnostic thermometers to tell us when the global environment is running a fever in respect to its oceans, atmosphere, hydrology, forests, fisheries and climate.

If and when one of UNEP's fever charts sets off the international alarm bell, the heaviest adjustments would fall on the American people as the world's champion polluters. In addition to the several useful steps Americans have already taken, we may have to move in one or all of the following directions:

• Install fuel-cleaning equipment on all vehicles and in power plants using fossil fuels.

• Reduce use of nitrogen and phosphate fertilizers.

• Install sewage treatment plants in all communities and recycle sewage for use as an ecologically safe fertilizer.

• Ban aerosol sprays, foam plastic, and cooling systems utilizing fluorocarbons.

• Ban detergents and production techniques releasing phosphates or other ingredients that contaminate rivers, lakes, and oceans.

Americans will have to become more accustomed to bearing the costs of the war on pollution by paying either higher prices or increased taxes. We will also be concerned about the harm that pollution by other nations may cause. With the worldwide proliferation of nuclear power, faulty handling, theft, or governmental diversion of radioactive material in one country can endanger all the rest.

Severe damage to the planet could well be the unintended result of man's productive energies. The prospects of asphyxiating, irradiating, overheating, or partially freezing the earth loom before us as marginal possibilities—if present trends are not reversed.

MATCHING FOOD WITH POPULATION

With the population of our planet likely to rise from four billion to six billion or more by the end of the century, it may be ominous that all four basic agricultural resources—land, energy, fertilizer, and water—will be more difficult and costly to come by.

The recent fertilizer scarcity may be temporarily solved in another two or three years when the effects of underinvestment will be alleviated by what industry leaders fear may be overinvestment.

Problems with the other three essentials will be less readily solved. With the more easily farmed land already under cultivation, bringing new land under the plow or tractor will take more abundant inputs of energy, fertilizer and water. Energy will continue to be expensive. Water may be the most limiting factor of all in certain key countries, unless heavy investments are made in new storage and irrigation facilities. Weather, which some climatologists feel has been unusually kind to agriculture in recent years, is still unpredictable.

The United States is not immune to the impacts of these developments. In 1973, as a result of a combination of unusual circumstances, Americans found themselves in the uncomfortable position of competing with the rest of the world for bread.

Experts disagree on facts, analyses, predictions, and remedies. But some points are widely accepted. World grain supply has been growing by about 30 million tons a year to meet the rising demand caused by more people eating, and people eating more. Yet there are about 500 million persons suffering from malnutrition, thereby contributing to underdevelopment, and indirectly, to continuing high birth rates.

Theoretically, with the right technical and public policy ingredients, the developing countries could easily double their own food production. But for some time to come the United States will remain the primary source of food for countries not yet able to grow enough themselves.

America's own food production will increase but experts say that no major scientific breakthrough comparable to hybrid corn or DDT is forseeable in the next decade or two. Food prices may come down from their peaks but the era of "cheap food" is probably over.

What does all this mean for the world and for the United States? Are areas with exploding populations—Asia, Africa, and Latin America—headed for mass starvation? Will Americans be expected to tighten their belts or change their diets?

The answers depend to a great extent on how the American people and their government view the food question. If they regard food as primarily a domestic concern with marginal international aspects, they will act accordingly. The emphasis will be first on providing as efficiently as possible for the American table, and secondly, on the sale of food abroad, with the leftover surplus available for food aid.

Domestic priorities prompted the sudden U.S. cut-off of soybean exports in 1973 when soybean prices skyrocketed. The action ignored interdependence and forced the Japanese and other regular customers to look elsewhere for reliable suppliers.

If narrow domestic priorities supersede all other considerations, Americans will have no trouble maintaining their accustomed diets, barring unexpected agricultural setbacks or price rises. The average American consumes one ton of grain a year, mostly in the form of meat, milk, and eggs—five times as much as the average Asian or African. This diet could continue with little change, except possibly for periods when prices might make meat or some other food item unusually costly.

If, alternatively, Americans come to regard food as a global problem and the U.S. government acts on this premise, the long-term prospect could be more promising for the world, including the United States. The short-term outlook, according to one view, would be somewhat tougher for the American consumer.

Adopting a global approach, the United States would give a high priority to food aid in multilateral programs dealing with the interconnected problems of population control, economic development, and malnutrition—issues that will be high on the agendas of statesmen for the next two decades.

The lower birth rates in some developing countries have occurred in response to progress in agricultural productivity, rural development, economic security, literacy, female education, health, family planning programs, and nutrition. A prime motive for large families in many areas has been that of producing enough surviving male children to provide for parental economic security. Medical, agricultural, social, economic, and educational progress in rural sections strikes at the heart of this problem.

An assured food supply, based on American and world commitment to necessary levels of food aid, will make a significant contribution to the success of these development efforts.

Such a scenario, in the view of some experts, might require a number of consumer measures—in lean years at least—to free needed grain for export:

• Restraint in consumption of grain-fed beef
• Reduced waste of food in homes and public eating places
• Less non-essential use of fertilizer
• More home gardening and canning
• More careful and prudent shopping based on nutrition and economy

Other experts feel that the official encouragement of American agricultural production could result in great increases in food for the next decade or two. They see the U.S. as capable of providing three times as much food aid as the eight million tons currently proposed as a high option for foreign assistance, without interrupting the flow of comestibles to American supermarkets. The more stringent scenario might come into play sometime in the next century, they say, but only if the population problem is not brought under reasonable control.

Both schools of thought would agree that a substantial U.S. committment to food aid would involve American adjustment to a higher tax bill. An increase of perhaps 1-2% would provide for the transfer of food, capital, and know-how required to move the world's development and population problems closer to solution.

American farmers would need to shift from one crop to another in response to world demand patterns. They would have to be more alert than ever to the latest scientific aids to greater productivity.

The payoff of these adjustments in the United States would be fourfold:

• The increased welfare of the populations served
• Economic growth of the less-developed nations acocompanied by a reduction in their birth rates
• A better chance for the maintenance of a workable world order
• An ultimate easing of the strain on the resources of the planet

INVESTMENT NEEDED

An American action program designed to cope with the interrelated worldwide shortages of energy, resources, and food, as well as the problems of biospheric pollution, would require heavy new investment in several areas. Additional capital is essential to provide:

- Greater energy production from all sources—nuclear, fossil fuel, solar, wind, water, and geothermal.
- Improved transportation via railroads and other vehicles not run by oil.
- Increased industrial productivity, a sphere in which the United States has been losing ground.
- Advances in environmental technologies (air scrubbers, effluent cleaners, sewage treatment devices, recycling plants, solid waste disposal systems).
- Scientific and technical research into the development of substitutes for nonrenewable resources, toxic fertilizers, etc.
- Successful foreign aid programs that lead to development, good nutrition, and population planning in less-developed countries.

Each of these items will require large injections of capital, either from private sources or from public funds. Capital must come from the people in the form of voluntary savings, or forced savings through taxes or high prices. If the needed steps are taken by industry and by federal, state, and local governments, the average American will find that his real disposable income will not be growing as rapidly and regularly as it did in the recent past. This will be especially true in the early years of heavy capital formation before the investments in energy and industrial productivity have begun to bear fruit.

If investment is unduly delayed, it could lead to two periods during which real disposable income would be actually lower: (1) when declining productivity causes a reduction in the gross national product, as in 1974, and (2) when the nation struggles to make up for lost time with a crash program of capital investment, cutting into household consumption.

The pattern of consumption, in any case, will continue to change. For the past two decades the share of consumer expenditures going to services rather than goods has increased from 38% in 1950 to 42% in 1972. This trend may be intensified partly as a result of anticipated higher costs of materials, energy, and industrial pollution, and partly as a consequence of changing popular preferences. With more public funds allocated to social needs—health, education, environment—a larger portion of family income will have to be set aside for taxes.

Many economists are optimistic about the powerful momentum of the American economy, the plentiful resources available, and the ingenuity of U.S. technology and management. Even with somewhat diminished growth rates and changing patterns of consumption, these economists feel that most Americans can confidently expect their standard of living to continue to rise with little noticeable change for the next decade.

Others feel that, as a result of a price-tax squeeze, the average family may face hard choices. Certain expenditures may have to be cut in order to safeguard others. The key adjustment would then involve the need for onerous trade-off decisions: steak dinners versus the family vacation, a summer cottage versus a second car, living in the suburbs versus sending a child to college.

The burden of altered expectations may weigh more heavily on some income groups than on others. Some of the above choices may not seem burdensome to lower income groups in Calcutta or even in Chicago, but most individuals judge their progress from their own starting lines. If the general public senses that the sacrifices required to cope with interdependence are not equitably shared, however, the resulting political and civic atmosphere might be recriminatory.

Americans should be able to avoid the politics of confrontation if the government's action program is devoid of serious inequities and if an intensive effort is made to develop public understanding of national needs, priorities, and burdens to be shared in the common interest.

It is the perceived level of fairness more than the actual level of living that is the stuff of politics.

The timing of heavy investments can be sensibly modulated to put available industrial capacity and manpower to work when the economy is not in full tilt. To take the easy way and to postpone action altogether during periods of euphoria may court disaster and traumatic future adjustments.

NEW PSYCHO-SOCIAL PERSPECTIVES

Adjustments to interdependence will impinge sharply on our daily lives. Taken collectively, they will inevitably have a profound psychological effect on the American people. Long-cherished notions deeply embeded in the American psyche will have to be revised as we find we must accustom ourselves to new concepts of the world, the United States, ourselves, and our future.

GLOBAL REALITIES

Nonrenewable resources will become more expensive and in some cases more scarce. It comes as a shock to learn that massive extraction of minerals and fuels needed to support our way of life may suddenly be peaking before our eyes.

We are doing irreversible harm to the biosphere which sustains us. We are just beginning to understand that the wastes and emissions of our affluent life-styles are disrupting the ecological cycles which enable us to survive.

The population explosion may cause unmanageable problems. All of us, not just the developing countries, will be gravely affected by the inexorable growth in human numbers.

THE ROLE OF THE UNITED STATES

We are no longer sufficient unto ourselves. We are learning that our present state of interdependence is not merely the dependence of others on us (which is easy to take), but has in it a hard core of U.S. reliance on the outside world. Decisions and developments that deeply affect our lives can take place far from our own shores.

We are not invincible. We are still strong, but we have lost Olympic games and withdrawn in exasperation from small wars. The dollar is frequently not the strongest currency on the London, Zurich, and Hong Kong exchanges. Our influence in world affairs remains enormous but it has declined.

We will have to cooperate with others to attain common objectives. In important actions which affect other nations, the United States can no longer afford the luxury of acting unilaterally or consulting casually. Increasingly, we may have to yield some of our independent freedom of action in order to achieve a meshing of our own goals with those of our planetary neighbors, as in the Law of the Sea Conference dealing with mineral rights and fishing areas.

We cannot remain forever a rich island in a sea of poverty. Leaders of less-developed nations are beginning to insist on what they consider international "social justice" as a matter of right rather than charity. They are more interested in improved terms of trade than in development programs in which aid "trickles down" to them. We are not likely to accept any "leveling-down" process, but we will have to contribute our share to a "leveling-up" program. The continually growing gap between rich and poor nations is already becoming the centerpiece of multilateral politics.

PERSONAL LIMITATIONS

Our personal prospects of material advancement may be reduced. Because of long-term economic trends and newly developing resource restraints, we cannot expect the same growth in material consumption that we have enjoyed in the past.

We no longer can afford waste of energy and resources. We are finding that our international prestige and credibility currently hinge not only on our power, wealth, and generosity but also on our self-discipline and thrift. We shall have to stop saying and thinking that "There's always more where that came from." To reduce incentives leading to overuse of energy and resources, some restraints and modifications may be in order for the demand-creating professions of advertising and salesmanship. Preferably our adjustment will be voluntary, but at least one state is already legislating restrictions on advertising by power companies and appliance suppliers.

We will need to give greater attention to "fair shares" at home. When prospects are lower generally, the have-nots will harbor stronger resentment against the haves. Those who are better off may be required by public policy to make a greater contribution to economic balance in the society.

We may have to accept some further limitations on our freedom of action. Because of potential shortages, higher costs, environmental dangers, growing congestion, and increased safeguards against crime and terrorism, we will have to accept some unaccustomed restraints on our freedoms of movement, action, and ownership. Most of these restraints will be of a minor character, but their cumulative effect could be a disquieting sense of frustration among many Americans if leadership is inadequate to the task of demonstrating the necessity, rationality, and fairness of imposed restraints.

Limits on the material side of things may lead, paradoxically, to some advances in the quality of life. As our industrial society accepts environmental, energy, and resource constraints, growth will inevitably be channeled in new directions, and patterns of personal consumption will be considerably altered. For those no longer preoccupied with attaining a basic standard of survival, these changes will afford opportunities for qualitative improvements in the style, conditions, and satisfactions of living.

FUTURE PROBABILITIES

We will be living increasingly with major uncertainties. With each passing year, the likelihood of disconcerting surprises involving population, energy, resources, pollution, and food increases.

Not every problem will have a solution. In many cases, the solutions themselves create new problems. In particular, we need to recognize that technology is not always capable of coming up with answers to the problems it creates. It will take time to develop a more mature appreciation of the limitations of technology as well as of its immense potential for both good and evil.

Posterity will have to enter into all our calculations. In deciding what we take from or leave on our planet, it is increasingly obvious that we no longer can afford to ignore the needs of our descendants. A new inter-generational ethic impels us not to leave the planet in worse shape than we found it.

Our indices of growth should include minuses as well as pluses and should measure quality as well as quantity. Honest planetary bookkeeping requires a row of minus figures for estimated depletion of resources and damage to the environment alongside the pluses for output of goods and services. If we are sensible, we will alter our goals, values, and criteria for personal and national achievement to include considerations of quality of life as well as more easily quantified material possessions.

While Americans are struggling to assimilate these concepts, they will have to continue making important choices affecting their own personal prospects together with the prospects for their country and the world. They will be handicapped in their decision-making by two factors. One is the extraordinary range of projections, from imminent doom to limitless progress, offered by official and non-official statisticians, analysts and specialists who claim expertise in futurology. The other is the frequent appearance of mercurial short-term twists, such as temporary oil gluts, which serve to conceal long-term trends.

Americans will require a steadiness of nerve and a large measure of prudent judgement to make important long-term decisions in the face of contradictory expertise, facts, forecasts, and a multiplicity of options.

UNRESOLVED ISSUES

The problems of interdependence and the approaches the United States may take in solving them raise several questions about the future of American society:

How will we deal with the expanding role of government? With problems so vast and with an agenda for action so far-reaching, the responsibility of government—federal, state and local—will inevitably increase. Will Americans want to preserve as much freedom of choice for themselves as possible, or will they prefer a greater degree of governmental intervention to tell them what they must do, possibly in the interests of greater equity? At each point, political leaders will have to be sensitive to public moods to determine which method will gain the widest measure of public support.

Can democracy meet the challenge of the future? One thesis today is that our problems have become too vast, complex, and pressing to be dealt with by a system based on consent of the governed. The view is that representatives whose time horizon may be limited by the next election and whose position may depend on constituents with vested interests in the status quo are incapable of making hard decisions.

The opposing view is that democracies in crisis can produce strong leadership. Elected officials can move an informed citizenry to make needed sacrifices and to agree on personal limitations in order to safeguard the essence of liberty.

Will our democracy move fast enough? When dangers appear far-off, can we take necessary actions via the democratic process well in advance? Do we always have to wait for psycho-political shocks, such as Pearl Harbor or Sputnik, to galvanize us into action?

Other democratic societies will face similar questions. As the U.S. begins its third century of national independence, will we be prepared once again to offer encouragement and moral support to countries espousing the principle of government by the consent of the governed? If so, we will counter our developing reputation as the patron of dictators and revert to our original image as the champion of freedom. Or, will we be inhibited by our recent over-commitments abroad from demonstrating our preferences for free societies struggling for survival?

Will our priorities be global or national? As Americans strive to maintain their own living standards, will they authorize larger taxes to finance a substantial share of the world development effort? Will media coverage of deprivation abroad quicken or dull our sensitivity to the needs of others? The solution of many problems of interdependence will depend on cooperative arrangements among many countries and through multilateral bodies. How far will the American people be willing to combine their sovereignty with the sovereignties of other nations to tackle problems which demand international solutions?

The ultimate choices we make will hinge on our understanding of what is at stake. This will require a large measure of leadership and inspiration in the political sphere and a commitment by the educational system and the media to equip the American people with a sure grasp of the new realities. It will require also a responsible willingness to change on the part of industry, labor, agriculture, and the other institutions of American life.

2 HUMAN NEEDS, FAMILY AND COMMUNITY

Introduction

In assessing what is humane about the environments in which individuals live, the focus comes to those areas which are in closest proximity to the individual—families, neighborhoods, communities. Neither do family units exist in a vacuum, nor do these units exist only as an entity affected by the push and pull of the surrounding environments. Families operate with the internal dynamics of those units complementing, coexisting, and competing with the forces external to them.

As an entity, a family can have many different descriptions; the form most frequently detailed is the isolated nuclear family. Elise Boulding contends that the "optimal size includes in addition to the nuclear family some type of functioning kin network" (p. 77). Several authors of following articles support this position. If one can extrapolate from Setleis' argument that the family is the primary reality for the child, especially for the child with learning disabilities, then we may be able to expand his other arguments. His recommendation that " . . . perhaps the most practical thing to do is to develop a framework of the family that enables us to have direction, perspective, and the basis for establishing priorities that are important to each member of the family" (p. 63) seems to be supported by the other contributors.

Assertions for the improvement of the quality of the functions of families regardless of the structure are made by David Mace. Intentional extended families whether biological or fictional to protect the isolated nuclear family or the single individual from excessive pressure from external environments are proposed by Boulding. If the society and families which exist in that society do not address themselves to the ageism problems caused for both those considered to be adolescents and to be old, those elements of families will continue to live in inhumane environments. It is families that must change to meet the needs of the adolescent and the aged.

The expansion of one's environment from outside family structures is into a neighborhood in which, if one is fortunate, there exists a sense of community. In a nation that has become privatized in many ways, through the popularity of the private home, the private automobile, the private TV set in one's private bedroom, there is a growing concern that this increased isolation contributes to a distrustful, fearful and unloving citizenry. Margaret Mead contends that how one feels about one's neighbor—if indeed those experiences are warm and loving or cold and hostile—has a bearing on one's later experiences with persons outside one's family. How persons within one's neighborhood act, especially in an urban setting, is described by Stanley Milgram—that sense of belonging found by the city dweller and not expected in our romanticized search for a "place in the country." By dichotomizing abstractive and associative cultures, Gary Weaver provides another way of assessing whether neighborhoods, communities, and cultures support one's individuality or request that it be sacrificed if one is to become a "member of the system."

Needs of humans whether in families of ten or as single individuals are filled by many means, some identified as parts of communities and some as a combination of both families and communities. Support of life endeavors is most often exemplified by our ethics surrounding work. The way in which work is defined and valued allows one to give or withhold value from leisure. Studs Terkel asks that we redefine "work"—allowing machines to make things and workers to "go on to human matters." It is the meaning we place on our job that controls not only our feelings about ourselves, but according to Estelle Ramey determines also our sense of boredom. The external environment in which one is employed can be in conflict with one's human quality of creativity. Based on a discussion contained in this section, youth tend to support the belief that institutions in this country need to make "active and conscious efforts to enable every citizen to attain as high a level of physical, intellectual, and cultural well-being as possible" (Starr, p. 148). The work-leisure argument with its value-laden decisions can be resolved within families—and family cohesiveness can be improved through leisure sharing. A personal need for relaxation is filled by leisure, according to Dennis Orthner, but it is not necessary to downgrade work to raise the value of leisure.

Americans have a reputation for their use of television as an activity for leisure time. Perhaps this is in response to the inability of families to develop creative leisure as well as a lack of reinforcement for family leisure. As an example of one-way communication that cannot substitute for human companionship, Dorothy and Jerome Singer consider television a member of the family. They recommend a consultation service based on research in children's behavior, especially positive growth and imagination, as a positive reinforcement to families to help them keep this member of the family under control. Classified by Vincent Rue as an entertaining medium that teaches what it shows, whether it intends to do this or not, the television industry is more responsive to economic gain than to cultural enrichment. He states that adults need to be in command of the impact of television within families and need to be cognizant of the messages carried by this non-interactive media.

But what of those families where humaneness is not taught, and there is no climate for conflict resolution? Boulding contends that one of the harmful myths about families is that the family is a haven from pressures of social change in the external environments. Concurrence by Murray Strauss indicates that the greatest danger to families comes from attacks by its own members. Statistics are cited that substantiate the numbers of injuries within families—what is not measurable is the psychological pain suffered by those persons and the extent to which such pain is persued from generation to generation. The thesis that Reginald Lourie presents lends substance to the request that within families one learn control of aggression. If his proposition that aggression is innate is accepted, then to "break the cycle of violence within families" will be a major task of adults in teaching children how to deal with violent feelings. It is how that teaching occurs that concerns Vincent Fontana—for the highest incidence of child abuse occurs during the ages of two and three, the same age range cited by Lourie for learning control. One begins to ponder the overriding concern about privatism and the extent to which that value influences the unwillingness of those outside the environment of a family to intercede for the welfare of those inside that environment. As Fontana raises the question, "If we worry about the future of our country, should we not be worrying about the children of today?" (Fontana, p. 189).

Commentary—Nancy Meredith, ed.

2A CHANGE AND THE FAMILY MODEL

A Philosophy of the Family as a Practical Necessity

by Lloyd Setleis

Whatever the state of its stability as a social institution, the family remains the primary reality for the child with learning disabilities

The disruptive quality of contemporary life has had its impact upon the viability of the American family. Whatever the state of its stability as a social institution, however, the family still remains the primary reality for the child with learning disabilities. The particular challenge such a child presents heightens his need for the family but also contributes to the strains and stresses that foster confusion, doubt, and frustration among the members of the family, which affect feelings about themselves and each other. In the interest of the child and the family, it is time for the family to be restored to the position of prominence it deserves as the essential social institution in the life of the child and, indeed, in the society. No other institution has so much significance in the lives of people. No other social arrangement has been created to replace it, especially in regard to the growth and development of the child whose ability to learn is impeded. The ability to order one's experiences is a requisite for human growth and development. It is essential to the process of an individual's forming of himself, of taking on the symmetry in appearance and behavior of those attributes that characterize the humanity of an individual. It is through the friction of this relationship with others, the yielding and embracing, the giving and receiving that the semblance of the human form emerges. The child with learning disabilities suffers the anguish his disabilities impose upon him in his struggle to achieve a meaningful ordering of his experiences.

From the moment of conception, when the biological processes hold the promise of a human being, the family is the primary reality. It is a reality where the gift of his past, the spark of his present, and the hope of his potential combine to set forth the drama which is his to unfold. It is in the family that all aspects of the human condition are enacted and experienced.

For the child with learning disabilities, irrespective of his therapies, educational programs, and special resources, his family is the source of sustenance, directing and sustaining his

This article is based on a paper presented at a meeting of the Pennsylvania Association for Children with Learning Disabilities, November 3, 1973, Philadelphia.

Lloyd Setleis, D.S.W., *Social Casework*, Vol. 55, No. 9, November 1974, pp. 562-67. Published by *Family Service Association of America.* Reprinted with permission.

Dr. Lloyd Setleis, D.S.W., is a consultant at Delta School, Philadelphia, Pennsylvania, and a professor at Wurzweiler School of Social Work, Yeshiva University, New York, New York.

struggle to grow and to develop. The family provides the form and substance of his life from which and with which he can achieve the outline of his person and the stuff of his personality in terms of his own self-organization. The family offers the axis along which he can evolve, the base line from which he can order his experiences and can pattern his life.

Eroded by social forces, modes of behavior prescribed by various social institutions have come to appear less related to the requirements of living. Not only are the purpose and function of the family subject to this social erosion, but the struggle to achieve a sense of one's identity, to know who and what one is, is heightened by distortions in values and confusion in life purposes and objectives. The crisis of our time is manifest in the way social institutions appear to be limping along just when the tempo of living is increasing. It is no wonder the family as a social institution is drifting in the swelling seas of a social storm. There are those who are abandoning it, writing it off as a disaster; others are holding on to it with a fervor that masks its condition. In less metaphorical terms, the family is subject to the whim of those who seek to clutch at a justification for all that is wrong in the larger social body. And yet, despite the desperate quality of the current scene, the family is still the vital force in the education, growth, and development of the child, especially for the child with impairments that impede learning. In a time when innovation often passes for progress and experts proliferate with changing fashion, the family remains the essential social arrangement with which the child can begin to make himself.

The members of a family constitute its human context. Their response to the child's needs is colored by their feelings, attitudes, and undergirding values that shape and direct their behavior. Often the particularities of the child's needs and behavior cause confusion and doubt about what they are doing and how they are doing it. Their concern for themselves and the child can directly or subtly create a condition in which the child becomes the family's primary reality, instead of the family's maintaining itself as the child's primary reality. When this transposition occurs, the child is denied what he needs from the members of the family and they in turn deny what they need and must have for themselves: The parents need to be man and wife as well as mother and father to the other children, allowing them to be children in their own right.

There is a trend toward family patterns in which relationships are differentiated in ways that are part of greater social and economic movements. There are the families in which the mother works, families that may be characterized as egalitarian in their relationships and responsibilities, families in which the child "finds himself" outside of the context, and families where the immediate moment becomes the central moment of living and the past becomes that from which one escapes rather than that which is brought into present living. There are families that see experimentation as a distinctive feature to be valued. However a family lives, the child requires consistency of form and clarity in direction.

In large measure, the family as a social institution is quite alone. It does not have the firmness of support from other institutions, as was the case in an earlier time. This deficiency in institutional support can leave the family and its members vulnerable to the vicissitudes of daily living. The subsequent effect can create psychological distortions and disturbances. Communication within more prescribed norms of behavior is difficult. While professional help can alleviate the anguish and relieve the pressure an individual or a family experiences, it does not necessarily lessen the need or demand for more help. To need help and to seek it is a positive assertion of the desire for more meaningful living, but it can also reflect a more profound desire for others to assume responsibility for directing one's life. It is safe to assert that at times all people feel this way. However, there is truth in what José Ortega y Gasset writes: "In the final analysis each one of us carries his own existence suspended in the hollow of his hand."[1]   Although professional helping may appropriately focus on psychological processes, modification of behavior, and so on, in view of the basically social nature of the individual, there is a need for an outer reality that provides a framework in terms of which these ways of work and modes of living can be given a meaning that incorporates a longer view, including yesterday and today and considering tomorrow.   What is wanted is the practical solution, but what is received is an expedient one.   A practical outcome takes in fundamental meanings.   We need to consider not only consequences, but how these consequences are consistent with our basic selves, selves that are the living material of the human condition.   Perhaps the most practical thing we can do is to develop a framework of the family that enables us to have direction, perspective, and the basis for establishing priorities that are important to each member of the family.   When confusion and doubt prevail, an anchor point allows the organization and ordering of ourselves.

The disruptive character of our times increases our consciousness of the patterns by which we live.   Our courage and spontaneity can be thwarted and it is not possible to fully rely upon yesterday's patterns.   We are capable, however, of constructing our lives and the tools we need to accomplish our objectives in the interest of restoring the family for ourselves and particularly for our children.   What are our choices?   Perhaps the family will need to carry functions that it originally created and maintained in an earlier time when the family was the unit of society and responded more completely to the needs of its members.   The framework may be found in a philosophy of the family.

The word *philosophy* evokes in some people the notion that it is removed from the details of daily living, that it belongs to a more distant order of reality, or that it is theoretical.   In fact, however, we are all living out philosophies.   As long as there are no obstacles to living, we are not challenged.   We can move along with the current of life without touching the rudder of our existence.   When a child whose efforts in growing move him into directions away from the mainstream, it becomes necessary to determine what is happening and where we are going.   At that moment, we draw on a philosophy that is more implicit and loosely formed than explicit and available in conceptual form.

What is meant by a philosophy is an overview, a stance that helps us develop a unitary conception of life in which we can see relationships between different events so that meanings can be derived which we can understand and with which we can persevere and continue.   A philosophy of the family provides a basis upon which its members can relate to themselves and each other.   Much of what is done in family living is well intentioned, but fragmented and unrelated to needs or circumstances.   Parents do what they feel they should, but often lack conviction.

Thus far it has been posited that the family is the child's primary reality, that it provides the form and substance with which he can form himself as an individual in his own right.   The basis for a philosophy of the family has been put forth.   In almost ten years of work with families at the Delta School in Philadelphia, Pennsylvania, it has been found that a central theme has underlain the concerns and questions with which parents have sought help.   Although families are unique and distinctive in character, composition, and disposition, the central theme concerns what members of a family are doing to, with, and for each other, as these actions become intensified by the particular needs of the child with learning disabilities.   It is as if the child increases the consciousness of family members and their actions.   Each action carries with it feelings, thoughts, and attitudes that give the human touch to what could be an otherwise mechanical action.   If examined through a grid that is essential to human development the significance of this theme sug-

[1] José Ortega y Gasset, *Man and Crisis* (New York: W. W. Norton, 1958), p. 89.

gests its character is less psychological or social than it is ethical—having principles of behavior that derive from the sanctity of life.

The grid is constructed from the following assumptions: (1) The individual is inherently a social being; (2) it is in actions with others that the definition and discovery of the self occur; (3) growth is a process in which struggle is inherent; (4) responsibility—the ability of the individual to call forth from himself what life requires of him—is essential to human growth and development; and (5) in the family, a tension exists between each member who seeks separateness yet needs to be an integrated part of the family.

THE ETHICAL IMPERATIVE

At the quintessence of the human relationship, in its most biological form, lies the ethical basis upon which the family exists. If life is to survive and continue, we have to act on the very thing we create—the child. There is built into the very nature of conception an ethical requirement. The nub of the fertilized egg, from conception to birth, has in it all the requirements for bringing to life the new creation. It is as though the pattern for an ethically based behavior is laid out. Human action within the family is geared to the individual's survival and continuance. The behavior we assume by choice grows out of an ethical imperative. We have the choice to respond to what the other person evokes in us by virtue of his need or we may choose to let him die. Thus, we struggle to deal with this growing and developing being for whom we have chosen responsibility. The ethical imperative requires that our behavior respect the value, the integrity, the self of the other and that we act in accordance with norms that define and specify ethical behavior.

As the baby develops in terms of his sociality, we provide him with the behavioral guidelines with which he furthers his growth and shapes his behavior. We struggle continuously with the question of how to relate to him as he changes. Behind the struggle there is an obligation; if we are to sustain and nurture this life, then we are obliged. Something beyond our self-interest as such must be satisfied. The need of the child requires not only the fulfillment of an obligation but an assurance that there will be a continuity of the obligation; it requires, also, a loyalty each to the other, a cohesive material that holds members together, if the ethical imperative is to be fulfilled. Obligation and loyalty as aspects of the ethical imperative are not one-way mechanisms for behavior; they are reciprocal. There is a mutuality of investment, an investment that is assured by the continuity of the family. The ethical imperative provides the skeletal structure of the family as an organization of individuals bound to each other by history and biological necessity for the enhancement of their humanity.

CONSERVER OF VALUES

The ethical commitment of parents for the welfare of children, of children for the parents, and of each for the other provides a regulating line in terms of which the family lives. This line represents an assurance against the capriciousness of life's surprises and deviations that impinge upon the integrity of the family.[2] In the daily struggle with the wider world, there are external pulls that may threaten the stability of the family. The family can not move as quickly as the changing society without doing violence to itself. In this regard, the family conserves values that relate to how its members live individually and collectively. Where the ethical imperative provides the impetus, the family's direction is guided by a purpose and a function.

[2]The concept of the regulating line has been taken from the field of architecture and is elaborated on by Le Corbusier in his book, *Towards a New Architecture* (London: Architectural Press, 1946).

PURPOSE AS GENERATING PRINCIPLE

At the most basic organic level of human existence, purpose prevails as a generating principle. It represents the objective to be fulfilled and sparks the process of growth and development. At the biological level, purpose is in us, but at the level of conscious living we need to choose and create a purpose in order to give our lives significance and meaning. It is as though we latch on to an inherent part of ourselves and by creating a purpose we are able to generate our lives.

The family, too, must have a purpose so that it can become to itself and to its members whatever it needs to become. Purpose enables the family to sort out what is important and necessary in the experiences of its members, so that living can be fulfilled. It helps ask such questions as: What kind of people do we want to be? Toward what end should education aim? Purpose helps us to order and form our concerns and act upon our wishes in a way that is relevant and economical. How the family shall move in terms of its purpose is a question that relates to its function.

FUNCTION AS ORGANIZING PRINCIPLE

The function of the family is one of the most confusing issues in today's world, especially as it relates to the child with learning disabilities. With the involvement of special schools, recreational programs, and psychological and psychiatric services in the life of the child, there can be for the child and the family an overlapping of efforts that pull apart the family as the primary reality.

Function deals with how purposes are fulfilled. It helps organize our actions so that behavior becomes significant and meaningful. It delineates who does what and how it shall be done in accordance with purpose and the ethical imperative.

The function of the family is differentiated from other organized efforts in that it humanizes its members. It is different from socialization. Although humanization and socialization are often referred to interchangeably, they represent different functions. The family offers its members a distinctive opportunity to live out the fullness of their lives. There is a continuity in the opportunity to use the family as a stage where experience is shared, reflected upon, and ordered into a form that can become internalized as part of the self, a self that has its basis in the family. It is in the family that pain and joy, certainty and uncertainty, disappointment and achievement, and self-worth and self-doubt all find an avenue for expression and response in the shared concern that has its roots in the ethical imperative. In the family the full humanity of the child is given its freest and widest range of opportunity to be seen, felt, and sustained, limited only by that which may destroy either the child or the family.

The process of socialization occurs in areas outside the family, where behavior and action are more limited by other purposes and functions and where the fullness of the child's involvement is more specifically focused and directed. In humanizing the child, the family provides him with the opportunity to develop the art of living; in socialization, the child learns the science of living. This distinction is clearly observed when parents report that the child seems more capable than his school reports. More often than not, the parents are right, but what they report is a capability that is more consistent with the humanization of the child than with his socialization at the school. The phenomenon they observe is the child's behaving with a wisdom that represents his ability to perceive inner qualities and relationships in his experiences with others. Some of the most profound and poignant observations about the human condition have come from children with severe impairments.

For example, a nine-year-old hyperactive boy announced he wanted to do "what the other kids do." At his insistence and with his family's encouragement, he joined a swimming class at the local YMCA. His poor physical coordination limited his learning. He left swimming and turned to baseball. Again failure. Despair diminished his determination to learn. One evening, his parents, his older brother, and his younger sister were each reading a book. In another effort to do as others, he took a book from his school bag and leaned on his mother's lap. He relaxed and read aloud. He did quite well with familiar stories. A new story, however, tested his ability. Again the struggle to learn heightened his dispair and difference from his contemporaries. Instead of an outburst or aimless moving about, however, he turned to his mother. With his elbows anchored in the softness of her lap, he looked at her eyes and asked, "Mommy, when am I going to be a person?" She held him closely. She assured him he was very much a person to her. In time, she added, he would learn to do what he could do, and she told him that she loved him for what he tried to do. He put his head against her breast. For a moment never felt before, the mother experienced a dimension of her son made obscure by nine frenzied years of his trying to do what others his age could. In this moment, she saw her son being rather than doing.

What is often forgotten is that the human emotion is a powerful force for surviving and negotiating the complexities of living, no matter its distortions. It is with emotions that experiences are felt and become an indelible part of the self. There has yet to be developed a wisdom quotient, nor are children graded or evaluated on this basis, for wisdom derives from the art of living which intensifies, clarifies, and interprets experience. Irwin Edman has stated:

> *The realm of art is identical with the realm of man's deliberate control of that world of materials and movements among which he must make his home, of that inner world of random impulses and automatic processes which constitute his inner being. The breaking of a stitch in the building of a hut, a skyscraper or a cathedral, the use of language for communication, the sowing or harvesting of a crop,* the nurture *[emphasis added] and education of children . . .* [3]

And so we come to earth again. It is appropriate to ask of what use is this philosophy of the family? If human behavior is to be formed and a child is to become what he is to become, the family is the structure that as a primary reality offers the child the form with which he can make himself.

The identification of the family as a social unit held together by an ethical imperative, directed by a consciously chosen purpose, and organized by a particular function makes possible a framework that allows for the ordering of priorities in terms of what each member can do and can act upon in response to the needs of other members of the family. It provides a context that gives meaning to psychological and intellectual processes and a stability for each member of the family in maintaining a bearing so necessary in learning and living. It is possible to understand that man, collectively and individually, orders his world and his experiences so that he may live. He tames into manageable units of knowledge the complexities of his universe, increasing the chances for survival of the species. Regardless of an individual's capabilities in engaging himself with his world, whether it is to master the mysteries of the universe or the requirements of everyday life, there is a basic need to limit the canvas on which he perceives the scenes of his life, to infuse it with the color of his emotions, and to comprehend it with the light of his intellect. In the continuum of our lives, each scene becomes part of the repertoire of ourselves that we

---

[3] Irwin Edman, *Arts and the Man* (New York: New American Library, 1949), p. 11.

bring to each encounter with what life presents to us. It is toward this end that the family is a vital force in the lives of all children, but perhaps more so for the child with learning disabilities.

In Defense of the Nuclear Family

by David R. Mace

A newspaper columnist, reviewing some notable features of the decade of the sixties, made special reference to the attack on the nuclear family. This represented, he said, a dramatic reversal in our value system, because it implied a rejection of the very foundation on which our traditional culture was built.

Surprisingly enough, the attack has not stimulated a very vigorous defense. Ill-founded accusations against the nuclear-family system have been received with indifference or even complacency. In this short essay I propose to examine the matter a little more closely.

WHAT IS THE NUCLEAR FAMILY?

Harold Christensen defined the nuclear family as "the least common denominator of family organization." It consists of one husband, one wife, and the children born to them. According to G. P. Murdock, it normally performs four basic functions: control of sexual access, control of procreation, education of children, and economic cooperation. It could still function if these roles were diminished in number or in degree—but not if all were eliminated.

Structurally the nuclear family is, as its name implies, a *nucleus.* It can be "extended" in three ways: first, by adding blood relatives and their dependents—grandparents, brothers and sisters, nieces and nephews, with their respective relatives by marriage; a second form of extension could be brought about by introducing multiple marriage; a third could occur through the adoption or inclusion of unrelated persons.

Extended families do not, of course, stand in contrast to nuclear families, as is often implied. Most extended families use nuclear families as building blocks. In this sense, the nuclear family has been regarded as universal. Murdock, in his monumental and much-quoted study *Social Structure,* found it in every one of the two hundred fifty human societies he examined. M. J. Levy and L. A. Fallers have, however, pointed out that, although nuclear families are indeed components of most extended families, in some cases nuclear functions are so diluted that the extended families are not effective units.

In sharp contract to these diluted nuclear families, Talcott Parsons has drawn attention to the "isolated nuclear family" in our contemporary society. Industrialization has brought high social mobility, which has weakened extended-family ties, while urbanization has broken down the close neighborhood communities in which families supported each other. The result is that many nuclear families have been forced to rely too exclusively on their own resources, and this has led in some instances to acute relational stress.

WHY IS THE NUCLEAR FAMILY UNDER ATTACK?

A sampling of the polemical literature soon reveals that the reasons for the attack on the nuclear family are seldom related to any serious attempt to understand its functioning. In nearly every instance, the attack is really against something else, and the nuclear

This article first appeared in *The Humanist,* Vol. XXXV, No. 3 May/June 1975, pp. 28-29, and is reprinted with permission.

Dr. David R. Mace is Professor of Sociology at the Behavioral Sciences Center for the Bowman Gray School of Medicine in Winston-Salem, North Carolina.

family is used as a convenient scapegoat. Here are four examples of the oblique reasoning that occurs frequently:

1. Marriages today are breaking down at an increasing rate so there must be something unworkable about our contemporary family system, which is the nuclear family.

2. Many parents and children are alienated from each other. This "generation gap" must be the result of the nuclear family; so we must find a better family system where it won't occur.

3. Individual freedom is being stifled in the tight, close, authoritarian atmosphere created by family life. The nuclear-family system must be to blame for this.

4. The sense of true community has been lost in our culture. The nuclear-family system must be the cause. We must therefore break it up in favor of more-open community groupings.

All the misfortunes listed here—the brittleness of our marriages, the alienation of the generations, the loss of the sense of personhood, and the superficial competitive character of community life—are perfectly legitimate causes for complaint and cry out for remedial action. However, they are all incidental results of vast social changes, to which neither our society in general nor our family system in particular have yet been able to accommodate themselves. To accuse the nuclear family of being the *cause* of this situation, when it is in fact a *victim* of it, is poor reasoning and gross injustice. In fact, I believe that enabling nuclear families to function effectively could do more to mitigate these evils than almost any action we could take at the present time. In other words, the attack on the nuclear family is a classic example of the mistaken policy of throwing out the baby with the bath water.

FAMILIES IN TRANSITION

Prophets of doom are today telling us repeatedly that marriage and the family are outworn and obsolete institutions in the final stages of decay and will soon be replaced by something better. This picture is irresponsible, dangerous, and grossly inaccurate.

The family is a most durable and, surprisingly, a most flexible institution. It has been with us for a very long time and has weathered many storms. As Panos Bardis has expressed it, "In view of man's nature, as well as of the conditions prevailing on our planet, the family is a virtually indestructible institution, which, throughout history, has been capable of resolving seemingly insoluble problems, and surviving cataclysmic catastrophes."

What Clark Vincent has called the "adaptive function" of the family has been grossly underrated, because for a long time in our Western culture it has not been brought into play. The chief role of the family is to provide a secure foundation upon which the culture may build, by feeding into our communities a steady stream of new citizens who understand, accept, and will uphold the values that make the culture distinctive. Consequently, the family responds very slowly and cautiously to cultural change. The result is that it appears to resist change; although what it is actually doing is demanding time to make the necessary adaptation.

This is the situation with which we are presently confronted. Today's unprecedented range and rapidity of cultural change, well documented in Alvin Toffler's *Future Shock,* is exerting tremendous pressure on the family, as on all other social institutions. It is now quite clear that many of the characteristic features of our traditional marriage and family system cannot and should not survive. A process of reconstruction is actively taking place, of which there is abundant evidence.

So the family is now in transition. But what is the nature of that transition? It is our failure to understand this clearly that has, I believe, caused most of our confusion.

It has been vigorously contended that the only way to deal with the traditional family, which admittedly is functioning poorly, is to change its structure. The blame for all our troubles has been placed on the pattern that the family has assumed in our Western society.

But what if it should happen that the real cause of the trouble lies not in the structure—the particular persons involved or the way in which they are grouped together—but in the manner in which they perceive each other and interact with each other? Suppose that our real need is not change of structure, but change of function?

THE NEW COMPANIONSHIP EMPHASIS

The "companionship family" is not a new idea. Ernest W. Burgess, the "father" of American family sociology, saw it clearly a generation ago. In 1945 he published, with Harvey Locke as co-author, a large book entitled *The Family—From Institution to Companionship.*

This title exactly describes the nature of the change that is now actively taking place in our family system. The families of the past were rigidly structured, legally fenced in, hierarchical, and often tyrannical; their relationships were dominated by custom, ritual, and predetermined roles. Families took this form because the societies they served were so fashioned. The traditional family was, quite properly, the foundation stone of the traditional culture.

The new emerging family is quite different. Our contemporary open society requires, not citizens schooled to conform and to obey, but men and women with a strong sense of autonomy, fully aware of their identity, and able to assume responsibility for their actions and to make creative use of freedom. The traditional family was simply not "tooled up" to turn out such products, and it must therefore be reconstructed in order to do so. The "companionship family" is the form we now need. It is an entirely workable pattern. Millions of such families are already operating successfully in our culture, though they are receiving little or no attention.

These highly successful families retain the nuclear pattern. Indeed, they demonstrate that *the nuclear family works much better on a companionship basis.* The traditional nuclear family was essentially a power structure based on a system of authority and submission that was unable to foster creative relationships in an atmosphere of love and intimacy. The new companionship emphasis makes such creative relationships its central goal.

This new nuclear family is, therefore, ideally suited to the task of raising and training citizens for our new society. In "What I Have Learned About Family Life" (*The Family Coordinator,* April 1974), I said:

> *The functioning nuclear family provides at once the model and the training school for the kind of human society we are trying to build. It is a microcosm of that larger world in containing both sexes and a variety of ages. In a manageable setting it enables its members to give and to get in just proportion. It trains them to be sensitive to the needs of others, to work together for common goals, to succor each other in times of crisis, and to find joy and gladness in shared delights. Its product is the kind of citizen who has learned to respect law and order; who is conscientious in his work, honest in his dealings, kind and charitable in his judgments, warm and affectionate in his friendships. We desperately need large numbers of just such people. And I frankly know of no way to get large numbers of them except to work for the increase of the kind of families that produce them.*

FACILITATING FUNCTIONAL, NOT STRUCTURAL, CHANGE

But why, if this new form of the family is emerging to replace the old, are marriages breaking down and parents and children alienated from each other on such a scale? Some degree of disintegration is of course inevitable in a culture passing through sweeping social change. But that does not fully explain our present predicament. The real problem is that *we have made a tragic error in estimating what is wrong and what must be done to put it right.*

Motivated often by high idealism, we have been trying to improve human relationships by destroying the structure of the family, instead of helping to change its functioning. We have looked to "alternative life-styles" to bring about improved human relationships and embarked on a series of social experiments that while interesting and valuable in themselves could not possibly produce a viable and durable substitute for family life.

What we need to change is not the way in which people are grouped together in social systems, but *the manner in which they interact with each other as persons.* It is not the nuclear family that is at fault. It represents a magnificient natural grouping that provides the ideal setting for learning to relate to others. What is wrong is that the nuclear family has not yet been renovated to produce the new kind of people who are needed to live in our new kind of world. So our culture is full of malfunctioning nuclear families, many of which are breaking down. We need to enable them to function in the new mode.

How can this be done? Ernest Burgess made it clear that the transition in our family life would not go smoothly unless we provided the services that would be necessary. He tried to spell out what these services would be. But another decade was to pass before Nelson Foote and others began to see clearly that a new kind of training for relationships was going to be needed. He coined the term "interpersonal competence" in 1955, and it became increasingly clear that the old ways of training people to relate to each other needed to be supplemented, and even replaced, by new patterns. Learning to perform prescribed roles, like actors on a stage, was not enough. New and more flexible ways of interacting could alone make possible the kind of depth relationships we now saw to be essential for creativity and personality growth.

SOME PROMISING NEW DEVELOPMENTS

We now stand on the threshold of exciting and promising new insights that can free nuclear families to function at very high levels of creativity. But this can only happen through intensive and extensive retraining in the skills needed for depth communication, for empathy, and for conflict resolution for the constructive management of anger in intimate relationships. Progress made in the past five years could be spectacular.

The new approach is gaining ground. We are at last beginning to see that true personality growth means learning to relate effectively to others, that *the unit of human society is not the individual but the dyadic relationship.* This new understanding will lead us to rediscover the power of the nuclear family as the natural unit of society, in which the ideal conditions exist for effective relational growth. A grass-roots movement is already taking place across North America that is leading to a proliferation of programs for marriage enrichment and parent effectiveness. An attempt is already being made to coordinate these new beginnings through the Association of Couples for Marriage Enrichment (ACME), which my wife and I helped to establish in 1973. Professional interest in this field is growing quickly—in the areas of research, preventive clinical services, and education and training.

Our attempts to jettison the nuclear family will not succeed. They have already cost a high price in terms of a disturbing increase in social pathology. We would be better employed in well-planned and sustained efforts to enable nuclear families in our midst to make the transition from the institutional to the companionship emphasis. This transition will not be easy, and it will take time. But I am personally convinced that helping to bring it about represents the best hope for the future of our society.

Familism and the Creation of Futures

by Elise Boulding

SPECIAL CHARACTERISTICS OF THE FAMILY AS AN AGENT OF SOCIAL CHANGE

The family is normally thought of as an instrument for the maintenance of social stability, as a primarily conserving social institution. It is perfectly possible, however, to look at it as an agent of potentially revolutionary social change. This paper will examine those transcultural properties of the family that lead to changes in other social institutions, and also the trends in the patterning of the family itself as a social group.

The family group has a unique relation to the future, different from that of all other types of social groups for two reasons. One, owing to the age-span of its members, it is a cluster of representatives of different population cohorts who have been exposed to historically different social stimuli at comparable ages. Thus each cohort representative will have a different sense of what is "possible" in the way of social happenings. Second, the family as a unit is continually in transition from one stage of the family life cycle to the next, so no one role constellation works for very long. The family can therefore never be in an equilibrium position. It is useful to think of family life as consisting of a swiftly moving series of identity crises as members of various ages with cohort-specific life experiences engage more or less effectively in anticipatory socialization for new social roles. The sum of these individual crises adds up to more than the constituent parts since the image of the family as a whole held in the minds of its members is also subject to this same set of identity crises. The pre-schooler who faces the crisis of becoming a kindergartner has parents who face the crisis of narrowing horizons that hits adults in their late twenties when the future no longer seems wide open, and grandparents who are facing the crisis of retirement. The teen-ager who faces the crisis of taking a role inside one of the many subsets of cultures and counter-cultures available to him in his late teens has parents who face both the empty nest crisis and the crisis of unrealized aspirations as the zenith of career activities is passed, and grandparents who face the crisis of no longer having sufficient health to be able to live independently in their own apartment. Needless to say, the image of the family as a whole will be different for each of these persons.

Pick any member of a family and focus on the particular identity crisis they are moving into or out of, and you can trace out a whole constellation of different yet concurrent identity crises for every other member of the family, the sum of which provides the family setting for the coping behavior each engages in. In addition to the internally generated crises that stem from bio-social aging, and from individual bio-social pathologies, there are the externally triggered crises that may result in unemployment, separation, injury and death of family members. One of the strangest mythologies perpetuated in contemporary family sociology is the mythology of the family as a psychological and physical haven from the pressures of social change in the outside world. The rate of change of role behaviors within the family, and the continual uncertainty about what responses to expect from

This paper has been published in condensed form under the title, "The Family as an Agent of Social Change," *The Futurist,* Vol. VI, No. 5, October 1972; and in complete form in *IDOC Seminar,* Number 47, October 1972, with original title. Reprinted with permission.

Dr. Elise Boulding is Professor of Sociology and Project Director, Institute of Behavioral Science, University of Colorado, Boulder, Colorado.

other family members because of life-cycle triggered role changes, makes the family a con-fusing setting for its members from start to finish.

Fortunately, the identity-crises people go through do not make them unrecognizable to one another, so there are constants as well as flux, and the group culture created by every family unit that lives together over time provides a patterning to the flux that does in-deed provide some security and stability for individual members. But by focusing on the continual shifts in required role performance and the accompanying identity crises, we can see the family as a workshop in social change instead of as a guarantor of the social order.

Since people are undergoing similar role changes in the non-family settings in which they perform daily, the fact of individual growth and change is not in itself a unique property of the family. What is unique, however, is that only in the family are people intimately confronting role changes in others widely removed from their age grade. Thus the family setting continually prods individuals to locate themselves in space and time in relation to other family members. Thus parents gain a special awareness of their own past as their offspring enact childhood in the historical present, and a special awareness of their own future as their own parents move into old-age roles. Since the enacted child-hood of their children is clearly very different from their own recollected childhood, due to the impact of changing technology and culture, children then become teachers of their own parents about the nature of ongoing social change through the attitudes and role behaviors they adopt. At the same time, the "traditional" parental role of socializ-ing children into acceptable social behavior in the adult world goes on. But this tradi-tional socialization, more easily recognized in societies with slower rates of change, is only a small part of the learning that goes on in the family. In reality, every family mem-ber is participating in the resocialization of every other, from the youngest sibling to the oldest grandparent or great grandparent, as different interpretations of social reality con-front one another in the family setting. The dynamics of this mutual resocialization may be masked by an authoritarian structure in which older members of a family refuse to give overt recognition to differing perceptions of younger members, but even then a co-vert resocialization is going on.

The wide age-span of members and shifting medley of role behaviors is characteristic of all types of family groupings in all societies, regardless of culture-specific definitions of kin structures. Exposure to the very old and the very young may not take place under the same roof, but takes place within some type of visiting-kin network. Extended family networks may be more visible in some societies than others, but they are present even in societies as acutely obsessed by the nuclear family phenomenon as the U.S.

These structure-specific characteristics of households give a special quality to other basic human behaviors when they take place in the family setting. The capacity for social bonding fostered by the nurturant responsibilities of adults for each other and for chil-dren can expand into a rich repertoire of empathic and caring behavior when a high value is set on nurturance. By the same token, the repertoire may be severely restricted in societies that do not set a high value on nurturance. The multi-age group, however, pro-vides the optimal setting for learning to give and receive love, since many styles of re-sponse, partly dependent on physical and emotional maturation, are interacting and mutually "freeing each other."

At the same time, the play instinct finds its first expression in the family setting. The family is the first "play community." If play is indeed the ultimately serious work of culture-creation that Huizinga describes in *Homo Ludens*,[1] then culture-creation begins in the family group. If describing the family as a play community rings hollow in an era of

suburban household misery and high divorce rates, it must be remembered that we are looking at transcultural features of the family that are more or less evident in different cultures
and eras.

The skill in social bonding and play-creativity, developed in a setting of intimate interaction with others of different chronological age and social experience, in a situation of
patterned instability created by constant identity crises of family members, becomes under
the right historical circumstances a powerful capacity for envisioning alternative futures and
creating them. What are "the right historical circumstances"?

THE FAMILY IN SPECIFIC HISTORICAL CONTEXTS

There have been historical eras when the future has seemed wide open, when the human
capacity to envision The Other, the totally different society, has flowered in a profusion of
images of divine-human utopias. Sometimes God appears as the main designer, sometimes
man, sometimes the two are conceived of as co-partners in creation. I have discussed
elsewhere[2] Fred Polak's work on the image of the future[3] which traces out the interaction
between the imaged future and the dynamics of the ongoing social process in the present.
Polak analyzes the different qualities that images of the future have in different eras,
depending on the balance of utopian and eschatological elements in the prevailing thought
of the era.

Polak gives less attention to the process by which the images of the future are generated
than to the effects of the images once created. I am suggesting here that the family is a
potentially powerful contributor to the generation of alternative images of the future because of the unique combination of experiences it offers the individual growing up within
its boundaries. In the "quiet" periods of history, the times of relative stability, when few
demands are made on the adaptive capacities of individuals or groups, or in periods of severe repression, the futures-creating capacities of the family may remain undeveloped. In
periods of rapid social change, when each cohort group represented in the household has
experienced critically different stimuli and pressures from the larger society at comparable
ages, the futures-creating capacities of the family may become highly developed if the social bonding is strong. We are accustomed to thinking of periods of rapid social change as
periods of weak family bonding, with high rates of family dissolution. Historically, however, there have always been identifiable subcultures in such eras of flux in which familistic groups have exhibited extraordinary intra-family stability and have acted as change agents
on the society around them.

In a recent international discussion on education for a peaceful alternative society[4] a
participant pointed out that for a hundred years preceding the French revolution household groupings in France were continual seminars on social change as parents, grandparents
and children of the more educated classes discussed and argued with servants, craftsmen
and peasants, in both rural and urban settings, about possible features of a new equalitarian society. It was this passionate intellectual interaction in household settings, reenforced by other social bonds, that made the ferment of new ideas about society such a
powerful one. Specific subcultures such as the Hugenots in France, pietistic sects such as
the Family of Love and the Brethern of the Common Life in Germany, and later the Meth-
odists and the Quakers in England, were all organized around a strongly bonded family
life with solid traditions of transgenerational communication.

Clarkson's *Portraiture of Quakerism*[5] gives a delightful contemporary picture of 17th
century Quakers, whose chief recreation, according to Clarkson, was "domestic bliss."
That domestic bliss, however, produced children who at a very young age were able to
carry on the social revolution while their parents were in jail—as they frequently were. The

first generation of Quakers in the late sixteen hundreds counted a number of twelve- to fourteen-year olds such as the gifted James Darnell, among their public preachers.6 Although many of the subcultures mentioned happen to be religious, the spheres of activity for which members of these groups are historically noted are economic and political, and are closely linked with the industrial revolution itself as well as with the political restructuring that led to a more equalitarian society both in England and on the continent.*

Although non-conformists were politically disfranchised until the 1830's, non-conformist sects throughout England cooperated in various ways from the 1660's on7 for the abolition of poverty and the removal of social inequalities. After political enfranchisement figures like the Quaker John Bright brought a non-statist, essentially anarchist approach to both national and international affairs into parliament as he worked for the removal of coercive privileges of state and aristocracy.

The cultural revolution in the People's Republic of China must similarly be traced back to the generation of mothers and fathers of the student group of which Mao Tse Tung was a part. These parents taught their children to be revolutionaries, and their parents had in turn taught them, in a tradition of both peasant and intellectual radicalism that goes back a long way in Chinese history.

Similarly today, in the U.S., young radical parents, black and white, are systematically teaching their children to be the constructors of the new society from a very early age.9 The children's liberation movement which is sweeping some elementary schools in our larger cities under pre-teen-age leadership, cannot be understood apart from the family settings in which these children have been nurtured.10

The illustrations given here provide at least a hint that if we look at any period of rapid social change, we will probably find certain subcultures that nurture strong familistic groupings which in turn produce powerful change agents operating out of the double context of the family bond and a special community solidarity. It is no accident that parental training for revolutionary change occurs chiefly in special subculture settings, since a powerful re-enforcement is needed in order to enable parents systematically to engage in new types of behaviors themselves, and to present new patterns to their children. Parents who were trying to raise their children as pacifists in Europe and the U.S. in the forties know how important a community of reference was in giving courage to them and to their children in the face of the hostility of the larger society.

TYPES OF FAMILISTIC GROUPINGS

By using terms like household and familistic grouping in the previous sections I have skirted the issue of defining the family in terms of specific membership patterns. The whole debate about whether the nuclear family is the basic unit in all societies seems to me largely irrelevant in the face of the great variety of household patterning we find both between societies and within any one society at a given time. This variety is found at all levels of societal complexity, and at various levels of industrialization. Rather than positing one optimal size and configuration for the universal family, as Levy11 does, or an evolutionary sequence from extended to nuclear family as Parsons,12 Winch13and others do, I suggest that each society has an optimal household size including some variant of an extended kin network suited to its particular type of socio-economic and political organization, given conditions of relative stability. In times of rapid change or catastrophe, this size will shrink (or expand) to maximize its adaptive potential. With the return of relative stability, the family will either return to the old optimum or establish a new one.

*See Raistwick's *Quakers in Science and Industry* for an account of the role of Quakers in the industrial revolution.8

For the purposes of this paper, I will have to bypass the knotty problem of providing an operational definition of "optimal" size in any given situation. I suggest, however, that the optimal size includes in addition to the nuclear family some type of functioning extended kin network. Accepting Litwak's[14] analysis of the family as that social institution best able to cope with idiosyncratic events, particularly in a complex highly bureaucratized society, it is clear that society as such is too much for either the single individual or the isolated nuclear family.

The very network of helping institutions in modern society that is designed to assist the family in its functioning is in itself so complex and demanding, that individuals and families require the cushioning effect of extended kin ties, whether biological or fictional, to protect them from excessive pressure from outside.

The family as a household group responsible for (at the least) the physical nurturance of its members, can be thought of on a continuum from the individual isolate householder to a multi-generation cluster of household groupings that may consist of biologically related individuals curturally defined as an extended family, or of a voluntary association of individuals living as an extended family. In order to emphasize the commonality between the culturally defined extended family and the household as a voluntary association, I will use the term Expanded Family to cover both.* Ron Roberts' book *The New Communes,*[15] quotes from the brochure of a New York City organization calling itself the Expanded Family for a definition of this term. The expanded family

can be simply a close friendship of trust and respect; it may be a convenient symbiotic arrangement involving shared outings, some mutural baby-sitting and perhaps a shared vacation. . . It can involve friends who rent apartments in the same building, friends who set up home together, or it can be a fully-fledged commune or a group marriage.[17]

This same range of potential shared functions can be found in the biologically-based extended family, including the features of group marriage in those (admittedly rare) extended families that practice what society then labels incest.

Ranged along our continuum, then, are the following general types: 1) the one-person household; 2) informal couple arrangements of varying degrees of permanency, with or without children; 3) the nuclear family with a more or less active kin network; and 4) the expanded family, biological or intentional.

Note that Roberts' definition of the expanded family includes a variety of combinations of adults and children in one or more houses, showing many or few domestic fuctions. No hard and fast line can be drawn between the expanded family and the intentional community, in which individuals and families share a common tract of land and have a well-defined mutual purpose beyond that of shared maintenance functions.

My hypothesis about the cyclical expansion and contraction of familistic groupings according to the exigencies of the times, within some overall parameters of optimal size for a given society, implies that any given society will have experienced various household patterns at different historical stages. It further implies that there is nothing historically unique about either the isolate householder or the expanded family experiments, of the twentieth century.

A quick trot through European history shows first the small-family groupings of the nomadic tribes of Gaul and then the small freeman landholder and his family, each being superseded by the large-family system of the early feudal society from the ninth to the

---

*The distinction between the biologically based extended family and the fictional extended family is not really a tenable one, of course. As Lloyd Fallers points out,[16] many societies create fictionalized kin structures. He mentions the Jie of Africa who maintain permanent lineage systems of equal size over time simply by fictionally re-grouping individuals to correspond with the ideal lineage system.

eleventh century. The large family system embedded in the familistic super-structure of feudalism developed because the individual freeman could not protect his family in the face of continual attack from seafaring norsemen.

The large-family system was gradually whittled away as a result of the population explosion that followed upon increases in agricultural productivity in the relative social peace from the eleventh century on. People driven off the land provided an urban labor pool that led to economic boom for the merchants and unemployment for the masses. The result was the alternation of economic and social advances with wildly disruptive mass movements that characterized medieval Europe. Henri Pirenne has given a vivid description of the crowds of footloose vagabonds who drifted through Europe, available for adventure in war, trade or politics, in the era which ushered in the Crusades.[18] These isolates were not only cut off from the traditional rural family household, but even from the possibility of independent nuclear family life in the city. We are indebted to Philippe Aries for descriptions of family life in medieval France.[19] He points out that by the fifteenth century, married workers in urban centers, if they were lucky, were housed dormitory style in the homes of their employers. Privacy was non-existent, for rich or poor. In the "big houses" of the rich beds were put up at night, taken down by day, in rooms overflowing with people twenty-four hours a day. For those not so quartered, there were tiny, often windowless, rooms for married couples and the youngest of their children. No traditional nurturance functions took place in these rooms—even meals were taken at taverns. Visiting took place in the village square. Infants were sent to wet nurses in the country when possible, and children were put out to apprenticeships at the age of seven.

The impossibility of drawing social boundaries around a familistic grouping, even the nuclear family, for urban masses in this period of European history staggers the modern imagination. With increasing (relative) prosperity as Europe moved toward the industrial revolution the reaction against the enforced deprivatization of the early middle ages took some interesting forms. Not only was the private extended family re-invented by the more affluent middle and upper class, but many urban communal ventures were undertaken, sometimes under church auspices. Marc Bloch describes communal households of up to 200 persons organized on a voluntary basis, in his *Feudal Society*.[20] Many women's communes were established (forerunners of today's women's lib communes?) for single working women who wished to live free of harrassment in an urban setting.*

A proliferation of religious and secular utopian communes and communities characterized the Europe of the sixteenth and seventeenth centuries. Eighteenth century affluence led to an emphasis on biological expanded families, and an accompanying decline in these experiments, but the nineteenth and twentieth centuries have each seen a new wave of expanded family ventures. Each new wave of expanded family experiments has on the one hand been related to periods of social and economic upheaval (particularly economic depressions)** and has in turn had a creative impact on the larger society. This impact has taken the form of agricultural or technological innovation in some cases, of models for subsequent social welfare legislation or educational practice in others. A systematic study of the contributions of expanded family experiments to economic and social innovation has yet to be undertaken, but the flavor of the type of contribution made can be gotten from a reading of Frank Manuel's *Utopias and Utopian Thought*.[22]

THE CHANGE POTENTIAL IN CONTEMPORARY FAMILISTIC GROUPINGS

Drawing a parallel with the experience of Europe from the middle ages through the

---

*The beguinages are an example of this.
**This point is emphasized in Charles Nordhoff's *Communisitic Societies of the Unites States*.[21]

industrial revolution, we can see that in a highly condensed sequence the U.S. has moved through a period of early industrial urbanism characterized by a substantial immigrant influx of single householders and nuclear families living both isolated and deprivatized lives. Thomas and Znaniecki's *Polish Peasant*[23] provides the classic documentation of this. The retreat to the privacy of the modified extended family has taken pathological forms in U.S. suburbia not (yet) observed in Europe, probably because of unique affluence levels in the U.S. This retreat has been paralleled however by two waves of communal ventures. The first began in the early eighteen hundreds and was largely religiously motivated.* The second, and largely secular wave began in the twenties, took a new start in the late forties after World War II as young men released from conscientious objector camps and their families decided to create alternatives to a society they had rejected, and has a new impetus today in the communes started out of the civil rights movement in the sixties.

The familistic experiments of the twenties and forties got very little attention, partly because they were undertaken by a very tiny and not very visible minority.** Today's experiments possibly get more attention than they warrant, but in terms of social impact their significance is not small.

How do these experimental expanded families fit into the total picture of the family in the U. S. today, and what do they offer for the future? No one knows the exact proportion of Americans living in communal ventures of various kinds, but the figure is probably well below one half of one percent.*** One thing social scientists have established through trend analysis is that in general social change at the level of the macrosystem is glacially slow. Changes in the age at marriage, number of children born, divorce rates, remarriage rates, and frequency of extra-marital sex may in the short run be subject to apparently abrupt fluctuations, but in the long run smooth out into steady trends. System breaks and trend reversals occur, but not often.****

It has frequently been commented that contemporary Americans are the marryingest people in the world. Parsons pointed out in 1965[26] that the U.S. now has the largest number of persons of marriageable age and not widowed living with their spouses and children ever recorded in the history of this country. If the divorce rate is rising, so is the remarriage rate. While it is true that the age of marriage is no longer dropping, but has started rising again, the fondness for marriage will not disappear quickly from the American scene. The best prediction about the families of tomorrow is that they will be like the families of today. That, however, is not a very interesting prediction. Moreover, in the light of my own hypothesis about expanding and contracting household groupings, it is not likely to be true. We have been in a stage of contracted nuclear households and we are probably moving toward an expansion, if not of household size, of shared services and facilities.

Who will the initiators of such change be? In general, middle America is very aware of the existence of the hip community and sees in the lice-infested crash pads of urban centers, and the higgeldy-piggeldy structures and equipment of the farm communes, a nightmare vision of a deteriorating society in which communal sex and drug orgies replace the

---

*This first wave of communal experiments does not fit the reaction-to-urbanism model, since many European immigrants went straight into these communities without intermediate urban experience in the U.S. To the extent that Euro-North America needs to be treated as a geo-historical unit, however, the phenomenon fits the model.

**Some idea of the family base of the ventures in the twenties can be gained from Charles Chatfield's *For Peace and Justice: Pacifism in America 1914-41*.[24] Staughton Lynd's Non-Violence in America also gives some clues on these developments.[25]

***Benjamin Zablocki estimates that approximately a million and a half people move in and out of the straight world.[27]

****See for example the trend charts in "Quality of Life, U.S.A.: Costs and Benefits of Urbanization and Industrialization, 1900-1970," by Elise Boulding and Patricia Bolton Trainer.[28]

ordered family routine of surburbia. Those who are experimenting with non-conformist approaches to familistic living can be divided into two groups.

One is the reactive. The reactors are the hippie "drop-outs" and street people who leave school, jobs, parental home and wander from crash pad to crash pad, commune to commune. The reactors are middle class young people protesting against what they feel are phony social relationships at every level from the family to the public civic sphere. Zablocki[29] after six years of studying communes, estimates that about one-half of these drop-outs return to the straight world after intense communal and drug experiences. They cut their hair, marry and live in arty middle class houses. They usually feel positively about their drop-out years, and feel the experiences made them more appreciative of the middle class world. Many belonging to the other half are probably permanently downwardly mobile and will drift into the cracks of society.

The other group of experimenters can be called the creatively alienated. Their response to becoming aware of the shortcomings of an affluent and insensitive society is to make a long-range commitment to building an alternative society. These creators may be found side by side in the same communes with the reactors, but they will be part of an identifiable creative core, never at the margins. If one looks at the life histories of the creatively alienated who founded the communities of the forties, one sees that now in the middle years of life these men and women are still creating new social forms and new movements, whether in educational systems or in economic and political structures.*

Looking ahead to the family forms of the future, then, we must not expect substantial changes to come from the reactor-drop-outs. These young people will either be back in the mainstream or form part of the permanently drifting sub-sulture that every society supports to some degree. The creatively-alienated are a likelier source of long-run alternative family forms.

Which of today's subcultures are producing tomorrow's social forms? Eight may be briefly mentioned. There is the white liberal subculture that produced a cohort of creatively dissenting young people who moved from the civil rights movement of the early sixties through various protest movements into a variety of experiments in new politics, alternative schools, communal living and community building. Then there are the ethnic subcultures, including black, chicano, Amerindian, and Amerasian. Each of these subcultures is producing some young people with distinctive family life styles that are self-consciously different from the middle class anglo style, and a commitment to social change consonant with this distinctive style.

The red power, brown power, yellow power and black power movements, while each contains enormous internal diversity, all have an identifiable thrust toward the development of viable family patterns for the future that draw on their respective strengths from the past. In each case this involves some concept of the expanded family. The concept of community for each of these groups is somewhat different than the middle class anglo concept of community, often involving a tighter integration of the family into the life of the subculture community.

The women's movement in the U.S. dating back to the early 1800's has produced a weak but identifiable subculture that is now taking on new life through the women's liberation movement. The contribution of this movement to the restructuring of the family is in the direction of removing traditional concepts of the division of labor and visualizing the family as a flexible working cooperative of people of various ages. Another weak but identifiable subculture is the gay liberation group. This movement is helping society

---

*A follow-up study on the communitarians of the forties really is needed. An outstanding representative of these communitarians is David Dellinger, the only member of that generation to stand trial with the famous Chicago 7 in 1969.

to free up its ideas of the composition of viable households for the maintenance and nurture of human beings. The children's liberation movement, largely a product of the same
anglo middle class subculture that produced the dissenting youth culture of the sixties, adds
a new dimension to the conception of the family as a working cooperative as it works to
remove archaic notions of age-graded status in family, school and society.

Other subcultures could be mentioned, but these are enough to give an idea of the diversity of sources for new patterns of familistic living. Within each of these subcultures there
is a creatively alienated minority who are actively experimenting, in their own lives, with
new patterns. The thought experiments that find their way into the literature are important, but the living experiments are even more important, because they provide for reality
feedback as to the viability of new patterns.

It would take another paper to outline the features of the new family emerging from
these experiments, and I have been here concerned to focus rather on the social dynamics
of changing family forms as a continuing historical process. This seemed important because of the tendency to regard today's experiments as examples of the disintegration of
the family. A few things can be said about the common features of the creative family experiments in the eight subcultures referred to above, however. Each of them involves a
strong rejection of certain privatistic family values of middle America, and seeks a new conception of the relationship of the family living group to neighborhood and community.
Approaches to that new relationship vary considerably, however, from subculture to subculture. Each is concerned about a more equitable distribution of economic resources,
and the exploration of ways to enlarge the stock of public goods and services to be equally
available to all. This does not usually imply a devaluing of private family space, but a reevaluation of it, and an exploration of alternative patterning of that space.

Each is also concerned with a more equitable distribution of role responsibilities and opportunities for personal growth among family members. This means freeing up the entire
world of non-domestic occupations for women, and opening the entire world of domestic
responsibilities to men (including the possibility of child-bearing through womb-implan-
tation surgery).

We can identify a trend of broadening the definition of the family itself, as people come
together with a commitment to maintaining a common household in groups not necessarily
based on one conjugal pair, and rearing children not necessarily born to the household.
Since these households have in recent times had a notoriously high rate of dissolution, a
pattern of impermanence and irresponsibility has been ascribed to them. This is an inevitable by-product of the anomic times, and often in fact reflects a lack of serious commitment
to familistic living on the part of the participants. Rosabeth Kanter pointed out several
years ago[30] how important commitment to common values and group discipline has been
in the success of communities in the past. Expanded family experimenters are becoming increasingly conscious of this, and the number of expanded families with a common religious
orientation (the factor most closely associated in the past with community success) may
well be increasing. Ron Roberts emphasizes the quality of commitment in his study of *The
New Communes,*[31] and comes up with a more favorable prognostication for their future
than most other students of communes.

The phenomenon of temporary households, whether couples simply shacking up, or group
marriages that continually dissolve and reform, is a very old one at least in the urban West,
and should not be confused with serious experiments in family living. While the possibilities of birth control and abortion on request make temporary arrangements somewhat
easier, the testimony of the hippie drop-outs who return to the "straight" community to
marry and live in suburbia is that transient human relationships are not satisfying in the
long run.

The new expanded households all testify to the necessity for an enormous emotional investment in family and community living, and the fact that people make these investments over long periods of time is an indication of the depth of their dissatisfaction with existing society and its conventional nuclear family living. I would like to quote from the letter of a fifty-year-old colleague who belongs to the conscientious objector cohort of the forties, and was personally involved in intentional living experiments after the war. He and his wife have just this past year begun a new venture, out of a lifetime of commitment to ventures that have changed form and membership over the years, but have always been carried out in the context of a dedication to the Christian peace movement. They have raised five children who are also creative community builders:

Amazingly enough we are under way—about 50 of us in several locations— Daybreak, The Gathering, Spring Garden House, Fat Mans Jug Band, Pine Street Collective, and Thorncroft, out in Chester County—small groups working out their problems of day to day living and sharing with other groups—an expression of mutual aid which can and is growing steadily. And there are various collectives through which we work—the Movement Building Collective, Training Collective, Trainers Collective, Community Justice Collective, Radical Education Collective, Community Associates, (a partnership open to all for economic purposes of sharing our resources, skills,and dividing them amongst us); and other things spin on and on.

Of course there are problems; living in community is not easy even when we are well prepared for it. But we have a good spirit and are hopeful we can survive and thrive in community—the name of one of our work-shops! . . .

The first year of the effort is hard, and exciting; the following years may be even harder because they may not be so exciting. The long pull is what will count, and probably prove most exhausting. But we are trying to guard against all of this—to be focusing on the now with an ear to the past and an eye to the future.[32]

The kind of expanded family these collectives represent is one grounded in profound intention to work for a new society. The children reared in these collectives will all have been reared in the context of these intentions, and if the testimony of the non-conformist subcultures of seventeenth and eighteeneth century Europe and England is any guide, the children so reared will themselves also be change agents. This is a far cry from the "hands off," "let them do their thing" attitude towards children in the communes described in Bennet Berger, et. al.,[33] where parents who have dropped out watch their children rejecting their own back to the land movement and drifting back to crash pads in the city. These communes lack the structure of social intention.

Family living in the twenty-first century will probably provide more options than are open to today's individuals seeking familistic groups. It will still be possible to live as the majority of today's families live, but neighborhood institutions that provide for sharing of family responsibilities including care of the very young and the very old will be much more generally available to modify the burdens of privatism. Pressure of dwindling environmental resources will probably also help along the trend towards an increase in all kinds of community-shared maintenance facilities for family units. The pioneering for this kind of sharing is coming now from the expanded family experiments we have been mentioning.

The future of intentional expanded families is wide open. As experience accumulates, these expanded families may acquire the kind of stability expanded families have had in pre-industrial eras. They will probably never be widespread, since they make special demands on human commitment and capacity for self-discipline. The climate which they create, however, will make more humanized family living possible in more humanized neighborhood communities, for the average family. More important, they will provide a steady reservoir of ideas for the continual reconstruction of society.

[1]Johan Huizinga, *Homo Ludens: A Study of the Play Element in Culture* (Boston: Beacon Press, 1950).

[2]Elise Boulding, "Futurology and the Imaging Capacity of the West," in *Human Futuristics,* Magorah Maruyama and James A. Dator, eds. (Honolulu: Social Science Research Institute, University of Hawaii, 1971), 29-54.

[3]Fred L. Polak, *The Image of the Future,* translated from the Dutch by E. Boulding (New York: Oceana Publications, 1961).

[4]Participant, International Peace Research Association Biennial Congress, Bled, Yugoslovia, October 1971.

[5]Clarkson, *Portraiture of Quakerism* (New York: S. Stansbury, 1800).

[6]Walter Joseph Homan, *Children and Quakerism* (Berkeley: Gillick Press, 1931).

[7]Auguste Jorns, *The Quakers As Pioneers in Social Work* (New York: Macmillan, 1931).

[8]Raistwick, *Quakers in Science and Industry* (New York: Kelley, 1968).

[9]Anon. "Saying Hello in Panther Language," *Village Voice,* 1971.

[10]Verbal communication from Robert A. Dentler, Member—U.S.A. Task Force on "The Future of Man and Society in a World of Science-Based Technology," Director—Center for Urban Education, New York City.

[11]Marion J. Levy, "Aspects of the Analysis of Family Structure," in the book of that title by Coale, Fallers, Levy, Schneider, and Tomkins (Princeton, New Jersey: Princeton University Press, 1965).

[12]T. Parsons, and R. Bales, *Family Socialization and Interaction Process* (New York: Free Press, 1955).

[13]Robert Winch, *The Modern Family* (New York: Holt, Rinehart and Winston, 1963).

[14]Eugene Litwak, "Extended Kin Relations in Industrial Democratic Society," in *Social Structure and the Family* (Englewood Cliffs, New Jersey: Prentice-Hall, 1964).

[15]Ron Roberts, *The New Communes* (Englewood Cliffs, New Jersey: Prentice Hall, 1971).

[16]Lloyd A. Fallers, "The Range of Variation in Actual Family Size," in *Aspects of the Analysis of Family Structure.*

[17]Roberts, op. cit.

[18]Henri Pirenne, *Medieval Cities* (New York: Doubleday, 1956; first edition, 1925).

[19]Philippe Aries, *Centuries of Childhood,* translated from the French by Robert Baldick. (New York: Vintage Books, 1965).

[20]Marc Bloch, *Feudal Society* (Chicago: University of Chicago Press, 1961).

[21]Charles Nordhoff, *The Communistic Societies of the United States* (New York: Shocken Paperback, 1965; first published in 1875). The communes studied by Nordhoff in some detail are the Shakers, Rappists, and Zoarites.

[22]Frank E. Manuel, (ed.), *Utopias and Utopian Thought* (Boston: Beacon Press, Daedalus Library, 1965).

[23]W. I. Thomas and Florian Znaniecki, *The Polish Peasant in Europe and America* (New York: Knopf, 1927).

[24]Charles Chatfield, *For Peace and Justice: Pacifism in America 1914-1941* (Knoxville: University of Tennessee Press, 1971).

[25]Staughton Lynd, *Non-Violence in America: A Documentary History* (New York: Bobbs-Merrill Co., Inc., 1966).

[26]Talcott Parsons, "The Normal American Family," in *Family in Transition,* Arlene S. Skolnick and Jerome H. Skolnick, eds. (Boston: Little, Brown and Company, 1971).

[27]Zablocki, Benjamin, interview, Boulder *Daily Camera,* 1971

[28]Elise Boulding and Patricia Bolton Trainer, "Quality of Life, U.S.A.: Costs and Benefits of Urbanization and Industrialization, 1900-1970," in the proceedings of the Special Session on Environmental Awareness of the 17th Annual Meeting of the Institute of Environmental Sciences, April 26-30, 1971 in Los Angeles, California, pp. 1-13.

[29]Zablocki, op. cit.

[30]Rosabeth Kanter, quoted in Ron Roberts, op. cit., p. 35.

[31]Ibid.

[32]George Willoughby in a personal letter to E. Boulding, dated October 25, 1971.

[33]Bennet Berger, *Looking for America: Essays on Youth, Suburbia, and Other American Obsessions* (Englewood Cliffs, New Jersey: Prentice-Hall, 1971).

Resources for the Aged
Reflect Strongly Held Social Myths

by Carl Eisdorfer

It is almost impossible to talk about the problems of the aged unless we talk about the problems of people more broadly defined. The aged are people and, from maturity on, become less and less alike. Thus "the aged" are actually the most heterogenous group in our population.

We see some aged persons who are intensely intelligent, capable human beings involved with the problems of their time. We see others living on the edge of a vegetative state.

Aging—a unilateral process for the living—is a bio-psycho-social phenomenon. We have really only begun to understand the biological processes of aging, and we need much more research in this area. Not only are some of the professionals who work with the aged insensitive to the need for biological research, but we appear to have a government which has been almost totally unaware of the tremendous needs in this field.

The 1971 White House Conference on Aging was in one sense a success, and for totally unexpected reasons. As part of the preconference research, two hundred thousand older people were polled. In the process, many useful contacts were made with older people, literally dozens of programs on aging were broadcast on local radio and television stations, and countless stories on the older people appeared in the press.

But, to keep this in perspective, the total budget for extramural aging research in the United States in fiscal 1972 was two and a half million dollars. That was not enough to continue the research already funded, and it meant that out of every hundred grants on research in aging, only one was being supported with federal money.

It is clear that there is a "politics of aging." At the same time that we have a broadening popular understanding of aging—spurred by White House conferences—there is an undercutting by the federal government of funds for fundamental research on the subject.

Regarding the psychology of aging, I have already stated the interesting fact that, statistically, the variance in psychological experiments increases as a direct function of age. The notion that adults, by virtue of arriving at a certain age, such as sixty-five, all fall off the edge and become senile and incompetent is both ludicrous and frightening. It is frightening because, like any other group that bears the weight of discrimination and the deprivation of resources by the rest of society, a rationalization takes place among the members of the older group—a rationalization that, in effect, accepts for itself the evaluation put on it by the larger society. In one sense the most destructive part of the white society's bigotry against blacks in this country was not what the whites did to blacks, but what blacks did to themselves in terms of self-stereotyping and self-resentment. In my view, the black-is-beautiful concept was the single most important thing to come out of the civil-rights movement. Blacks began to recognize that blacks are not lazy, are not stupid, and do not all tap dance.

The older person in our society must realize that it is not at all clear what aging does to people psychologically. Until about five years ago, psychologists thought that there was an

Reprinted with permission from *The Center Magazine*, Vol. 8, No. 2, March/April 1975, pp. 13-18, a publication of the Center for the Study of Democratic Institutions, Santa Barbara, California.

Dr. Carl Eisdorfer is Chairman of the Department of Psychiatry and Behavioral Sciences at the University of Washington School of Medicine in Seattle.

inverse relationship between age and intelligence. Actually that view can still be found in most undergraduate and graduate psychology textbooks. But in 1973, the task force on aging of the American Psychological Association in effect discarded that notion, not because of social consciousness (which would have been the wrong reason), but because the data on which the notion was based turned out to be wrong. When I was a youngster, everyone thought that intelligence peaked at age fourteen because the Stanford-Binet intelligence test in those days, was used to measure the intelligence of youngsters, and it simply stopped measuring accurately after adolescence. Then, just before World War II, David Wechsler came along and standardized his tests at Bellevue in New York. The subsequent Wechsler-Bellevue intelligence scale, which peaks at age twenty-one, is the first adult intelligence scale.

When Wechsler got a bit older he revised his tests to the now well-accepted Wechsler Adult Intelligence Scale. That one peaks at twenty-six or twenty-seven and goes down from that point.

The data are right, but the interpretations are usually false since they are based on a cross-sectional study. The mistaken assumption is that an individual's intelligence will continue to develop until his mid-twenties, and that he will go downhill from that point on longitudinally. It's reminiscent of our college courses in developmental psychology in which we spend six months worrying about the first three or four years of human life; then we devote two weeks to adolescence; and, after that, well, lots of luck—by implication it has all happened—as if we were some sort of bullet or shell whose target velocity and trajectory were determined in the early moments of propulsion.

We've learned to do this culturally with our "superfluous people." These are people for whom we have no use and about whom we have very little information, and so we act as if they do not exist, and we mediate resources to them as if they do not exist. Then we must justify our behavior and so we close the circle by maintaining that they cannot utilize resources because they don't have the competence.

The change in our understanding of the intelligence of the older people came after a half-dozen longitudinal studies were made. That is, a cohert, a group, of older people was followed for a period of ten years. At Duke University, we studied a sample of people between the ages of sixty and sixty-nine, and we fully expected that their intelligence would drop off after ten years. But with one notable exception, their intelligence, after ten years, was undiminished. The one exception was those persons who had significantly high blood pressure: they showed a drop in intelligence.

That raises another issue. When we talk about aging, do we really mean sickness? The aged are more likely to be sick than are younger people. But being old and being sick are two quite different things. Unfortunately, too many of us are guilty of the correlative fallacy which assumes that if two things are correlated—for example, if aging and sickness are found in the same people—there is an etiology. We assume that aging causes sickness, and that the two are somehow synonymous.

Aging is, of course, a process that is associated with a number of losses—"associated with," not necessarily etiologically related. What are the losses of aging? They say you can't teach an old dog new tricks. That's garbage. Not only is it not true of dogs, it does not apply to people. Older people do learn and some learn well. As a group they have several interesting properties. The current older group of people were not nearly as well-educated as are the majority of Americans. A decade or less ago, there were approximately a million functional illiterates in the older group. These were largely people who were never educated.

But older persons can learn. Their main disability as observed by some psychologists is that they tend to become more physiologically upset in the learning system and more reluctant to venture possible wrong responses than are younger persons. As a result, the older person gives the appearance of not learning. Older persons in our culture are so accustomed to being put down that they want to be secure; they would rather risk appearing ignorant by not answering than answer and be wrong.

So the learning strategy of the older persons tends to be different. But that strategy can be changed if you tell older people it is all right to make mistakes. They need a cultural system that says, "Yes, you can act in a different way." The point is that the notion that older people are unable to learn is a socially mediated notion. If we believe, for example, that only children can learn, the social consequences of that belief are clear. We proceed to put virtually all of our educational resources at the disposal of children.

A wise society prepares its people for their whole future, not a part of it. The average life expectancy for a white male American born today is about seventy-two years of age. The white American male who reaches sixty-five can expect to live to seventy-seven or seventy-eight. For a woman, it is even longer—women live four to six years longer than men in this country.

This situation is full of social ambiguities. If we have a child with leukemia, for instance, how much of our resources should we spend to keep that child alive for, say, five years? That is a tough question, but most of us would err on the side of saying, "Let's pull out all the stops to keep him alive. Maybe there will be a cure for cancer in five years." Historically, that is the way our society has been answering that question. We do pull out all the stops. We are sympathetic; all we have to do is close our eyes and picture a leukemia ward for children.

It is a little more difficult to think about nursing homes and the older persons in our society and to make sound judgments about the resources we should deploy for these people. It is a fact that if nursing homes and homes for the older persons are made into places for dying, people in them tend to die very rapidly. If they are made places in which to live, if we develop programs for the living, then people in them tend to live longer. Such data have been known for ten years now, but for some reason nobody has made use of them yet.

The biological, psychological, and social variables in aging are interrelated; they affect and are affected by each other in profound ways.

About five per cent of our aged population—that is, about one million out of twenty million aged—are in full-term custodial care. The U.S. Senate's Special Committee on Aging recently produced a report, researched and written by Val Halamandaris, which is a heavy indictment of nursing homes in this country. Nursing homes alone are a problem that deserves many television documentaries. The Senate hearings describe nursing-home staff administering drugs on a plate to whoever the staff thinks can be made more quiet by them; nonexistent medical care; lack of therapeutic or activity programming; and the fact that this kind of care of the aged is costing taxpayers about four to five billion dollars a year, money that could be used in so many better ways for the older people.

But the indictment is not of the nursing-home industry. Nursing homes only reflect the prevailing society. As I have suggested elsewhere, if saving money is our only objective, we could save more simply by following Kurt Vonnegut's suggestion in *Welcome to the Monkey House.* He handles the aging problem very simply. He pictures, next to some restaurant, such as a Howard Johnson's, a parlor where people can go between their sixty-fifth and sixty-sixth birthdays and have their lives terminated. Vonnegut's parlor is staffed by attractive men and women skilled in discovering the best method to do away with people. Sometime before a person's sixty-sixth birthday he walks into the future Howard Johnson's, gets a free meal, then walks next door and, against a background of soothing music, has the death of his choice.

Of course, an alternate solution would be to begin by recognizing why older people are with us. They are with us because they are people. If you separate out twenty million older human beings, call them superfluous, develop a set of concepts about these older persons which have little or no basis in reality, and then systematically cut them off, you have compromised all people. What is at stake here is the whole value structure of a society.

What are the problems that the older people themselves say they have? The first problem most of them mention is insufficient money. That is not surprising. All of us, regardless of age or income, feel our income is inadequate.

But for older people, this happens to be largely true. Insufficient money is indeed a cruel problem. Anyone on a fixed income is in serious trouble during a time of protracted inflation such as we are now experiencing. Older people need money, and since they are often at the bottom of our economic ladder, a lot of older people need a lot of money. The National Council on Senior Citizens, the American Association of Retired Persons, the National Retired Teachers Association, and others have accomplished a good deal by forcing the country and Congress to take a hard look at Social Security and the Supplementary Security Income program.

I might add that while we do need a careful reappraisal of the system, some of the attacks being made on the Social Security program in the media are ill-informed and destructive. Many critics of Social Security do not know what they are talking or writing about. Some have managed to frighten a lot of older Americans who are not themselves too well-informed about Social Security, how it was instituted, and how it works. Several groups are now very carefully addressing the problem. This is a subject that could be the basis of a most useful documentary on television, because everybody—not just the older citizens—is interested in what happens to the money they have been paying into Social Security and how the benefits are paid.

In addition to money, health is a critical problem for older people. More than half the older population is suffering from some illness or impairment. If you define "older Americans" as those sixty-five and older, then three-quarters of them are suffering from some chronic disease. But the term "chronic disease," as used by a physician, can be anything from arthritis to hemorrhoids. So simply saying that somebody is "chronically ill" does not tell us much, nor does the term "suffering" help much in that phrase.

Of more importance, about thirty-seven per cent of older people say they have some disability in work or leisure activity due to poor health. But then, people of all ages have some disability. Anybody who must wear eyeglasses has a disability. The question is, what can be done to minimize a disability and to maintain a level of functioning? This is a largely untapped area vis-à-vis the aged.

In New York City and other urban centers, a principal problem expressed by older people is neither money nor health; it is the violence. Older New Yorkers fear being mugged, robbed, beaten, or murdered. They feel a need for protection.

Another problem of the older person is the fear of a prolonged, chronic, deteriorating illness. Older people are much more afraid of that than they are of dying. Younger people fear death. Older people fear being dependent and incapacitated.

What can be done about these and other problems associated with aging?

I have said that as long as we continue to devote almost all of this nation's educational resources to children and youth, we will continue to have a problem, not only with regard to the older people, but all up and down the generational line. Today, medical students know that ten years after they leave school, much of their knowledge will be outmoded. Lawyers realize that they must constantly keep up with the law. Accountants are going back to school to study changes in tax law. We live in an extraordinary time in which knowledge is coming at an extremely rapid rate, especially in technologically developed countries such as ours. To limit the investment of educational resources is to insure obsolescence and the creation of a subgroup cut off from the mainstream. Here the media could play a role for which they are particularly qualified.

I believe that it is absurd to think that educating and/or training people from roughly the age of six to the age of eighteen—or, at most, twenty-six—will give them an adequate educational base for the next forty to sixty years.

In a sense, aging is a less serious problem in the less developed countries for several reasons. First, people die at a younger age; second, there is a transmission of relevant knowledge from the old to the young in those societies; third, often the aged control or own the resources. In a less developed country—usually an agrarian society—someone who has been farming for sixty years is, all things considered, a better farmer than someone who has been farming for forty years; that is, until the information-base changes. In a developed society, if you were a trolley-car conductor, for example, and the city switched to buses, you probably could not make it and would be given "early retirement." Changes in production technology in a developed society will have a similar effect.

Another difficulty facing all people in our society is fear about what aging may be like. A recent study of a thousand people in the Pacific Northwest was focused on the issue of preparing for retirement. Most of those studied were upper-middle-class technicians between the ages of thirty-five and sixty-five. Ninety per cent of them said their income was not adequate. But when these same people were asked in a different part of this quite elaborate questionnaire whether they thought they had an adequate retirement income in prospect, eighty-six per cent of them said, "yes," despite the fact that their present "inadequate" income would be cut by more than half when they retire.

This illustrates an incredible denial of what it means to be old in our society. I try to point out to older folks that people tend to spend more when they are no longer busy at work.

We use the figure "sixty-five" as a social convenience to designate the "older" person. But there is no reason why any other age cannot be adopted. People can now retire at sixty-two under Social Security if they agree to take a little less money per month. The United Auto Workers will retire people at fifty-five if they promise to leave the auto industry.

About five years ago, a group of economists reported to a Senate subcommittee that the present economic structure in this country—as projected over the next quarter of a century—would not be able to sustain blue-collar workers for more than twenty years. Blue-collar workers will have to get out of the labor force after twenty years to make room for new workers. If they began working at age nineteen, they would be retired at age thirty-nine, and that will be the new entry point into aging. Sounds stupid, silly, absurd—except that about a year ago an officer of the A.F.L.-C.I.O. said that more than sixty per cent of the union's members had either retired before age sixty-five or had contracts that would retire them before that age.

A Banker's Trust study of eight and a half million workers in the greater New York area stated that the retirement contract of forty years is dead, the contract of thirty years is becoming a thing of the past, and that we are now seeing twenty-year retirement contracts. So the absurd predictions of five years ago are becoming the realities of today.

We will have to develop a new mentality about forty-year-olds, because if we cling to the concept that "older people" are superfluous, I predict that we will adopt the same attitude toward forty-year-old retired people as we have adopted toward today's sixty-five-year-olds. The younger citizens will say that forty-year-olds are incapable of learning; they will be denied access to long-term health care because it is too expensive to be wasted on older people. Forty-year-olds will begin to shift their psychology from a need-achievement mentality (which got us to where we are today, because it says it is important to try and that there is a basic need to achieve) to a self-protective, defensive mentality based on a fear of failure. The culture will no longer be dominated by people aged thirty-five to fifty; it will be dominated by those who are thirty to thirty-five, because the thirty-five-year-olds will be only five years from retirement.

Most of our society's behavior toward its older people is based on rationalizations that are mental garbage. For several years, we have been receiving a soft-sell message. Presumably it has something to do with another problem, but it really has to do with aging. If you look at our soft-drink bottles, you will find embossed the legend, "No deposit—no return." That message has really got across, and it is one that must be counteracted. How can that be done?

First, we must educate older people about a variety of things. The educational process itself is terribly important. Exercising one's cognitive function is as important as exercising one's heart. If it is not exercised, there will be the kind of cohort effect I mentioned earlier.

Second, older people, typically, are deprived of services, some of which are available but of which they are ignorant. They must be kept informed.

Third—and this is a major issue—the attitude of the dominant part of our society about getting old, together with the denial about what it means to be old, must be changed. Actually the chances are nineteen to one that when you are old you will still be mentally alert, involved, active, rather than winding up like a vegetative patient in a nursing home. I have been trying to persuade people that there can be a joy in aging and that many old people are happy, particularly those who prepared for this stage of their life.

Fourth, and this is related to the point I just made, what kinds of investments can we make so that one's older years will be an exciting and creative period in one's life? No one has touched this problem, but it can be met if we give it the attention and economic support it must have. For example, what can we do to prevent some of the deterioration of aging? How much of it is preventable? What are useful roles for older persons to play? How can we foster creativity?

The most important thing we can do is to break out of this whole business of denying the realities of aging and the fear of what aging involves. I recently attended a conference on death and dying. One of the most salient things that came out of that conference— which was made up of about 125 health-care professionals, nearly all of whom had worked with dying patients—was that most people who are dying are comfortable in talking about their death, they want to talk about their death. They are not nearly as depressed about the fact of their impending death as are the people who are taking care of them and who cause "the problem" by running away from the issue. That is really where we are now with aging and the fear and ignorance of aging.

Older people are increasing in number at a faster rate than younger people. By the end of the century, we will have twenty-nine million older Americans. Older people are a tremendous untapped resource in our country. The question is whether we will merely create a larger pool of "superfluous" human beings out of our older citizens or integrate everyone into the total society.

Adolescent Girls: A Two-Year Study

by Gisela Konopka

The Center Quarterly Focus is on the findings of a 2-year nationwide study of the adolescent girl directed by Dr. Gisela Konopka.

At an all-day conference October 7, 1975, in the St. Paul Student Center, University of Minnesota, some 500 persons — students, faculty, practitioners — reacted to and discussed in small groups, materials developed out of the study begun in October, 1973.

Supported by a grant from the Lilly Endowment, Incorporated, Dr. Konopka and a staff of specially trained researchers in 12 different states undertook to identify the wide variety of needs, aspirations and concerns of young women 12 to 18 years old. The 920 women, interviewed in both rural and urban settings, represented every racial, religious and ethnic group and a range of socioeconomic backgrounds. One-third of the women were adjudicated delinquent, one-third were active in youth organizations, and one-third fell into neither category. An informally structured but open-ended 60-90 minute interview with each girl was taped. Subsequently, these sessions were analyzed according to the girl's views, beliefs and feelings on education, careers, marriage, children, the women's movement, adults, friends, drugs and alcohol, sexuality, social and political concerns, relationships with adults, experiences with and recommendations for youth organizations.

Three literature searches were completed: (1) a review of the professional literature in the past ten years on adolescent girls, (2) youth agency publications, and (3) fiction written for and read by adolescent women.

Gisela Konopka's book containing her findings and recommendations based on them was published by Prentice-Hall under the title *Young Girls: A Portrait of Adolescence* in December, 1975. Poems by the girls quoted in the following presentation are taken from the book.

This Quarterly, which does not purport to cover the wide range of opinions expressed by the girls, is organized into two parts: Gisela Konopka's remarks at the conference (edited for publication), and selected questions and responses relating primarily to practice. Certain findings are dealt with at some length — others, not at all. Questions relating to practice also are limited. However, the questions from the participants do reflect some of the current concerns in their work with adolescents at this time.

All of the materials generated by the study are available to scholars, students and practitioners in the offices of the Center for Youth Development and Research. It is hoped they will be used. The Related Readings in this Quarterly were taken from the extensive, annotated Bibliography available also in the Center office.

Miriam Seltzer, Editor,
Center Quarterly Focus

Center Quarterly Focus, published by the Center for Youth Development and Research, University of Minnesota, St. Paul, Minnesota.

Dr. Gisela Konopka, D.S. W., is Professor and Director of the Center for Youth Development and Research at the University of Minnesota, St. Paul, Minnesota.

I have always maintained that when we set out to talk about people we should first let them talk about themselves. I cannot bring 920 girls here to speak to you in person, but I can let a few speak through their poetry. They write beautiful poetry. This poem was written by a 15-year-old girl in a delinquency institution. She talks about herself and her generation.

I am a bottle
Sealed with feeling
too deep for anyone else.
I am a bottle
floating in an eternal ocean of people
trying to help.
I am a bottle
keeping my fragile content inside it,
always afraid of breaking and exposing me.
I am a bottle
frail and afraid of the rock and afraid of the storm,
for if the storm or rocks burst or crack me
I sink and become part of the ocean.
I am a person, I am a person
In the people of the world.

Though I have to generalize about what we found in our study, it is important to remember that *every person is somewhat different from any other.* I also want to say at the outset that I am talking about reality — what we actually heard, not necessarily what we wished to hear. This poem by a 16-year-old speaks to individuality.

I used to be a grape in a bunch
and all the other grapes were the same,
But now I am an apple, crisp and fresh
and everyone is different.
My, how life has changed.

These 12- to 18-year-olds were born into national and international strife with the beginning of inflation and depression. The general environment of their parent generation was characterized by prosperity, though it does not follow that all of them participated in prosperity. Their grandparents lived through the depression of the 30's. Each generation grows up in a different kind of context. The girls we interviewed hold high hopes of better justice for all. Their generation comes after the fighting generation, and they are experiencing the harsh reaction against the preceding rebellion. They are very self-conscious adolescents, even more so because they are female. Though we rarely heard the girls talk abstractly about their self concepts, everything they said was permeated by their concept of self.

I shall try to report what they said according to what I thought was significant to them: (1) their present drives, their dreams for the future; (2) their family, important as a supporting and limiting power; (3) their friends, important as mirrors of themselves; (4) the organizations they joined; (5) the school, again important as a supporting and limiting power; and (6) the political and social scene.

LIFE GOALS

Marriage

This generation of young women wants both marriage and a career. They have thought it through in rather a calm way. In general they do not expect to marry early. "I want to get married when the time comes and the time is right. I don't want to rush it because I want to make sure. It's like if there was a problem you have to pay so much money to get a divorce and I don't think it's right. If two people love each other they should be able to stay together without those laws between them." I'm not saying there will be no teenage marriages, but on the average they think after 22 is a good time to get married. One thing stands out: marriage means a great deal to them but they do not want to be married to a domineering male. Again there are exceptions, but this is feared with great realism, particularly in the poverty area. "I would rather be more like friends with my husband. That comes first." "I just want to marry someone who shares a lot of the same interests I do and we can get along with each other."

Children

Many girls want children, but they know they have a choice as to when and how many. Most of them wanted three; many wanted fewer; very few wanted more. They thought of raising children mostly in terms of very young children. This business of really raising a human being had not sunk in very deeply.

Divorce

We found an extraordinary fear of divorce. When they talked freely this terrible fear came through. Typical statements: "What is the use of getting married if you just get divorced?" "The children will be hurt."

Careers

The choice of careers is influenced by life experiences—by what we might call adult models. Organizations and schools have given them very little conscious exposure to such models. Counselors in schools seemed to be especially ineffective. "Talking to them is like talking to a brick wall." White collar jobs are preferred. The most tradition-bound group were the adjudicated girls.

SEX

Sex is talked about very calmly by most of the girls. They accept themselves as sexual beings. This is not to say they all wanted to have premarital sex, but practically all of them were very tolerant of others who do. Even if they said, "That's not for me," they were tolerant. "I want to wait until I get married, but I don't look down on a friend."

There was enormous fear, however, of being used sexually. They believed a boyfriend should be an equal, a friend, "gentle, nice, someone who listens." *Listens* was written large. Practically none of the girls would want to just go from one love affair to another.

Sexual Abuse; Incest

We found that first sex experiences which had been disastrous and harmful usually happened to girls in their own homes. I'm not talking exclusively of incest. Sometimes it was the father, of course, but often it was a brother, another relative, or the mother's boyfriend. The tragedy is that these girls, when they run away from an intolerable situation, are treated as offenders, not as victims. We do exactly the most harmful thing in such a situation: we put them into institutions where they are separated completely from men and cannot learn any healthy relationship to the other sex. Furthermore, they are labeled. As one of the girls said, "Well, if they put me there, I am bad." This increases their sense of inferiority. They become outcasts.

Pregnancy before Marriage

The attitude of most of the girls toward pregnancy before marriage again is one of tolerance. This is not a militant generation. Many would want to keep the child, but tend to think of the child only as a baby. Some talk about adoption. They discuss abortion openly. About half of the group were strongly for abortion, half were strongly against it.

Sex information was incredibly poor — an absolute disgrace in 1975. To be sure, there were exceptions. One girl said, "When I first found out I was pregnant I didn't even know what pregnant meant and I went to the nurse and she told me 'that means you're going to have a little baby,' and I said 'What?' And then I told my parents and then I thought I had really been bad." Many did not even know about menstruation.

To summarize, I don't think we found a sex revolution, but there is greater tolerance for premarital sex. There is still an enormous need to help people understand sex. The institutionalized girl was the worst off. She had gone through horrible experiences and most of the time was a victim. She was treated as the offender and made to feel an outcast.

RELATIONSHIP TO ADULTS

Generation Gap

I would like to discuss the relationship of the girls to adults in terms of three myths that we must destroy. One is the much publicized generation gap. Naturally there is always a generation difference, but I would not say it is a great gap. The values the girls hold are often quite similar to those of the adult world. What they expect of people is what we expect of people, too. Negative qualities of adults they mentioned were "phony, nosey, grouchy, greedy, self-conscious; they stereotype us, they don't like us." Positives named included "fun to be with, understanding, respect us, will listen, care, trust us and deserve trust, are patient, fair and just."

Relationship to Parents

The second myth is that the family is totally falling apart, that young people want to get out of the family. We found they want a family very badly, yearn for a family if they don't have it. A girl who was thrown out by her family said in a poem: "Loneliness is missing your family, it's not knowing what to say."

Really surprising to us was that the most significant adult named by a majority of the girls was mother. They want to be related to mother and often have very good relationships with their mother. "She is just fantastic. She can yell at us, but we really respect her. She is always there to help. She understands, she works, and she knows who she is." That last sentence was rather typical. The nonsense about the working mother being the worst is not true. I think young people are quite realistic about parents.

Next in rank among significant adults was father. Yet he showed up as more authoritarian, often less communicative, and tending to lose contact when the girls reach adolescence. Fathers, it was reported, don't want daughters to grow up; they want them to remain their little girl. "Oh, he's quite tolerant about a lot of things, but, oh boy, if I go out, oh my little girl, that shouldn't happen."

Another finding, not startling but exciting, was the warm relationship with the grandparent generation. These are real people whom the girls love. This is also true of uncles and aunts. "I can talk with them. My grandmother tells me she wasn't always good, but my mother would never say that."

Permissiveness

The third myth I want to hit hard is that this is a permissive society. We found incredibly authoritarian families, the vast majority in fact. We found the battered adolescent. "When I do something wrong he beats the shit out of me. If I wouldn't clean the table right, or especially if I talked back, or if I started to cry or showed any feeling, my stepfather would beat me up." Or, "She wouldn't let me go nowhere. She beat me with braided ropes, extension cords, yardsticks, boards, whatever she could find when she was mad." A girl described being brought in by police for something she had done. The parents turned to the policeman and said, "What would you do?" He said, "Well, if she were my girl I'd give her a good beating with a police belt." "All right," the father said, "give me the belt" (it has a big buckle) and in front of everybody the girl is beaten with the belt. She gets hysterical, falls on the floor, starts laughing and laughing. The more she laughs the more they beat her. Then she walks upstairs and vomits all day. Again, as with sex offenses, these girls are not treated as victims, always as offenders. With some exceptions, the treatment in delinquency institutions is abominable. Too much still is done to degrade the girls. One girl said, "My mother always told me, 'Whenever you see anyone crying, just try to talk to them.' But up here you can't do it because they will start yelling at you, 'You shut your mouth or you will get three days strict you know.' Being locked up, that's the worst. You can't get out, you can't say what you want, you can't do what you want. They bust teenagers for just anything. There is nothing you can do. They're just over you." The hate such conditions create is illustrated by one girl's solution: "Blow everybody up and get people to know what they are doing." Some institutions do try to provide help, especially those that are smaller. Quoting another interviewee: "Our counselor here will try to help you. If you don't want to go to her you can talk to one of the girls."

PEERS

Another important subject we explored was how adolescent girls feel about their peers. What about the loneliness that showed up so strongly in my previous study?* It is still there. Friends of their own age are very important, but adults are just as important. The girls stressed that friends must be trustworthy and you must be able to talk to them. That goes for both boys and girls, not just girls. What they do when they are with friends is pretty much the same, whether the group includes boys or not. Some have sex relations, but they want the boy also as a friend. The delinquent girls talked a great deal about how their boyfriends support them, give them some sense of value. This prop is taken away the moment they are placed in an institution. These girls also suffer from distrust by the community. One interviewee who had become pregnant before marriage was not allowed to go to the same school she had attended, a youth organization of which she was a member immediately excluded her, the parents of her friends did not allow their daughters to communicate with her, and she became a total isolate. This kind of thing we heard frequently.

We found few gang activities. Where they existed, girls were part of the gang, not just the auxiliary. Though there was violence in the gangs and they retaliated with violence, most girls disliked the violence.

Suicide attempts were frequent in our survey population. The reasons are the same as those found in any other population. Enormous loneliness, which we find again among the aged, is one. I was interested in a couplet quoted to us by girls across the country:

Loneliness is a silent jail
Without cellmates, parole or bail.

Other reasons for suicide attempts were severe conflicts, either with the boyfriend or with the parents. Occasionally they were related to depressive drugs, especially alcohol. I am often asked if we found much homosexuality or lesbianism. The answer is we didn't. We certainly found it in the delinquency institutions, but all of us know it flourishes there because of the total segregation from boys. Oddly enough, in terms of attitudes, homosexuality was the most disliked quality. Tolerance about sex did not seem to extend to homosexuality or lesbianism.

---

*Konopka, Gisela, *The Adolescent Girl in Conflict,* Englewood Cliffs, N.J.: Prentice-Hall, 1966.

DRUGS AND ALCOHOL

Not surprisingly, we found an increase in alcohol use, partially because there is less conflict with society about it and partially because it is often fostered by the parents. The girls themselves stressed the negative effects of hard drugs. They see them as a danger, but as for marijuana — most of them hardly consider it a drug. They want it to be legalized. Half of the girls said they do not use drugs but they all knew of them. That applies just as much to rural areas as to urban areas. A question we asked was: "Why do you think girls take drugs? Is it different from why boys take drugs?" They said no, it was kind of the same: curiosity, peer pressure, finding drugs agreeable. But they thought boys also take drugs to prove their masculinity. Whether they evaluated the boys correctly I don't know.

We thought drug information often increased curiosity, but on the other hand it showed quite well the different effects drug use can have. We felt that strong motivation is required to stop taking drugs. "My boyfriend doesn't want me to take drugs and I want to please him." Or "I want to have healthy children, so that's why I stopped." They feel they cannot talk to adults about drugs. Most of them thought their parents did not know it when they took drugs. Among girls who belonged to youth organizations (one-third of our sample) most knew about or had taken drugs, but they said, "Oh my goodness, we would never mention it there!"

SOCIAL AND POLITICAL INVOLVEMENT

My first impression when I looked at this part of the material was: this is really catastrophic! They are terribly self-concerned, they don't know how to participate in the political scene, they are disenchanted about things political, they don't feel responsible as citizens. After more careful reading of the material and discussion with my researchers, I recognized that first of all we must think of adolescence as a period of basic self-concern anyhow. Second, many adults do not participate in the political scene either. We were interviewing at the height of Watergate, so that had a strong influence. Finally, we have to remember that the girls actually were very concerned about issues but they did not know how to translate their concern into action. This was the first time they had been asked what their thoughts were. They talked about war, about government cheating, about race relations, and about issues relating to youth — e.g., the draft and the juvenile court. We also talked with them about the women's movement. Very often they saw only the extremes in the movement, which they didn't care for. But when we probed a little deeper we saw that they have simply accepted as their due what others fought for: equal pay for equal work, open opportunities for women, etc. So although they are not revolutionaries, they are involved, as this poem illustrates. It was written by a 16-year-old who has dropped out of school but wants very much to be a lawyer.

You talk about the problems of the world
and I am not allowed to speak because I am just a little girl.
But there is something I would like to say to you, you know
It's my world too.
You think that you can understand more than anyone at all
But mister, you are really short when you think you are tall.
And I'm not allowed to give my opinions because I'm not as big as you.
Try not to forget
It's my world too.
They talk about young people all the time
But they don't think of others who are out of line

And some problems mean nothing to you
But while I am living here
It's my world too.
What I want is the best for everyone
Cuz thinking of yourself is not good in a long run.
So think about what you want for me and you
And while you are thinking, remember
It's my world too.

SCHOOL

School was often seen as very positive, mostly because the girls find friends there. Race discrimination hurts deeply, especially when teachers insult minority girls or show fear of them. Their anger at being treated differently flares out, "What do they think I am, an animal?" Many girls experience enjoyment in school. When we asked what they expect of school they spoke of friendship and understanding, but also of learning. Often the subjects they preferred were those we consider difficult. Exceptions were the delinquent girls who usually have been treated abominably and feel that school has nothing for them.

YOUTH ORGANIZATIONS

We found it rather sad that youth organizations seem to have little meaning to the girls. In general they found them childish. Perhaps the most serious finding was an indirect one: when we asked them about significant adults, two girls out of 920 named two people from youth-serving organizations. The girls do not think they can talk with youth workers if they have problems. "Organizations are only for the good ones."

I read an article recently stating that nobody knows what kind of people we want to develop. If we don't know that, then I think we should really give up. Every society has to decide what kind of people it wants. To my thinking it is really quite simple. I go to the ideals of the Bill of Rights, which I did not invent: (1) an open free society based on the proposition that the purpose of government is to advance and protect human rights; (2) a representative form of democratic government which means that citizens must be encouraged to participate in their own fate and have the necessary knowledge to do so, otherwise it will not survive; (3) a society ruled by law; (4) an egalitarian non-discriminatory society with equal opportunity for everybody; (5) a pluralistic society with opportunity for groups to have a variety of life styles without harming others or feeling that one or the other style is inferior. If we combine these ideals we get a sense of direction, a sense of how to deal with our youth in the family, in schools, in youth organizations and in corrections. The time has passed for rigid, laid-out programs for young people. Most significant are the people who work with them. They not only must understand these youngsters but must consciously see how they themselves relate to people. They must be able to listen to and respect young people and permit their genuine participation. I felt very strongly that these young girls were asking us not only to listen to them but to convey something of the meaning of life to them. They want to talk, they want to think things through, they want absolute honesty.

The young people we talked to were very sober. We must help them feel that there is hope, that there is compassion, that joy and commitment actually are possible. So I will end with a thought from Morris West who understands the stark reality of life but also understands it beauty.

To reject the joy of living is to insult Him who provides it,
And who gave us the gift of laughter along with the gift of tears.

Our young population has that gift. We squelch it far too often; we do not enhance it enough.

Questions and answers related to practice

DOGMA AND DIRECTION

Q. How do we move between the two extremes of trying to impose ideals upon young people (making them what we think they should be) and not giving them any direction at all?

G.K. This seems to me to be one of the philosophic questions that I hope everybody can go back and discuss with the girls themselves. To think through the difference between dogma and direction is an exciting experience at almost any age. I don't expect we will ever find the complete answer. But if our ideal is a population capable of making choices on two grounds (1) consideration of other people and (2) facts, then we have to learn to look at facts, to assess them, and to develop a measuring stick for making choices. I think we can help people learn how to make choices without imposing our own styles on them. We must allow them a large number of alternatives.

BUILDING TRUST

Q. In what ways can a worker cooperatively build trust between group and leader?

G. K. First of all, you surely don't build trust with gimmicks. Kids very quickly spot phoniness. I don't learn trust in a weekend therapy session, by falling back blindfolded and being caught before I drop. Since the whole "bag" at that moment is to create trust, I assume they won't let me drop. Does that mean I can trust the next guy I meet in the community who wants to cut my throat if I disagree with him? No.

Another way some of us try to build trust is by sitting across the desk from a person saying, "You know I understand who you are and what you think, and you must trust me." It doesn't work. Trust is built slowly, through experience. When you are working with people, be honest. By that I don't mean be brutal. But be open; don't pretend the world is all good when you know it is not. When they need you, be available. It takes time to build trust.

If you are asking me how to build trust with very distrustful young people I would need an hour to discuss it. You have to undo so much. But it is not as difficult as most adults seem to think. What came out over and over in our study was this incredible yearning to have somebody to talk to.

MEETING NEEDS – TOWARD GREATER EFFECTIVENESS

Q. Should every girls' organization try to meet all the needs of all girls, or are there some basic needs or concerns that all organizations should broaden their base to meet?

G. K. In my opinion no organization and no individual can ever serve all the needs of all the people. That's impossible. So it's all right sometimes to say we will just cut out a certain slice from the whole pie and, let's say, provide services for a particular neighborhood, or serve girls in a particular area of interest. What I think is dangerous though, is separation on the basis of delinquency or race or ethnic background.

Now, are there basic needs all organizations should meet? I think so. We may not always agree on all needs and concerns but we have to know them and develop our thinking and our programs around them, based on some philosophy. I talked about this in the Bill of Rights context. For instance, if we believe people must be able to make choices, otherwise our democracy will die, then it behooves all organizations to provide experience in making choices rather than having authoritarian leaders who set the program and expect everyone to work by the book.

If we agree that self-esteem is the basis for respecting other people, then we have to provide the ingredients which enhance self-esteem: real participation in decision-making, for instance, not just asking for opinions; genuine acceptance of young people as equals, not just as pre-adults. We can translate almost every one of these basic "shoulds" or ideals, combine them with what we understand, and make them part of our programs.

So, I would say all youth organizations have to fulfill some of the basic needs of human beings and serve a wide variety of young people, yet they cannot reach all of them.

Q. You mentioned earlier that the girls had quit some of the organizations when they were in junior high school. Can you elaborate on that — what they liked about some organizations and disliked about others?

G. K. Okay, what do they like? Written very big is opportunity for adventure—the real possibility to get out and do things that are different, not the tame camping or the usual kind of summer program. I don't mean necessarily running the rapids but just going somewhere else, meeting totally different people, discussing new and exciting things. Wish for excitement is very big in that age range.

I don't usually name names, but 4-H got a good press so I'll use it as a concrete example. One thing the girls liked there was the coed organization which allowed them to be with boys at some times. We found kind of a general feeling: "No, we don't want always to be with boys but we like to have the opportunity to work with them and not just to party with them." Second, they liked individualized projects — not programs where everybody has to do the same thing. They liked the feeling of doing something distinct and getting recognition for it. Third, they liked being allowed to travel. "It wasn't just going on a vacation. We did something, we exhibited something, we worked on something together, and we were somewhere else." Being involved in actual helping also is important to them, as is the kind of adult they meet. Their most negative reaction is to the adult who treats them like little kids and looks down on them.

I think all organizations could be more effective. One of my great hopes is that we will get away from the notion of compartmentalization — school is for learning, youth organizations are for fun, parents are for nurture. We have to work together and eliminate the jealousies among us. For that we need the right kind of people. Partially they have to be found, but partially they can also be developed through training. At the Center we are starting a two-year project, funded by the Lilly Endowment, Incorporated, in which we hope to train 400 significant personnel within eight youth-serving organizations plus some staff from corrections.

REACHING TROUBLED ADOLESCENTS

Q. Do you have any ideas on how organizations and resources can better reach troubled adolescents?

G. K. First of all, do not segregate them. Why do we call one "troubled" and another "untroubled?" I have not yet seen an adolescent who is not troubled at times. In fact, I have not seen a person who is not troubled at times, regardless of age, but in adolescence everything is worse. It's a more touchy age. Almost every experience is brand new. The ability to see failure in perspective has not yet been developed. For instance, you have fallen in love and the boy leaves you. You haven't experienced this before and you are ready to commit suicide. In contrast, I feel scared before I give a speech but I have experienced over and over that somehow it will work out. So I am anxious, but not desperate.

My answer then is: first, don't segregate; second, take the troubles seriously, but don't look on the "troubled" as a group apart; third, understand the enormous range of normalcy.

In general, much of what we consider emotionally disturbed is normal.

Q. What are the alternatives to traditional ways of dealing with runaways?

G. K. Certainly they vary. Sometimes we treat runaways as offenders rather than as victims, and then things get worse and worse and worse. I think definitely this has to stop. There have been some very good places for runaways here in the Twin Cities — open places where a girl could go and stay. But some changes are taking place that worry me. The current approach seems to be "now that we have been good enough to take you in, we expect you to bare your soul. Tell us all about yourself." That's not what I call an alternative. Neighborhood houses used to offer people refuge, but few such residences exist any more. Desperately needed, I think, is a network of residences all over the country (not only in the cities) where young people can stay for a time and where they will find helping people to talk to if they wish, but only if they wish. These residences might be called youth hostels— not runaway houses or half-way houses. We who work with youth often have gold in our hands, not yet tarnished by the taste of being something bad. Why label prematurely a person in the making? Just because our young people take to the road we don't have to label them runaways.

CHANGING STRUCTURES THAT OPPRESS YOUTH

Q. What can be done politically to change the structures that oppress youth and especially female youth?

G. K. I do not think that youth is totally "oppressed." Perhaps the most important structure in need of change is the family structure where double standards still prevail. Girls in our study often complained that they were not allowed to go out in the evening but their brother was, or the boy was allowed to hike in summer with a group but the girl wasn't. And this distinction was not made on the basis of age; it was strictly boy/girl. Sexuality is not the only basis for uneven treatment, but it certainly is the strongest one.

I see changing the family structure not so much in terms of making a new structure but rather in terms of moving away from the male dominated authoritarian structure. I also see the family structure as a mirror of the political structure. That means in the old monarchies in authoritarian countries the family followed the same pattern. Most people in this country come from this kind of background where the king was at the helm and below him were the people subservient to him. Now it is odd that change in political structure does not necessarily result in change in other structures. It didn't follow in the family; frequently it didn't follow in the schools. But these are structures that need to be changed.

Another structure that definitely must be changed is the one surrounding status offenses. Boys and girls are brought before the courts because they are not going to school. Americans feel very embarrassed because our delinquency figures are so high. Naturally they are when we count every kid that plays truant as a delinquent. I don't know of any other country which does that. If the status offender (the offender who has committed an act that would not be a crime for an adult) were to be taken off the courts, most girls wouldn't even be offenders. Most of the time they are in that category because of "sexual misconduct" which is not considered misconduct among the boys, even today. This will be changed and the change will come through the legal profession. Who will then take care of these girls? Who will work with them? I say it is the responsibility of people in the neighborhoods and of the youth organizations in the community.

Other structures — vocational education, for instance — need to be changed, too. But enough for now.

REACHING YOUNG PEOPLE

Q. How can we change our approach to young people so that we can reach them?

G. K. They are not so hard to reach. They want to be reached. They want to be listened to; they don't want to be talked down to; and they don't want to be constantly told that they must be exactly what someone else is. I'll finish up with an illuminating poem from a 16-year-old girl:

> *I used to be the cocoon all wrapped up*
> *in what I thought then was safety*
> *insulating myself from all the hurts and joys of life.*
> *Afraid of so much of love, strangers, of being rejected*
> *Of trying new things, of being wrong, of being laughed at.*
> *Or of just being.*
> *Snuggled in my security blanket, I miss so much.*
> *Now I am the worm, just breaking through the cocoon*
> *Crawling slowly, inching my way towards the light.*
> *Crawling a little, a little, each day, I hope.*
> *Trying not to slip back a foot for every inch I gain.*
> *Some day I will be that butterfly, free and glorious,*
> *not afraid of everything I do.*

The message I get: Don't make young people feel they have to be afraid; let them be creative; try not to crush the butterfly; let them think, live, be concerned and develop.

RELATED READINGS

Conger, John Janeway. *Adolescence and Youth.* New York: Harper and Row, 1973.
   Related physical development and self concept. Outward appearance and inner self-image are more closely bound together for females than for males.
Gottlieb, David, ed. *Youth in Contemporary Society.* Beverly Hills: Sage Publications, 1973.
   Contributors identify and analyze anticipated trends in youth behavior. Focus is on implications for programs and policies dealing with youth in the decade ahead. Includes good chapter on drugs and one on "the real generation gap."
The Mood of American Youth, 1974. Reston, Virginia: National Association of Secondary School Principals, 1974.
   A poll was conducted of 2,000 high school students sampled nationwide by the Gilbert Youth Research Division of Herff-Jones. Outlines the national issues of concern to youth. Reflects a determined and ambitious generation of students who are committed to their own individual goals.
National YWCA Resource Center on Women. *Teen Women Tell About Their Needs.* New York: National Board, YWCA, 1974.
   Questionnaires were sent to 1,111 adolescent women and four workshops were held, to determine young women's concerns. Subject areas are: jobs, sex, recreation, drugs, child care, counseling, racism, women's changing roles. Implications for programs are evident. The project was planned and carried out under the leadership of teen women.

2B A SENSE OF COMMUNITY

Neighbourhoods and Human Needs

by Margaret Mead

Human beings must be brought up among human beings who have learned from other human beings how to live in a particular way. There are very few cultural differences when we discuss basic human needs; that is, the floor below which the human being must not be permitted to fall.

Primarily, the neighbourhood is the place where children are brought up to become members of their own society. Inevitably, within a neighbourhood, children encounter various older adults from whose experience they learn how to adapt themselves to the kind of society into which they are growing. In a static society, older experienced people who have learned nothing new in their lifetime are the greatest asset, for they transmit the entire heritage to the children. But in a society that is changing, grandparents who are continually learning and who have themselves participated in change have the highest potentiality for transmitting a sense of adaptation. The neighbourhood, where children learn to meet basic human needs and to move toward the use of higher human capacities, is where they first encounter adults—parents and grandparents and unrelated adults of these two generations. The older people may not include their own grandparents (for in some parts of the world there is an extraordinary lack of tolerance of one's own relatives), but there will be some members of the grandparental generation who are treated with consideration.

Of course, any neighbourhood that we design, or that we attempt to ameliorate, must meet the basic physiological needs for all human beings—the essential needs that human beings share with animals; the need for food, water, space, sleep, rest, and a minimum of privacy.

Of these, privacy is one of the most variable. There are societies that have no word for privacy, and when the idea is explained to them they think it is horrible. In one society in which I worked—Samoa—a curtain hung between me and other members of the household gave me a certain privacy; but in a house without walls nothing separated me from the rest of the village, from whose eyes, obviously, I did not need the protection of privacy. Nevertheless, some sort of privacy, some small, identifiable spatial territory of one's

"Neighbourhoods and Human Needs," by Margaret Mead, *Ekistics,* February 1966, Vol. 21, No. 123, pp. 124-126. Reprinted with permission.

Dr. Margaret Mead, author and anthropologist, is currently with the Department of Anthropology, Columbia University, School of General Studies, New York, New York.

own—even if it is only a hook on which to hang one's own hat—seems to be a basic human need.

A second basic need is for some continuity in human relationships. It need not be affectionate or even kind. One society that I studied—the Mundugumor—reared their children to be effective and happy cannibals, but Mundugumor methods of child rearing would seem very harsh to us. It never occurred to a mother to give her baby the breast when it cried; instead, she put it in a flat scratchy basket, which she hung up high so the baby could see what was going on. Then, when the baby became restless, she scratched the outside of the basket, making a sound like the squeak of chalk on a blackboard, and the baby stopped crying. It was not an affectionate sound, but it was a sound that assured the baby of continuity in its human environment.

The idea that a baby must be brought up by its biological mother and that it will be traumatized by the mother's absence for a week derives from a recognition of this need for continuity. But, in fact, the child who is reared from birth to be accustomed to eight different human beings, all of whom are close, can be given a sense of continuity by any one of them. And where the immediate environment—the shape of its bed and the smell of its room—is part of what is continuous, the child can stand a greater variety of persons close to it.

This means that in planning neighbourhoods for the future, various possibilities are open to us. We can turn the family car into a house, and when the child, together with the cat and the dog and familiar toys, is moved to a strange place the car will still be a familiar home. Or we can bring children up to live in the same place every summer but in a different place each winter. We can do a great many different things, providing we keep in mind the basic need for continuity and familiarity. There is considerable evidence that failure to take this need into account may lead to severe conflict in young children, and so we are faced with the problem of how to move children safely from highly familiar to entirely unfamiliar environments, with nothing to bridge the gap. A familiar and trustworthy environment is necessary for the child to learn that things will be here tomorrow that are here today and that its hand, reaching out, will find what it is seeking for. But we must also recognize that continuity can be provided for in many different ways.

If children are to be ready to live in a changing world, they must also be prepared to deal with strangeness almost from the day of their birth. For those who live in the modern world, it is a disabling experience to grow up knowing only their own relatives. The fewer the relatives, the more disabling an experience it is. And yet, all over the world, as older forms of the extended family are breaking down into small, isolated nuclear family groups, the child is becoming disastrously overdependent on its two parents. Disastrous in the sense that living in large cities is disastrous for those who have not learned to deal with a variety of people and who have not learned to expect that the strange will be interesting and rewarding or to recognize that it must be treated with a certain wariness.

The inclusion of the strange has implications for the size of the basic neighbourhood. That is, the neighbourhood cannot be modeled on the primitive village where everyone knows everyone else and everything is familiar. There are, however, some people who would like to keep everything within a safe, closed environment—keep all the cars out, keep all the strangers out, and turn the neighbourhood into a grass plot where all the children can run. There is no doubt that a neighbourhood must have something that is child-scale, some place where children can walk about. I am inclined to think that if children can walk enough, the question of whether or not adults are walkers is less serious. Adults can tolerate enormous specialization—even many kinds of deprivation—if, as children, their senses have been stimulated. One striking example of this can be seen in the experience of people who have suffered deafness, blindness or paralysis in later life, but who still can draw on earlier experience of hearing, vision and movement. Helen Keller is probably the best example of such a person. She could hear and see up to the time she learned her first word, and this early experience preserved for her a sense of the world that carried her through her later incredible sensory isolation. All this suggests that the better we can build into neighbourhoods ways of humanizing the small child in the fullest sense of the word, the greater tolerance the adult will have for the strangeness and stresses of a world in which some people may be physically highly restricted for long periods as they move into outer space or deep in the sea—experiences for which human beings have had little evolutionary preparation. Certainly, we need areas where young children are safe, and where they can move on their own legs (and this, of course, will affect the location of nursery schools and primary schools); but we also need to provide for their living dangerously part of the time, even while they are very young. Strangeness and danger are part of living in an urban environment.

The anonymity of the city is one of its strengths as well as—carried too far— one of its weaknesses. Even the young baby, growing up to live in a city, needs to have windows on the unknown world. The shopping center, in which the child encounters strangers and sees its mother encountering strangers, is one such window. But at the same time, the child needs the grass plot, the protected walk, and the nursery school where everything is close and familiar. Only in this way can the small child achieve the autonomy that is necessary at every stage of development. There must be play places in front yards where children can walk safely without fear of traffic. When children move into a newly built housing estate that is inadequately protected from automobiles, parents may be so frightened that the children—who have no preparation for dealing with traffic—will run under the wheels of the cars, that they give the children no freedom of movement at all. In one tribe I know of, the village was located at some distance from a big river. Then, one year, the river changed its course and ran right through the village. The adults, who had no idea what to do, were terrified of the water and, of course, their children fell into the river. In contrast, another people who had lived on the river for a long time knew how to teach their children—and their children were safe. Today, we have to teach our children not only about rivers, but also about traffic: to realize its dangers and be wary of them and also to know how to take chances safely. So, too, in every neighbourhood, there must be places where older children can move freely away from the familiars with confidence, trust, and toleration of strangers and the strange.

Children also need multisensory stimulation. There are several reasons for this. Because of tremendous individual differences, we do not know whether a particular child will be most dependent on hearing, sight or touch: Moreover, in different contexts, there may be a greater emphasis on the use of the eyes or the use of the ears. The child who, as a small child, has lacked multisensory stimulation will be handicapped in making the necessary transition from one to the other. But, beyond these considerations, there is evidence that multisensory cross-referencing is a very creative source of innovation in thought, and we want to bring up children who have the capacity for innovation in a dynamic world.

Children need an environment in which they can learn fine discrimination—in which they can hear small sounds and learn to differentiate between footsteps, learn to hear slight differences in tones of voice, learn to wake and know what time it is. Some peoples have a greater sensitivity to noise and want to shut more of it out than other peoples do. This is something in which whole cultures can be differentiated one from another. But in all cultures, human beings—in order to be human—must understand the non-human. They must have some understanding of plants and animals, water and sunshine, earth, the stars, the moon and the sun. People who have not appreciated the stars cannot really appreciate satellites; they are confused as to which is which. This need to know about the non-human also affects what is necessary for a good neighbourhood. There must be water, preferably water that moves, for moving water is one of the major experiences through which a child's senses are amplified. There must also be earth—not merely a sandbox. There must be animals, although not necessarily large animals. A child can learn about animals as well from fish in a pond as from buffalo on a prairie, and he can dig in a miniature garden as well as in a great field.

Providing the pattern is complete, the scale can be reduced and the details of the arrangement can be different in different neighbourhoods. The child needs to learn what lives in the water, what lives in the air, what lives on earth, and how human beings are related to these growing, living, singing, fighting and playing creatures. Any environment is crippling if it cuts the child off from such experiences. The child who has grown up in peach country—who has learned to register, as he wakes up, a drop in temperature and knows how this will affect what people will do—has acquired a lifetime familiarity. He can live in a city for forty years, but when he goes back to the peach country and sees the peach blossoms, he can still wake up at two o'clock in the morning and say what the people are going to do. Experience of this kind is never lost.

A principal aim in building a neighbourhood must be to give the child trust, confidence, and the kind of autonomy that can be translated into a strength to bear the strange, the unknown, and the peculiar. So children need some experience of the range of humanity in its different versions. It is nonsense that children do not have racial prejudices. Of course, they do not know which race is "superior," and this is the root of racial prejudice. However, children are sensitive to differences in physique, and a child to whom only dark-skinned people are familiar may get used to seeing white faces but shriek with terror at the sight of a white man in a bathing suit. Equally well, a white child may get used to seeing dark faces but be terrified at the discovery that the middle of someone's back is dark. We need an environment in which the child experiences differences in colour, type and physique, with sufficient range so that no one group is solely associated with unskilled labour or with the exercise of some highly skilled profession. Instead of being presented with stereotypes by age, sex, colour, class, or religion, children must have the opportunity to learn that within each range, some people are loathsome and some are delightful.

I think we must also consider how children can be presented with models of the kinds of thinking that will be required of most educated adults. Though not all children will learn in the same way, in general it is known, for example, that children who have grown up in rooms that conform to ordinary geometric forms later learn geometric thinking with relative ease. Similarly, children can learn about volumes and ratios from blocks long before they learn words to express the ideas they have grasped. And today they need somehow to learn that their own language is only one of many languages. They need to experience the fact that this object—this container for holding liquids—is called "glass" *in English*. This is something that must be learned very early, but it is part of learning that one's own culture is one of many cultures. It is part of acquiring freedom of movement in the modern world.

In building a neighbourhood that meets human needs, we start with the needs of infants. These give us the groundwork on which we can build for contact with other human beings, with the physical environment, with the living world, and with the experiences through which the individual's full humanity can be realized. For every culture, the criteria must be modified. We cannot set our sights too low, but we can aim at any height, for we have as yet scarcely begun to explore human potentialities. How these are developed will depend on the learning experiences we can provide for children through the human habitat in which they live.

The Experience of Living in Cities:
A Psychological Analysis

by Stanley Milgram

Adaptations to urban overload create characteristic qualities of city life that can be measured

> *"When I first came to New York it seemed like a nightmare. As soon as I got off the train at Grand Central I was caught up in pushing, shoving crowds on 42nd Street. Sometimes people bumped into me without apology; what really frightened me was to see two people literally engaged in combat for possession of a cab. Why were they so rushed? Even drunks on the street were bypassed without a glance. People didn't seem to care about each other at all."*

This statement represents a common reaction to a great city, but it does not tell the whole story. Obviously cities have great appeal because of their variety, eventfulness, possibility of choice, and the stimulation of an intense atmosphere that many individuals find a desirable background to their lives. Where face-to-face contacts are important, the city offers unparalleled possibilities. It has been calculated by the Regional Plan Association (1) that in Nassau County, a suburb of New York City, an individual can meet 11,000 others within a 10-minute radius of his office by foot or car. In Newark, a moderate-sized city, he can meet more than 20,000 persons within this radius. But in midtown Manhattan he can meet fully 220,000. So there is an order-of-magnitude increment in the communication possibilities offered by a great city. That is one of the bases of its appeal and, indeed, of its functional necessity. The city provides options that no other social arrangement permits. But there is a negative side, also, as we shall see.

Granted that cities are indispensable in complex society, we may still ask what contribution psychology can make to understanding the experience of living in them. What theories are relevant? How can we extend our knowledge of the psychological aspects of life in cities through empirical inquiry? If empirical inquiry is possible, along what lines should it proceed? In short, where do we start in constructing urban theory and in laying out lines of research?

Observation is the indispensable starting point. Any observer in the streets of midtown Manhattan will see (i) large numbers of people, (ii) a high population density, and (iii) heterogeneity of population. These three factors need to be at the root of any sociopsychological theory of city life, for they condition all aspects of our experience in the metropolis. Louis Wirth (2) if not the first to point to these factors, is nonetheless the sociologist who relied most heavily on them in his analysis of the city. Yet, for a psychologist, there is something unsatisfactory about Wirth's theoretical variables. Numbers, density, and heterogeneity are demographic facts but they are not yet psychological facts. They are external to the individual. Psychology needs an idea that links the individual's *experience* to the demographic circumstances of urban life.

One link is provided by the concept of overload. This term, drawn from systems analysis, refers to a system's inability to process inputs from the environment because

Excerpted from *Science,* 1970, 167, No. 3924, 1461-8 (copyright ©1970 by the American Association for the Advancement of Science), with permission of the author and the publisher. A 51-minute film depicting the experiments described in this article is available to educational groups. It is entitled THE CITY AND THE SELF and is distributed by Time-Life Films, Inc., Time-Life Building, Rockefeller Center, New York, New York 10020.

Dr. Stanley Milgram is with the Graduate School of the University Center of New York, Graduate Center, New York, New York.

there are too many inputs for the system to cope with, or because successive inputs come so fast that input A cannot be processed when input B is presented. When overload is present, adaptations occur. The system must set priorities and make choices. A may be processed first while B is kept in abeyance, or one input may be sacrificed altogether. City life, as we experience it, constitutes a continuous set of encounters with overload, and of resultant adaptations. Overload characteristically deforms daily life on several levels, impinging on role performance, the evolution of social norms, cognitive functioning, and the use of facilities.

The concept has been implicit in several theories of urban experience. In 1903 George Simmel (3) pointed out that, since urban dwellers come into contact with vast numbers of people each day, they conserve psychic energy by becoming acquainted with a far smaller proportion of people than their rural counterparts do, and by maintaining more superficial relationships even with these acquaintances. Wirth (2) points specifically to the "superficiality, the anonymity, and the transitory character of urban social relations."

One adaptive response to overload, therefore, is the allocation of less time to each input. A second adaptive mechanism is disregard of low-priority inputs. Principles of selectivity are formulated such that investments of time and energy are reserved for carefully defined inputs (the urbanite disregards the drunk sick on the street as he purposefully navigates through the crowd). Third, boundaries are redrawn in certain social transactions so that the overloaded system can shift the burden to the other party in the exchange; thus, harried New York bus drivers once made change for customers, but now this responsibility has been shifted to the client, who must have the exact fare ready. Fourth, reception is blocked off prior to entrance into a system; city dwellers increasingly use unlisted telephone numbers to prevent individuals from calling them, and a small but growing number resort to keeping the telephone off the hook to prevent incoming calls. More subtly, a city dweller blocks inputs by assuming an unfriendly countenance, which discourages others from initiating contact. Additionally, social screening devices are interposed between the individual and environmental inputs (in a town of 5000 anyone can drop in to chat with the mayor, but in the metropolis organizational screening devices deflect inputs to other destinations). Fifth, the intensity of inputs is diminished by filtering devices, so that only weak and relatively superficial forms of involvement with others are allowed. Sixth, specialized institutions are created to absorb inputs that would otherwise swamp the individual (welfare departments handle the financial needs of a million individuals in New York City, who would otherwise create an army of mendicants continuously importuning the pedestrian). The interposition of institutions between the individual and the social world, a characteristic of all modern society, and most notably of the large metropolis, has its negative side. It deprives the individual of a sense of direct contact and spontaneous integration in the life around him. It simultaneously protects and estranges the individual from his social environment.

Many of these adaptive mechanisms apply not only to individuals but to institutional systems as well, as Meier (4) has so brilliantly shown in connection with the library and the stock exchange.

In sum, the observed behavior of the urbanite in a wide range of situations appears to be determined largely by a variety of adaptations to overload. I now deal with several specific consequences of responses to overload, which make for differences in the tone of city and town.

SOCIAL RESPONSIBILITY

The principal point of interest for a social psychology of the city is that moral and social involvement with individuals is necessarily restricted. This is a direct and necessary function of excess of input over capacity to process. Such restriction of involvement runs a broad spectrum from refusal to become involved in the needs of another person, even when the person desperately needs assistance, through refusal to do favors, to the simple withdrawal of courtesies (such as offering a lady a seat, or saying "sorry" when a pedestrian collision occurs). In any transaction more and more details need to be dropped as the total number of units to be processed increases and assaults an instrument of limited processing capacity.

The ultimate adaptation to an overloaded social environment is to totally disregard the needs, interests, and demands of those whom one does not define as relevant to the satisfaction of personal needs, and to develop highly efficient perceptual means of determining whether an individual falls into the category of friend or stranger. The disparity in the treatment of friends and strangers ought to be greater in cities than in towns; the time allotment and willingness to become involved with those who have no personal claim on one's time is likely to be less in cities than in towns.

Bystander Intervention in Crises

The most striking deficiencies in social responsibility in cities occur in crisis situations, such as the Genovese murder in Queens. In 1964, Catherine Genovese, coming home from a night job in the early hours of an April morning, was stabbed repeatedly, over an extended period of time. Thirty-eight residents of a respectable New York City neighborhood admit to having witnessed at least a part of the attack, but none went to her aid or called the police until after she was dead. Milgram and Hollander, writing in *The Nation* (5), analyzed the event in these terms:

Urban friendships and associations are not primarily formed on the basis of physical proximity. A person with numerous close friends in different parts of the city may not know the occupant of an adjacent apartment. This does not mean that a city dweller has fewer friends than does a villager, or knows fewer persons who will come to his aid; however, it does mean that his allies are not constantly at hand. Miss Genovese required immediate aid from those physically present. There is no evidence that the city had deprived Miss Genovese of human associations, but the friends who might have rushed to her side were miles from the scene of her tragedy.

Further, it is known that her cries for help were not directed to a specific person, they were general. But only individuals can act, and as the cries were not specifically directed, no particular person felt a special responsibility. The crime and the failure of community response seem absurd to us. At the time, it may well have seemed equally absurd to the Kew Gardens residents that not one of the neighbors would have called the police. A collective paralysis may have developed from the belief of each of the witnesses that someone else must surely have taken that obvious step.

Latané and Darley (6) have reported laboratory approaches to the study of bystander intervention and have established experimentally the following principle: the larger the number of bystanders, the less the likelihood that any one of them will intervene in an emergency. Gaertner and Bickman (7) of The City University of New York have extended the bystander studies to an examination of help across ethnic lines. Blacks and whites, with clearly identifiable accents, called strangers (through what the caller represented as an error in telephone dialing), gave them a plausible story of being stranded on an outlying highway without more dimes, and asked the stranger to call a garage. The experimenters found that the white callers had a significantly better chance of obtaining assistance than the black callers. This suggests that ethnic allegiance may well be another means of coping with overload: the city dweller can reduce excessive demands and screen out urban heterogeneity by responding along ethnic lines; overload is made more manageable by limiting the "span of sympathy."

In any quantitative characterization of the social texture of city life, a necessary first step is the application of such experimental methods as these to field situations in large cities and small towns. Theorists argue that the indifference shown in the Genovese case would not be found in a small town, but in the absence of solid experimental evidence the question remains an open one.

More than just callousness prevents bystanders from participating in altercations between people. A rule of urban life is respect for other people's emotional and social privacy, perhaps because physical privacy is so hard to achieve. And in situations for which the standards are heterogeneous, it is much harder to know whether taking an active role is unwarranted meddling or an appropriate response to a critical situation. If a husband and wife are quarreling in public, at what point should a bystander step in? On the one hand, the heterogeneity of the city produces substantially greater tolerance about behavior, dress, and codes of ethics than is generally found in the small town, but this diversity also encourages people to withhold aid for fear of antagonizing the participants or crossing an inappropriate and difficult-to-define line.

Moreover, the frequency of demands present in the city gives rise to norms of noninvolvement. There are practical limitations to the Samaritan impulse in a major city. If a citizen attended to every needy person, if he were sensitive to and acted on every altruistic impulse that was evoked in the city, he could scarcely keep his own affairs in order.

Willingness to Trust and Assist Strangers

We now move away from crisis situations to less urgent examples of social responsibility. For it is not only in situations of dramatic need but in the ordinary, everyday willingness to lend a hand that the city dweller is said to be deficient relative to his small-town cousin. The comparative method must be used in any empirical examination of this question. A commonplace social situation is staged in an urban setting and in a small town—a situation to which a subject can respond by either extending help or withholding it. The responses in town and city are compared.

One factor in the purported unwillingness of urbanites to be helpful to strangers may well be their heightened sense of physical (and emotional) vulnerability—a feeling that is supported by urban crime statistics. A key test for distinguishing between city and town behavior, therefore, is determining how city dwellers compare with town dwellers in offering aid that increases their personal vulnerability and requires some trust of strangers. Altman, Levine, Nadien, and Villena (8) of The City University of New York devised a study to compare the behaviors of city and town dwellers in this respect. The criterion used in this study was the willingness of householders to allow strangers to enter their home to use the telephone. The student investigators individually rang doorbells, explained that they had misplaced the address of a friend nearby, and asked to use the phone. The investigators (two males and two females) made 100 requests for entry into homes in the city and 60 requests in the small towns. The results of middle-income housing developments in Manhattan were compared with data for several small towns (Stony Point, Spring Valley, Ramapo, Nyack, New City, and West Clarkstown) in Rockland County, outside of New York City. As Table 1 shows, in all cases there was a sharp increase in the proportion of entires achieved by an experimenter when he moved from the city to a small town. In the most extreme case the experimenter was five times as likely to gain admission to homes in a small town as to homes in Manhattan. Although the female experimenters had notably greater success both in cities and in towns than the male experimenters had, each of the four students did at least twice as well in towns as in cities. This suggests that the city-town distinction overrides even the predictably greater fear of male strangers than of female ones.

TABLE 1. PERCENTAGE OF ENTRIES ACHIEVED BY INVESTIGATORS FOR CITY AND TOWN DWELLINGS (SEE TEXT).

Experimenter	Entries Achieved (%)	
	City*	Small town†
Male		
No. 1	16	40
No. 2	12	60
Female		
No. 3	40	87
No. 4	40	100

* Number of requests for entry, 100. †Number of requests for entry, 60.

The lower level of helpfulness by city dwellers seems due in part to recognition of the dangers of living in Manhattan, rather than to mere indifference or coldness. It is significant that 75 percent of all the city respondents received and answered messages by shouting through peepholes; in the towns, by contrast, about 75 percent of the respondents opened the door.

Supporting the experimenters' quantitative results was their general observation that the town dwellers were noticeably more friendly and less suspicious than the city dwellers. In seeking to explain the reasons for the greater sense of psychological vulnerability city dwellers feel, above and beyond the differences in crime statistics, Villena (8) points out that, if a crime is committed in a village, a resident of a neighboring village may not perceive the crime as personally relevant, though the geographic distance may be small, whereas a criminal act committed anywhere in the city, though miles from the city-dweller's home is still verbally located within the city; thus, Villena says, "the inhabitant of the city possesses a larger vulnerable space."

Civilities

Even at the most superficial level of involvement—the exercise of everyday civilities—urbanites are reputedly deficient. People bump into each other and often do not apologize. They knock over another person's packages and, as often as not, proceed on their way with a grumpy explanation instead of an offer of assistance. Such behavior, which many visitors to great cities find distasteful, is less common, we are told, in smaller communities, where traditional courtesies are more likely to be observed.

In some instances it is not simply that, in the city, traditional courtesies are violated; rather, the cities develop new norms of noninvolvement. These are so well defined and so deeply a part of city life that they constitute the norms people are reluctant to violate.

Men are actually embarrassed to give up a seat on the subway to an old woman; they mumble "I was getting off anyway," instead of making the gesture in a straightforward and gracious way. These norms develop because everyone realizes that, in situations of high population density, people cannot implicate themselves in each others' affairs, for to do so would create conditions of continual distraction which would frustrate purposeful action.

In discussing the effects of overload I do not imply that at every instant the city dweller is bombarded with an unmanageable number of inputs, and that his responses are determined by the excess of input at any given instant. Rather, adaptation occurs in the form of gradual evolution of norms of behavior. Norms are evolved in response to frequent discrete experiences of overload; they persist and become generalized modes of responding.

Overload on Cognitive Capacities: Anonymity

That we respond differently toward those whom we know and those who are strangers to us is a truism. An eager patron aggressively cuts in front of someone in a long movie line to save time only to confront a friend; he then behaves sheepishly. A man is involved in an automobile accident caused by another driver, emerges from his car shouting in rage, then moderates his behavior on discovering a friend driving the other car. The city dweller, when walking through the midtown streets, is in a state on continual anonymity vis-à-vis the other pedestrians.

Anonymity is part of a continuous spectrum ranging from total anonymity to full acquaintance, and it may well be that measurement of the precise degrees of anonymity in cities and towns would help to explain important distinctions between the quality of life in each. Conditions of full acquaintance, for example, offer security and familiarity, but they may also be stifling, because the individual is caught in a web of established relationships. Conditions of complete anonymity, by contrast, provide freedom from routinized social ties, but they may also create feelings of alienation and detachment.

Empirically one could investigate the proportion of activities in which the city dweller or the town dweller is known by others at given times in his daily life, and the proportion of activities in the course of which he interacts with individuals who know him. At his job, for instance, the city dweller may be known to as many people as his rural counterpart. However, when he is not fulfilling his occupational role—say, when merely traveling about the city—the urbanite is doubtless more anonymous than his rural counterpart.

Limited empirical work on anonymity has begun. Zimbardo (9) has tested whether the social anonymity and impersonality of the big city encourage greater vandalism than do small towns. Zimbardo arranged for one automobile to be left for 64 hours near the Bronx campus of New York University and for a counterpart to be left for the same number of hours near Stanford University in Palo Alto. The license plates on the two cars were removed and the hoods were opened, to provide "releaser cues" for potential vandals. The New York car was stripped of all movable parts within the first 24 hours, and by the end of 3 days was only a hunk of metal rubble. Unexpectedly, however, most of the destruction occurred during daylight hours, usually under the scrutiny of observers, and the leaders in the vandalism were well-dressed, white adults. The Palo Alto car was left untouched.

Zimbardo attributes the difference in the treatment accorded the two cars to the "acquired feelings of social anonymity provided by life in a city like New York," and he supports his conclusions with several other anecdotes illustrating casual, wanton vandalism in the city. In any comparative study of the effects of anonymity in city and town, however, there must be satisfactory control for other confounding factors: the large number of drug addicts in a city like New York; the higher proportion of slum-dwellers in the city; and so on.

Another direction for empirical study is investigation of the beneficial effects of anonymity. The impersonality of city life breeds its own tolerance for the private lives of the inhabitants. Individuality and even eccentricity, we may assume, can flourish more readily in the metropolis than in the small town. Stigmatized persons may find it easier to lead comfortable lives in the city, free of the constant scrutiny of neighbors. To what degree can this assumed difference between city and town be show empirically? Judith Waters (10), at The City University of New York, hypothesized that avowed homosexuals would be more likely to be accepted as tenants in a large city than in small towns, and she dispatched letters from homosexuals and from normal individuals to real estate agents in cities and towns across the country. The results of her study were inconclusive. But the general idea of examining the protective benefits of city life to the stigmatized ought to be pursued.

Role Behavior in Cities and Towns

Another product of urban overload is the adjustment in roles made by urbanites in daily interactions. As Wirth has said (2): "Urbanites meet one another in highly segmental roles. . . . They are less dependent upon particular persons, and their dependence upon others is confined to a highly fractionalized aspect of the other's round of activity." This tendency is particularly noticeable in transactions between customers and individuals offering professional or sales services. The owner of a country store has time to become well acquainted with his dozen-or-so daily customers, but the girl at the checkout counter of a busy A & P, serving hundreds of customers a day, barely has time to toss the green stamps into one customer's shopping bag before the next customer confronts her with his pile of groceries.

Meier, in his stimulating analysis of the city (4), discusses several adaptations a system may make when confronted by inputs that exceed its capacity to process them. Meier argues that, according to the principle of competition for scarce resources, the scope and time of the transaction shrink as customer volume and daily turnover rise. This, in fact, is what is meant by the "brusque" quality of city life. New standards have developed in cities concerning what levels of services are appropriate in business transactions (see Fig. 1).

McKenna and Morgenthau (11), in a seminar at The City University of New York, devised a study (i) to compare the willingness of city dwellers and small-town dwellers to do favors for strangers that entailed expenditure of a small amount of time and slight inconvenience but no personal vulnerability, and (ii) to determine whether the more compartmentalized, transitory relationships of the city would make urban salesgirls less likely than small-town salesgirls to carry out, for strangers, tasks not related to their customary roles.

To test for differences between city dwellers and small-town dwellers, a simple experiment was devised in which persons from both settings were asked (by telephone) to perform increasingly onerous favors for anonymous strangers.

Within the cities (Chicago, New York, and Philadelphia), half the calls were to housewives and the other half to salesgirls in women's apparel shops; the division was the same for the 37 small towns of the study, which were in the same states as the cities. Each experimenter represented herself as a long-distance caller who had, through error, been connected with the respondent by the operator. The experimenter began by asking for simple information about the weather for purposes of travel. Next the experimenter excused, herself on some pretext (asking the respondent to "please hold on"), put the phone down for almost a full minute, and then picked it up again and asked the respondent to provide the phone number of a hotel or motel in her vicinity at which the experimeter might stay during a forthcoming visit. Scores were assigned the subjects on the basis of how helpful they had been. McKenna summarizes her results in this manner:

People in the city, whether they are engaged in a specific job or not, are less helpful and informative than people in small towns; . . . People at home, regardless of where they live, are less helpful and informative than people working in shops.

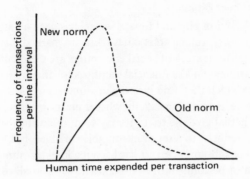

Figure 1. Changes in the demand for time for a given task when the overall transaction frequency increases in a social system. (Reprinted with permission of the publisher from R. L. Meier, *A Communications Theory of Urban Growth,* **1962. Copyrighted by M.I.T. Press, 1962.)**

However, the absolute level of cooperativeness for urban subjects was found to be quite high, and does not accord with the stereotype of the urbanite as aloof, self-centered, and unwilling to help strangers. The quantitative differences obtained by McKenna and Morgenthau are less great than one might have expected. This again points up the need for extensive empirical research in rural-urban differences, research that goes far beyond that provided in the few illustrative pilot studies presented here.

At this point we have very limited objective evidence on differences in the quality of social encounters in city and small town.

But the research needs to be guided by unifying theoretical concepts. As I have tried to demonstrate, the concept of overload helps to explain a wide variety of contrasts between city behavior and town behavior: (i) the differences in role enactment (the tendency of urban dwellers to deal with one another in highly segmented, functional terms, and of urban sales personnel to devote limited time and attention to their customers); (ii) the evolution of urban norms quite different from traditional town values (such as the acceptance of noninvolvement, impersonality, and aloofness in urban life); (iii) the adaptation of the urban dweller's cognitive processes (his inability to identify most of the people he sees daily, his screening of sensory stimuli, his development of blasé attitudes toward deviant or bizarre behavior, and his selectivity in responding to human demands); and (iv) the competition for scarce facilities in the city (the subway rush; the fight for taxis; traffic jams; standing in line to await services). I suggest that contrasts between city and rural behavior probably reflect the responses of similar people to very different situations, rather than intrinsic differences in the personalities of rural and city dwellers. The city is a situation to which individuals respond adaptively.

FURTHER ASPECTS OF URBAN EXPERIENCE

Some features of urban experience do not fit neatly into the system of analysis presented thus far. They are no less important for that reason. The issues raised next are difficult to treat in quantitative fashion. Yet I prefer discussing them in a loose way to excluding them because appropriate language and data have not yet been developed. My aim is to suggest how phenomena such as "urban atmosphere" can be pinned down through techniques of measurement.

The "Atmosphere" of Great Cities

The contrast in the behavior of city and town dwellers has been a natural starting point for urban social scientists. But even among great cities there are marked differences in "atmosphere." The tone, pacing, and texture of social encounters are different in London and New York, and many persons willingly make financial sacrifices for the privilege of living within a specific urban atmosphere which they find pleasing or stimulating. A second perspective in the study of cities, therefore, is to define exactly what is meant by the atmosphere of a city and to pinpoint the factors that give rise to it. It may seem that urban atmosphere is too evanescent a quality to be reduced to a set of measurable variables, but I do not believe the matter can be judged before substantial effort has been made in this direction. It is obvious that any such approach must be comparative. It makes no sense at all to say that New York is "vibrant" and frenetic" unless one has some specific city in mind as a basis of comparison.

In an undergraduate tutorial that I conducted at Harvard University some years ago, New York, London, and Paris were selected as reference points for attempts to measure urban atmosphere. We began with a simple question: Does any consensus exist about the qualities that typify given cities? To answer this question one could undertake a content analysis of travel-book, literary, and journalistic accounts of cities. A second approach, which we adopted, is to ask people to characterize (with descriptive terms and accounts of typical experiences) cities they have lived in or visited. In advertisements placed in the *New York Times* and the *Harvard Crimson* we asked people to give us accounts of specific incidents in London, Paris, or New York that best illuminated the character of that particular city. Questionnaires were then developed, and administered to persons who were familiar with at least two of the three cities.

Some distinctive patterns emerged (12). The distinguishing themes concerning New York, for example, dealt with its diversity, its great size, its pace and level of activity, its cultural and entertainment opportunities, and the heterogeneity and segmentation ("ghettoization") of its population. New York elicited more descriptions in terms of physical qualities, pace, and emotional impact than Paris or London did, a fact which suggests that these are particularly important aspects of New York's ambiance.

A contrasting profile emerges for London; in this case respondents placed far greater emphasis on their interactions with the inhabitants than on physical surroundings. There was near unanimity on certain themes: those dealing with the tolerance and courtesy of London's inhabitants. One respondent said:

> When I was 12, my grandfather took me to the British Museum . . . one day by tube and recited the Aeneid in Latin for my benefit . . . He is rather deaf, speaks very loudly and it embarrassed the hell out of me, until I realized that nobody was paying any attention. Londoners are extremely worldly and tolerant.

In contrast, respondents who described New Yorkers as aloof, cold, and rude referred to such incidents as the following:

I saw a boy of 19 passing out anti-war leaflets to passersby. When he stopped at a corner, a man dressed in a business suit walked by him at a brisk pace, hit the boy's arm, and scattered the leaflets all over the street. The man kept walking at the same pace down the block.

We need to obtain many more such descriptions of incidents, using careful methods of sampling. By the application of factor-analytic techniques, relevant dimensions for each city can be discerned.

The responses for Paris were about equally divided between responses concerning its inhabitants and those regarding its physical and sensory attributes. Cafés and parks were often mentioned as contributing to the sense that Paris is a city of amenities, but many respondents complained that Parisians were inhospitable, nasty, and cold.

We cannot be certain, of course, to what degree these statements reflect actual characteristics of the cities in question and to what degree they simply tap the respondents' knowledge of widely held preconceptions. Indeed, one may point to three factors, apart from the actual atmospheres of the cities, that determine the subjects' responses.

1) A person's impression of a given city depends on his implicit standard of comparison. A New Yorker who visits Paris may well describe that city as "leisurely," whereas a compatriot from Richmond, Virginia, may consider Paris too "hectic." Obtaining reciprocal judgment, in which New Yorkers judge Londoners, and Londoners judge New Yorkers, seems a useful way to take into account not only the city being judged but also the home city that serves as the visitor's base line.

2) Perceptions of a city are also affected by whether the observer is a tourist, a newcomer, or a longer-term resident. First, a tourist will be exposed to features of the city different from those familiar to a long-time resident. Second, a prerequisite for adapting to continuing life in a given city seems to be the filtering out of many observations about the city that the newcomer or tourist finds particularly arresting; this selective process seems to be part of the long-term resident's mechanism for coping with overload. In the interest of psychic economy, the resident simply learns to tune out many aspects of daily life. One method of studying the specific impact of adaptation on perception of the city is to ask several pairs of newcomers and old-timers (one newcomer and one old-timer to a pair) to walk down certain city blocks and then report separately what each has observed.

Additionally, many persons have noted that when travelers return to New York from an extended sojourn abroad they often feel themselves confronted with "brutal ugliness" (13) and a distinctive, frenetic atmosphere whose contributing details are, for a few hours or days, remarkably sharp and clear. This period of fresh perception should receive special attention in the study of city atmosphere. For, in a few days, details which are initially arresting become less easy to specify. They are assimilated into an increasingly familiar background atmosphere which, though important in setting the tone of things, is difficult to analyze. There is no better point at which to begin the study of city atmosphere than at the moment when a traveler returns from abroad.

3) The popular myths and expectations each visitor brings to the city will also affect the way in which he preceives it (14). Sometimes a person's preconceptions about a city are relatively accurate distillations of its character, but preconceptions may also reinforce myths by filtering the visitor's perceptions to conform with his expectations. Preconceptions affect not only a person's perceptions of a city but what he reports about it.

The influence of a person's urban base line on his perceptions of a given city, the differences between the observations of the long-time inhabitant and those of the newcomer, and the filtering effect of personal expectations and stereotypes raise serious questions about the validity of travelers' reports. Moreover, no social psychologist wants to rely exclusively on verbal accounts if he is attempting to obtain an accurate and objective description of the cities' social texture, pace, and general atmosphere. What he needs to do is to devise means of embedding objective experimental measures in the daily flux of city life, measures that can accurately index the qualities of a given urban atmosphere.

EXPERIMENTAL COMPARISONS OF BEHAVIOR

Roy Feldman (15) incorporated these principles in a comparative study of behavior toward compatriots and foreigners in Paris, Athens, and Boston. Feldman wanted to see (i) whether absolute levels and patterns of helpfulness varied significantly from city to city, and (ii) whether inhabitants in each city tended to treat compatriots differently from foreigners. He examined five concrete behavioral episodes, each carried out by a team of native experimenters and a team of American experimenters in the three cities. The episodes involved (i) asking natives of the city for street directions; (ii) asking natives to mail a letter for the experimenter; (iii) asking natives if they had just dropped a dollar bill (or the Greek or French equivalent) when the money actually belonged to the experimenter himself; (iv) deliberately overpaying for goods in a store to see if the cashier would correct the mistake and return the excess money; and (v) determining whether taxicab drivers overcharged strangers and whether they took the most direct route available.

Feldman's results suggest some interesting contrasts in the profiles of the three cities. In Paris, for instance, certain stereotypes were borne out. Parisian cab drivers overcharged foreigners significantly more often than they overcharged compatriots. But other aspects of the Parisians' behavior were not in accord with American preconceptions: in mailing a letter for a stranger, Parisians treated foreigners significantly better than Athenians or Bostonians did, and, when asked to mail letters that were already stamped, Parisians actually treated foreigners better than they treated compatriots. Similarly, Parisians were significantly more honest than Athenians or Bostonians in resisting the temptation to claim money that was not theirs, and Parisians were the only citizens who were more honest with foreigners than with compatriots in this experiment.

Feldman's studies not only begin to quantify some of the variables that give a city its distinctive texture but they also provide a methodological model for other comparative research. His most important contribution is his successful application of objective, experimental measures to everyday situations, a mode of study which provides conclusions about urban life that are more pertinent than those achieved through laboratory experiments.

TEMPO AND PACE

Another important component of a city's atmosphere is its tempo or pace, an attribute frequently remarked on but less often studied. Does a city have a frenetic, hectic quality, or is it easygoing and leisurely? In any empirical treatment of this question, it is best to start in a very simple way. Walking speeds of pedestrians in different cities and in cities and towns should be measured and compared. William Berkowitz (16) of Lafayette College has undertaken an extensive series of studies of walking speeds in Philadelphia, New York, and Boston, as well as in small and moderate-sized towns. Berkowitz writes that "there does appear to be a significant linear relation between walking speed and size of municipality, but the absolute size of the difference varies by less than ten percent."

Perhaps the feeling of rapid tempo is due not so much to absolute pedestrian speeds as to the constant need to dodge others in a large city to avoid collisions with other pedestrians. (One basis for computing the adjustments needed to avoid collisions is to hypothesize a set of mechanical manikins sent walking along a city street and to calculate the number of collisions per unit of time, or, conversely, the greater the frequency of adjustments needed in higher population densities to avoid collisions.)

Patterns of automobile traffic contribute to a city's tempo. Driving an automobile provides a direct means of translating feelings about tempo into measurable acceleration, and a city's pace should be particularly evident in vehicular velocities, patterns of acceleration, and latency of response to traffic signals. The inexorable tempo of New York is expressed, further, in the manner in which pedestrians stand at busy intersections, impatiently awaiting a change in traffic light, making tentative excursions into the intersection, and frequently surging into the street even before the green light appears.

VISUAL COMPONENTS

Hall has remarked (17) that the physical layout of the city also affects its atmosphere. A gridiron pattern of streets gives the visitor a feeling of rationality, orderliness, and predictability but is sometimes monotonous. Winding lanes or streets branching off at strange angles, with many forks (as in Paris or Greenwich Village), create feelings of surprise and esthetic pleasure, while forcing greater decision-making in plotting one's course. Some would argue that the visual component is all-important—that the "look" of Paris or New York can almost be equated with its atmosphere. To investigate this hypothesis, we might conduct studies in which only blind, or at least blindfolded, respondents were used. We would no doubt discover that each city has a distinctive texture even when the visual component is eliminated.

SOURCES OF AMBIANCE

Thus far we have tried to pinpoint and measure some of the factors that contribute to the distinctive atmosphere of a great city. But we may also ask, Why do differences in urban atmosphere exist? How did they come about, and are they in any way related to the factors of density, large numbers, and heterogeneity discussed above?

First, there is the obvious factor that, even among great cities, populations and densities differ. The metropolitan areas of New York, London, and Paris, for example, contain 15 million, 12 million, and 8 million persons, respectively. London has average densities of 43 persons per acre, while Paris is more congested, with average densities of 114 persons per acre (18). Whatever characteristics are specifically attributable to density are more likely to be pronounced in Paris than in London.

A second factor affecting the atmosphere of cities is the source from which the populations are drawn (19). It is a characteristic of great cities that they do not reproduce their own populations, but that their numbers are constantly maintained and augmented by the influx of residents from other parts of the country. This can have a determining effect on the city's atmosphere. For example, Oslo is a city in which almost all of the residents are only one or two generations removed from a purely rural existence, and this contributes to its almost agricultural norms.

A third source of atmosphere is the general national culture. Paris combines adaptations to the demography of cities and certain values specific to French culture. New York is an admixture of American values and values that arise as a result of extraordinarily high density and large population.

Finally, one could speculate that the atmosphere of a great city is traceable to the specific historical conditions under which adaptations to urban overload occurred. For example, a city which acquired its mass and density during a period of commercial expansion will respond to new demographic conditions by adaptations designed to serve purely commercial needs. Thus, Chicago, which grew and became a great city under a purely commercial stimulus, adapted in a manner that emphasizes business needs. European capitals, on the other hand, incorporate many of the adaptations which were appropriate to the period of their increasing numbers and density. Because aristocratic values were prevalent at the time of the growth of these cities, the mechanisms developed for coping with overload were based on considerations other than pure efficiency. Thus, the manners, norms, and facilities of Paris and Vienna continue to reflect esthetic values and the idealization of leisure.

COGNITIVE MAPS OF CITIES

When we speak of "behavioral comparisons" among cities, we must specify which parts of the city are most relevant for sampling purposes. In a sampling of "New Yorkers," should we include residents of Bay Ridge or Flatbush as well as inhabitants of Manhattan? And, if so, how should we weight our sample distribution? One approach to defining relevant boundaries in sampling is to determine which areas form the psychological or cognitive core of the city. We weight our samples most heavily in the areas considered by most people to represent the "essence" of the city.

The psychologist is less interested in the geographic layout of a city or in its political boundaries than in the cognitive representation of the city. Hans Blumenfeld (20) points out that the perceptual structure of a modern city can be expressed by the "silhouette" of the group of skyscrapers at its center and that of smaller groups of office buildings at its "subcenters" but that urban areas can no longer, because of their vast extent, be experienced as fully articulated sets of streets, squares, and space.

In *The Image of the City* (21), Kevin Lynch created a cognitive map of Boston by interviewing Bostonians. Perhaps his most significant finding was that, while certain landmarks, such as Paul Revere's house and the Boston Common, as well as the paths linking them, are known to almost all Bostonians, vast areas of the city are simply unknown to its inhabitants.

Using Lynch's technique, Donald Hooper (22) created a psychological map of New York from the answers to the study questionnaire on Paris, London, and New York. Hooper's results were similar to those of Lynch: New York appears to have a dense core of well-known landmarks in midtown Manhattan, surrounded by the vast unknown reaches of Queens, Brooklyn, and the Bronx. Times Square, Rockefeller Center, and the Fifth Avenue department stores alone comprise half the places specifically cited by respondents as the haunts in which they spent most of their time. However, outside the midtown area, only scattered landmarks were recognized. Another interesting pattern is evident: even the best-known symbols of New York are relatively self-contained, and the pathways joining them appear to be insignificant on the map.

The psychological map can be used for more than just sampling techniques. Lynch (21) argues, for instance, that a good city is highly "imageable," having many known symbols joined by widely known pathways, whereas dull cities are gray and nondescript. We might test the relative "imagibility" of several cities by determining the proportion of residents who recognize sampled geographic points and their accompanying pathways.

If we wanted to be even more precise we could construct a cognitive map that would not only show the symbols of the city but would measure the precise degree of cognitive significance of any given point in the city relative to any other. By applying a pattern of points to a map of New York City, for example, and taking photographs from each point, we could determine what proportion of a sample of the city's inhabitants could identify the locale specified by each point (see Fig. 2). We might even take the subjects blindfolded to a point represented on the map, then remove the blindfold and ask them to identify their location from the view around them.

One might also use psychological maps to gain insight into the differing perceptions of a given city that are held by members of its cultural subgroups, and into the manner in which

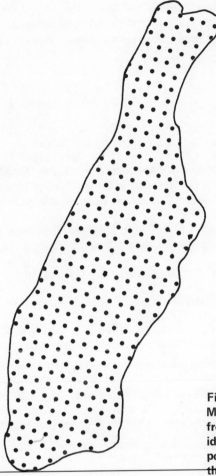

Figure 2. To create a psychological map of Manhattan, geographic points are sampled, and, from photographs, the subjects attempt to identify the location of each point. To each point a numerical index is assigned indicating the proportion of persons able to identify its location.

their perceptions may change. In the earlier stages of life, whites and Negroes alike probably have only a limited view of the city, centering on the immediate neighborhood in which they are raised. In adolescence, however, the field of knowledge of the white teen-ager probably undergoes rapid enlargement; he learns of opportunities in midtown and outlying sections and comes to see himself as functioning in a larger urban field. But the process of ghettoization, to which the black teen-ager is subjected, may well hamper the expansion of his sense of the city. These are speculative notions, but they are readily subject to precise test.

CONCLUSION

I have tried to indicate some organizing theory that starts with the basic facts of city life: large numbers, density, and heterogeneity. These are external to the individual. He experiences these factors as overloads at the level of roles, norms, cognitive functions, and facilities. These overloads lead to adaptive mechanisms which create the distinctive tone and behaviors of city life. These notions, of course, need to be examined by objective comparative studies of cities and towns.

A second perspective concerns the differing atmospheres of great cities, such as Paris, London, and New York. Each has a distinctive flavor, offering a differentiable quality of experience. More precise knowledge of urban atmosphere seems attainable through application of the tools of experimental inquiry.

REFERENCES AND NOTES

1.   *New York Times* (15 June 1969).
2.   L. Wirth, *Amer. J. Soc.* 44, 1 (1938). Wirth's ideas have come under heavy criticism by contemporary city planners, who point out that the city is broken down into neighborhoods, which fulfill many of the functions of small towns. See, for example, H. J. Gans, *People and Plans: Essays on Urban Problems and Solutions* (Basic Books, New York, (1968); J. Jacobs, *The Death and Life of Great American Cities* (Random House, New York, 1961); G. D. Suttles, *The Social Order of the Slum* (Univ. of Chicago Press, Chicago, 1968).
3.   G. Simmel, *The Sociology of Georg Simmel,* K. H. Wolff, Ed. (Macmillan, New York, 1950) [English translation of G. Simmel, *Die Gross-stadte und das Geistesleben Die Grosstadt* (Jansch, Dresden, 1903)].
4.   R. L. Meier, *A Communications Theory of Urban Growth* (M.I.T. Press, Cambridge, Mass., 1962).
5.   S. Milgram and P. Hollander, *Nation* 25, 602 (1964).
6.   B. Latané and J. Darley, *Amer. Sci.* 57, 244 (1969).
7.   S. Gaertner and L. Bickman (Graduate Center, The City University of New York), unpublished research.
8.   D. Altman, M. Levine, M. Nadien, J. Villena (Graduate Center, The City University of New York), unpublished research.
9.   P. G. Zimbardo, paper presented at the Nebraska Symposium on Motivation (1969).
10.   J. Waters (Graduate Center, The City University of New York), unpublished research.
11.   W. McKenna and S. Morgenthau (Graduate Center, The City University of New York), unpublished research.
12.   N. Abuza (Harvard University), "The Paris-London-New York Questionnaires," unpublished.
13.   P. Abelson, *Science* 165, 853 (1969).
14.   A. L. Strauss, Ed., *The American City: A Sourcebook of Urban Imagery* (Aldine, Chicago, 1968).
15.   R. E. Feldman, *J. Personality Soc. Psychol.* 10, 202 (1968).
16.   W. Berkowitz, personal communication.
17.   E. T. Hall, *The Hidden Dimension* (Doubleday, New York, 1966).
18.   P. Hall, *The World Cities* (McGraw-Hill, New York, 1966).
19.   R. E. Park, E. W. Burgess, R. D. McKenzie, *The City* (Univ. of Chicago Press, Chicago, 1967), pp. 1-45.
20.   H. Blumenfeld, in *The Quality of Urban Life* (Sage, Beverly Hills, Calif. 1969).
21.   K. Lynch, *The Image of the City* (M.I.T. and Harvard Univ. Press, Cambridge, Mass. 1960).
22.   D. Hooper (Harvard University), unpublished.
23.   Barbara Bengen worked closely with me in preparing the present version of this article. I thank Dr. Gary Winkel, editor of *Environment and Behavior,* for useful suggestions and advice.

American Identity Movements: A Cross-Cultural Confrontation

by Gary R. Weaver

If we were to assess the significant, long-term results of the civil rights and anti-Vietnam war movements of the 1960's, we would probably place at the top of our list the numerous court decisions barring discrimination, the development of massive opposition to the Vietnam war, and the 18-year-old right to vote. While all of these developments are indeed important, I suggest that by far the most significant long-term consequence of both movements is the growth of popular questioning of cultural assumptions held by Americans for generations. Rather than having values of a subcultural group dissipated and absorbed by the dominant culture, these two groups have undermined the values and assumptions of the dominant culture.

The net results of these two movements has been a drive toward true pluralism of cultures and subcultures—including such "subcultural" identity groups as Women's Lib, Gay Lib, Chicano, American-Indian, and many other groups. No longer are individuals denying their identities to fit into an abstractive, Anglo-male society. They are asserting their uniqueness and wholeness while taking it for granted that they are entitled to their fair share of society's benefits.

THE MELTING POT MYTH

Foremost among the numerous assumptions which are now questioned by many Americans is the long-standing "melting pot" myth of cultural equality of people of all races. We would have to search diligently to find evidence of Chinese, Latin, Middle-Eastern, Indian-American, African, or of even Eastern or Southern European ethnic patterns of behavior and thought being absorbed into the American culture. The pot melted no further than corn, shop suey, spaghetti, pork chops, and shish kebab. Each ethnic group has not contributed its own cultural traits equally to the whole. Rather, there has been a cultural shaping by a white, male, Protestant, Anglo-Saxon cookie cutter. This leveling (not "melting") has now been challenged by numerous subcultural groups as they fight for their own life styles, values, perceptions, and interests, which are often contrary to the mainstream mold.

This cultural imperialism (not cultural pluralism) was a result of racism, liberalism, and rapid technological and urban growth. It was obviously easier to identify non-whites and to reject not only their cultural, but their individual, identities. The dynamics of racism are now apparent to most Americans. The more subtle effects of liberalism are less apparent. In fact, the community-focused, equality-directed characteristics of liberalism seem to be contrary to any sort of racism or cultural imperialism. Yet, the belief that all men are equal is perhaps as responsible for this cultural leveling as any sort of overt racism, primarily because it denies the reality of physical, cultural, and psychological differences among men.

Let us contrast the positions of the overt racist and the so-called liberal regarding racial attitudes. The racist would maintain that whites and non-whites are inherently different, and that non-whites are inferior to whites. The liberal would maintain that whites and non-whites

Reprinted with permission from *Intellect*, Vol. 103, No. 2364, March 1975, pp. 377-380.

Gary R. Weaver is Director, Community Programs and the Pride/American University Institute, The American University, Washington, D.C.

are basically the same, except that non-whites have not been treated equally. This liberal contention appears very humane, yet could easily be translated to mean the only reason non-whites are different is that they are pathologically white. If their culture were the same as the white culture, everyone would be equal. This denies the very real fact that there are non-white subcultures and that non-whites are not only physiologically different, but also culturally different. Accepting these differences does not lead us back to racism, because there is no concurrent need to assume superiority or inferiority.

The break-up of fairly isolated communities and ethnic groups by industrialism, urban growth, and technological advancement, especially in the mass media, has abetted the liberal drive for homogeneity and the consequent imposition of an Anglo-Saxon cultural cookie cutter. This shaping and leveling is expressed by Daniel P. Moynahan as he suggests that the lack of a biological father in many black homes is responsible for much of the economic and social ills in ghettos around the country. The assumption is that the Western model of the family is ideal, and that the black model is pathological. There are literally millions of families around the world that do not have the biological father present, yet there is a low incidence of crime, few riots, and the social fabric seems quite healthy. Thus, it is anthropologically unsound to assume that the Western family model is "normal" or best. Indeed, numerous scholars are beginning to feel that the Western family model may be responsible for many contemporary ills in Western society today.

THE QUALITATIVE REVOLUTION

Blacks and students towards the mid-1960's began to resemble each other in terms of opposition—they were against the system. Until then, this was not necessarily true—that is, the black civil rights movement was geared to allow increased participation in the system. To this extent, it was very much like the labor movement and previous revolutionary movements. Its objective was *quantitative*—a piece of the socioeconomic and political pie. The student movement, on the other hand, was primarily *qualitative*. For many, the pie was not worth eating in the first place. By the mid-1960's, however, black leaders began to question the quality of the pie and, indeed, began to develop cultural styles in opposition to the pie.

This opposition to the system extended throughout the student movement around the technologically advanced world. Regardless of nationality, students seemed to oppose any way of life or thought which appeared systematic, rule-bound, and impersonal, as opposed to the spontaneous, the free, the intensely and, therefore, personally felt. However, this opposition is true mainly of the technologically developed cultures. In the less technologically developed countries, student revolts were much less qualitative. For example, in January, 1972, there was a university student revolt in Sierra Leone, in which the major issues included ironing boards in the dormitories, more allowance, and better food. There was little effort to change "the system" of Sierra Leone.

Whereas the 1950's was the era of conformity, the 1960's was the era when nonconformity was paramount. In the late 1950's "everyone" smoked Marlboros, college men (black or white) wore Ivy League clothes, and, while McCarthy purged, the Korean War killed hundreds of thousands, an economic crisis pervaded, and Emmett Till was killed, young people ran through college dormitories yelling for panties before rushing to their favorite fraternity or sorority parties. In the 1960's, cigarettes became available for the *exceptional* man or woman, students could come to class nearly nude without arousing more than a hearty ho-hum, a President announced that he wanted to make the world "safe for diversity," and massive movements were led against racial discrimination and war. Students occupied the university president's office to protest discrimination, war, and lack of participation in decision-making. Fraternities and sororities were dying.

I suggest that many of these phenomena were not only reactions to the leveling process of the pre-1950's, but an effort to retain subcultural and personal identity, and to prevent the sense of meaninglessness and the rush toward an Orwellian *1984* from becoming a reality. That is, they were not signs of cultural disintegration, but, rather, efforts to truly maintain cultural integration of all ethnic and subcultural groups without the cultural imperialism of the past overwhelming individual and group identity.

No longer are various subcultural groups willing to pay the price of loss of individual and cultural identity to get their fair share of the systemic pie. If gaining a quantitative advance means qualitative loss in lifestyle to accommodate the mass-society cookie-cutter, then the alternative is no longer one of copping out, as the Beat Generation did, but one of altering the dominant cultural system to allow for retention and enhancement of cultural identity while offering a share of the pie. This new awareness may be termed "Consciousness Level III" or a "prefigurative culture," but the net result is that, with the 1970's, it has grown to include Women's Lib, Gay Lib, the Chicano movement, the American-Indian movement, and even various communal efforts.

THE ASSOCIATIVE VS. ABSTRACTIVE CULTURE

What is the qualitative American cultural revolution all about? It is a struggle between two modes of thought, reflecting two cultures which seem in opposition. More importantly, it represents a struggle between two ways of organizing society, its values, and perceptions. It has been described as a struggle between associative and abstractive cultures, rational vs. analytic thought, or as a struggle between members of a *Gemeinschaft* or community and members of a *Gesellschaft* or more complex society.

The struggle is very much analogous to the culture clash of technologically advanced mass societies and non-technologically advanced, community-oriented cultures. Although this clash has been described as occurring between East and West, this is greatly oversimplified and misleading. In actuality, it has no absolute geographic parameters, but, rather, socioeconomic, philosophic, and experiential demarcations, with no sharp line dividing one culture into the associative grouping and another into the abstractive grouping. While the associative, non-Westernized grouping might include parts of Latin America, Asia, and Africa, there are "hybrids" of sorts—such as Japan, urbanized Latin America, and perhaps even urbanized Nigeria.

This oversimplified model of culture is intended to offer a way of contrasting and comparing two basic culture-and-personality systems. It is primarily descriptive, yet may lead us to understand that the clash between generations, races, and identity groups today is indeed a culture gap, not a generation gap. It is no accident that young people today have developed music styles similar to the realism of blues or the free-style of jazz, that youth prefer bright clothing, or that self-actualizing students use Eastern philosophies to guide their lifestyles while young blacks seek their African roots.

To illustrate this, let us consider the following linguistic example. As an undergraduate, I often joined my fraternity brothers at Howard University as they met outside one of the women's dormitories to evaluate the quality and quantity of incoming coeds during the first few days of the fall semester. This was a popular male, chauvinistic activity which allowed the brothers to get together and talk. As we sat there, I noticed that a particular brother, John, was not with the group. I asked a fellow brother, "Where's John?" "Oh he's not hanging out. He's got a nose job." At the moment I thought it extremely odd that John, who was fairly handsome, would have his nose altered surgically. A few weeks later, I again noticed that John was not hanging out at a local bar with his fraternity brothers. Again, I inquired as to the whereabouts of John. Again, the reply was, "He's got a nose job."

Finally, I broke down and asked, "What do you mean, a nose job?" "You know, a young lady has him by the nose." To have a "nose job" was to be deeply involved with a girlfriend, consequently being unable to hang out with his friends. Out of cultural context, and translated literally, the phrase made absolutely no sense.

Here we find a characteristic of associative or relational language. It is a product of small, intimate groups or people who subconsciously share similar experiences. For example, every language has a standard and non-standard form—the so-called King's English and patois. The non-standard form is usually a subcultural form. In no way is the non-standard language a sign of lack of intelligence. In fact, it is often more sophisticated than the standard language in its verbal, spoken form. Seldom is it written, making it necessary to communicate face-to-face vocally, sharing more than simply words, but also the physical presence of another. Body language, tone of voices, and who is speaking to whom are all important. Everything is associated with everything. It is more intimate than standard language, which can be written and translated quite easily to everyone, regardless of who wrote it, where only words are relevant and abstracted or selected out of the communications scenaria.

BLACK DIALECT: AN ASSOCIATIVE LANGUAGE

Let us consider a non-standard form with which we are all somewhat familiar—black dialect, or black patois (sometimes termed ghettoese). Not only does it have a very consistent grammatical form, but, in terms of verbal usage, it is much more sophisticated than standard English. For example, if a teacher asked a child to have his mother come to school tomorrow, the child might respond, "No, she can't. She be sick." The teacher then asks, "Would you please have her come in next week, then?" The child responds, "No. She can't. She be sick." What is happening? Is the child making up an excuse? On the contrary, the child is expressing herself very clearly, using the verb "to be" in a tense which is no longer used in the English language, but is found in Shakespearean English, to indicate an ongoing process—that is, her mother is ill, and will be ill, an ongoing process. This verb tense is found in many non-written languages around the world and in many non-Western languages such as Greek. Interestingly, "to be" (ascription) is the most common verb in black dialect and many non-Western languages, while "to do" (achievement) is the most common verb in standard English.

Associative verbal interaction is highly developed. A popular activity among children in ghetto areas is an activity called Joning, the Dozens, or the Numbers. It is a form of interaction where one child tries to out-insult another, usually poetically, by referring to his mother. Often, this game can go on for hours and requires a good verbal command, the ability to tie words together associatively, use of vocal and body messages, and a very quick wit. Few standard-speaking children could handle the English language as deftly as these children do.

"Toasting" is another very common usage of non-standard English. A toast is a very long story in poetry fashion which is passed on and added to as it is passed along. Many famous toasts, such as "Stagger Lee," were developed in jail. Not only are toasts indicative of a highly sophisticated language form, they often have been passed down in perfect iambic pentameter form. The same is true of many of the lyrics to blues music.

In fact, all artistic work is, by definition, associative. That is, a work of art is meaningful because it sets off a series of emotional associations in the viewer/listener. It is somewhat misleading to term much modern art "abstract art." Although it does abstract from a totality of lines, colors, and forms only those which are basic to a particular theme, feeling, tone or mood, abstract art is art because the viewer can associate spontaneously with the message of the artist, without the clutter of extraneous lines, colors, and forms. To a greater extent, this is perhaps the purest form of association, similar to the glass bead game of Herman Hesse.

Poetry and music are whole works which can not be divided into separate parts, however much pedantic critics might wish to do so. They ignite a series of deep associations in the listener's head, and he feels what the poet or composer felt. The words and sounds bring to his conscious mind feelings which were long buried in the unconscious. Is it any wonder that poetry is perhaps the most difficult written form to translate into another language?

A contrast of mainstream, white poetry and black poetry illustrates the associative element in the black culture. Black poetry is usually read aloud, and voice tone, gestures, and the presence of both poet and listener is essential (e.g., Gil Scott Heron, Nikki Giovani). White poetry is usually not read aloud, but, if it is, it is done in a monotone, non-emotional voice.

Lastly, we all speak associative languages with loved ones and friends. Labels we give loved ones have developed by usage and are intimate ways of expressing feelings. Most of us would be offended if a stranger called our wife "bunny," or our husband "sugar." Who says what to whom is vital, and the meaning is all in the situation.

MASS SOCIETY: THE ABSTRACTIVE CULTURE

Of course, we all can speak abstractive language. It is technical and provides a common language for performing tasks without considering who is saying what to whom. The message, not the communicator, is all that is important. Thus, it can be easily written, but communicates little feeling. It is eminently rational, logical, practical, and simple. In fact, much of what the Anglo-male culture values is typically abstractive (objectivity, aloofness, rationality), and is exactly the opposite of what is considered associative—and often feminine (subjectivity, personally and emotionally involved).

These two styles of expression not only represent two ways of thought, but two ways of organizing society. The abstractive is typical of complex societies, where individual differences or subgroup differences are leveled to provide a common mode of communication. The associative represents a homogeneous community, where everyone shares the same collective unconscious, has similar values and perceptions, and has similar childhood experiences. The small, isolated village would be an associative community, while the larger urban areas or the total U.S. would be an abstractive mass society.

People come together in groups because they either trust each other or because there is mutual predictability. In a community, there is natural predictability, because all share the same collective values and behavior patterns. Everyone knows his or her place and belongs to the community. There are spontaneous similarities between all members of the community, and one can therefore infer from one's own behavior the behavior of others. This is very common in all homogeneous groups where there is no need for written rules to govern behavior, because what is proper is unconsciously known.

Ten years ago, in a small, white community, roles were ascribed. If you came from a wealthy, landed family or one with a long "noble" heritage, you could be the dumbest citizen in the community and still have the highest status. On the other hand, if you were the most intelligent black in the community, your role would be ascribed as having the lowest status. Communities are in-group oriented, unconsciously very tradition-directed, rigid, and difficult to belong to unless you were born into the culture. This is very illogical for organizing talents in the culture, but very human.

Abstractive societies are made up of groups of people who do not know each other well enough to trust one another spontaneously. People come from various ethnic groups, value systems, perceptual systems, etc. Status, ideally, is achieved generally in economic terms, and social trust is maintained through a system of explicit rules, which every member of the society must learn, and which must be enforced to protect the rights of all. Thus, what a person is becomes irrelevant to the system—only what a person does is important. This is much more logical and humane than the associative community, but much less human. In fact, it is a schizoid organization, where the totality of a person is discarded—whether he is Protestant, black, sad, happy, etc., is of no consequence unless it interferes with his task.

This schizoid nature of abstractive societies has led to the sense of alienation one feels. The boss really doesn't give a damn if your mother died last night. We have difficulty communicating feelings, and, in fact, we find we can not really feel anything. It has reached the point where the schizoid nature of the abstractive system has created inefficiency. Thus, businesses and government are supporting such devices as sensitivity sessions to break down the inability of people to relate as human beings, instead of merely as task performers.

In many ways, the abstractive society is more humane—that is, it is more objective and not as in-group oriented. A black would not be logically rejected simply for being black, because blackness is irrelevant to task performance. There is a larger and less rigid frame of reference, but, also, there is an inability to grant the wholeness of people and to take into account such supposedly irrelevant criteria as ethnic identity, personal feelings, and individual egos.

The associative community is more human—it gives a sense of wholeness and belonging—but it also excludes the outsider and is often very inhumane. The abstractive society is more humane—it does not necessarily reject the outsider and allows for advancement in terms of achievement, but it is also less human, as it treats individuals in a schizoid manner. The associative community seems very illogical, because behavior is determined by custom and numerous factors are associated with particular behavior, whether logically or not. For example, a few years ago I was in Honduras, visiting a Peace Corps contingent there. Numerous women volunteers were having trouble in their village. The men no longer respected them, yet they had done nothing to earn this disrespect. Upon closer analysis, it was found that the American women chose to wear slacks, because they were much more practical in the jungle. However, the local culture frowned upon women who wore slacks. Generally, women who wore slacks were prostitutes. Thus, associated with wearing slacks was the suggestion of prostitution, and the American women are being associated with these so-called "bad" women.

TRUE PLURALITY TODAY

Both the abstractive and associative cultures have their excesses. The associative community gives a sense of belonging, spontaneity, wholeness, predictability, in-group identity, and is very human, but it also is often rigid, ascriptive, exclusive of outsiders, inhumane in extreme, and can even be turned fascistic. The abstractive society is very logical, achievement-oriented, and humane, but it also leads to alienation, lack of whole self-identity, a schizoid personality, and, consequently, is very inhuman. Economically (capitalism), politically (liberalism), and socially (mass societies of heterogeneous ethnic groups), the abstractive culture has clearly conquered most subcultural groups. However, the student movement was certainly a reaction to this system, as are the ethnic minority and various identity movements today.

Young people have asked themselves what price one has to pay to become a member of the abstractive system. Is life really meaningful if one earns $50,000 per year, but has sacrificed his individual identity and feels like an insignificant cog in a societal machine that determines his worth by what he does rather than who he is? Blacks and other minority groups have also asked themselves whether they must necessarily give up their individual and group identities to melt into the pot—can not one be black, and still be American? Was it an accident that other ethnic groups that melted so easily were termed Italian-American or Irish-American, while, until recently, those who could not melt were termed American Indians and American Negroes? Clearly, certain identifiable groups were treated as castes within the class system, and getting into the system seemed paramount. Thus, many blacks did straighten their hair and attempt to lighten their skin, many women did feel as if they must sacrifice their femininity to become achievers, and many homosexuals did marry and live miserable lives to keep their jobs and status in the society.

Presently, the qualitative revolution demands that these groups participate with equal opportunity in the class system without giving up group or sub-cultural identity, because the white, male, Protestant, Anglo-Saxon mold is increasingly questioned and challenged in terms of its quality and worth. In fact, even white, male, Protestant, Anglo-Saxons have begun to join the revolution.

2C LIFE SUPPORT AND LEISURE

Why Should Sammy Run Anymore?

by Studs Terkel

A re-examination of the American work ethic

Work, by its very nature, is about violence—to the spirit as well as to the body. It is about ulcers as well as accidents, about shouting matches as well as fistfights, about nervous break-downs as well as kicking the dog around. It is, above all (or beneath all), about daily humil-iations. To survive the day is triumph enough for the walking wounded among the great many of us.

The scars, psychic as well as physical, brought home to the supper table and the TV set, may have touched, malignantly, the soul of our society. More or less.

Work is about a search, too, for daily meaning as well as daily bread, for recognition as well as cash, for astonishment rather than torpor; in short, for a sort of life rather than a Monday through Friday sort of dying. Perhaps immortality, too, is part of the quest. To be remembered was the wish, spoken and unspoken, of the heroes and heroines.

There are, of course, the happy few who find a savor in their daily job: The Indiana stone-mason, who looks upon his work and sees that it is good; the Chicago piano tuner, who seeks and finds the sound that delights; the bookbinder, who saves a piece of history; the Brooklyn fireman, who saves a piece of life. . . . But don't these satisfactions, like Jude's hunger for knowledge, tell us more about the person than about his task? Perhaps. Nonetheless, there is a common attribute here: a meaning to their work well over and beyond the reward of the paycheck. For the many, there is hardly concealed discontent. The blue-collar blues is no more bitterly sung than the white-collar moan. "I'm a machine," says the spot-welder. "I'm caged," says the bank teller, and echoes the hotel clerk. "I'm a mule," says the steelworker. "A monkey can do what I do," says the receptionist. "I'm less than a farm implement," says the migrant worker. "I'm an object," says the high-fashion model. Blue collar and white call upon the identical phrase: "I'm a robot." "There is nothing to talk about," the young accountant despairingly enunciates.

As the automated pace of our daily jobs wipes out name and face—and, in many instances, feeling—there is a sacrilegious question being asked these days. To earn one's bread by the sweat of one's brow has always been the lot of mankind. At least, ever since Eden's slothful couple was served with an eviction notice. The scriptural precept was never doubted, not out loud. No matter how demeaning the task, no matter how it dulls the senses and breaks the spirit, one must work. Or else.

Lately there has been a questioning of this "work ethic," especially by the young. Strangely enough, it has touched off profound grievances in others, hitherto devout, silent, and anonymous. Unexpected precincts are being heard from in a show of discontent. Communiqués from the assembly line are frequent and alarming: absenteeism. On the evening bus, the tense, pinched faces of young file clerks and elderly secretaries tell us more than we care to know. On the expressways, middle management men pose without grace behind their wheels as they flee city and job.

There are other means of showing it, too. Inchoately, sullenly, it appears in slovenly work, in the put-down of craftsmanship. A farm equipment worker in Moline complains that the careless worker who turns out more that is bad is better regarded than the careful craftsman who turns out less that is good. The first is an ally of the Gross National Product. The other is a threat to it, a kook—and the sooner he is penalized the better. Why, in these circumstances, should a man work with care? Pride does indeed precede the fall.

Others, more articulate—at times, visionary—murmur of a hunger for "beauty," "a meaning," "a sense of pride." A veteran car hiker sings out, "I could drive any car like a baby, like a woman changes her baby's diaper. Lots of customers say, 'How you do this?' I'd say, 'Just the way you bake a cake, miss.' When I was younger, I could swing with that car. They called me Lovin' Al the Wizard."

Dolores Dante graphically describes the trials of a waitress in a fashionable restaurant. They are compounded by her refusal to be demeaned. Yet pride in her skills helps her make it through the night. "When I put the plate down, you don't hear a sound. When I pick up a glass, I want it to be just right. When someone says, 'How come you're just a waitress?' I say, 'Don't you think you deserve being served by me?' "

Peggy Terry has her own sense of grace and beauty. Her jobs have varied with geography, climate, and the ever-felt pinch of circumstance. "What I hated worst was being a waitress. The way you're treated. One guy said, 'You don't have to smile; I'm gonna give you a tip anyway.' I said, 'Keep it. I wasn't smiling for a tip.' Tipping should be done away with. It's like throwing a dog a bone. It makes you feel small."

In all instances, there is felt more than a slight ache. In all instances, there dangles the impertinent question: Ought not there be an increment, earned though not yet received, from one's daily work—an acknowledgement of man's being?

The drones are no longer invisible nor mute. Nor are they exclusively of one class. Markham's Man with the Hoe may be Ma Bell's girl with the headset. (And can it be safely said, she is "dead to rapture and despair"? Is she really "a thing that grieves not and that never hopes"?) They're in the office as well as the warehouse; at the manager's desk as well as the assembly line; at some estranged company's computer as well as some estranged woman's kitchen floor.

Bob Cratchit may still be hanging on (though his time is fast running out, as did his feather pen long ago), but Scrooge has been replaced by the conglomerate. Hardly a chance for Christmas spirit here. Who knows Bob's name in this outfit—let alone his lame child's? "The last place I worked for, I was let go," recalls the bank teller. "One of my friends stopped by and asked where I was at. They said, 'She's no longer with us.' That's all. I vanished.") It's nothing personal, really. Dickens' people have been replaced by Beckett's.

To maintain a sense of self, these heroes and heroines play occasional games. The middle-aged switchboard operator, when things are dead at night, cheerily responds to the caller, "Marriott Inn," instead of identifying the motel chain she works for. "Just for a lark," she explains bewilderedly. "I really don't know what made me do it." The young gas meter reader startles the young suburban housewife sunning out on the patio in her bikini, loose-bra'd, and sees more things than he would otherwise see. "Just to make the day go faster." The auto worker from the Deep South will "tease one guy 'cause he's real short and his old lady left him." Why? "Oh, just to break the monotony. You want quittin' time so bad."

The waitress, who moves by the table with the grace of a ballerina, pretends she's forever on stage. "I feel like Carmen. It's like a gypsy holding out a tambourine and they throw the coin." It helps her fight humiliation as well as arthritis. The interstate truckdriver, bearing down the expressway with a load of seventy-three thousand pounds, battling pollution, noise, an ulcer, and kidneys that act up, "fantasizes something tremendous." They all, in some manner, perform astonishingly to survive the day. These are not yet automata.

There are cases where the job possesses the man even after quitting time. Aside from occupational ticks of hourly workers and the fitful sleep of salaried ones, there are instances of a man's singular preoccupation with work. It may affect his attitude toward all of life. And art.

Geraldine Page, the actress, recalls the critique of a backstage visitor during her run in *Sweet Bird of Youth*. He was a dentist. "I was sitting in the front row and looking up. Most of the time I was studying the fillings in your mouth. I'm curious to know who's been doing your dental work." It was not that he loved theater less, but that he loved dentistry more.

At the public unveiling of a celebrated statue in Chicago, a lawyer, after deep study, mused, "I accept Mr. Picasso in good faith. But if you look at the height of the slope on top and the propensity of children who will play on it, I have a feeling that some child may fall and be hurt and the county may be sued. . . ."

Is it any wonder that in such surreal circumstances, status rather than the work itself becomes important? Thus, the prevalence of euphemisms in work as well as in war. The janitor is a building engineer; the garbage man, a sanitary engineer; the man at the rendering plant, a factory mechanic; the gravedigger, a caretaker. They are not themselves ashamed of their work, but society, they feel, looks upon them as a lesser species. So they call upon promiscuously used language to match the "respectability" of others, whose jobs may have less social worth than their own.

Not that these young men in white shirts and black gloves are so secure, either. The salesman at the advertising agency is an account executive. "I feel a little downgraded if people think I'm a salesman. Account executive—that describes my job. It has more prestige than just saying, 'I'm a salesman.' " A title, like clothes, may not make the man or woman, but it helps in the world of peers—and certainly impresses strangers. "We're all vice-presidents," laughs the copy chief. "Clients like to deal with vice-presidents. Also, it's a cheap thing to give somebody. Vice-presidents get fired with great energy and alacrity."

At hospitals, the charming bill collector is called the patients' representative! It's a wonderland that Alice never envisioned. Consider the company spy. With understandable modesty, he refers to himself as an industrial investigator. This last—under the generic name, Security—is among the most promising occupations in our society today. No matter how tight the job market, here is a burgeoning field for young men and women. Watergate, its magic spell is everywhere.

In a further bizarre turn of events (the science of medicine has increased our life expectancy; the science of business frowns upon the elderly), the matter of age is felt in almost all quarters. "Thirty and out" is the escape hatch for the elderly auto workers to the woods of retirement, some hunting, some fishing. . . . But thirty has an altogether different connotation at the ad agency, at the bank, at the auditing house, at the gas company. Unless he/she is "with it" by then, it's out to the woods of the city, some hunting, some fishing of another sort. As the work force becomes increasingly younger, so does Willy Loman.

Perhaps it is this specter that most haunts working men and women: the planned obsolescence of people that is of a piece with the planned obsolescence of the things they make.

Or sell. It is perhaps this fear of no longer being needed in a world of needless things that most clearly spells out the unnaturalness, the surreality of much that is called work today.

As some occupations become obsolete, others come into being. More people are being paid to watch other people than ever before. A cargo inspector says, "I watch the watchman." He neglected to tell who watches *him*. A young department head in a bank finds it amusing. "Just like Big Brother's watching you. Everybody's watching somebody. It's quite funny when you turn and start watching them. I do that quite a bit. They know I'm watching them. They become uneasy."

Here, too, grievances come into play. The most profound complaint, aside from non-recognition and the nature of the job, is "being spied on." There's the foreman at the plant, the supervisor listening in at Ma Bell's, the checker who gives the bus driver a hard time, the "passenger" who gives the airline stewardess a gimlet eye. . . . The indignation of those being watched is no longer offered in muted tones. Despite the occasional laugh, voices rise. Such humiliations, like fools, are suffered less gladly than before.

Perhaps it is time the "work ethic" was redefined and its idea reclaimed from the banal men who invoke it. In a world of cybernetics, of an almost runaway technology, things are increasingly making things. It is for our species, it would seem, to go on to other matters. Human matters. Freud put it one way. Ralph Helstein puts it another. He is president emeritus of the United Packinghouse Workers of America. "Learning is work. Caring for children is work. Community action is work. Once we accept the concept of work as something meaningful—not just as the source of a buck—you don't have to worry about finding enough jobs. There's no excuse for mules any more. Society does not need them. There's no question about our ability to feed and clothe and house everybody. The problem is going to come in finding enough ways for man to keep occupied, so he's in touch with reality." Our imaginations have obviously not yet been challenged.

But there are stirrings, a nascent flailing about. Though "Smile" buttons appear, the bearers are deadpan because nobody smiles back. What with the computer and all manner of automation, new heroes and anti-heroes have been added to Walt Whitman's old work anthem. The sound is no longer melodious.

Nora Watson may have said it most succinctly. "I think most of us are looking for a calling, not a job. Most of us, like the assembly line workers, have jobs that are too small for our spirit. Jobs are not big enough for people."

Boredom: The Most Prevalent American Disease

by Estelle R. Ramey

Welcome to the banquet of life: Ennui sits at the head of the table, Tedium below the salt

If you really want to know what's bothering a lot of Americans, don't read the articles in the medical journals; read their advertisements. One such sociomedical vignette showed some busy mothers decorating the school gym for a PTA non-event. Off in a corner is a lone, dispirited woman. The caption under the picture diagnoses her disease as: "M.A. (Fine Arts) . . . PTA (President-elect) . . . representation of a life currently centered around home and children, with too little time to pursue a vocation for which she has spent many years in training . . . a situation that may bespeak continuous frustration and stress: a perfect framework for her to translate the functional symptoms of psychic tension into major problems. For this kind of patient—with no demonstrable pathology yet repeated complaints—consider the distinctive properties of Valium."

In other words, our heroine is dying of boredom. Short of a personal and cultural revolution, the root causes of her sickness can't be treated. Her brain is starving. A convenient way to adjust her to her proper duties is to "tranquilize" her with a mind-dulling drug. It will also get her off her doctor's back.

Boredom is a grossly underestimated malady. It causes mischief and destruction; it is socially very expensive. Erich Fromm identifies it as the insidious cause of catastrophes ranging from drug addiction to violence. Bertrand Russell said that "boredom is a vital problem for the moralist since at least half the sins of mankind are caused by fear of it." Yet boredom per se gets little or no attention from the public health establishment. For one thing, most victims do not identify it as the origin of their difficulties. They tend to think of it as a trivial complaint that afflicts only the decadent and jaded. This is nonsense; in our society boredom is endemic and increasing.

If poverty is economic deficit, then boredom is psychic deficit. Like poverty, its consequences must be cured by social changes, not by medicine. From the medical point of view, therefore, both poverty and boredom are no-win problems. Patients come to the doctor complaining of a myriad of physical symptoms, and most resist treatment. Such patients are a drag on themselves, their families, their doctors. The big traffic in prescription tranquilizers probably reflects the boredom of the doctor more than the needs of the patient.

Aside from the medical costs of boredom, this neural disorder exacts a social price in many other ways. Schoolteachers have known for a long time that children who are bored in the classroom are a menace to everyone around them—the older the child, the more extensive the damage. Rising suicide and divorce rates reflect, in large part, higher and more broadly democratic demands for "meaningful" experiences, and an unwillingness or inability to tolerate monotony. Educated people are bored. Uneducated people are also bored. The old are bored, and so are the young.

What is boredom and who is most susceptible to it? It is a painful condition resulting from a deficit of sensory responsiveness to the external world. Every human being is vulnerable because of the fundamental nature of our nervous system. There are no class, race, age, or sex lines in its distribution, but it seems most agonizing after sustained intellectual challenge or prolonged stimulation of the senses. Starving or force-feeding the highest center of the brain will induce its characteristic discomfort, while high sensory or intellectual expectations will intensify its symptoms.

Most studies of boredom have concentrated on the pathological effects of monotony on people or animals under controlled laboratory conditions. The results are directly applicable to many real situations—men stationed in distant Antarctic outposts, prisoners of war, prisoners of peace, lonely housewives, truck drivers on long solo runs, space probers, and airplane pilots. Every piece of evidence we have supports the eloquent statement of Christopher Burney, who, as a British secret agent during World War II, was caught and imprisoned by the Nazis: "I soon discovered that variety is not the spice but the very stuff of life. We need the constant ebb and flow of wavelets of our consciousness; now here, now there, keeping even our isolation in the ocean of reality so that we neither encroach nor are encroached upon."

Emotional and intellectual health depends on an appropriate amount of action in a varied environment; there is no reason to believe that women need less variety than men, or children less than adults. It has been a complacent male assumption that intelligent women don't mind doing the kind of tedious tasks that would send an intelligent man right up the wall. However, studies done on sex differences as a factor in tolerance to a monotonous environment have shown that women may respond even more irritably than men to such constraints. D. V. Biase and his colleagues used a group of male and female college students and subjected them to a uniformly uninteresting environment. They were well fed and put singly into soundproof rooms of a comfortable temperature, with a dim, diffused light (or no light) and either a low, unchanging background hum or no sound at all. The subjects could lie down but were not allowed to sleep. A device like a lie detector was used to monitor their nervous response. None of the subjects could stand the boredom for long.

The absolute monotony quickly produced emotional disturbances sometimes verging on the violent. Women showed a lower tolerance than men for isolation and tedium, and they were more likely to verbalize their distress. In what Biase calls "the Colonel Glenn syndrome," however, some of the men persisted in denying that they had difficulty coping with the torment of sensory deprivation, even though they had been observed during the course of the experiment to be moaning and writhing. Our culture, it appears, does not like its men to be anything but strong and stoical in public. When anguished, they keep a stiff upper lip and perforate their ulcers. Women have the right, for what it's worth, to complain.

Whatever the culturally permissible responses, it is a fact that every aspect of brain function, in both men and women, was disturbed after even a few hours' exposure to sensory deprivation. Their reaction time, sensory acuity, power of abstract reasoning, and internal motivation to move or to daydream or to think, all decreased. They became as empty of responsiveness as the environment was empty of input. Nothing in, nothing out is apparently the credo of the human nervous system. (Physical exercise, incidentally, appears to tone up the entire nervous system. When the subjects were allowed to move around or to exercise, their tolerance for environmental monotony increased.)

We come by our hungry brains in a natural progression. Even rats can get bored in an unchallenging environment. Anita Hatch took some laboratory rats and put them singly in warm cages with plenty of food and water but with little visual or aural stimulation or handling. After three months in this suburban rat heaven, the animals began to act like caricatures of the lonely housewife or her unemployed spouse. They became jumpy, irritable, and aggressive. They nibbled constantly and became fatter than their peers out in the exciting world. The bored rats then began to show signs of organic disorders. They developed nervous twitches and scaly tails. If they had had access to a rat doctor, they would have run up high medical bills and would have been put on tranquilizers. It wouldn't have helped them to have to go back to the same old cage.

Those rats didn't need a doctor. They needed some variety and stimulation. Just putting them back in a lively rat community for one week reversed all their pathology. It should be noted, however, that if the rat community gets too crowded and too lively, the rats once again begin to develop diseases, and these disorders of satiation are little different from those of deprivation. Thus either too much or too little nervous stimulation leads to unresponsiveness. A good environment provides just enough sensory input to maintain a sense of well-being—for mice, women, and men.

The need for exploration and novelty seems to be built into brains and the more complex the brain, the more the need for variety. It is not only men who climb mountains just because they are there. Laboratory animals trained to run a maze to get food will learn the easiest and fastest path to the food, and then, after a while, the little beasts begin to experiment with more difficult ways to get fed. If even a rat brain is willing to sacrifice a quick meal for a change of pace, what can we expect from the voracious human brain? Exactly what one might think—it will go to remarkable lengths to escape boredom.

The trouble is, we don't know how. Ennui is so pervasive and so nebulous. Whose fault is it that so many people are bored with their lives? Mrs. M.A. Fine Arts, because of her underutilized brain, has psychic tension, but just turn the page of that same medical journal and meet her husband—the male mainstay of the tranquilizer industry. This drug ad shows a middle-aged, middle-management executive with overflowing in- and out-boxes and three phones ringing at once. Tranquilizers will keep him going until his coronary occlusion makes further medication unnecessary. His is the other face of boredom—psychic tension from overload and satiation. Life is unsatisfying. Tranquilize it.

Clearly, it's not simply the occupation that creates the pervasive sense of tedium that many Americans are experiencing. Large numbers of stereotypic housewives are not bored by the PTA or their daily routines. They enjoy them. There is, in fact, far more potential flexibility and variety in running a home than in being a file clerk, a bank teller, a sentry at a missile base, or an assistant to an assistant editor at *Penthouse.* Many workers in what seem to be deadly, boring jobs do not report unhappiness with the work. Others in occupations that are far more interesting (to the observer) quit in rage and despair at the boredom of their lives. The depression and anxiety of boredom seems to be generated by one's perception of the value of the work and the degree of envious awareness of more exciting possibilities. It is not the job itself but the sense of control, power, and status it engenders that determines whether you'll suffer the pain of boredom.

A research scientist may have to perform many repetitive operations to obtain useful data, but the publication of that data and the recognition of her unique contribution make the work exciting. A psychoanalyst hears some stupefying stories during a day's work, but his status, his income, and his God-like importance to the patient make up for the tedium. An accountant spends his day with endless columns of numbers, but there is apparently a satisfying symmetry to his balanced additions and subtractions that compensates for the intrinsic monotony of his life's work. Of course, accountants do get bored. Some take to squirreling away large numbers of $100 bills to enliven the day. Psychoanalysts, too, get bored and start investing in real estate or racehorses, and research scientists get bored and become ineffectual scientist-administrators.

It's nice to have options. But what happens to someone who is fixed in a job or a household like a bug in amber? When there are no other viable choices, boredom is endured. But human beings always get some of their own back; they strike out with whatever power they have against the society that inflicts this torment upon them.

You can't tranquilize everybody. The bright child, bored by a tedious, unimaginative educational system and too little physical activity, tries to enliven things by throwing spitballs. Bored adolescents form rampaging gangs to provide the excitement that their routine, impoverished lives don't generate. They don't all live in slums. You'll find them in the best suburbs, ripping off the local stores just for the hell of it.

Men on assembly lines get so bored that they develop a free-floating hostility. On a recent television program, a man was shown moving an auto from one spot to another a few feet away, after which he went back to get another car, and so on and so on all day long— the ant and the grains of sand. He was asked whether he ever detected any faults in the cars in the process of moving them. He said, "Sure I do." He was asked if he reported them. His answer was succinct: "No." He was being screwed by "them." Screw "them."

There's nothing new about boredom, just as there's nothing new about its emotional cognates—sloth, despair, hopelessness, alienation, passivity, and anomie. It's simply that we are less willing to endure the condition than our bored forebears. The desire for change is now accepted as a justification for almost any kind of behavior. The divorce rate is escalating in all age groups but is most dramatic in marriages of twenty to thirty years. More than 95 percent of all those late divorces are requested by the bored, middle-aged husbands. Most bored wives are still willing to settle for a tranquilizer, but then, an older woman's options are pretty much limited to that. The husband, however, can opt for a hedonistic thrashing around that used to be culturally unacceptable. Even politicians, those sensitive barometers of social sanctions, can now seek out new young bed companions without suffering a drop in the polls. Their constituents seem to understand that marriage to the same woman for thirty years can get damned boring. Everybody understands, except maybe the politician's old wife.

Our society regards its women's capacity for being bored in a curiously contradictory way. Women no longer have to be pregnant all the time, and they don't have to be ignorant. At last, they can be seen as strong, intelligent, vigorous persons. At the same time, however, they are seen as weak, nonintellectual, and by nature fit only for the protected atmosphere of a harem. The same man who insists on sending his daughter to the most elitist and intellectually demanding college can't understand why women aren't satisfied with a nice home, husband, and children. His mother was. What right have these pampered women to be bored?

It is true that in an industrial society, most jobs are sedentary, monotonous, and impersonal. They have one big advantage, though, over housework. They provide money as an index of personal worth and, along with that money, a subtle but important sense of independence. The tranquilized housewife is bored, and so is her husband, but he at least has some economic ego assurance. And working men do get out of the house every day and into a world of other adults. Even the assembly-line worker can get some relief from his tensions by relating to his co-workers as in a tribal rite, and every evening he can leave his tedious job and find a change of pace in his "after-work" activities. There is little change of pace for his wife.

The forlorn wife and mother in the pharmaceutical blurb suffers not only from a lack of "meaningful stimuli," as one psychiatric reference book puts it, and an "inability to become stimulated" by her daily activities; she also compounds her psychological problems by feeling guilty about her attitude. She doesn't necessarily want a paid job, but the "libidinal and aggressive strivings" that were necessary when she was a student are now counterproductive and must be denied. One way to deal with this is to take on still more obligations (president-elect PTA) and then to complain about having too much (not too little) to do. Obviously, she does have a lot of very necessary functions. Her harried day has been catalogued ad nauseam—the constant chauffeuring of the children, the volunteer work that nobody appreciates, the gourmet cooking classes, the PTA wheel-spinning, the care and feeding of her semi-detached husband, and the endless shopping trips. Somehow, though, she can't work up that old zest. Neither can her husband, but the dynamics are different.

Medical counseling for the bored of either sex usually comes at a high price. But there is general agreement in the profession that women far outnumber men in the category of time-wasting, neurotic goldbrickers. Doctors complain bitterly about the bored housewives who clutter their waiting rooms and "have nothing the matter with them." Such women place a heavy load on our medical-care delivery system because boredom—with its accompanying depression, guilt, and anxiety—mimics just about all organ system disorders—skin rashes, head-aches, backaches, chronic fatigue, dizziness, shortness of breath, sexual dysfunction, insomnia, excessive sleeping, stomach pains, menstrual disorders, personality changes, and chest pains. Unfortunately, "psychogenic pain" hurts just as much as any other kind of pain and all good doctors are obliged first to rule out grim organic diseases that can present the same symptoms. This takes a lot of time and money.

Dr. William A. Nolen, a surgeon, writing recently in a popular women's magazine, describes the problem this way: "Women who are 'all tired out' account for a substantial segment of most medical practices. They're difficult—almost impossible—patients to treat. Most are in the thirty-five-to-forty-five age group. They've been married ten to fifteen years, their children are all in school, their husbands are earning a reasonably comfortable living. Very few of them have jobs outside the home. When a woman with this complaint comes to my office, I almost always find the same thing. She may be slightly overweight—who isn't?—but other-wise, physically, there's not a darn thing wrong with her." Dr. Nolen then speaks directly to these maddening females: "Most of you are tired for only one reason. You're bored." The good doctor is exactly right, but his Rx for cure shows a curious lack of insight.

Nolen advises these women to take the $10 or $15 that an office visit might cost and spend it on a "relaxed lunch at a restaurant" or on a "good movie." What happens to his patient when the movie is over and the lunch is digested? She comes back for another prescription for her sickness. But even this Band-Aid treatment of a destructive disease is preferable to the Dra-conian "cure" some doctors use to treat chronic boredom. Dr. Nolen describes a typical, rest-less patient named Beth, aged forty-two, who "was referred to me by a reputable family doc-tor as a candidate for hysterectomy." The referring doctor suggested the operation because Beth was "anemic due to prolongation of her menstrual periods." It turned out Beth was not anemic and that she "needed a hysterectomy about as much as I did."

But, if Beth shops around long enough, she will almost certainly find a doctor prepared to yank out a healthy uterus or prescribe expensive iron shots or tranquilizers or energizers or prolonged psychoanalysis. In fact, Beth may insist upon such mistreatment in order to have a socially acceptable reason for her terrible malaise. Being bored out of your mind is not con-sidered a serious ailment, but a hysterectomy has clout. So does a nervous breakdown or alco-holism.

It's not only the women who can afford the casual hysterectomy, the endless psychoan-analysis, who are caught up in the tedium of high expectations and minimal satisfaction. Tradi-tionally, the working-class woman was supposed to be uninterested in anything other than her home, her church, her children, and her man. Not for her the luxury of yearning for fulfillment. All she needed was a full uterus, a full belly, and shining kitchen linoleum. Where McGinty sat was the head of the table, and that's how she liked it (he said). Boredom was for those fancy ladies uptown. In actual fact, her life was stultifyingly boring most of the time, and so was her husband's; but neither was encouraged to do any soul-searching about the full life. Times have changed. Working-class women, like their richer sisters, don't have to be pregnant all the time, and, when they do go to work to help keep the family in shoes, they learn about another dimension of themselves. They like the give and take of the working world. They are finding in themselves the ability to be independent.

No woman—upper-, middle-, or working-class—gets bored with her daily routines because Gloria Steinem and Betty Friedan told her to be unhappy. Boredom is a predictable consequence of the pill, educational opportunities, and the financial demands of an expanding economy. Recent books that cry havoc because women are no longer satisfied with lives of undeveloped potential and unrealized dreams are trying to preserve a social structure that is already a shambles. To understand what's going on, their authors would do better to look at the indignities we inflict on older, retired men. As life expectancy and our expectations of life increase, so does our vulnerability to boredom. Healthy men who are forced to retire and "enjoy" their well-earned leisure often find themselves sickened by the deprivation. Dr. Jay A. Winston of Harvard described a typical retired man:

> *Mr. G., a self-employed businessman, had delayed his retirement until age 72. His health had remained good: His work had been personally fulfilling. Retirement was actually his wife's idea. Mrs. G. was looking forward to the relaxing lifestyle that her husband's retirement would finally allow.*
>
> *Mr. G. expected he would travel, develop new interests, and spend more time with his family. But his work had been at the center of his life. He had never developed hobbies. While he had enjoyed providing his family with the means to entertain themselves, he had not partaken in many of the activities himself.*
>
> *His business sold, Mr. G. found he was bored, frustrated, resentful. He arose each day and wandered around the house without a sense of purpose. His personal habits began to change—he became uncharacteristically sloppy, changed his clothes less often. He was irritable. And his mental capacities were suddenly failing. He would walk downstairs only to discover he had forgotten what he was looking for, or what he wanted to do. He began to forget people's names.*
>
> *Disturbed at these changes, Mrs. G. sought help for her husband. A thorough medical examination revealed no organic basis for his symptoms, which were classic signs of early senility. As part of a psychiatric evaluation of the problem, Dr. Shader decided to initiate a "life review" with Mr. G.*
>
> *Mr. G. admitted he never really wanted to retire, and he acknowledged anger and resentment towards his wife for forcing him to do so. Eventually he was able to confront his wife and express his anger, which re-opened communications between them.*
>
> *Things improved after that. He was able to arrange to do part-time consulting work for the new owners of his life-long business enterprise. He and Mrs. G. soon found they were beginning to enjoy their new-found leisure time together. After 16 weeks of therapy, Mr. G.'s memory problems and other signs of senility had disappeared.*

Not many old men can afford such therapy. They just disintegrate.

When sensory activation and intellectual curiosity are suppressed by a dull environment, the brain responds with a protective withdrawal from the real world. In his work with institution-bound patients, Dr. Frank R. Mark has found that revitalization of almost moribund human beings can often be achieved by the simple technique of making available things that they can handle and examine and manipulate. When you engage their interest, it is like engaging the wheels with the motor; they start to move. Doctor Mark calls loneliness, anxiety, and boredom America's major diseases.

Our society has thus created the apotheosis of a physiological dilemma. For some, satiation is the problem. The phones on the desk never stop ringing. Crisis follows crisis. The rock music gets louder, the strobe lights whirl faster, the movies become bloodier, movement from place to place becomes more frenetic, relations with others increase exponentially, and the ability to respond decreases constantly. The sound must be turned up even higher as deafness supervenes, and even then the excitement diminishes. Catch-22. For others, nothing exciting or new happens as each day mimics every other day. Little is asked, little is given.

History is full of examples of the extraordinary things that women and men will do to avoid satiation or boredom. The only thing that is new is the great increase in the number of people who have joined the chase for diversion or fulfillment. Ennui used to be strictly an upper-class disease that affected a few lords and ladies of the realm. The rest of their contemporaries were struggling desperately to survive. It is only when primal hungers are comfortably blunted to mere appetites that other human needs—love, respect, creativity—come to the surface of consciousness. It is absurd to speak of the intellectual boredom of a starving woman or man.

In the United States, although there is terrible poverty for some, most Americans are well fed and have more than a modicum of shelter, education, leisure, and freedom. Advanced technology and splendid natural resources made this possible and simultaneously made boredom more democratic. The rich and the ruling have always put a lot of energy into staving off ennui. They invented fetes, fancy clothes, hunts, racing, political intrigue, chivalry, gambling, sex games, and that most exciting game of all—war. It takes a lot of ingenuity to stay viable in the face of total leisure. Most of these diversions are now available to large numbers of Americans. They don't seem to be enough.

Rich men are going into politics—making money is not stimulating enough. Rich women are taking jobs; so are the not-so-rich women. Older people are swarming back to school to get retraining or simply to get back into the real world again. Everybody seems to have decided all at once that he or she has just one life to live, and to live with "gusto." A resigned acceptance of boredom as part of the inescapable pain of living is becoming less common. Inevitably this makes for chaos at every level of the social structure. Somebody has to do the boring work to get the papers filed, the refuse collected, the cars assembled, the letters typed, and the laundry washed. But who should be saddled with these jobs? Not me. Let it be you.

Women and men don't have much sympathy for each other's pain. Yet for all of us in America it's not easy to be young, it's harder to be middle-aged, and it's terrible to be old. It seems that our best hope is to try to help each other reach for the Greek definition of happiness: the use of all of one's powers to achieve excellence. If we put our fertile brains to designing an environment in which people who do the necessary monotonous jobs are rewarded richly for their daily boredom, in which retraining for new occupations is a normal phase of every life, and in which women and men complement instead of wounding each other, boredom will not be so pervasive.

A country that can produce the Constitution can produce a more enriching and fulfilling environment with less noise and more music. First, however, we must recognize the destructiveness of boredom, and then ask how this disease can be minimized. It will mean a massive cultural reevaluation.

Creativity in Conflict

by E. Bruce Peters

Creativity and the organization are always in conflict. Drawing the first organizational blocks establishes a system "inhospitable to a great and constant flow of ideas and creativity" (1). Any reshuffling of the blocks will threaten someone or reward someone disproportionately.

But it is not just a question of putting in a new organizational block for a creativity division. Creativity already exists and is paramount in at least one division, usually called R & D. In a successful organization, creativity must pervade the whole environment—the climate of human relationships, the overall efficiency of an enterprise, the attitudes of top management, and the creative leadership exerted.

Unlike products which can be counted, measured, analyzed, or otherwise quantified, creativity is supremely human and ethereal. Given these qualities, the study of creativity can properly start with man, followed by other pertinent factors of organization.

THE CREATIVE PERSON

Since the creative person himself is the starting point, consideration of the method by which he first becomes a member of an organization is appropriate. Recruiting creative individuals varies little from recruiting any other type of individual who is in short supply and great demand.

Shortcomings in corporate recruiting of individuals from major business schools have been tallied (2). These include inept interviewing, a poor schedule, one-sided interviews, slowness in reimbursing travel expenses, etc. These same ineptitudes apply with even greater force to attempts to recruit creative individuals, since creative individuals—be they MBAs, scientists, engineers, or whatever—are only a small percentage of the total.

To aid in locating these scarce individuals, it should be noted that "it takes a thief to catch a thief." The creative individual is not likely to fit the common mold of organizational activities. Those individuals who have demonstrated the greatest creativity are the ones most likely to recognize the quality in others. Therefore, the screening process for candidates will have to be done by other creative individuals, rather than by administrators in the personnel section.

WORKING WITH THE CREATIVE PERSON

Once the mutual assessment is complete, and the creative individual has become a member of the organization, what are the conflicts between the organization and the individual? To function effectively, the creative individual must be granted an autonomy and independence completely foreign to that of other employes.

Some firms have abolished office hours and given each of these employees his own key to the building. This is possible, because the creative person is driven by his work, rather than by directives from his boss. But that drive may not be readily apparent to other employes

Reprinted with permission from *Industrial Research,* Vol. 17, No. 4, April 1975, pp. 69-72.

Dr. E. Bruce Peters directs International Sociotechnical Systems, specializing in applications of behavioral science to R&D management.

and administrators. Consequently, there is plenty of room for misunderstanding, jealousy, and bickering.

Without considerable education, the personnel department will have difficulty adjusting ratings, personnel evaluation procedures, and pay scales to an individual who doesn't turn out a recognizable piece of work at regular intervals—and also doesn't follow normal hours, much less punch a clock. Unless they have been exposed in their own development to this type of individual, executives of line divisions can hardly be expected to look favorably on such an unusual type of activity—especially when budget-cutting time arrives.

But it doesn't end there. Frequently, the creative individual has the power to make or break the company—by suggesting new products, new activities, or new fields of endeavor, or by being alert to the necessity for curtailing current activities at the right time.

Despite his potential effect on the company, the creative individual is usually limited in the degree to which he can climb in the company without switching over to an administrative capacity. He has been hired because of his originality, freshness of view, independence of thought, and critical ability. It's not surprising that he applies these talents to the organization of which he is a part—with the result that he often has difficulty fitting in as a team worker or an effective administrator.

Yet the unfortunate fact is that a changeover to an executive position is the only way his advancement can be assured. This results in a double fault, bad for him and bad for his co-workers. To remedy this difficulty, many companies have established a parallel hierarchy by which a creative person could make as much as the company president. Despite the logic of such a system, this is another point of friction built into the organization.

COMMUNICATIONS

Size is another stumbling block. The tendency of modern business is to increase in size. This tendency is brought about by economies of scale, by the increasing size of investments required in meeting ever-increasing costs of machines, labor, and raw materials, and by increasing capabilities of centralized management.

In this environment, the organization's built-in resistance to change increases. Minor decisions which would affect only a few persons in a small organization now affect the entire colossus.

The necessity for transmitting messages back and forth through so many different levels slows reaction time and feedback. Filtering occurs at each level, so that ideas are shorn of their audacity, the emphasis changed, or completely blocked.

In addition to the frustration of individuals in a creative group, pertinent information concerning organizational needs and possibilities also is blocked. Contributions of the creative group diminish or become less related or organizational goals. General dissatisfaction ensues.

An alternative is the assurance that information missions are established to convey just this type of information back and forth across organizational lines. In fact, considerable research shows that some recognizable individuals are particularly adept or influential as information gadflies. But again, the organization works against their potential effects on overall creativity by failing to recognize, reward, or give scope to their free-wheeling tendencies.

Communications within the organization are important, but they're also important between organizations. In a few industries, companies can encourage full disclosure of all new developments, either on an exchange basis with other companies, or by publication in an appropriate journal.

This exchange of information is like flint striking steel. It produces showers of sparks—new ideas which can be carefully kindled into the full fires of progress. But here also, we find that the nature of the competition or company policies frequently block this means of fostering creativity.

CONTROLS

Another major area in which the organization is at odds with its own creative and adaptive forces is that of the controls it applies. Controls in this context mean evaluating, budgeting, and planning, as well as information transfer and leadership.

Evaluation—The conflict between the organization and a creative person is exemplified in the accompanying account from a talk by Prof. James W. Mosel (3). The example quoted clearly explains that neither the creative person nor his work can be evaluated according to the "tried-and-true" principles learned in business school. Instead, his performance must be judged in the light of his contribution or potential value in reaching the overall goals of the company.

EVALUATION OF CREATIVITY

"I know a systems analyst (in those days he was called a management engineer). He almost had a nervous breakdown trying to apply scientific management principles to the Manhattan Project during World War II. He tried to functionalize and standardize and specialize the work of mathematical physicists. He tried to set up standards. He tried to develop an appropriate appraisal form.

"His first difficulty, the most traumatic, was that he found it impossible to describe the work. He couldn't even produce a job description. He went into the cubicle of a theoretical mathematician and said, 'All right, what are your tasks, duties, and elements?' The fellow said 'What's that?' He went through it again. The fellow finally answered, 'Well, what I am trying to prove is that locally compact sets are not dense in themselves in Hilbert space.' The engineer asked, 'That's a duty? Show me these things.' The fellow said, 'I can't because they don't really exist. They are just abstract ideas which we invent.' The systems analyst exploded. 'You are working with something that doesn't exist? Come on now, tell me your tasks, duties, and elements.'

"Eventually the engineer went to the second page in a book, published by the U.S. Employment Service, which tells how to analyze a job. It says, "If you don't make any sense of what the incumbent says, watch what he does.' So he began to observe.

"Well, the mathematical physicist did only three things. He drank coffee in the office, he looked at books, and he wrote on the blackboard. That's all he did. Obviously, my analyst was getting nowhere.

"He went to the man's boss, who really wasn't his boss because it turned out that the man really didn't have a boss. 'What's this fellow doing?' he asked. The boss said, 'We don't know what he is doing. If we knew what he was doing, we wouldn't have him doing it.' Astonished, the analyst asked, 'Do you mean to tell me that you don't know the tasks, duties, and elements of this subordinate?' The boss responded, 'Hell, no. That's why we've got him doing it. He's the only man in the country who understands this sort of thing.'

"So the analyst went on to the next part of the interview form. 'Now tell me,' he asked the boss, 'how do you know when he is doing the job well? What are the criteria?' The boss answered, 'I haven't the slightest idea.' When the analyst persisted, he finally said, 'Well, I guess he is doing it

well when he tells me so.' 'Do you mean to tell me,' shouted the analyst, 'that you depend on a subordinate to tell you when he is doing a job right?' The boss stood his ground. 'That's absolutely true. He's the only person in this country who can understand the proof of these theorems. If he says he's doing it right, he's doing it right. That's why we have him doing it.' " (3)

Budgeting—In a free-wheeling situation, budgeting also is a problem. How is it possible to allocate funds on a continuing basis to an enterprise which doesn't produce a tangible result on a regular basis? —But then, when it does click, it's like hitting the jackpot at Las Vegas.

In some creative fields such as advertising, it is possible to establish dollar relationships based on the cost of ads, TV time, etc. An industrial organization has a more difficult time. Even in boom periods, the different portions of the organization will be competing for a limited amount of funds. In periods when the organization is cutting back, those units with quantifiable outputs will certainly win out over any creative group when it comes to a contest for funds.

Planning—While the allocation of funds is the ultimate in controls, another type of control is the planning process. When planning is done efficiently, all portions of the organization become involved in the development of the plans for the future. In so doing, they try to visualize the need for change and become more disposed to accept its inevitability.

Planning is no panacea, however, because in the process of visualizing future trends and future activities, most people feel most comfortable with what they already know. Consequently, their planning centers around better ways of doing present activities. They have difficulty considering any radical departure from present practices. In addition, there is considerable difficulty in planning while carrying out the day-to-day activities which make the company prosper in the near term.

Creative transfer—While planning may constitute a control to regulate future activities, it also overlaps into the transfer process, the process by which a creative idea becomes a reality. Properly done, planning is a key portion of the process.

But the difficulties go beyond outlining future activities. We mentioned these difficulties in the discussion of large and small organizations. Even more to the point is the following quotation from James Brian Quinn (4).

"As one vice president of research said, 'A new product is like a baby. You can't just bring it into the world and expect it to grow up and be a success. It needs a mother (enthusiasm) to love it and keep it going when things are tough. It needs a pediatrician (expert information and technical skills) to solve the problems the mother can't cope with alone. And it needs a father (authority with resources) to feed it and house it. Without any one of these, the baby may still turn out all right, but its chances of survival are a lot lower.' "

The points to note in connection with creativity are the effects of failure. The creative individual is perhaps more motivated than most by seeing his ideas translated into reality. Unwarranted changes or cancellations of creative programs, brought about by a failure in the transfer process, will have a depressing effect.

The consideration of the transfer process is the most difficult part of transforming an idea into reality. This concept involves not only technical aspects but also the planning of change and the problems of restructuring an organization.

Leadership—The final conflict area is that of leadership. This commodity is always in short supply. But no group will react so strongly to leadership—good or bad—as the individuals engaged in creative activity. Creative individuals simply cannot be forced to produce usable ideas on a regular, measured basis.

Although the stress of competition or need is a valuable incentive for most of them, creative persons react unfavorably to new edicts regulating their activity or putting them on a par with other workers. One of their distinguishing characteristics is their sense of feeling different. As a result, they must be treated differently.

A highly participative type of leadership and management is indicated. In addition to all of the usual managerial skills, the leader of a creative group must have a high degree of sensitivity to human relations. Any group singled out for such special handling will induce cross-stresses in an organization.

SYNTHESIS

Thus, the confrontation of ideas leading to change may cause conflicts with the entrenched status quo of the remainder of the organization. But an organization can be optimized for creativity.

Of course, the proposed optimization could not be wholly adopted by any real-life organization, since no organization has the sole objective of optimizing creativity. There are other objectives, such as financing the enterprise and turning out some sort of saleable product. This synthesis merely provides a descriptive model, a catalog of attributes, from which suitable segments could be taken and applied. What then are the characteristics of an organization which help to resolve the innate conflict and favor creativity?

First, the creative part of the organization should be in small units. Individuals rather than teams will be identified with specific projects wherever possible. When work by teams is required, two smaller teams will perform the same task, rather than trying to work as one large team.

Coordination and cooperation between teams will be encouraged by providing equal rewards to each for a successful solution to the problem. At worst, the assignment of the same task to two teams will impose an acceptable kind of stress. At best, it will provide a selection of alternative solutions.

As individuals and teams demonstrate greater creativity, they will be rewarded by more profound problems and a greater share of the budget. Successful individuals will be promoted and given raises, but permitted to remain in their fields.

As they show greater capabilities, the entire operational budget might be turned over to them to divide among salaries, operational expenses, equipment, etc., as they see fit. A certain degree of slack would be maintained in order to capitalize on any favorable development.

The creative workers would be physically separated from the rest of the organization in order to cater to their idosyncrasies and provide individual liberty to the maximum extent possible. Their installation would be comfortable and serviceable, but not luxurious—providing high-quality equipment of the type needed to accomplish their task.

In addition, there would be some sort of experimental or pilot facilities to aid in proving the feasibility of any ideas generated. In this fashion, some conflict with the rest of the organization would be reduced.

The transfer of ideas to reality would be bridged by a planning group which would be separated from day-to-day operational tasks. But the planning group would have one foot on each side of the bridge, aiding the process of communications.

Communications would be further helped by occasional retreats, something along the order of religious retreats. Separated from the cares and pressures of ordinary activities, top management could explain its objectives to the creative group. Similarly, the creative group could describe the scope and possible outcomes of their endeavors.

Those individuals who were the informal opinion leaders and information carriers would be identified, their contributions recognized and rewarded. They would be given latitude to perform their self-appointed tasks.

Finally, the leadership of this particular group would be the best available in the organization. The type of management would have to be participative to an extent which would seem extreme in other portions of the organization. Yet out of this type of leadership, an orientation in the general direction of movement of the company would emerge. And this is the capstone on the development of a descriptive model optimizing conditions for creativity.

REFERENCES

1. Levitt, T., *Harvard Business Review,* May-June 1963, p. 81.
2. *Wall Street Journal,* Nov 25, 1968.
3. Mosel, J. W., "Group Relationships and Participative Management," a talk delivered at the Industrial College of the Armed Forces, Sept 26, 1967.
4. Quinn, J. B., *Harvard Business Review,* Jan-Feb 1963.

Color the New Generation Very Light Green

by S. Frederick Starr

How do young Americans view the System? An obvious question for the bicentennial, perhaps, but not one that was asked with any frequency before the 1960's. Now it is heard on every side, and not just because of the upheavals of a few years ago. Back in 1955 those under thirty constituted only about 19 percent of the electorate; now they are 29 percent. During the same period their absolute numbers in the labor force doubled, to more than 33 million. Through these and other developments, young Americans and the System have become inextricably linked with each other.

In recognition of this, a veritable industry has grown up to explain the young worker or student to the nation at large. The American Council on Education introduces us to the incoming college freshmen each fall, and at intervals the Yankelovich organization turns out a detailed profile of the age group as a whole. A bevy of pollsters periodically checks out the behavior of youth on the campus, at the ballot box, on the assembly line, and in bed. The results are reported widely and in detail, but all too often with an eye for short-term fluctuations rather than less sensational long-term trends.

Thus we are told that young people are "conservative" (*Newsweek*) and "politically withdrawn" (an authority on higher education); that college students spurn learning for the sake of the "paper chase" (*New York Times*); and that the noncollege majority is "dissatisfied and frustrated" (Daniel Yankelovich). All this may well be true. Undeniably, it makes vivid copy.

Images, as historian Daniel Boorstin has noted, threaten to usurp the place of reality in our culture, and images of youth are no exception. They are everywhere. So surrounded are young Americans by media-made images of themselves that at times they become the perpetuators of these images, presenting them to interviewers and pollsters as substitutes for their own perceptions. For example, the young head of the United Auto Workers local at Lordstown, Ohio, just after the much-publicized G.M. strike there, began an interview with Studs Terkel by observing that "*Someone*" [emphasis mine] said Lordstown is the Woodstock of the workingman." This "someone" surely produced a compelling image. But in the end it is only an image—and, incidentally, one that baffles the many participants in the strike who view their experience in more traditional labor terms.

THE NEW FOCUS ON WORK

One aspect of the present reality that few would deny is that "the System" does not mean the same today as a decade ago. If during the Sixties higher education and the draft provided a young person's most immediate contact with our complex of national institutions, today it is work, or the lack of it. This is true for everyone to some extent, but it is particularly so for youth, whether they are "last in, first out" at the factory or B.A.'s out pounding the pavement. With unemployment in the sixteen-to-twenty-nine age bracket running at 14 percent, compared with just above 6 percent for those thirty and over, this is not so surprising. For blacks under thirty the unemployment picture is still grimmer. Nor are degree holders

Reprinted with permission from *Fortune,* Vol. XCI, No. 4, April 1975, pp. 174-175.
Dr. S. Frederick Starr is with the Kennan Institute, Smithsonian Institute, Washington, D.C.

with jobs immune from feeling a pinch, since in recent years students as a group built up several billion dollars of debts; even young doctors take an average of five years to pay off theirs.

With the new focus on work, education may be slipping from the central place in the System as young people perceive it. The gap between the earning power of men with sixteen years of education and those with twelve has shrunk recently and is now down to $2,100 a year in the twenty-five-to-thirty-four age bracket, reports economist Stanley D. Nollen of Georgetown University. In the past few years, awareness of this trend, together with the mounting cost of schooling, has brought a noticeable drop in the proportion of high-school graduates electing to go on to college—from above 61 percent at the end of the 1960's to below 58 percent last autumn. The happy marriage of education with success, which has long characterized the American System, may be ending in separation, at least temporarily.

If young people's contact with the System is now primarily through work, then the reported decline in dedication to one's job cannot be passed over lightly. Several analysts have claimed to find such a decline. Daniel Yankelovich has documented growing doubts among young people in the labor force that "hard work always pays off," while the Department of Health, Education, and Welfare has placed its imprimatur on the concept of a spreading "blue-collar blues."

It would be premature, however, to prepare the wake for the Protestant ethic of work and the desire to "get ahead." Take, for example, the evidence for college students. The Educational Testing Service found that, among 21,000 college seniors whom it surveyed, the principal factor in choosing a vocational field was the possibility for leadership. In the same sample, those who went on to graduate school cited "self-discipline and determination" as the most essential qualities needed to reach their educational goals. And for what it is worth, a recent cover story in *Glamour* magazine posed the questions "How Much Can You Make? How Far Can You Go? How Soon Can You Get There?"

A CLASS OF LOSERS

While granting all this, some observers point to a reverse trend among young workers. The increase in absenteeism, the spread of drugs to the factory, and declining productivity are all evidence, they say, of a profound malaise among working youth. Its roots are often traced to the monotonous nature of much factory work. Young industrial workers, it is said, are less tolerant of mindless work than their parents might have been. A far more pessimistic explanation is that the close linkage of success with education over the last generation has turned those who didn't go to college into a new class of losers who see themselves as having been shut out from success in the American System. According to this view, such people have already made low performance a way of life.

Against both of these diagnoses of malaise are ranged a number of authorities who flatly deny that the young American worker is indifferent either to his job or to work in general. Dr. Iradj Siassi, clinical psychiatrist at the University of Pittsburgh, bases his denial on studies of workers at various automobile plants. In each case, he found job satisfaction and dedication to work to be quite high for all ages. The discontent that did exist was mainly linked with workers' doubts about whether they would be adequately rewarded for their efforts. In regard to surveys indicating that young workers take work less seriously than their counterparts in earlier days, Siassi points out that this is quite natural for a generation which has been able to assume jobs would be there when wanted. As it becomes scarcer, he reasons, work will move up fast on young people's scale of values.

This is already happening. Political scientist Roberta Sigel of Rutgers University interviewed a thousand Pennsylvania high-school seniors last spring and found "personal drive and ambition" to be a primary value among them, including those headed directly for jobs. One may wonder just how different this is from a while back, but when William Winpisinger, a general vice president of the International Association of Machinists and Aerospace Workers, began five years ago to proclaim that "the work ethic is alive and well among young Americans," many of his listeners winced. Today they wouldn't.

ON THE PLATFORM WITH ARCHIE BUNKER

So America's young people do retain an eagerness to work and a rather old-fashioned optimism about what work will bring them. But precisely these attitudes make the pink slip or the graduate-school rejection more difficult to face. The large recent increase in demands by young people for psychiatric services both on campuses and in factories may be traceable in part to the fear of not making it in a society that encourages one to want to do so. No Michael Stivic relishes the thought of ending up on the loading platform beside his father-in-law, Archie Bunker. Yet downward mobility could become as American as upward mobility.

Despite all the blame heaped upon the System a few years back, young people still tend to interpret failure in personal terms. Yankelovich still finds a prevalent belief that a "strong" person can control his own life, and those who share this belief will probably view lack of such control as evidence of their own weakness or insignificance. But no neat line separates feelings about one's self from feelings about one's environment.

It has been argued that young people are not so much actively hostile to the political and economic system as passively alienated from it—"turned off." Many observers have found support for this conclusion in the fact that only half of the eligible voters under twenty-five bothered to vote in 1972 and less than a quarter in 1974. If the apparent estrangement from civic life is genuine and enduring, the argument runs, then surely our public institutions are in trouble. Perhaps they are, but the voting figures do not prove it. Ward politicians have always known that new voters are less likely than others to turn out to register, and with the broadening of the franchise to include eighteen-year-olds, there are far more potential new voters than usual.

Ever since 1972, when the anticipated phalanx of new voters failed to materialize, we have been hearing that the activism of the Sixties is dead. Low voter turnout among youth, the declining number of recruits for public-interest projects, and the student preoccupation with careers have all been cited as proof that the interests of young Americans have shifted away from reforming the System. This may well be true of most young people nowadays, but then the activism of yore was a majority movement at only a few highly publicized moments. What those hailing or regretting the end of activism fail to appreciate is the extent to which activism has survived by becoming regularized and institutionalized as part of the System. The still-strong interest in various types of advocacy law is but one example of the continued vitality of youthful reformism.

A major reason activism among youth is less visible today than a few years back is that it has largely abandoned populist methods and become professionalized. A National Student Lobby campaigns actively for student-related measures before Congress. Young leaders of an activist Student Association of the State University of New York command a budget approaching $100,000, which they dispense in behalf of their favorite causes like the seasoned politicos they are. Purists may regret the passing of the naiveté of the Sixties, but by adopting the style of practical American politics, youth has doubtless become a more effective force than formerly. Even the unions are feeling the pressure, for as one young worker told the A.F.L.-C.I.O. journal, *The Federationist,* "participation means more than being permitted to drive the beer truck to the local's annual picnic."

VOICES IN A DIVERSE CHOIR

It appears, then, that many of the reigning images of youth today are open to question. Young people seem better disposed toward work and personal achievement, less negative toward the System, and less startlingly unique in their political behavior than may be generally acknowledged. Nonetheless, it is well to be reminded that "youth" does not connote just one state of mind or one attitude toward the System, if it ever did. Marked distinctions within the age group persist. These partly correspond to differences in education, but one may wonder whether the most significant differences in outlook may not come to follow lines of poverty and wealth.

By any measure, "youth" is less distinct a category today than it has been for some while. The principal factor affecting young people at present—the tightening economy—affects almost the entire population in some degree. Inevitably this will make for closer interaction between generations than has recently existed. No one who has been on an American campus recently can fail to have been struck by how closely students and parents are working together in order to meet the staggering costs of education, and how deeply many students understand and appreciate their parents' plight. The shared problems facing youth and the rest of us increase the likelihood that any reassessments of the System will be carried out by the society as a whole, with youth singing as one or several voices in a single choir made up of all age groups.

Having recognized the elements of diversity within the under-thirty generation as well as the common ground between that generation as a whole and its elders, we should also recognize one additional point: that rich or poor, educated or uneducated, white collar or blue collar, young Americans today expect more from the System than has any generation in the past.

Specifically, they tend to believe that America's institutions must make active and conscious efforts to enable every citizen to attain as high a level of physical, intellectual, and cultural well-being as possible. In this regard, they recognize no sharp distinctions between public and private institutions, or between national and local bodies. All must in the long run further this same end.

A BROADENED SOCIAL CONTRACT

Some observers speak of this point of view as a new "psychology of entitlement," while others disparage it as a "welfare ethic." Either way, it is by no means so alien to the experience of most young people as one may at first think. Postwar prosperity brought to our grade schools and high schools any number of services that scarcely existed earlier: a range of special educational programs, preventive medicine, career guidance, psychiatric counseling, etc., etc. For better or worse, a desirable school became the one that could provide the maximum number of such services, just as a desirable job could be measured in terms of its benefits, and a desirable multiversity in terms of the number of "opportunities" it offered. Such a standard could readily be applied to society at large, which is precisely what is happening.

For some young people, such expectations may well prove to be little more than a welfare ethic. For others, however, this emerging mentality may become part of a renegotiated and broadened social contract. Should this prove to be the case, increasing numbers of younger citizens will be measuring their freedom in terms of what the System does for them as well as what it does not do to them. Reciprocally, they will have to be willing themselves to be measured in terms of diligence on the job and the persistence and responsibility with which they exercise a civic sense. Can that reasonably be expected? The answer is clearly yes.

Familia Ludens: Reinforcing the Leisure Component in Family Life

by Dennis K. Orthner

Leisure is examined as a normal and potentially vital component in the contemporary family. Consideration is given to the interplay between work and leisure and the means by which leisure facilitates companionship and family interaction. Specific attention is given to the lack of reinforcement of family leisure in present institutions and the important role leisure can play in marital, child, parent-child, and retirement adjustment.

In his study of the march of civilizations, Johan Huizinga (1949) carefully examines the role of play in culture. He concludes that man appears to develop the presence of the play element as an integrating force for his institutions and society as a whole. The playing man, "homo ludens," is recognized by Huizinga as a viable and natural condition of mankind with myriad permutations. An offshoot of this concept led a number of recreation groups to adopt the slogan: "the family that plays together, stays together." The family from this point of view, is perceived of as utilizing play to facilitate its integration or solidarity. In other words, familia ludens becomes a measure of the health and vitality of a family. At a higher level, the reinforcement of companionship as a means of integrating the modern family as an institution presupposes the element of togetherness and sharing found in the playing family.

Play, however, is but an active form of leisure and it is important to understand leisure before we can adequately test the above family related assumptions. There is little question that today the family is being influenced by a change in perspectives of and opportunities for leisure. New conceptions of work, job, career, leisure, play, and recreation are challenging the structure of the family. Leisure has been hailed the harbinger of ill as well as the source of new life for the family (Hobart, 1963). Somewhat surprisingly, little attention has been given the leisure factor by family life professionals. As an indication of this lack of awareness, an examination of marriage and family texts reveals that very little, if any, mention is given the role of play, recreation, or leisure in the modern family.[1] Lack of research in the area can partially explain this but the dearth of speculation beyond the "do things together" cliché is difficult to understand. Perhaps it is time to consider familia ludens and explore several questions: Is leisure really an important consideration for the family and why; should leisure reinforcement be a function of family life specialists; and if so, what should the principle concerns be in this area?

It is important first of all to examine what is happening in the worlds of work and leisure. Work, for many in the post-industrial society, is increasingly losing much of its earlier meaning (cf. Reisman, 1958; Goodale and Aagaard, 1974). This is especially true in the case of the job or occupation.[2] Kaplan states that "the familiar ticket to life—work—seems in danger of

---

[1] A notable exception to the above is the text by Robert O. Blood, *Marriage* (Free Press, 1969) which devotes a chapter to "Companionship in Leisure."

[2] For an excellent discussion of the difference between job and work, see Thomas F. Green, *Work, Leisure, and the American Schools* (N.Y.: Random House, 1968).

From *The Family Coordinator*, April 1975, pp. 175-183. Copyright 1975 by National Council on Family Relations. Reprinted by permission.

Dr. Dennis K. Orthner is Professor in the Department of Child Development and Family Relations, University of North Carolina at Greensboro, North Carolina.

having outlived its acceptability" (1971, 26). The definition of who we are is usually answered by an occupational reference-lawyer, professor, plumber, and so forth. But what if you find little meaning in your job, your required hours of "work" are being reduced, and the economy cannot support your continuing to "moonlight"? The idea that any occupation can provide a sense of accomplishment if only the proper job enrichment techniques are employed or if children are reared with the proper orientation toward work is highly questionable. What Jacques Ellul calls the "autonomous monolithic technological society with its scientistic values" (1968, 38) strains to reduce each task to its simplest component and man becomes the servant, not the master.

Families are encouraged, nevertheless, to reinforce the work ethic. "Parents, regardless of social class, do a great deal to determine whether a child will be work-oriented or a sluggard, whether he will seek or avoid responsibility" (Lipsett, 1962, 46). The implication is made in this statement that the option to a work orientation is a loathesome state and that persons selecting another life orientation are somehow avoiding responsibility. While the case for vocational education on the part of parents is not denied (Shoffner and Kelmer, 1973), it is questionable whether the work ethic, as it has been reinforced, is truly functional any longer.

As discretionary time becomes more available, the work ethic fails to allow genuine freedom. Working at play becomes the norm. Vacations are pre-planned to the most minute detail. Weekends are an endless string of "things to do." Even sex is defined in terms of schedules and techniques (Lewis and Brisset, 1967). According to Alexander Reid Martin (1961):

The complete inability to relax even for a moment is a common complaint and evidence of neurotic disturbance. The widespread and characteristic symptoms of our so-called age of anxiety stem from a fear of relaxation and leisure. This reaches its most intense expression in many individuals who are unable to take vacations, in those who are beset by severe after-work irritability, and in those who suffer from what is called the Sunday neurosis.

If support for the work ethic as the dominant life force in man is increasingly dysfunctional or inappropriate as it appears to be, perhaps even worse would be the lack of support for an adequate replacement. There is particular danger in supplanting the work ethic with no ethic. Not surprisingly, this is already occurring and having a negative effect on the family.

The increase in middle-class youthful deviancy can partially be explained as an inability to creatively utilize discretionary time. This should not be taken as an attack on the alternative life styles of youth who are attempting to develop a different ethical foundation for their lives. Many of these latter persons are opting out of the so-called "work-trap" in favor of a preferred orientation toward creative leisure. But what of the "T.V. generation" that has been fed only the pablum of vicarious participation and entertainment, controlled activities with defined leadership, and a notable lack of clear-cut work goals? Many of them get into trouble simply out of boredom. Without proper leisure socialization, this probably will increase.

Another problem resulting from a lack of leisure reinforcement is that free time increasingly becomes less "free." As an example, Walker (1969) reports that labor-saving devices have not had as much effect on relieving the homemaker from household tasks as many believe. What usually happens is that standards shift, filling the potentially released time. For example, when clothes were washed by hand, they were usually worn longer and washed less frequently. Today, we expect a change of clothes daily and a clean wardrobe from which to select our garb for the day. Without education for leisure, increases in non-work time will probably continue to lead to a disconcerting rise in standards and a loss of freedom for all family members.

WHY IS LEISURE IMPORTANT?

Leisure offers a new source of family integration suited to the age toward which we are moving. John Neulinger (1974, 120) recently stated:

It is not necessary that we downgrade work in order to raise the value of leisure. Leisure is not non-work; leisure is not time left over from work. Leisure is a state of mind; it is a way of being, of being at peace with oneself and what one is doing.

Free time, therefore, is not leisure; it only releases the possibility of leisure. As the potential for this freedom is increasing, it would be appropriate to discuss what leisure can do for the family.

First, leisure fulfills needs for personal relaxation. It cleanses the mind and frees one to consider alternatives. In effect, leisure should help release persons from the conventionality which tends to restrict individuals in their decision-making and their opportunities for alternative modes of interaction. There is a tendency for roles to become increasingly defined over time, especially in the family. It is only during leisure that persons become free to consider other means of handling tasks.

This spontaneity and reduction in inhibition is very important in developing interpersonal understanding. If persons interact primarily in defined roles, then the feedback they receive limits both the realization of their self as well as that of the other. The result is the "role-playing" so common in many families with the necessary reduction in communication to reduce the threat of structural instability. Interpersonal communication is enhanced by leisure. The realization of the other beyond the constraints of a particular role improves the level of understanding and offers further possibilities for exchange. In addition, leisure allows the release of normal pressures and tension, the opportunity to share frustrations, and the ability to compensate for inadequacies in other areas.

The cohesiveness of the family can be improved through the sharing of leisure. By enjoying a common experience, the participants develop a sense of exclusiveness and come to know one another better. Stone and Taves (1956) report that a "combat metaphor" is common among family campers who come to view their experience as a means of improving their social solidarity. The wilderness trip, for example, is perceived of as a struggle only able to be won if each person understands one another. This strengthening of family ties among campers has also been reported in studies by West and Merriam (1970) and Lay and Devall (1974).

The sense of solidarity, however, is increased by more than just the experience of the shared activity itself. In many cases, a great deal of planning and preparation is done before the activity is even engaged in. The family that plants a garden together may spend weeks deciding what will be grown, where it should be located, what procedures need to be followed, and so on. After the activity, the process of recollection often reinforces the cohesiveness of the family and opens the communication of the members revealing new opportunities for interaction.

But not all leisure activities function in the same way for families (Orthner, 1974). Individual activities may provide relaxation for the persons involved but they also develop their own set of commitments that reduce possibilities for communication and sharing. A high proportion of time spent in individual activities has been found to be negatively related to marital satisfaction (Orthner, 1975). On the other hand, "joint" activities, those which require interaction, are most likely to be associated with family solidarity. Games, camping, and most forms of play allow persons to explore their environment with greater freedom and to test themselves in new situations. Family roles are less clearly defined in such activity and role exchange becomes possible: the husband might cook, the wife pitch the ball, or the children control the rules.

"Parallel" leisure activities, a third possibility, offer the promise of sharing but produce an actual reduction in participant interaction. The spectator oriented activities dominate this pattern of leisure with television viewing their forte. As a recreational resource, the television provides an opportunity for the family to be together, to vicariously experience something in common, but with few necessary requirements for sharing. Planning is provided by the networks and the "T.V. Guide" and recollection is handled through re-runs and magazines. Parallel activities, therefore, may give the family a feeling that they are "doing things together" and yet hide the underlying tension and needs for interpersonal reinforcement that are handled in joint activities.

A central issue is whether families know how to develop their capacities for leisure and how to select those activities that contribute to their solidarity. Somewhat optimistically, Dumazedier feels that "family cohesion is not threatened with the new society, but renewed—thanks to leisure and semi-leisure relationships and activities" (1971, 197). But he is assuming acceptance of the "new society" with a leisure ethic, while for many persons this is not going to be an easy adjustment. The anxiety that exists with free time and the inability to select those activities that integrate the family are going to become critical issues in the immediate future. Guidance will be necessary for many families to find fulfillment in leisure.

TOWARD LEISURE REINFORCEMENTS

The responsibility for a reorientation toward leisure should be shared by each of the institutions of society. But family-shared leisure, as a special case, certainly is not receiving the reinforcement it needs. As an example, socialization in leisure is usually associated with schooling and, specifically, with physical education. These programs, however, tend to have several strikes against them in facilitating gratifying family leisure: activities tend to be sport oriented, skills are rewarded more than pleasure, and sex-division is usually practiced. This results in competition being encouraged instead of cooperation, the continuation of the "work at play ethic," and the separation of men and women in leisure when they need to learn to relax and enjoy these periods together.

Other recreation groups have done little better. Most recreation programs are geared to a separation of family members. Men do these things, women do those things; boys do this, girls do that. Women have been barred from various recreational establishments of men, including golf courses. With few exceptions, girls are presently not allowed to participate in Little League baseball with boys. It may be expected that if a man wished to join the garden club, he would cause considerable consternation. Given this separation, it is little wonder that recreation leaders report that "the tremendous forces, positive and negative, shaping modern family life are in some ways seemingly beyond the influence of recreational forces in our society" (Miller and Robinson, 1963, 257).

Neither economic nor religious institutions have been particularly noteworthy in their reinforcement of family recreation. The non-family orientation of American business has been aptly criticized (Koprowski, 1973) and there are few indications of a major change. Forced overtime, extensive business travel, relocation, the "company-first" attitude, and other factors reduce leisure possibilities. Churches, likewise, seem to develop programs that separate family members. While we rarely find a church today that forces men to sit on one side and women the other or deplores mixed swimming, total family activities are often hard to find. As an example, a local church held a family week culminating in a picnic at which the men played baseball and the boys and girls played other separate games, while the women cooked, cheered, and talked with one another. Only rarely did family members see, play, or even eat with one another after they had arrived.

This brings us to the central problem: Many families, if not most, do not know how to develop and reinforce in themselves the creative use of leisure. They become dependent on outside sources of interest to relieve them of the boredom, tension, and insecurity they often feel with one another. Certainly, summer camps become this for many children when their parents no longer find them comfortable to have around. It is interesting to watch the current flak over Little League and the revolt of parents who see their children being dehumanized in this "sport." A boy must work very hard, risk ridicule as well as other punishment, and conform to strict adult control over other areas of his life to "play" ball. What ever happened to sandlot ball and other spontaneous forms of play? It appears that parents have felt more comfortable in sending their children into organized activities where "responsible" adults are in control. One wonders, however, if this is not simply another means of shifting their responsibility and especially, an indication of their own insecurity with play and leisure.

This inability to creatively develop free time resources is probably best seen in the growth of television. The fact that the average family views its television set over six hours per day (Rue, 1974) is only an indication of its influence. Most important, families have become dependent on this recreational source as the mainstay of their perception of family-oriented leisure.

The above suggests that families do need guidance in effectively developing their leisure resources and that this guidance is presently not available to any significant extent. This is not to say that the family is losing its recreational function, but rather that many families are not prepared for the possibilities of leisure. Family life professionals should be concerned over the divesting of responsibility for family leisure that appears to be occurring, especially since free time without a positive leisure ethic may be a factor in familial disorganization.

It is not being advocated that a new subject be added to all the programs that are now being offered. However, it is important that this dimension be appropriately integrated into those subject areas that are relevant to leisure education. This is not a new idea. Buckland (1972) has hailed the productive use of leisure as an important element in parent education. Davy and Rowe have said that families need to be aware of their role in providing "an atmosphere conducive to the cultivation of creative interests" (1964, 80). Koprowski (1973) and Rue (1974) have emphasized the need for more knowledgeable control over television viewing. In addition, Kraus (1964) has proposed that courses in home and family living explore the function of leisure and recreation in terms of their effect on building desirable family relationships.

SOME SPECIFIC AREAS OF CONCERN

Marital Adjustment

In sympathy with the Mace view that good family strategy must first concentrate on the marital dyad (1974), husbands and wives need reinforcement for sharing their discretionary time together. There is a tendency for roles to be increasingly divided over the marital career and separate interests to develop. Orthner (1975) found in his study a rather steady decline in jointly shared leisure activities over the marital career. Because shared leisure is a major determinant of companionship, this decline may be a primary reason for the marital disenchantment reported in most research (cf. Rollins and Feldman, 1970).

Couples should be encouraged to order their priorities so that joint participation in leisure activities is possible. All too often marriages get boring, even in the early years when emphasis is placed on individual pursuits or parallel activities such as television. When children arrive, expenses increase and parental role demands may make it difficult for husbands and wives to have time together alone. This may mean allocating scarce financial resources for baby sitting services but parents need to be aware of the relational costs of not having this time to share.

In addition to parenthood, other areas of marital stress can be resolved easier if some leisure is shared. Conflict is inevitable and a genuine understanding of the other is necessary for any issues to be effectively dealt with.   Shared leisure facilitates this process because persons are more likely to communicate with and understand someone with whom they have had a common experience. The camaraderie that develops also aids conflict resolution by providing a perception of common goals rather than the separation of interests and outlooks common to many marriages.

Husbands and wives also should be encouraged to view sexual relations from the point of view of play and leisure. Miller and Robinson emphasize that "making love is the greatest, most beautiful form of play we know. In its purest, mose wholesome form it is the uninhibited and enthusiastic sharing by husband and wife in the entrancing, fascinating, aesthetic games of sexual relations" (1963, 264). The popularity of Alex Comfort's *The Joy of Sex* certainly lends credence to this perspective. Yet, many couples are held back from this experience by outmoded concepts and lack of knowledge. Other persons are so concerned with technique that a sexual experience takes on work-life overtones. Certainly, sex educators need to stress the importance of a leisure setting with free time, reduction in anxiety, and the freedom to enjoy one another as vital to sexual satisfaction.

Child Adjustment

In a recent television commercial, a mother is pictured calling out to her son: "Johnny, I hope you are not doing anything!" This seems to speak to the anxiety of parents over the free time of children. There is a sincere lack of recognition of the value of play as a means of learning in the young. Children practice alternate roles, they create, they become more physically adept, they learn; in general, children use their leisure as a valuable tool in becoming more aware of themselves, others, and the world around them.

The 1960 White House Conference on Children reported that adult values of leisure had an overriding influence on the free time perspectives of children (Sorenson, 1961). The 1970 Conference contained a plea by the children themselves: "We want the opportunity to learn to make decisions during our free time" (Chandler, 1971, 204). As an antidote for the "uselessness and worthlessness" felt by many children, it was recommended that children should have a voice in shaping their own leisure, especially in the planning of activities and programs that influence them. Furthermore, it was encouraged that "in the family, child-parent discussions about the use of leisure time should be commonplace" (Chandler, 1971, 204).

But are most parents realistically prepared to handle the responsibility of this guidance? Probably not, if the data on how parents use television as a baby-sitting service are even close to being correct (Looney, 1971; Rue, 1974). It is especially important for young children to learn to use leisure creatively and constructively because if severe constraints are placed on their perceptions of leisure as youth, it is doubtful that they can free themselves from these constraints as adults. Education for leisure assumes that people are "exposed early and long to experiences that will help them develop appreciations and skills that will help the flowering of their personalities as leisure becomes increasingly available to them" (Brightbill, 1960, 94).

Parents are going to need aid in examining alternate activities, developing insights into the role of play for children and adults, and establishing guidelines on how to develop in their children the means of selecting pursuits that relieve their frustration and tensions while developing themselves personally.

Parent-Child Adjustment

The relationship between parents and children can also be helped by the creative use of leisure. Just as husbands and wives can increase their understanding of one another through sharing some of their leisure together, parent-child communication can likewise be enhanced. Parents need to be encouraged to do things with their children. When a child's free time is only spent with peers, coaches, recreation leaders, or teachers, he becomes more dependent on them for his self-concept development and personal satisfactions than his parents. He is likely to shift his authority to persons other than the parents because he perceives that they are more concerned and care for him. If the trend toward children spending less time with their parents continues, it may be expected that they will be increasingly less influenced by them as well. As child nurturance is a primary function of the contemporary family, this appears to be an abdication of parental responsibility. In support of this line of thinking, Nye (1958) found that juvenile delinquents were more likely to have negative concepts of family recreation, probably because they had not experienced it.

Children, themselves, seem to want family recreational activities. Some of the most fondly remembered experiences of youth are times spent with parents but interestingly, away-from-home activities yield the most positive memories (cf. Conner, Johannis, and Walters, 1955; Stone, 1960). This may be because the sharing of new experiences is more likely to open communication between parents and children, especially when children are allowed more exclusive parental attention. In a study of high-school students, Stone (1960) found that 54 percent desired to do more with the family while only six percent desired less family recreation. It would appear then that parents are a major factor in not providing the opportunity for these experiences, even among adolescents. Guidance needs to be given to parents so that they can learn to utilize these needs of their children to better the overall family relationship. As an indication of one common misunderstanding, a young father recently told the author that he was working very hard and long hours now so that when his children get older, he will have more time to give them. Not only was he unaware of the non-family commitments he was establishing for himself, but also he did not realize that when he finally is ready for his children, and his wife for that matter, they will probably be unable to establish the kind of relationship for which he is hoping. He may simply be too late.

Adjustment to Retirement

Another area that should be of critical concern to family professionals is retirement adjustment. Despite differences in life expectancy between men and women, most persons reach retirement age married. Suddenly, they are faced with the prospect of having to deal with more potential leisure than they could have dreamed of. It has been estimated that a retired person will have more available discretionary time than the amount of time spent at work over the previous 20 years (Kaplan, 1960). Reduced incomes usually require husbands and wives to spend much of this time together in a smaller residence. If the work orientation that dominated much of their life is not properly channeled, frustrations and anxieties are likely to create marital problems. It is little wonder that many wives dread the prospect of their husband's retirement.

CONCLUSION

We return now to the basic issue: Is familia ludens a viable concept and is there utility in reinforcing this leisure component in family life? First, it is apparent that some qualifications need to be placed on the concept of family play. It is not being recommended that families do everything in concert so that familia ludens becomes an all encompassing life style. Individuals often need time to be alone, to reflect and relax in the presence of no one. At other times, interests may develop with non-family members that are satisfying and meet needs that cannot be enjoyed or shared with the family. In addition, it is recognized that for many families, stability is dependent upon defined roles and reduced communication, variables that might be altered in shared play.

An additional problem that must be reckoned with is the overall anxiety regarding leisure on the part of many. For some persons, this manifests itself in a fear of personal and interpersonal freedom, an inability to relax. The old adage that "idle hands are the devil's workshop" seems to characterize this type of person. Work becomes the driving force in life and leisure the enemy of productivity. For other persons, leisure anxiety manifests itself in a somewhat neurotic search for pleasure and fulfillment, the unusual and different experience. These latter persons measure a good vacation by the number of miles travelled, the number of kodachromes taken, and the number of waterfalls visited. The fact that every movie nominated for an award has been personally viewed becomes a status symbol. Experiences are evaluated in terms of quantity, not quality. This type of leisure is competitive and difficult to share despite the presence of others.

On the one hand, it should be emphasized that each family has to learn to find its own satisfactions, those things that allow personal fulfillment and interpersonal nurturance. On the other hand, it is evident that the family depending upon companionship as a means of integrating itself cannot establish the rapport necessary for this without the sharing of experiences together. This is not to say that "togetherness" and leisure are the same but rather that family integration based on intimacy, open communication, and interpersonal support requires a component of interaction during moments relatively free from the constraints of everyday responsibilities, i.e., during leisure. Failure to realize and experience this, for whatever reason, is likely to result in separation of interests, closure of communication channels, and stress during those times when shared leisure does occur. This is why there seems to be considerable value in encouraging the active mode of leisure implied in familia ludens. Again, it must be recognized that not all families require this and all persons need support for independence in leisure as well as sharing, but reinforcement of sharing has not received proportionately the attention it deserves, that is the point of this paper. This is also why training people in skills such as tennis, photography, gardening, or whatever, as good as they may be for each of us, is not the entire answer. There is a deeper need, if you will, for socialization toward leisure in the broadest sense. Recreation for both the individual and the family should be the re-creation that the term implies.

The author has an old watering can with the words on it: "Don't hurry; don't worry; and don't forget to stop and smell the flowers." In a world rushing by us so fast, it can be hard to develop this kind of leisure perspective. The eminent sociologist Robert M. MacIver recognized this plight in the following:

> Back in the days when unremitting toil was the lot of all but the very few and leisure still a hopeless yearning, hard and painful as life was, it still felt real. People were in rapport with the small bit of reality allotted to them, the sense of the earth, the tang of the changing seasons, the consciousness of the eternal on-going of birth and death. Now when so many have leisure, they become detached from themselves, not merely from the earth. From all the widened horizons of our greater world a thousand voices call us to come near, to understand, and to enjoy, but our ears are not trained to hear them. The leisure is ours but not the skill to use it. So leisure becomes a void, and from the ensuing restlessness men take refuge in delusive excitations or fictitious visions, returning to their earth no more (1955, 54-55).

REFERENCES

Blood, Robert O., Jr. *Marriage.* New York: The Free Press, 1969.

Brightbill, Charles K. *The Challenge of Leisure.* Englewood Cliffs, NJ: Prentice-Hall, 1960.

Buckland, Clare M. Toward a Theory of Parent Education: Family-Learning Centers in the Post-Industrial Society. *The Family Coordinator,* 1972, 21, 151-162.

Chandler, Barbara A. The White House Conference on Children, A 1970 Happening. *The Family Coordinator,* 1971, 20, 195-207.

Comfort, Alex. *The Joy of Sex.* New York: Simon and Schuster, 1972.

Conner, Ruth, Theodore B. Johannis, Jr., and James Walters. Family Recreation in Relation to Role Conceptions of Family Members. *Marriage and Family Living,* 1955, 7, 306-309.

Davy, Thomas J. and Lloyd A. Rowe. Precis of the Conference on Leisure in America. In James C. Charlesworth (Ed.), *Leisure in America: Blessing or Curse.* Philadelphia: American Academy of Political and Social Science, 1964.

Dumazedier, Joffre. Leisure and Post-Industrial Societies. In Max Kaplan and Phillip Bosserman (Eds.), *Technology, Human Values, and Leisure.* New York: Abingdon Press, 1971.

Ellul, Jacques. Technique, Institutions, and Awareness. *American Behavioral Scientist,* 1968, 11, 38.

Goodale, James and A. K. Aagaard. The Four Day Week. *Behavior Today,* September 30, 1974, 250.

Green, Thomas. *Work, Leisure, and the American Schools.* New York: Random House, 1968.

Hobart, Charles W. Commitment, Value Conflict, and the Future of the Family. *Marriage and Family Living,* 1963, 25, 405-412.

Huizinga, Johan. *Homo Ludens: A Study of the Play Elements in Culture.* Trans. by R. F. C. Hull. New York: Roy Publishers, 1949.

Kaplan, Max. *Leisure in America: A Social Inquiry.* New York: Wiley, 1960.

Kaplan, Max. The Relevancy of Leisure. In Max Kaplan and Phillip Bosserman (Eds.), *Technology, Human Values, and Leisure.* New York: Abingdon Press, 1971.

Koprowski, Eugene J. Business Technology and the American Family: An Impressionistic Analysis. *The Family Coordinator,* 1973, 22, 229-234.

Kraus, Richard. *Recreation and the American Schools.* New York: Macmillan, 1964.

Lay, Richard and W. B. Devall. Perception of Recreation Site, Satisfaction and Sociability: A Comparison of Wilderness and Developed Campground Users. Paper read at the Annual Meeting of the Pacific Sociological Association. San Jose, California, March, 1974.

Lewis, Lionel S. and Dennis Brissett. Sex as Work: A Study in Avocational Counseling. *Social Problems,* 1967, 15, 8-17.

Lipsett, Lawrence. Social Factors in Vocational Development. *The Personnel and Guidance Journal,* 1962, 40, 432-37.

Looney, G. The Ecology of Childhood. In *Action for Children's Television.* New York: Avon Press, 1971.

Mace, David R. What I Have Learned About Family Life. *The Family Coordinator,* 1974, 23, 189-195.

MacIver, Robert M. *The Pursuit of Happiness.* New York: Simon and Schuster, 1955.

Miller, Norman P. and Duane M. Robinson. *The Leisure Age, Its Challenge to Recreation.* Belmont, CA: Wadsworth, 1963.

Neulinger, John. On Leisure. *Behavior Today.* April 29, 1974, 120.

Nye, F. Ivan. *Family Relationships and Delinquent Behavior.* New York: Wiley and Sons, 1958.

Orthner, Dennis K. Toward a Theory of Leisure and Family Interaction. Paper presented at the annual meeting of the Pacific Sociological Association. San Jose, CA: March, 1974.

Orthner, Dennis K. Leisure Activity Patterns and Marital Satisfaction Over the Marital Career. *Journal of Marriage and the Family,* 1975, 37, 91-102.

Reisman, David. Leisure and Work in a Post-Industrial Society. In Eric Larrabee and Roy Meyersohn (Eds.), *Mass Leisure.* Glencoe: The Free Press, 1958.

Rollins, Boyd C. and Harold Feldman. Marital Satisfaction over the Family Life Cycle, *Journal of Marriage and the Family,* 1970, 32, 20-27.

Rue, Vince. Television and the Family: The Question of Control. *The Family Coordinator,* 1974, 23, 73-81.

Shoffner, Sarah and Richard Klemer. Parent Education for the Parental Role in Children's Vocational Choices. *The Family Coordinator,* 1973, 22, 419-427.

Sorenson, Roy. Implications of the White House Conference on Children and Youth for Recreation. Selected Papers of the 42nd National Recreation Congress. New York: National Recreation Association, 1961.

Stone, Carol. Family Recreation, A Parental Dilemma. *The Family Coordinator,* 1963, 12, 85-87.

Stone, Gregory P. and Marvin J. Taves. Camping in the Wilderness. In Eric Larrabee and Roy Meyersohn (Eds.), *Mass Leisure.* Glencoe: The Free Press, 1958.

Walker, Kathryn E. Homemaking Still Takes Time, *Journal of Home Economics,* 1969, 61, 621-624.

West, Patrick and L. C. Merriam, Jr. Outdoor Recreation and Family Cohesiveness: A Research Approach. *Journal of Leisure Research,* 1970, 2, 251-259.

Children and TV

by Jerome L. Singer and Dorothy G. Singer

In most households in America, and increasingly throughout the world, television is a member of the family. In this country more than 96 percent of the homes have television sets, and surveys suggest that they are turned on throughout much of the day and well into the evening. Like an imaginary companion, a big brother or a surrogate parent, the TV set is there providing stimulation and talking to the smallest child in a way that has never before been a part of human experience. Into the humblest of homes it pours out a vast panoply of incidents from royal weddings, Papuan tribal ceremonies, disasters, high-kicking chorus girls in Busby Berkeley movies and great quantities of violent incidents, real and fictional—plus commercials, badgering, seducing and teasing everyone into wanting hundreds of products.

Confronted with this vast new presence, what role can a university play in helping us to understand its impact on children and adults, to identify its dangers and enhance its constructive potential? A group of researchers and students in the Yale Child Study Center has begun systematic studies of the effects of television on children and developed a plan for university involvement with television's role in child development and family life.

Our interest first grew out of a continuing research project on the nature of children's imagination and spontaneous play behavior. Make-believe games, pretending or socio-dramatic play in children represent a miracle and a mystery in human development. It is fascinating to watch five-year-olds as they manipulate blocks or plastic toys, simulate different voices and sound effects, and introduce settings and characters not present in their immediate environment. Such observations may also provide important clues as to how our imagery capacities develop into the complexities of adult thinking.

While almost all children engage in make-believe play as early as the second year of life, our studies indicate that the complexity of such play depends on additional stimulation from parents or other adults. Telling children stories, engaging with them in fantasy games, reading aloud or encouraging them to read imaginative literature seems to be important in enhancing their spontaneous resort to make-believe.

Our observations were also directed to the content of make-believe games that children played. Here it was obvious that many of the themes involved material learned from television—in fact, that television programming was having a major impact on the imaginative development of children. Yet just 10 years ago there had been almost no systematic research on this subject. The gap has been only partially redressed by the research of the Surgeon General's "Committee on Television and Social Behavior of the United States Public Health Service." Its report, produced in 1972, focused on the impact of television violence on actual violent behavior and attitudes in children, and, to a lesser extent, in adults.

Dr. Dorothy G. Singer is Professor of Psychology and Director of the School Psychology Program at the University of Bridgeport, Connecticut. Dr. Jerome L. Singer is Professor of Psychology and Director of Yale University's Clinical Psychology Training Program.

TV and Violence

Let us summarize the main findings of the Surgeon General's Committee and some subsequent research on violence. Keep in mind that while in most American homes there are some spankings and occasional fights between children, the actual amount of violence that any person is likely to witness is very small. Indeed, the vast majority of Americans saw nobody killed throughout World War II. Only a small percentage of the armed services participated in combat. By contrast, consider that 40 million people saw Jack Ruby shoot Lee Harvey Oswald on TV.

Surveys of the number of violent incidents occurring typically on commercial television indicate little change from year to year, with as many as eight violent episodes occurring per hour. A commercial for one movie alone, shown in viewing time when many children would be likely to watch, included 11 instances of violence in a one-minute spot. Seventy-one percent of programs Saturday morning—a prime children's viewing period—involved at least one violent action.

This massive exposure to TV violence undoubtedly has complex effects on us all. The major finding of most research up to now has been that children who are already showing signs of overt aggressive behavior—getting into fights with other children—are also the ones who, exposed to violent shows on television, will increase the level of their destructive behavior.

Thus, while we cannot say that all children exposed to violence on TV become more aggressive by imitation, even if the number amounts to only five percent (and the odds are that the percentage is much larger), television is producing a massive mental health problem and increasing the probability of fighting behavior in our society. There is now experimental evidence, for example, suggesting that children who view a good deal of violence become desensitized and are less likely to become upset when they see aggressive actions.

Violence and "Good Guys"

There is also a more subtle effect. Consider all the detective and police stories now presented on television which, in the interest of a dramatic ending, conclude with the police or other "good guys" shooting down the criminals, or at least beating them into submission. Even kindly old Barnaby Jones often ends up shooting and killing. The implicit message is that it's O.K. for criminals to be brought to justice by violence if you're a "good guy." Of course, we're all convinced that we are on the side of right. The profound importance of the concept of due process in a democratic society is lost in the flurry of quick endings—an unfortunate message for children and adults.

Still another example of the power of television is reported by George Gerbner of the University of Pennsylvania. He finds that people who view television with even moderate frequency will greatly over-estimate the chances that they will be involved in a violent incident. Even highly educated people believe that the amount of violence that they see represents the probabilities of such incidents in their own life. On children the effects are equally contagious. A series of accidents to children was traced to their viewing of Evel Knievel's motorcycle jump last summer.

CHILD CREATIVITY AND TV

Our task as researchers is not to condemn television out of hand or to call for censorship. Certainly in view of the great public education provided by the Watergate Committee and the House Judiciary Committee Hearings, one would have to credit television with many useful contributions to our society. Can television producers also develop self-restraint in the depiction of violence, particularly in relation to children? Can they develop a broader range of programming that will entertain and also promote such constructive social values as altruism and cooperation?

TV Industry and Parents Need Help

Research is needed to explore how children respond to specific types of programming. We need to be able to identify such differing predispositions in children and to communicate our findings to parents and teachers. The industry and parents need help in understanding its role in the development of a child.

Our own recent experiments have focused mainly on how television programs can be used to develop positive emotional growth and imaginative skills in children. A specific program that we have emphasized has been "Mister Rogers' Neighborhood." While "Sesame Street" is better known because of its high entertainment value combined with an emphasis on reading skills, "Mister Rogers' Neighborhood" also has a wide following, especially among pre-schoolers.

By contrast with "Sesame Street" it is a relatively slow-paced show centering on the gentle and sensitive personality of Fred Rogers, who talks to children as if on a one-to-one basis. His intent is to help the child's social and emotional development, to prevent unnecessary fears and to give the child a sense of being cared about and being "special." Many adults are turned off by the program because of its slow pace and almost "goody-goody" content. It is less lively and has less of a "showbiz" quality than most other national TV productions for children. Nevertheless Fred Rogers is a psychologically knowledgeable man.

Our interest in this show grew partly out of experiments by Drs. Aletha Stein and Lynnette Friedrich of Pennsylvania State University, which indicated that pre-school children exposed to it for only a few programs showed more co-operativeness and friendliness in their subsequent play and less overt aggression under certain conditions. Our own research on imagination in children had indicated that they can benefit from exposure to adults who encourage them to carry out make-believe or fantasy games, and we wondered if a program such as "Mister Rogers' Neighborhood" would have a similar impact. If so, parents and day-care and kindergarten teachers could be encouraged to have children watch the show knowing that it would have constructive behavioral benefits.

The experiment that we carried out was designed to meet reasonably high scientific standards, with observers watching children before, during and after the experiment. The observers were trained to rate the children's behavior along relevant dimensions but did not know the objectives of the study and therefore couldn't influence it in a particular direction. Our study was not conducted in the rarefied atmosphere of a laboratory; we established a relationship with a private day-care center in a small industrial city near New Haven and arranged to do the research with the consent of individual parents.

This enabled us to convince the parents not only of the value of our experiment but to enlist their help in giving us information about their family viewing habits and their attitudes about the role of TV in the child's life. It also encouraged them to come to us with questions that they might have about their children or about issues related to television. We embedded a research process on child development within a consultative relationship to a small community group.

Experimenting with Children

The experiment involved the comparison of a control group of children, who went through the usual nursery school routines, with three experimental groups. One group of 15 watched "Mister Rogers' Neighborhood" every day for two weeks; a second group watched it for the same period but with an adult who served as an intermediary, helping the children to relate to the program's imaginative content. A third experimental group watched no television but met for the same time with a teacher who gave them exercises and games involving imagination and make-believe play.

The results indicate pretty clearly that the children exposed to the live adult without television subsequently showed the greatest increase in their spontaneous imagination and pretend play. Those who watched "Mister Rogers' Neighborhood" with the adult intermediary showed the next greatest gain. Exposure to the program alone, without an adult, led to only a small increase in imaginative play. By contrast, the control group of children who had no TV or special training decreased in imaginative play.

Incidentally, those who showed an increase in imaginative play seemed happier thereafter during free-play opportunities around school. We did not, however, find any particular changes in the amount of aggression shown by the children as a result of their watching the television show. Those who were exposed to the live adult training did show somewhat less aggressive behavior.

These results indicate that a program like "Mister Rogers' Neighborhood" can be useful particularly if an adult plays an active role in helping the child to orient himself to the viewing situation—especially if it is in a public setting such as a nursery school or a day-care center where children are likely to watch in larger groups and to distract or interrupt one another. Indeed, Mr. Rogers' major assumption is that he is addressing an individual child, and of course this condition was not duplicated in our crowded setting.

TV AND FAMILY VIEWING PATTERNS

Another phase of our research involved collecting data about family viewing patterns. One fact which emerged is that these families watch a considerable amount of television, particularly "All in the Family," "I Love Lucy" and currently popular detective or police shows such as "Mannix," "Columbo" and "Kung Fu." A typical pattern would involve the child watching TV in the late afternoon on returning from school and often staying up quite late into prime adult viewing time.

Although the parents all saw themselves as well-intentioned, it had never occurred to most of them that some negative consequences might result from their children seeing so many violent programs shown during the late hours. (In this particular city, public television was not available, so the children couldn't see such benign shows as "Mister Rogers' Neighborhood.") It became clear to us that these basically responsible parents were paying little attention to the content or extent of their children's TV viewing.

Parents Eager for Help

We did find that children who were more spontaneously imaginative in their play, before the experiment began, were more likely to have mothers who valued "personal self-worth" traits such as ambition, confidence, creativity and idealism. Mothers of less imaginative children were more likely to emphasize "social self-worth values" such as attractiveness, compassion, friendliness and generosity. In other words, there was some subtle transmission of parental values to the children in the degree to which imaginativeness in play was being encouraged. Parents who rated themselves higher on "social self-worth" values reported that their own and their child's favorite programs were those involving aggressive or violent components—notably "Daktari," "Kung Fu" and "Gun Smoke."

It became clear from our group meetings that many of these modestly educated young parents were eager for help in learning how to use television more effectively. They often felt that they could not control the set and were eager for suggestions on how to set reasonable limits on viewing. They also needed help in confronting some of their own prejudices or attitudes. Many women, for example, tended to regard the low-keyed and gentlemanly Mr. Rogers as being perhaps too "effeminate"—that they ought not to expose boys to watching someone like this. This was particularly true of women from a strongly traditional female orientation.

One of our tasks, we realized, was to help them recognize that boys, as well as girls, need models who can represent sensitivity, tenderness and concern.

CONSULTING SERVICES FOR TV

We feel that the time is now ripe for universities to confront the psychological and social impact of television on our children. It seems to us that a university ought to include—among its programs relating to psychological, social and mental-health aspects of child care—a center which could provide a triple approach to television's role.

Universities Can Help

The first might be called "production and industry consultation." It would include consultation between behavioral scientists, mental health specialists and media professionals as well as artistic and dramatic groups in the university who could develop program material for use by TV stations when child viewing is at its maximum. The mental health specialists could advise on content and evaluate the effectiveness of new programming on children. We still have a great deal to learn about how much attention children pay to programs, how much they comprehend about what is intended for their benefit and what behavioral consequences result from their viewing. Psychology can now analyze such data, given a co-operative relationship with producers.

A second unit might emphasize systematic research on children's imagination and the ways in which current programming influences behavioral patterns. This branch would be most closely related to "pure" research in the psychology of child development and the mental-health aspects of television viewing, with an emphasis on understanding—in the deepest sense—the psychological meaning of the TV set in the homestead.

The third sphere would involve establishing a clinical section—a family television consultation service which would be open to the local community. Here families could be brought together to discuss their viewing habits, how to evaluate available programming, and how to avoid the worst and take the best for their children's sake.

Commercials versus Programs

Meanwhile, the continuing clinical facilities of the university could establish panels of families who would be willing to try to modify their viewing styles. Recent research on television commercials indicates that mothers can be trained to be careful observers of how children react to commercials and the extent to which they can either grasp or be misled by a commercial. It has been found, in fact, that young children often confuse commercials with the main programming and are susceptible to appeals from commercials that lead to family disputes over purchases. A consultation service could help families to define what families want from TV and begin to give them control over what they feel has become an insidious monster in their own homes.

Our own view is that television is here to stay. Censorship remains abhorrent to most Americans, though wise self-regulation and more constructive programming by producers would be welcome. Centers of the kind that we have described here could bring the university, the community and the industry together to help us understand how to make best use of this magical medium.

Television and the Family—
A Question of Control

by Vincent M. Rue

While television consumes nearly one fourth of our existence, attempts to investigate and control this medium have largely been sporadic and ineffectual. Typically, parents are uninvolved, as are child development and family relations specialists. Given the existing network programming philosophy and the tentativeness of research on televised violence and viewer aggressiveness, the case for parental control in addition to concerted efforts of networks, sponsors, and the federal government is presented. Concurrently, the circularity of TV broadcasting sustenance is also discussed relating to effective points of interventive responsibility. Ten recycled principles are proposed for remedial reconsideration and action.

With the click of an "on" switch some 25 years ago, a new era of communication had unknowingly been illumined. Whether or not the "medium is the massage" as McLuhan (1967) would have us believe, or merely the message, is peripheral to the extent of its social penetration and pervasiveness. Phenomenologically, television is more common to us than any race, creed, or political affiliation, electromagnetically living in 98.5 percent of American homes (*Television Factbook,* 1969-70). The medium is both modern yet moldy, master yet mistress, magnificent yet merciless, and mindful yet often mindless. As a unique intervening variable in mankind's development, television is a present composite of these paradoxes and more, more than we now know, and more than we might have ever suspected. This paper will discuss the significance of television in family life. It will highlight pertinent viewing influences on family members, patterns of control, and present suggestions for improvement.

As far back as 1948, television was perceived as "practically a member of the family" (Coffin, 1948, 550). Today, the average American family views television some 6.12 hours per day, representing one fourth of a lifetime, or well over one third of all one's waking hours.[1] When these figures are broken down to account for individual use, the impact of television use is startling.[2] In short, television has become a constant resident in the American home.

Ironically, however, this electronic invader, so intimately ingrained in family life, is not oriented toward the family. Instead, it caters to the individual who may or may not be a member of a family. In the presence of the TV, the family tends to observe behavior that is more parallel, or individual-oriented, than interactive (Walters and Stone, 1971). In this sense, television is a familial activity only in the limited sense of one's being "in the same room with other people" (Maccoby, 1951, 427). Consequently, the tendency to decrease family conversation is increased in TV families, transforming them from a "social group characterized by conversation, to an audience . . . silently gazing" (McDonagh, 1950, 122). Research by Bogart (1956), Coffin (1948), and Pearlin (1959) confirms television's major reorganizational

[1]Nielsen survey, cited in *Change,* February, 1972, 11.
[2]According to Looney (1971, 55): "By the time a child is fourteen and in the eighth grade, he has watched the violent assault or destruction of nearly 18,000 human beings on television. During an average year, an older child attends school 980 hours and watches TV 1,340 hours, so that by the time he graduates from high school, he will have spent between 11,000 and 12,000 hours in the classroom and more than 22,000 hours in front of the television set, with perhaps 5,000 of those hours consumed by 350,000 commercial messages."

From *The Family Coordinator,* January 1974, pp. 73-81. Copyright 1974 by National Council on Family Relations. Reprinted by permission.

Dr. Vincent M. Rue is the Associate Director of the Sir Thomas More Clinic, Downey, California.

effect on family life in recreational-leisure time activities with a general overall decrease in the amount of family communication. A simple behavioral circle might be constructed on the basis of these studies and others: the more we watch, the less we talk; the less we talk, the more we need to watch. All of this has led one author to proclaim: "either burn all television sets in the home or learn how to use them more judiciously" (Koprowski, 1973, 234).

THE NATURE OF TELEVISION

Any mention of control of television use by parents, adults, adolescents, or children must necessarily include the contribution of those who make the programs possible, namely, the television industry itself.

First and foremost television is a money-making enterprise whose profit-making motives for existence must supercede all other considerations. At the same time television exists for citizens, since, in a real way, the airwaves are owned by the public (Communications Act, 1934). In order to balance these two competing interests the Federal Communications Commission regulates the broadcasting industry through licensure which demands that television stations be responsive to the public interest, convenience, and necessity of their local audience.[3]

Any change in the existing structure or function of the television industry must then be understood in terms of its circular sustenance. Both responsible and irresponsible TV broadcasting is usually born of the networks, sponsored by independent commercial interest, unseen by federal agencies, bypassed by educators, nurtured by uninvolved (perhaps even uninterested or unsuspecting) parents, and consumed by indigested young and old. In turn, these viewers are influenced by what they see (violent or not violent), paired with multitudinous sponsoring advertisements: what they see, they are told, they must become. Viewers are then transformed into consumers of TV goods and philosophy which, in turn, promotes conglomerate commercial interests reinforcing the networks to continue producing a particular type of program. The bulk of this happens with almost nonexistent federal government involvement, nor investigative concern by child development and family relations specialists.

It should be remembered, however, that the medium of television is inherently neutral, in that it is an entertaining informational platform extending over time and the populace. In effect:

It teaches law-breaking and law-enforcement equally well. It teaches the evil and the brutal as easily and completely as the good or the kind. What it teaches depends on the hands that control it, however wisely or ignorantly or innocently. It will teach what it shows, no matter whether it intends to teach this or not (Skornia, 1970, 2).

PATTERNS OF TELEVISION CONTROL

Amidst inclement responses of industry abuse, the positive functions of family television viewing bear goal-oriented explication. In its own unique way television (1) provides infor-

---

[3]The networks are not licensed. They are essentially a specialized service industry which provide programs to the affiliated stations over lines rented for the most part from the telephone company. Each commercial network owns and operates five licensed stations, the maximum permissible for one corporation. The networks sell advertising time on their programs, and give 30 percent of that revenue to the local stations which accept a program. The sale price of a commercial minute and the station's share are a direct function of audience size. Typical prices of popular shows are $60,000 to $75,000 per commercial minute, running $100,000 or more for specials. The above considerations mean that networks and stations choose their programs so that they have the largest possible audience at the lowest production cost consistent with audience drawing power (adapted from "The Advocates," October 3, 1971).

mation, fun, enjoyment, and pleasure; (2) it brings parents and children a broader view of life than exists in or around the family context; (3) it makes the unspeakable discussable by providing opportunities for expressing emotions which have never had occasion to surface, such as love, hate, ambition, and accomplishment; and (4) it makes possible vicarious learning experiences for experimentation and self-growth (cf. Ziferstein, 1966).

The impact of television on children has received widespread attention in the literature, but little concern on the air. While there have been hundreds of studies in this area, 35 out of 44 major market television stations do not have as many as fourteen hours per week of children's programs (Jennings and Jennings, 1971).[4]

Perhaps the two most comprehensive studies ever undertaken regarding children and television were done in England by Hilde Himmelweit, A. N. Oppenheim, and Pamela Vince (1958), and in North America by Wilbur Schramm, Jack Lyle, and Edwin Parker (1961). Both studies found that the greater part of children's TV is adult programs, e.g., Westerns, crime, drama; that TV is most often used as a form of entertainment and escape; that TV reorganizes leisure time activities, reducing play time and dominating the child's leisure; that the greater the degree of parent-child conflict, the more television watched; that children are more frightened by realistic rather than stylized violence; that too early exposure to violent and stressful programs is also frightening; that TV to some extent makes children passive; and that TV makes its biggest impact when the child cannot turn to parents or friends for additional information. Schramm found little to no discrimination of adult program viewing by adults or children. Very often in cases where the TV is left on children view indiscriminately, like their parents. Schramm recommends that parents use their examples as potently as possible (cf. Dominick and Greenberg, 1972), and attempt to guide their children, through a viewing process, pointing out some of the "reality opportunities" as they are broadcast.

The case for discriminating use of television and parental control for children can be made in that it is taken as axiomatic here that children are human beings, not adults, and are a special interest group, with special and unique capabilities, needs, and interests in amusement, stimulation, discipline, education, recreation, moral development, imagination, and others. The following hour analysis of television air time might also lend credence to the need for selectivity in the programs children watch. A typical week for the 63 network prime-time hours broadcast looks like this: 35 hours—violent and melodrama series, and movies; nine hours—drama; nine hours—comedy; seven hours—variety; two hours—sports; and one hour— public affairs (*Better Radio and Television,* 1973, 2). According to Gerbner's TV violence index, the 1972 fall shows have a higher violence rating than ever: NBC—71 percent, ABC— 67 percent, and CBS—57 percent (*Behavior Today,* October 2, 1972, 2).

Yet abundant evidence indicates that there is generally little control of television viewing by parents for their children. In 1962, Hess and Goldman found that (1) while mothers view themselves as the most competent in regulating the television their children watch, they apparently are making little effort to supervise and regulate either type or quantity of TV viewing, (2) the father's role is mostly marginal, and (3) the young child is left to regulate his own viewing.

[4]This is not to say there are no high quality TV shows for children. Recent specially produced children's TV fare should be cited and lauded. For example, the Corporation for Public Broadcasting (CPB) enables Sesame Street, Mr. Roger's Neighborhood, and The Electric Company. This Fall, ABC hosts The ABC Afternoon Special, Kid Power, Curiosity Shop, Make a Wish, The Jackson Five, The Osmonds, and The Saturday Superstar Movie. NBC hosts Take A Giant Step, Talking with a Giant, and Mr. Wizard. CBS hosts Captain Kangaroo, In the News, You are There, and Children's Film Festival.

In 1970, preschool children were watching an average of 54 hours of TV a week, nearly 64 percent of their waking hours (Looney, 1971, 55). Lyle and Hoffman (1972) found that television was extremely popular with the 158 preschoolers they studied, and that they frequently made their own programming decisions.[5] Musgrave (1969) found that 53 percent of the 600 parents of eleven-year olds studied did not prohibit their children from watching any programs and 40 percent did not encourage the watching of specific programs. Steiner (1963) reported a laissez-faire attitude on the part of most parents who oppose television and practically no restrictions by those parents who only show signs of concern. While Rarick (1973) found a significant degree of concurrence between mother and father as to the desirability of a TV program for their child, he found that in only half of the 24 families studied did parents discuss programs with their children. Conjointly, one third said that they attempted to control the kinds of programs their children viewed, but only one out of twelve parents actually prevented their children from viewing undesirable programs.

Generally, the parents who do control their children's television do so for two broad reasons: (1) fear that their child may be adversely affected by premature exposure to the adult world and (2) a general belief that TV viewing is less important for a child than other activities (Barcus, 1969). But the dilemma of control is compounded by a number of factors. There is some support to indicate that restricting the child's viewing of TV may actually do more harm than good (cf. McLeod, Atkin, and Chaffee, 1972). Moreover, one study found that children do not prefer the kinds of programs their parents feel are most desirable for them to see (Rarick, 1973).

Barcus (1969) made a major contribution in this area by presenting a typology of parental controls over children's TV viewing (see Figure 1). The question of control of television use then becomes a matter of definition of type, degree, and temporality. In his studies, Barcus found evidence to suggest that there is both positive and negative parental controls exerted on both formal and informal levels. Conceivably, the type and degree of control can appropriately vary by age of the child and the viewing occasion, but more research is needed to determine the appropriate levels of intervention and the effects of this control in relation to group viewing where different age children are simultaneously viewing the same TV set.

The apparent fact that most parents do not control the TV their children watch might be explained by any of the following reasons: parents hold a generally positive attitude about TV and its use; the negative effects of programs are overridden by the overall positive effects achieved; lack of time for continuous supervision or discussion; inexperience or unwillingness; the futility of uni-directional value development; the lack of experience, confidence, knowledge, or skills to discuss TV with their children; the non-differentiation between an entertaining and learning context.[6] In short, parental control of TV use mirrors myriad paradoxes:

> . . . *television helps to educate the child, but watching it interferes with his education. It helps keep him busy and out of mischief, but it also keeps him too busy to do his chores. It keeps the kids in when you want them in,*

[5]For a detailed examination of television in the lives of preschool-age children, see J. Cazeneuve and P. Bendano, La Television y Los Ninos Menores de Cinco Anos (Television and Children under Five Years Old). *Revista Espanola de la Opinion Publica,* 1971, 23, 49-54.

[6]Industry inattentiveness and the lack of parental concern and action in controlling children's television has prompted the establishment of a number of educational and advocacy-oriented organizations which provide helpful publications for parents, teachers, etc.: Action for Children's Television, 46 Austin St., Newtonville, Mass.; National Association for Better Broadcasting, 373 N. Western Ave., Los Angeles, Calif.; Citizens Communication Center, 1812 N St., N.W., Washington, D.C.; and Action on Safety and Health, 2000 H St., N.W., Washington, D.C.

which is good, except for some of the bad things they see. And it keeps them in when you want them out, which is bad even if they see good things (Steiner, 1963, 95).

While there is some indication that parents might be more concerned about the development of moral values than violence (Rarick, 1973), beyond a doubt, the most insistent public focus on TV has been regarding violence in society and its antecedent stimuli, pervasive in the mass media (cf. Emery, 1959; Mussen and Rutherford, 1961; Zion, 1963; Wilson, 1971; Halloran, Brown, and Chaney, 1970; Steiner, 1963; Feshback and Singer, 1971; and Bandura, 1971). That the issue remains heated is testimony to the inconclusiveness of past research efforts and the cumulative contradictions amassed in the Kefauver hearings of 1951, the Dodd hearings of 1961-62, the Report of the National Commission on the Causes and Prevention of Violence in 1969, and now the recent Report of the Surgeon General's Scientific Advisory Committee on Television and Social Behavior in 1972.

A basic unanswered question has perplexed the empirical study of televised violence and viewer response: What is the relationship of what children bring to television to what television brings to them? The polarization of scientific opinion that televised violence adversely affects viewers is represented in the affirmative by the studies of Bandura and associates (1971), and in the negative by the research of Feshback and Singer (1971).

The most costly and comprehensive examination of television and violence has recently been completed by the twelve-member Surgeon General's Scientific Advisory Committee (*Television and Growing Up: The Impact of Televised Violence,* 1972). Undoubtedly marred by conservative membership selection, vested interests, and overly vague conclusions (Sterling, 1973), it nonetheless concluded its two million dollar study with the following two implications:

1. While imitative behavior is shown by most children in experiments on that mechanism of behavior, the mechanism of being incited to aggressive behavior by seeing violent films shows up in the behavior of only some children who were found in several experimental studies to be previously high in aggression. (The same held true for the field studies.)

2. There are suggestions in both sets of studies that the way children respond to violent film material is affected by the context in which it is presented. Such elements as parental explanations, the favorable or unfavorable outcome of the violence, and whether it is seen as fantasy or reality may make a difference (18).[7]

Regardless of these findings, the power of television would seem to be significant in that the billion dollar TV advertising market yearly bears witness to the effectiveness of TV's influencing not only what you buy, but more importantly, who you are. Why not also in regard to violence?

From a slightly different perspective, for many children television has become a soothing pacifier and an effective one, because "like a sorcerer, it can tell stories, spin dreams, play enchanting music, make children laugh, even teach them jingles to sing—in short, it is an unfailingly entertaining companion" (Hayakawa, 1971, 106). But when TV's companionship role is escalated is it not conditioning children to over-expect ever stimulating interaction and uni-directional-giving friendships? For adults so encompassed, entertained, and consoled by television's unreality, is it not probable that their reality will inevitably become irritating? Perhaps television is saying something of the caliber of family interaction that in its constant luminescence we fail to see.

[7]For a capsule view of this work, see C. Atkin, J. Murray, and O. Nayman. The Surgeon General's Research Program on Television and Social Behavior: A Review of Empirical Findings, *Journal of Broadcasting,* 1972, 16, 21-35.

Figure 1. Theoretical model of types of parental controls over children's TV viewing.*

		Control Prior to Viewing	*Control During Viewing*	*Control After Viewing*
Positive Forms of Control	Formal	Screening Selecting Suggesting program for child	Discussion Interpretations Changing channel to another program	Answering questions Discussion of things viewed
	Informal	*De facto:* adult selection & viewing	Viewing with children Explaining	Praising things learned

Negative or Restrictive Forms of Control	Formal	Restrictions on:
		
		1. content, programs
		2. time
		  a) no. hours permitted
		  b) certain hours
		3. until completion of other activities
			Shutting off set
			Switching channels
				Forbidding future viewing

	Informal	*De facto:* adult selection & viewing	Scolding child while viewing	Scolding child for things learned

*Reprinted with permission of *Television Quarterly*, the journal of the National Academy of Television Arts and Sciences.

Someone once chided: we are what we eat. What does a steady diet of soap operas say about a housewife's marriage, particularly her information-stimulation inputs, i.e., her husband and friends? For that matter, what games are played by an uninterested husband who eagerly turns on television sports, but turns off marital or familial interaction? Television not only provides a diagnostic glimmer of relationship adequacy, but it also presents unlimited materials for classroom and family discussion of value development, love, marriage, family life, etc.

An additional point needs to be made about companionship and television use. Both from the perspective of the child and adult, human beings are very selective in choosing friends. The process of "friend selection" is usually ritualistic and elaborate. Yet television, in most cases uninvited, has been and is becoming more of an "ever attentive friend" for an increasing number of viewers as weekly hours of TV watching indicates. Because it poses no physical threat as would an undesirable stranger, TV has all the time it wants to say and do whatever it wants. Maybe as we become citizens of a post-industrial society, its relationship role will become ever more critical for many.

From the viewpoint of socialization, who and how often should we be asking: "Are the values TV portrays good enough for emulation?" For the most part, television exhibits a simplistic world view, flirting with unreality. The complexities of human interaction are reduced to 22 or 44 minute miniatures.[8] One can't help but think then that life becomes like a sandwich. On one piece of bread are the "good guys" and on the other are the "bad guys," and violence, because it is faster and more appealing, becomes the repetitive spread. But is this really what families want? Or is it simply what they get? Or is it so because too many have abrogated their public responsibility in voicing concern? Or perhaps more cogently, is it so because families are unable to voice their concerns amidst the roar of the television industry and network domination?

IMPLICATIONS

By and large, parents expect the television industry to regulate and be responsible for itself. But network accountability is secondary to economic accountability, and this in turn very often supercedes program suitability to family preferences. Federal concern has been, for the most part, punting the responsibility back to the family living room. Consequently, all roads lead back to the family, which terminally pleads "stress-overload" and "over-expectation" but to ears that do not hear.

In conjunction with the recommendations made by the National Association for Better Broadcasting, this author posits ten recycled principles for remedial reconsideration and action in improving responsible television:

1. That controlled television use in the family is a requisite for individual and familial growth.

2. That parents watch at least some of the programs their children and adolescents watch, and in collaboration with them, establish rules and guidelines for the optimum use of television.

3. That open and frank discussion of television use, type of programs watched, and program content be encouraged by all family members, including marital units.

---

[8]This is not to say that there are no programs which starkly confront reality. "The Family Game: Identities for Young and Old" is a TV show produced by WQED which deals with problems and issues facing families today and attempts to bridge the generation gap. Public television's serial broadcast of the Loud family might serve as an excellent focal point for discussing communication and marriage and family relations within and outside of the context of the family living room.

4. That children and adolescents are special audiences of TV consumers, and as such, merit special protection and programming responsibility suitable to their appropriate level of growth and maturity; and that child development and family relations specialists play a major role in age-related maturity and capability specification, and identification of program suitability.

5. That parents have a major responsibility to communicate to their children their own judgments about taste, and attitudes toward television viewing, including crime, cruelty, violence, sex, profanity, and all forms of exploitation.

6. That TV programs which incorporate sadism, "crime for fun" brutality as the basis for entertainment, "the portrayal of violence as a solution, and the picturing of details of crime and sadism which blunt feelings of compassion and humanity" (N.A.B.B., Policy Statement) do not reflect adequate responsibility to the "public interest, convenience, or necessity" (F.C.C. Licensing Requirements), and hence, not be allowed the privilege of being publicly broadcast.

7. That both the television industry and independent commercial interests bear and share in all of the above mentioned responsibilities with special concern for exploiting the young, and adequate consumer participation in the type and amount of programs decided to be produced and broadcast.

8. That the federal government, through its regulatory arms (F.C.C. and F.T.C.) also share in this responsibility with the power of coercing the television industry to conform to these principles; that it establish as rules Action for Children's Television's three recommendations proposed in 1971; that it more actively and stringently enforce "truth in advertising"; that it prohibit existing commercial advertising practices from children's television; that it generally diminish the amount and type of advertising on adult programs; and that it keep television competition fair by insuring that those broadcasters who seek to be conscientious and initiate programming change are not penalized in doing so.

9. That responsibility for improving the quality of television rests first with the broadcasting profession, second with commercial sponsors, third with family TV viewers, fourth with educators, and fifth, with representative federal agencies.

10. That both the public and the television industry be educationally reminded that the air and airwaves are public property; that the privilege of using these airwaves is indeed a right given with corresponding responsibility expected, and that the implications of public ownership of television need greater identification, publication, and actualization for substantial broadcasting responsibility to be achieved.

CONCLUSION

These principles lay no claim to comprehensiveness or finality. Rather, they are presented as an initial attempt to counteract and correct the misnomer that primary television responsibility rests with the consumer. In conjunction with these principles, a number of unasked and unanswered questions have been raised and explored, especially regarding potential advantages and disadvantages of television use in the family. It is suggested that acknowledgement and concern for the resolution of these questions become a vital part of academic investigation in child development and family relations, rather than being sporadically subject to federal study or left to the vested interests of network sponsored research. Hence, even though television caters to individual interests, its mode, degree, and consequence of expression are all of familial and social concern. The aim of this presentation then is to prompt interest and impetus for changing a perspective which has given inadequate consideration to the importance of television as a family member and its social-psychological utility.

REFERENCES:

Bandura, A. The Impact of Visual Media on Personality. In J. Segal (Ed.) *The Mental Health of the Child.* Rockville, Maryland: National Institute of Mental Health, 1971.

Barcus, F. E. Parental Influence on Children's Television Viewing, *Television Quarterly,* 1969, 7 (3), 63-74.

Bogart, L. *The Age of Television: A Study of Viewing Habits and the Impact of TV on American Life.* New York: Frederick Unger, 1956.

Coffin, T. Television's Effects on Leisure-Time Activities. *Journal of Applied Psychology,* 1948, 32, 550-558.

Dominick, J. and B. Greenberg. Attitudes Toward Violence: The Interaction of TV Exposure, Family Attitudes, and Social Class. In *Television and Social Behavior.* Volume III: *Television and Social Learning.* Washington: U.S. Government Printing Office, 1972.

Emery, F. Psychological Effects of the Western Film: A Study in Television Viewing: II, The Experimental Study. *Human Relations,* 1959, 12, 215-232.

Feshback, S. and R. Singer. *Television and Aggression.* San Francisco: Jossey-Bass, 1971.

Halloran, J., R. Brown, and D. Chaney. *Television and Delinquency.* Leicester: Leicester University Press, 1970.

Hayakawa, S. Who's Bringing Up Your Children? *Catholic Digest,* May, 1971, 105-108.

Hess, R. and H. Goldman. Parents' Views of the Effects of TV on Their Children. *Child Development,* 1962, 33, 411-426.

Himmelweit, H., A. Oppenheim, and P. Vince. *Television and the Child.* London: Oxford University, 1958.

Jennings, R. and C. Jennings. *Programming and Advertising Practices in Television Directed to Children: Another Look.* Newtonville, Mass.: Action for Children's Television, 1971. (xerox)

Koprowski, E. Business Technology and the American Family: An Impressionistic Analysis. *The Family Coordinator,* 1973, 22, 229-234.

Looney, G. The Ecology of Childhood. In *Action for Children's Television.* New York: Avon Press, 1971.

Lyle, J. and H. Hoffman. Explorations in Patterns of Television Viewing by Preschool-Age Children. In *Television and Social Behavior.* Volume IV: *Television in Day-to-Day Life– Patterns of Use.* Washington: U.S. Government Printing Office, 1972.

Maccoby, E. Television: Its Impact on School Children. *Public Opinion Quarterly,* 1951, 15, 421-444.

McDonagh, E. TV and the Family. *Sociology and Social Research,* 1950, 35, 113-122.

McLeod, J., C. Atkin, and J. Chaffee. Adolescents, Parents, and Television Use. In *Television and Social Behavior.* Volume III: *Television and Adolescent Aggressiveness.* Washington: U.S. Government Printing Office, 1972.

McLuhan, H. M. *The Medium is the Massage.* New York: Random House, 1967.

Musgrave, P. How Children Use Television. *New Society,* 1969, 13, 277, 278.

Mussen, P. and E. Rutherford. Effects of Aggressive Cartoons in Children's Aggressive Play. *Journal of Abnormal and Social Psychology,* 1961, 62, 461-464.

Pearlin, L. Social and Personal Stress and Escape in Television Viewing. *Public Opinion Quarterly,* 1959, 23, 255-259.

Rarick, D. Parental Evaluations of Television Violence. *Educational Broadcasting Review,* 1973, 7(1), 34-43.

Schramm, W., J. Lyle, and E. Parker. *Television in the Lives of Our Children.* Stanford, Calif.: Stanford University, 1961.

Skornia, H. Television Teaches What It Shows. Reprint from *Better Radio and Television,* 1970. Los Angeles: National Association for Better Broadcasting.

Steiner, G. *The People Look at Television.* New York: Alfred Knopf, 1963.

Sterling, C. Broadcasting Textbooks 1971-72. *Educational Broadcasting Review,* 1973, 7(1), 44-53.

Surgeon General's Scientific Advisory Committee on Television and Social Behavior. *Summary Report to the Surgeon General: Television and Growing Up–The Impact of Televised Violence.* Washington: U.S. Government Printing Office, 1972.

Television Factbook 1969-70. Washington: Television Digest, 1969, 25.

Walters, J. and V. Stone. Television and Family Communication. *Journal of Broadcasting,* 1971, 15, 409-414.

Ziferstein, I. The Use and Abuse of Children's Time. Reprint from *Better Radio and Television,* 1966. Los Angeles: National Association for Better Broadcasting.

2D TROUBLED FAMILIES

The All-American Blood-Soaked Family

"If one is truly concerned with the level of violence in American society, the primary focus should not be on violence in the streets, but on violence in the home," University of New Hampshire sociologist Murray A. Straus told colleagues at the September 1975 convention of the American Psychological Association in Chicago. He offered some impressive evidence in support of his contention.

Data collected on homicides in over a dozen counties reveal that the most common relationship between murderer and victim is membership in the same family. Overwhelmingly, statistics show that women are not murdered by robbers or rapists in the streets, but by their own husbands. And when husbands murder wives, they tend to do so with exceptional brutality, carving the body with multiple stab wounds or pumping it full of lead. On the other hand, when women murder husbands, they tend to settle for a single well-placed knife wound or bullet hole.

HIGH FLIGHT LEVEL

Straus is undertaking a nationwide survey of marital violence. Pilot studies show 16 percent of a sample of middle-aged couples have violently and physically attacked one another during the last year. Another sampling using in-depth interviews found over half the couples questioned had fought physically at least once during their marriage, and one-fourth had done so with some frequency. Taken as a whole, this and other evidence indicates that "the typical adult is more likely to be attacked—verbally, physically and mortally—by his or her own spouse than by any other person," stresses Straus.

There is something in the family as we know it that makes it "preeminent in respect to all types of physical violence, from slaps to torture and murder," Straus believes. That something, he suspects, is sexism. The family is part of a social structure that keeps women subordinate, through force if necessary. The marriage license, according to this view, is a "hitting license" that legitimizes a man's right to keep his woman in line.

This cultural sanction was dramatically demonstrated by three psychologists at Michigan State University who staged a series of fights for unsuspecting passersby. Males aided a man being attacked by either a man or a woman and interfered when a woman was being attacked by another woman. But not a single male witness would interrupt a man beating a woman. The social code would seem manifest: men and only men have the right to hit women and only women.

CONJUGAL RITES?

Perhaps the men in those experiments just assumed that the man attacking the woman was married to her—and hence had the right to beat her up. Apparently this was an assumption in the notorious case of Kitty Genovese, who was murdered in a New York housing development while dozens of people stood by. When interviewed afterward, many said they did not interfere because they thought the attacker was her husband.

In other ways, the legal system legitimizes this code and enforces it, occasionally in the letter of the law and overwhelmingly in actual practice. The doctrine of "Spouse Immunity" prevents a wife from suing her husband for assault and battery in many jurisdictions. Studies show police will avoid making arrests for assault that would be automatic if it were not for the fact that the man and the woman involved were married. Studies of abused wives show large numbers endure such assaults for many years, perhaps because our society forces them into economic dependence on a man.

They may ultimately respond by killing the husband, leaving him if they can find some way of supporting themselves and their children, or, most futilely, attempting to secure a warrant for his arrest. But of over 7,500 women who attempted to acquire such warrants in Washington, D.C., in 1966, less than 200 were able to do so. Usually, the warrants did even those who got them little good. In another District of Columbia study, over three-fourths of the assault cases not involving marriage partners resulted in a trial or a guilty plea. Only one-sixth of those involving husbands and wives reached such disposition, and by the time such cases reached the courts, the crime had invariably been reduced from felony to misdemeanor. The reluctance of police, prosecutors and other public officials to act springs from our culture's belief that husbands have the right to chastise their wives, Straus believes.

CARRYING ON

Even aside from the role models thus provided children, the family is the prime educator in the use of physical force for the next generation, the researcher claims. At least 93 percent of the parents in one survey in the United States and Great Britain were found to use physical punishment on their children. The message to the child is clear, Straus believes—physical force is the means by which the strong impose their will on the weak. Children are encouraged to take up a violent creed among themselves (especially if they are male), and parents urge them to deal with aggression in others by fighting back when challenged. In one national survey, 70 percent of the parents said that they thought it was important for a boy to have fistfights when he is growing up.

"The myth of family nonviolence" has helped to idealize this basic social unit, Straus contends; but the black-and-blue facts are that family life hardly ensures domestic tranquility.

The Roots of Violence

by Reginald S. Lourie

Violence: An exertion of any physical force so as to injure or abuse. It implies intense, turbulent or furious action, often destructive. (Definition from Webster's Unabridged Dictionary*)*

Violence, and in particular violent behavior, has been a national and international problem in a variety of forms since the beginning of nations, with its roots in the behavior of individuals and groups. In recorded history it begins with Abel and Cain. In our recent history it can be identified by almost universally known names such as Oswald, Berkeley, Watts, and Hitler. Its manifestations are manifold, including individuals who are in the violence game for themselves, or as agents for others, or even in disguise as "invitors" of violence against themselves, i.e., a kind of "career" as a victim.

Violence, when it takes the form of group violence, ranges from gang, mass, or mob violence to war itself. It can be impulsive or cold and calculated. It can come from within the individual or from without, sometimes resulting from a kind of contagion. It can have a purposeful goal or be apparently senseless. It can be a method of communication, even an expected pattern of everyday, especially close relationships in specific persons or groups. It can thus be contained within the relationship to one individual, adult or child, in a family, or show up in the feuds between individuals, families, clans, gangs or nations. It can be contained in socially acceptable forms such as in sports or exhibitions or in adventure or hunting. It can be turned on the outside world, or, more specifically, society, either directly or indirectly, to achieve movement, change or obtaining specific goals. When it is indirect it can follow patterns of apparent nonviolence, most usually within families. In recent history, nonviolence, as used by some militant groups, large or small, appears to be calculated to stir up loss of control or violence in others. It can be used to create fear and thus control others.

Expressions of violence usually follow the rules an individual makes for himself. These rules can be with calculated disregard of society's rules and governed only by fear. In spite of usually good, sometimes strict rules for control, there can be impulsive violent action in response to inner or outer pressure created by the situation of the moment thus overwhelming the individual's own standards and basic concepts about control of violence, when it is used in service of the defense of one's life, to protect territorial rights, property, or honor. Behavioral scientists are increasingly being asked to take some responsibility for better ways of dealing with these phenomena, especially where violence is evidenced in an increasing problem in our cities in the form of violent crime and riots. While the nature and origins of violence are complex problems, there is always one common denominator when we look at their fundamental roots: the individual and how he came to be the way he is.

To understand the nature and roots of violence and the end result we must start with the fundamental makeup of the individual. We immediately encounter a controversial area in which there are two opposing schools of thought: on the one hand there is the group that feels that aggression is an innate drive (Freud, 1930; Lorenz, 1966). Greenacre (1960)

Ekistics, February 1975, Vol. 39, No. 231, pp. 96-108. Reprinted with permission.
Dr. Reginald S. Lourie is Director, Department of Psychiatry, Children's Hospital of the District of Columbia.

has taken the added step of attempting to trace its origins to forces which provide the impetus for growth and movement in the prenatal life of the foetus. The opposite view is summarized by Montagu (1968), who is one of the spokesmen for the group who feels that the human is not born with innate aggression. Lately Tinbergen (1968) and Goren (1968) have attempted to provide a synthesis.

I feel strongly that there is not only a basic aggressive drive—as one can see it even in infants—but also there are considerable individual variations from the beginning of life in the quantitative and qualitative patterns of expression of aggressive energy. While at present we cannot be clear about the organic bases for aggressive energy and impulse, we have some clues that there are genetic determinants of the amount of such drive in males with an extra Y chromosome (Money, 1969). Frank Erwin (1970) has demonstrated that pathology of the temporal lobe can be a determinant of episodic violence. In particular it has been shown that temporal lobe epilepsy can be the basis for outbursts of violence as a form of seizure equivalents. We also have some evidence from the work of Weinstein (1953) with brain damaged individuals that there are deep midline brain centers which can act as inhibitors of aggression, especially in its impulsive violent forms of expression, since when damaged, the individual displays impulsive violent behavior. There is also some evidence from lobotomized patients that the frontal lobes have an influence on inhibiting impulses and controlling violent behavior (Lourie, 1971).

There is newer information which provides a basis on which we might understand how the syndrome of minimal brain dysfunction influences the process of controlling aggression. Anohkin (1964) in his studies of "systemogenesis" has demonstrated in birds how there are brain nuclei in clusters responsible for specific functions. These nuclei are not completely activated at birth and contain multiple activating and inhibitory centers. In their sequential maturation there are therefore balances established which allow each function to develop with controls available to provide the basis for avoiding excesses. Can we postulate that if the inhibitory areas of a given nucleus are damaged, controls are more difficult to achieve? This may allow us to understand at least one basis on which some individuals' aggressive expression can more easily become out of control and end as violence.

Even though there is evidence which points to constitutional determinants in the level of aggressive energy available to an individual, from the beginning of life, its fate and its expressions are determined by life experience. It is the influence of the child's external world and his response to it which determines whether this form of energy is expressed in the form of violence. To begin with, when one starts life with a high level of aggression, there can be special problems with the development of inner controls if an imbalance exists from the start. This is particularly true in the individual who is born with organically based distortions in his neurointegrative capacities, making the individual vulnerable to impulse control problems. When there is poor internal monitoring of the impulses and therefore poor ability to control actions growing out of the aggressive drive, the child's environment, his everyday handling and relationships need to provide the controls to insure appropriate ways in which he responds to the drive. Ideally, there occurs a neutralization of aggression and/or a fusion of the aggressive drives with the others, particularly with the binding power of love. Failure of this neutralization or distorted fusions can result in what is presented to the world as aggressive or violent behavior.

As an example of how this works in life situations, let us begin with a child who has a high level of aggressive energy expressed in motor activity such as is seen in the hyperactive infant. When there is an imbalance between the level of drive and the ability to modulate or otherwise control, it becomes important for such a child to have controls available from the outside since they are not available from within, at least until he can develop his own internal controls (thus, inability to establish controls can represent a developmental delay and is not necessarily permanent). Now, if instead of controls being available, this type of child is over-stimulated, the level of drive which can result makes controls even more difficult. When such a child's motor begins to race and his brakes are not available, a pat can become a slap. Grasping an object can end with pushing it and causing it to fall and break. If there are still no controls available from the outside, the end result can be a feeling of helplessness which must be defended against at all costs. Thus, even in the first year of life, a child can establish the defense that hurting or breaking is intentional, not accidental. This is particularly true if other forms of pleasure and satisfaction are not available. A distorted fusion of drives can then take place in which the child says, "I not only want to hurt or break, but it is also my pleasure." Then the basis for violence as part of relationships and response to the environment can become rooted. Another basis on which poorly controlled violent behavior can take place is the over-control of aggressive, even exploratory behavior so that there is no opportunity to experiment with situations in which inner controls are necessary. Margaret Mead (1935, 1969) reports from her work in Bali that massacres result in societies where there is no permission for children to experiment with aggression.

The early aggressive energy is usually utilized to see that the needs of the organism for growth and safety are met. There is also the use of aggression in pleasurable ways. These fusions can lead to a variety of possible directions in the fate of the aggressive energy such as the use of aggression when survival needs are not met. Thus, some children grow up feeling that the only way one can have survival needs met is by violence. There can then be a fusion of violence with dependency relationships, i.e., the child has learned that aggressive energy should be expressed in violent forms and to picture violence as the only way to create movement and change.

When he acquires his first teeth, the baby experiments with biting. When he becomes concerned about people leaving him at eight months, he turns away from them and causes them to disappear again when they return, thus attempting to deal with helplessness in still another way. When he is discovering his own will, when he is toilet trained, when he is experimenting with sexuality, etc. he tests out how all these experiences can be used as an expression of aggression. Depending on the responses he encounters in these experiments, the outcome seen in some young children is preoccupation with one or another of these ways of expressing aggression. The physically abused child provides another example of identification with a violent form of aggression as a component of relationships which the individual child can make his own. Thus, many child beaters have been beaten children themselves. Still others, as examples of the repetition compulsion, invite and even need hurt as part of close relationships.

The most active experimentation with physical violence begins early in the second year when stamping, kicking and breaking are tentatively tried. The answers to fitting inner controls with societal norms and expectations begins here. One approach that delays appropriate answers or makes them unnecessary is "we must let him express himself." The key time in which the most lasting answers to what one does with aggressive drives and feelings appears to be between two and three years of age. During this time when the child is able to be exploring how he and his drives fit in with his expanding horizons in his world, he experiments with aggression in more direct forms in sometimes quite violent ways such as the use of sadism and other cruel approaches to aggressive expressions. During this period the young child is preoccupied with forms of being hurt and the ways in which others get hurt. The literature for this age group that has been handed down from generation to generation has many such themes, Jack and Jill fall down the hill; Humpty Dumpty falls off the wall; the cradle falls off the tree. When concerned adults attempt to "clean up" the naked violence and aggression in these nursery rhymes, the young children lose interest in them.

When the environment, including the cultural patterns to which the young child is exposed between two and four years of age, has a large component of violence involved in relationships, these can be readily identified with by the child. This was one of the most difficult areas of adjustment to the nursery groups in the South End study carried out in Boston by Pavenstedt and Malone (1969) as they report it in "The Drifters."

The methods by which controls are established (by no means comprehensive) involve neutralization of aggression, particularly by making it unnecessary, especially as a survival device, as well as encouraging healthy and appropriate fusion with pleasurable drives. Sublimations of aggressive and violent wishes if appropriate, can be effective control devices. For example, the child who is free to experiment with aggression can find that if you are not allowed to beat someone up, you can find that there are ways of beating him out instead. This, in turn, can be translated into useful investments of aggressive energy such as ambition and competitiveness.

The prevalent patterns of controlling aggression are accomplished by the use of language to express feelings rather than act them out. Child says "no" to himself as he hits – then with reinforcement, the "no" becomes automatic. Postponing or displacing the pleasure from violence can be accomplished by structuring, such as in games or by looking rather than doing, etc. The latter particularly explains one of the average child's interests in TV violence, and when he grows up, his preoccupation with newspaper headlines of murder and violent crime and the popularity of detective stories. One should also keep in mind the usefulness of this type of vicarious experiencing of violent forms of aggression, but also its most important service as a means of helping the individual to learn how to deal with violence from others.

There are many variations and combinations of overstimulated aggression and violence and attempts to control which are ineffective. One example is the overstimulated child controlled by fear, which can be effective only in direct violence being taboo. With the continuing pressure for expression of exciting and destructive wishes, the end result can be acting out in indirect ways such as fire setting.

The use of rules as a means of containing and channeling aggression is a very useful device and takes the form of strict repetitive patterns in early childhood even in games and later in "contained, licensed violence" in the form of boxing, football, etc. The development of an appropriate conscience, sense of right or wrong, good or bad, moral judgments, etc., are important control devices which are necessary in healthy personality development. Unfortunately, the child is exposed not only to the rules which fit in with an appropriate conscience, but also to the "superego lacunae" which are presented to the child in his environment (Johnson and Szurek, 1952), i.e., it learns you must be honest – except with insurance companies or income tax. It is in this context that the respect or disrespect for law is established as well as for the rights of others and property rights. Since superego development and identification involve models found in close relationships, there is an immediate hazard in the development of a proper conscience in the child who has never learned what it is like to be close to or part of another person. There is some feeling that the only true amoral, asocial, psychopathic personality is the individual who has never learned in the first five years of life what it is like to be part of another person. The entry into the delinquency system where violence can be a way of life, begins at eight or nine.

We should also comment further on the use of fear and reversals as methods used by the individual to control aggression. These fears and reversal mechanisms develop when the child is at the height of experimenting with aggressive experiences, especially in the form of violence and sadism; that is, between two and three years of age. The child's aggressive powers are enhanced by the use of his own magic power. However, this could stir up powerful aggression and violence in others and in the environment. Therefore, fear of bodily damage as a normal area of concern in this age period very often serves as a means of helping the individual make the decision that it isn't safe to be violently aggressive; in fact, it might be better to be passive or turn the aggression on oneself. Here, too, fear can result in still another defensive step where, on a counterphobic basis, violent aggression may come back into the picture in an attempt to negate the fear. This is often the psychology of the bully.

In all these approaches to finding their own answers, one sees how violence can become acceptable in children who are exposed to distortions in cultural values about dealing with aggression. Where contradictory messages about aggression are offered to them or they experience repeated frustrations or their models or ego ideals are using violence, the end result can be preoccupation with violence as a means of survival or pleasure or an acceptable, expectable way of life. Finally, there is the violence dictated by mental aberrations, such as mental distortions in perception of reality. This is reflected in paranoid thinking which calls for violent solutions to imagined danger. It is seen in hallucinations which dictate violent behavior. The end result of his early life experience is that each individual has become accustomed to a degree and form of violence. There is a particular type of violence and form of violence with which he has made peace. Each individual has his peculiar level of control and thickness of the veneer over his aggression and his conditions which can allow its breakthrough. The veneer can be dissolved by alcohol. Violence can also be part of group expression to show loyalty. It can emerge also when the individual is faced with fear which cannot be solved. There may be a need to be heard and recognized as a person and violence is the only way the individual can get such attention. Violence may also be a show of bravery, to show one's toughness, testing survival skills by taking risks. It can be his way of declaring group unity or his participation to repel invasion of the group from a subgroup or from the "dangers" in the community.

There are two basic approaches which the community has in dealing with socially unacceptable violence; to help an individual establish controls from within or to supply controls from without. When we must resort to controls from without, mostly this is accomplished by creating fears. When this form of fear does not work, attempts are made to devise ways of creating more effective fears and more effective external controls which include retaliation and punishment. To put this approach in perspective, it should be kept in mind that even the Biblical admonition of "an eye for an eye and a tooth for a tooth" is an attempt to modify overpunishing so that the punishment will fit the crime. It has been pointed out that the Biblical admonition is an attempt to remedy the pattern in ancient times in which when a slave attacked his master and destroyed his eye or tooth, he would be killed.

Only too often as behavioral scientists and mental health professionals we are asked by society to help devise new ways of helping individuals establish controls or to rework the control problems in a given individual or group. At the same time there is an understandable reluctance on the part of society to be concerned, as we are, with the nature and origins of violence as we see them in the earliest years of life. There is a great reluctance for us to look at the savage, which in one degree or another is a part of every human, with a thinner or thicker or more effective veneer of civilization covering it. It is the young child trying to find the answers to aggressive drives in himself who can tap in on the savage, who can scratch the surface and get through the veneer of even the most meek, soft, sweet parents in the world, and tap the underlying violence.

If we are truly to have more effective programs for dealing with the problems of violence and crime in our society (as well as institutionalized violence such as war), at least a good part of our effort needs to be aimed at those most important points in life when the young child finds his first and sometimes permanent answers to this part of his world. In Judge David Bazelon's terms: "We are more preoccupied with fire fighting than fire prevention."

The community points to the more and more destructive fires that need to be put out right now. By all means we need to have more and better fire fighting, but the much less glamorous job of fire proofing must be a major responsibility if we truly know where the fires of violence begin.

REFERENCES

Acquisition and Development of Values, report of a conference held May 15-17, 1968. Washington, National Institute of Child Health and Human Development (Govt. Printing Office 1969 — nos. 351-894).

Anohkin, A. (1964), "Systemogenesis: in the developing brain," *Progress in Brain Research,* vol. 9 (New York, Elsevier).

Freud, S. (1930), "Civilization and its discontents" (1930), in *Complete Psychological Works,* standard edition, vol. 21. Translated and edited by J. Strachey (London, Hogarth Press, 1961), pp. 59-145.

Gorer, M. (1968), "Man has no killer instinct," *New York Times Magazine,* Feb. 18.

Greenacre, R. (1960), "Considerations regarding the parent-infant relationship" *International Journal of Psychoanalysis,* vol. 41, pp. 571-84.

Johnson, A. and S. A. Szurek (1952), "The genesis of antisocial acting out in children and adults," *Psychoanalysis Quarterly,* vol. 21, pp. 323-43.

Lorenz, K. (1966), *On Aggression* (New York, Harcourt, Brace and World).

Lourie, R. (1971), "The first three years of life: an overview of a new frontier of psychiatry," *American Journal of Psychiatry,* vol. 127, no. 11, pp. 1457-63.

Malone, C. A. (1969), "Developmental deviations considered in light of environmental forces," in E. Pavenstedt (ed.), *The Drifters: Children of Disorganized Families* (Boston, Little, Brown).

Mark, J. H. and F. R. Ervin (1970), *Violence and the Brain* (New York, Harper and Row).

Mead, M. (1935), *Sex and Temperamental Deviations Considered in Primitive Societies* (New York, Morrow).

_____. (1969), "Violence and its regulation," *American Journal of Orthopsychiatry,* vol. 39, pp. 227-29.

Money, J. (1969), "XYZ, the law and forensic moral philosophy," *Journal of Nervous Mental Disorders,* vol. 149, pp. 309-11.

Montagu, A. (1968), *Man and Aggression* (London, Oxford University Press).

Tinbergen, N. (1968), "On war and peace in animals and man" *Science,* vol. 160, pp. 1411-18.

Weinstein, E. A., E. C. Alvord, Jr., and D. Mck. Rioch (1953), "Disorders associated with disturbances of brain function," *Annals of the American Academy of Political and Social Sciences,* vol. 286, pp. 34-44.

To Prevent the Abuse of the Future

by Vincent J. Fontana

It is difficult to accept the fact that in our society today inhuman cruelty to children appears to be rapidly increasing and that the perpetrators of this crime are, for the most part, not strangers but the parents themselves. The story of the battered child is one which has an unhappy beginning and, through the scars of inflicted trauma, and the emotional neglect and deprivation, leads to an unhappy ending. So serious has this problem become that it has been a subject of study by child welfare institutions in every state and by the federal government.

The maiming and torturing of children has been reported and discussed in the *Journal of the American Medical Association.* It stated that "the assaults on children, if complete statistics were available, could turn out to be a more frequent cause of death than such world recognized and thoroughly studied diseases as leukemia, cystic fibrosis, muscular dystrophy, and might even rank with automobile fatalities." There is a definite symptomatic connection between the violence and crime in our society today and the abused and battered child of yesterday. Maltreatment of children is one aspect of the social violence running rampant in our country today, and is symptomatic of an illness which is insidiously creeping into our society. Child abuse is a medical-social disease that has assumed epidemic proportions and encompasses a child rearing pattern which is becoming more entrenched in our population. It is a disease that is not only a time-limited phenomenon, but the cause and effect of a cyclical pattern of the violence reflected in all our statistics on crime.

The list of known injuries suffered by children at the hands of their parents has included parents throwing, shooting, stabbing, burning, drowning, suffocating, biting, sexually violating, and deliberately disfiguring their own infants and children. By far, the greatest number of injuries resulted from beatings with various kinds of implements and instruments. Some children have been strangled or suffocated with pillows held over their mouths, or plastic bags thrown over their heads. A number have been drowned in bathtubs.

Dr. C. Henry Kempe, of the University of Colorado School of medicine in Denver, in 1962, reported the results of a nationwide survey of hospitals and law enforcement agencies indicating a high incidence of battered children in a one year period. A total of 749 children were reported as being maltreated; of this number 78 died and 114 suffered permanent brain damage. In only a third of these cases did proper medical diagnosis initiate court action.

In New York City in 1972, there was more than a 500% increase in reported cases of abuse and neglect within the period of 1961 to 1970, and in 1973 over 18,000 cases of suspected child abuse and neglect were reported to the City Central Registry. In 1972, 200 children's deaths in New York City were attributed to maltreatment. Only a fraction of the neglected and abused children are taken to physicians or hospitals for medical attention. Many of these children go unrecognized, undiagnosed, and hence, unreported. We are probably seeing only the tip of an iceberg. Unfortunately, the true incidence rates and distribution patterns of child abuse and neglect are unknown at this time. The gathering of hard data is at the present being undertaken; it is a costly, complex, and time-consuming task, but if this work is properly organized and evaluated, perhaps the true incidence of this disease will be known in the future.

Reprinted by permission from "To Prevent the Abuse of the Future," by Vincent Fontana, *Trial Magazine,* Vol. 10, No. 3, May/June 1974, pp. 14-16, 18.

Dr. Vincent J. Fontana is Pediatrician-in-Chief of the New York Foundling Hospital Center for Parent and Child Development.

It must be recognized that the incidence rates of child abuse must be distinguished from the reporting rates since the actual occurrence rates are likely to be higher for the reasons previously mentioned. An important fact to keep in mind with reference to the actual incidence of child maltreatment is that in spite of child abuse laws in every state of our nation only a few laws exist that mandate the reporting of child fatalities due to maltreatment. In some states coroners and medical examiners are not required by law to report fatalities suspected to be due to maltreatment.

The neglect and abuse of children denotes a situation ranging from the deprivation of food, clothing, shelter, and parental love to incidents in which children are physically abused and mistreated by an adult resulting in obvious physical trauma to the child and often leading to death. Kempe described this repeated physical abuse of children and called it "The Battered Child Syndrome," Other reports in the medical literature have referred to this disease over the years as "unrecognized trauma," a term limited to a description of the bone lesions found in the maltreatment of children.

Unfortunately, both these terms do not fully describe the true picture of this often life-threatening condition. The more precise and descriptive term that could be applied to this clinical entity is that of "The Maltreatment Syndrome."

A maltreated child often presents no obvious signs of being battered but has multiple minor physical evidences of emotional and, at times, nutritional deprivation, neglect, and abuse. In these cases, the diagnostic ability of the physician coupled with community treatment and preventive child abuse programs can prevent the more serious injuries of inflicted battering that are significant causes of childhood deaths.

The maltreated child is often taken to the hospital or private physician with a history of "failure to thrive," malnutrition, poor skin hygiene, irritability, a repressed personality, and other signs of obvious physical neglect. The more severly abused children are seen in the emergency rooms of hospitals with external evidences of body trauma, bruises, abrasions, cuts, lacerations, soft tissue swellings and hematomas. Hypernatremic dehydration, following periodic water deprivation by psychotic mothers, has been reported as a form of child abuse. Inability to move certain extremities because of dislocations and fractures associated with neurological signs of intracranial damage can be additional signs of inflicted trauma.

Other clinical signs and symptoms attributed to inflicted abuse may include injury to abdominal organs. Abdominal trauma may result in "unexplained" ruptures of stomach, bowel, liver or pancreas with manifestations of an acute abdomen. Children manifesting the maltreatment syndrome give evidence of one or more of these complaints. Those with the most severe maltreatment injuries arrive at the hospital or physician's office in a coma, convulsions, or even death. The signs and symptoms indicating the maltreatment of children, therefore, range from the simple undernourished infant reported as "failure to thrive" to the "battered child," — often the last phase of the spectrum of the maltreatment syndrome.

Many of these maltreated children are not taken to the physician or hospital for medical care unless the child is in acute distress or the parents suspect impending death, because parents fear legal entanglements. If the infant or child is taken to a physician or hospital, the history related by the parents is often at variance with the clinical picture and the physical findings noted on examination of the child. The physician often discovers that the mother has taken the child to various hospitals and doctors in an effort to negate any suspicions of parental abuse. Difficulty in obtaining any type of history is often encountered and diagnosis is dependent on the physical examination, the x-ray findings, and a high index of suspicion on the part of the reporting source.

X-ray evidence of fractures may be present in various stages of reparative changes. On the other hand, if no fractures or dislocations are apparent on initial examination bone injury may remain obscure during the first few days after inflicted trauma. In these cases bone repair may become evident within weeks after the specific bone trauma. The more common findings on x-ray examination of these fractures reveal several diagnostic and unusual bone changes. Periosteal hemorrhages are frequently noted under the periosteum or the covering around the bone of infants since it is not securely attached to the underlying bone. This is followed by periosteal calcification which begins to appear on x-ray from five to seven days after the fracture. This layer of calcification around the shaft of the bone indicates incidence of previous trauma and suggests further investigation into the causes of the fracture.

Children who are abused and neglected tend to be in the young age group. Parental neglect and abuse may occur at any age, with an increase of incidence in children under three years of age. Several surveys have indicated that children upon whom more serious physical injuries were inflicted tended to be younger than those on whom less serious injuries were inflicted.

Many of these maltreated children are perceived as if they had the emotions and motivations of older children and adults. They often are expected to "mother" the mother and there is a reversal of roles with the mother's fears and misperceptions leading to inflicted abuse on the child. Older children oftentimes are physically abused because they are found to be unacceptable and offer a threat to the viability of the family unit. The mother will justify her actions on the basis of the child's imperfections using disciplinary actions that oftentimes lead to battering.

In evaluating our cases of child abuse and neglect at St. Vincent's Hospital and Medical Center of New York and The New York Foundling Hospital's Center for Parent and Child Development, it appears that the battered child is usually the victim of emotionally crippled parents who have had unfortunate circumstances surrounding their own childhood. The battering parent appears to react to his own child as a result of past personal experiences of loneliness, lack of protection, and love. Some of these mothers have been raised by a variety of foster parents during their own childhood. These mothers are unable to react normally to the needs of their own children.

The abusing parent frequently has a history of having been brutalized himself as a child and so the pattern of violent behavior perpetuates itself from generation to generation. These parents are unable to distinguish between their own childhood suffering and their vicious reactions toward their children. The parents were usually immature, narcissistic, egocentric, demanding, impulsive, depressed and aggressive. The parents appear unwilling to accept responsibility as parents. They appear to have a distorted perception of a particular child at a particular stage in its development. When the child is not able to perform, the parent may be triggered into a reaction leading to inflicted abuse.

Divorce, alcoholism, drug addiction, mental retardation, recurring mental illness, unemployment, and financial stress were important factors often present in the family structure of abusing parents. These stress factors all play major roles in leading the potentially abusive parent to strike out at a special child during a crisis situation. The three components, namely, a potentially abusing parent, a child, and a sudden crisis are the necessary ingredients that give rise to child abuse and battering.

It has been shown that infants and young children that have been abused and neglected at the hands of their own parents, if they survive, tend to carry out their injuries into adolescence. Many of these children as they approach adolescence, begin to show evidence of psychological and emotional disturbances leading to juvenile delinquency. These psychological changes that are noted in the maltreated children that survive are usually irreversible and pose a threat to society.

Dr. Carl Menninger has stated that every criminal was an unloved and maltreated child. He feels that the criminal is a child who survives his maltreatment physically but who suffers at the hands of unrestrained, aggressive, and psychotic adults. There has been concern among criminologists that the tendency of abused or battered children, if they survive, is to become tomorrow's murderers and perpetrators of other crimes of violence. It has been theorized that children so maltreated have an unusual degree of hostility towards parents and towards the world in general. It would appear, therefore, although certainly more investigative work is necessary and wanting to come to any reliable conclusions, that the maltreatment of children may well provide one of the sources of juvenile delinquency, future murderers, and perpetra-tors of violence in our society.

Strong consideration should be given to the thesis that treating the syndrome of the battered child may be a means of preventing not only possible permanent physical or mental injury or death of a child, but may also be a means of breaking the violence breeding violence generational cycle. A most important aspect of this disease is that the abused and maltreated children who survive will have emotional and psychological crippling which is passed on to succeeding generations with a sense of rejection and frustration leading to further crime and violence and the battering parents of future generations.

Efforts have been made throughout the country to protect the abused and battered child by the enactment of child abuse laws in every state of the nation. Fundamentally, these child abuse laws are only the first step in the protection of the abused and neglected child. It is what happens after the reporting that is of utmost importance. A multidisciplinary network of protection needs to be developed in each community to implement the good intention of these child abuse laws. It is our duty not only to report suspected cases of child abuse but also to initiate the necessary steps to prevent further maltreatment to the patient and other siblings in the family unit. We must become intimately involved in the social and legal actions taken to protect the child and assist in the treatment of the parents. The purposes of child abuse laws are to protect the parents when presented with invalid evidence; to protect the child by making it mandatory to report suspected cases of maltreatment; and to protect the reporter from possible damage suits by the parties involved.

Separating the child from the parent who neglects, batters and kills a child is totally inadequate unless it is coupled with a simultaneous concern to insure future adequate rehabilitation and preventive measures that will help eliminate the psychological and social environmental factors that foster the battering parent syndrome. If these parents are to be given any help or assistance they must be made to recognize their own intrinsic worth and potentials as human beings. This can only be accomplished by a recognition and cooperative effort by all professionsals and paraprofessionals. Only in this way can we provide the kinds of innovative treatment programs and services that will help eradicate this disease of child abuse in our communities.

At a recent Select Sub-Committee Hearing in Washington, D.C., Bryant Fraser, Staff Attorney for the National Center for the Prevention and Treatment of Child Abuse and Neglect in Denver, Colorado, described the legal and legislative status of child abuse in our 50 states. All 50 states, Washington, D.C., Puerto Rico, and the Virgin Islands, now have some form or other of mandatory reporting in cases of suspected child abuse. In 43 states, or 86% of the country, the privileged status of confidential communications has been abrogated in cases dealing with child abuse. This abrogation ranges from just those communications between husband and wife, or a doctor and patient to an abrogation of all privileged communications, except those of attorney-client. In 30 states some form of Central Registry for keeping track of suspected cases of child abuse has been established. At least three states have provisions for cooperating with other states to exchange this type of information, in an attempt to establish a Federal Central Registry. The Child Abuse Laws in 33 states provide criminal sanctions for failure to report suspected child abuse. New York has added a provision to their new law which would make a person civilly as well as criminally liable for failure to report child abuse. Previously, recovery for civil damages was through a negligence per se approach. Eight states give either a private physician or a hospital the right to retain custody of a child, without a court order and without the parent's permission. This is done if they believe it would be dangerous or life-threatening for the child to remain in his home environment. At the time of this writing, 19 states grant the child an absolute right to counsel in civil or juvenile proceedings involving child abuse. Four of the states have gone further and now require by law that a guardian be appointed to represent the child's interest in all cases of suspected child abuse. This guardian, which is to be appointed in every case of suspected child abuse to protect the child's interest, is more than just a simple legal advocate for a child – it connotes a legal representative to protect the child's interest in all legal proceedings and a guardian to protect the child's long-range interest.

In the field of child abuse legislation it is important to note the definition of child abuse is expanding to cover other forms of abuse, namely, sexual abuse, emotional abuse, and neglect. In 1973, the New York State Legislature passed a new comprehensive child protective services act and made pertinent additions and amendments to various sections on child protection in the Family Court Act. A new and broader category, "maltreated child," was created. A maltreated child is one "under 18 years of age now defined as 'neglected' in the Family Court Act; or one who has had serious physical injury inflicted upon him by other than accidental means." This effectively now encompasses not only the neglected children but also those physically maltreated children between 16-18 years of age who could not be included in the child abuse category because of its 16 years of age limitation. The legal definition of "abused child" means "a child less than 16 years of age whose parents or other person legally responsible for his care inflicts or allows to be inflicted upon such physical injury by other than accidental means which causes or creates a substantial risk of death, or serious or protracted disfigurement, or protracted impairment of physical or emotional health or protracted loss or impairment of the functions of any body organ."

The Child Protection Act of 1973 passed by the legislatures of New York can well serve as a model child abuse law for other states. It is all encompassing in its definitions of child abuse and neglect. It provides intervention for the protection of children and mandates investigative reports as well as intensive supportive services to rehabilitate families. It also mandates Commissioners of Special Services to receive and care for children who are maltreated by bringing such cases before the family court for adjudication.

Child maltreatment is the responsibility of all society and demands the involvement, understanding and cooperative efforts of the medical, social and legal disciplines of our country. If we worry about the future of our country, should we not be worrying about the children of today? Unless we help stem the tide of child maltreatment, one day we will be trying to cope with drug addiction, alcoholism, crime, violence and mental disorders of alarming proportions.

(References available upon request from Dr. Fontana)

3 GOVERNMENT- FAMILY INTERLOCK

192

Health Care Policy

Introduction

The interlock between government and families that will be examined in this section will include the following issues: the increasing interdependence of the citizen and regulation by the government, the place of the individual and family in public social policy, and selected areas of policy decisions that have the potential for value conflicts.

The Declaration of Independence embodied the Jeffersonian concept that that government is best that governs least. There are those who now voice alarm over the extent to which that basic tenet is being eroded. Regulatory agencies at cross-purposes with each other, the high cost of conforming to stipulations, enforcement supervision—these and more are the resulting paradox of protecting the consumer citizens from their own mistakes and from those of the marketplace. This increasing bureaucracy, coupled with computerized record-keeping and the concomitant invasion of privacy are ongoing issues that must somehow be balanced with the safety and security needs of the individual, family, and nation.

Second, there has always been the need to reconcile the differences between the haves and the have-nots among us. Whether we think of public social policy as affecting individual citizens or the aggregate of individuals that comprise households and families, it is aimed primarily at social justice for those who are not capable of participating in the economic mainstream or who have "fallen out," for whatever reason.

As Eldridge stated in "Economics in Conflict," the abuses of the economic system are corrected, if at all, in the political arena. Family policy, then, would seem to be an important part of the body politic since a fully functioning citizenry is essential to democratic ideals. Senator Walter Mondale (Dem., Minn.) has long supported the need for an assessment of "family impact" of various government programs. Although this might alert the politician and voter to the cause of family welfare, it gives little added power to the family itself as a corporate entity. In a subsequent article, Catherine Chilman states, "Public social policy should include, but not be separate from, public family policy. Just as it should recognize the complexity and interactional dynamics of social, economic, and political systems, so it should recognize the complex interactional dynamics of that smaller and weaker system—the family."[1]

Third, it is the ethical system that activates the intent of the political system, and it is here, particularly in child-care policy and in housing policy, that values have not been clearly defined. In Olmstead v. United States (1928), Louis D. Brandeis, dissenting, wrote, "Experience should teach us to be most on our guard to protect liberty when the Government's purposes are beneficent. Men born to freedom are naturally alert to repel invasion of their liberty by evil-minded rulers. The greatest dangers to liberty lurk in insidious encroachment by men of zeal, well-meaning but without understanding."[2]

The inclusion of articles on child care, housing, and health are meant to be a citizen's alert to the needs of individuals and families for dignity and equal status in the business of being governed.

Commentary—Evelyn Eldridge, ed.

---

[1]Catherine S. Chilman, "Public Social Policy and Families in the 1970's," *Social Casework,* Vol. 54, No. 10, December, 1973, p. 585.
[2]Olmstead v. United States. Brandeis, J., dissenting. 277 U.S. 438, 439, 479 (1927).

3A ONGOING INTERDEPENDENCE

Regulations—Quietly Pervading the Daily Life of a U.S. Family

by Brooks Jackson and Evans Witt

ALLENTOWN, PA. (AP)—at 7:45 A.M., Nancy Ruddell sits down for her first cup of morning coffee, adding an artificial sweetener containing saccharin.

"Contains no cyclamate" reads the little packet of sweetener. Cyclamate lacks saccharin's bitter aftertaste, but it cannot be sold for human consumption because of a U.S. Food and Drug Administration (FDA) ruling in 1969.

This day that started at 6:15 A.M. is a mostly unexceptional one for Tom and Nancy Ruddell. They take their two children to school; Tom goes to work at Pennsylvania Power and Light; Nancy makes two shopping trips; and they give a small party.

But throughout this day, and every other day, the Ruddells' lives—and those of every American—are shaped by federal regulations.

The extent to which federal regulations touch the Ruddell family is not unusual. Every family in this country is affected by the rules made in Washington, D.C.

This is a look at the regulations in a day in the life of one American family in this city of 109,000 in the rolling hills of eastern Pennsylvania.

6:15 A.M.—A burst from the alarm clock rouses the family. The clock reads 6:15 because Congress decreed Daylight Saving Time ended when October did.

6:25 A.M.—Geoffrey, age 5, slips out of his pajamas which are flame retardant because the Consumer Product Safety Commission requires sleepwear for children to be so treated.

6:50 A.M.—Three quarts of Abbotts homogenized milk are brought in by Geoffrey. Nancy makes a mix of milk and reconstituted Shop Rite Instant Non-Fat Dry Milk, cutting the drink's calories and cholesterol. But the resulting mixture is also cheaper than ordinary skim milk because the U.S. Department of Agriculture sets a higher support price for skim milk than whole milk.

HIS PROTEST

7:50 A.M.—Tom starts for work. The federally mandated seat belt alarm on his Audi sedan doesn't make a shrill buzz when he turns the ignition key. It's been disconnected. "It's my way of protesting the system," he says.

7:55 A.M.–Driving to work, Tom recalls the story of how a federal safety inspector ordered the wearing of hardhats and installation of guardrails at the workshop of the Trolley Museum in Kennebunkport, Maine. During the family's summer vacations, Tom spends much of his time working as a volunteer in restoring old trolley cars.

"They probably did us a favor, but, my Lord, it makes you think. They've even gotten to trolley museums," he says.

8:14 A.M.–Nancy backs her Volvo station wagon out of the garage on the way to take Jennifer to school. She pulls a small greyish box out of the glove compartment, presses its button and the garage door closes.

The box is a low-powered radio transmitter, a Wickes model 116-56, which was built according to Federal Communications Commission standards.

But FCC rules are not something Nancy thinks about. She notices the label on the back of the transmitter for the first time: "This label is required by FCC RULES. Do not remove."

8:19 A.M.–Jennifer carries her homemade lunch of a ham-and-tomato sandwich into the Union Terrace School. Many other students at Jennifer's public school will eat a lunch prepared at the school cafeteria, federally subsidized at about 23 cents for each lunch.

The U.S. Department of Agriculture requires that, to qualify for the subsidy, the school must serve a "Type A" lunch, which the department specifies must contain 2 ounces of meat or a meat substitute, 3/4 cup of at least two vegetables or fruits, bread, butter and a half pint of milk.

"PEANUT SPREAD"

8:35 A.M.–The federal government is constantly looking over Nancy's shoulder as she buys the family groceries at the big, brilliantly illuminated Shop Rite supermarket.

Nancy picks up a two-pound jar of Skippy peanut butter, which the FDA says can be called peanut butter because it is 90 per cent peanuts. Any less, the FDA says, and it must be called "peanut spread."

The label on the can of sliced peaches lists the vitamins, minerals and calories that each serving contains. The FDA again is responsible.

The Department of Agriculture set the standard that determines that the roast Nancy buys is "choice" rather than "prime." And it inspected the farm that was home for the cow that was the source for the $1.87-a-pound beef.

These regulations are not on Nancy's mind as she shops.

"I'm looking for food that I think is nutritional. I don't care what the government says is right," she explains.

12:17 P.M.–As if to underline her statements, Nancy makes her second shopping stop of the day at the Allentown Farmers Market, where mostly Pennsylvania grown produce is sold in stalls in the open-air market, largely free from federal control.

Nancy buys apples and cheese. Both are sold by farmers under federal agricultural marketing orders, which are designed to control supply and allocate income among producers. The federal government also props up the price of cheese by keeping foreign cheese out of the country and by buying quantities of American cheese when prices fall.

Much of the produce available at the market avoids federal regulation, for it is produced and sold inside Pennsylvania. For example, there is meat on sale that is not USDA inspected, because it is not shipped across state lines and thus is not in interstate commerce.

1:10 P.M.–Tom goes over a report at his office. It shows, based on a poll of the company's supervisory officers, that 23 federal bodies either receive reports from Pennsylvania Power and Light or affect its business in some way.

The Agriculture Department loans money for rural electric service, the Environmental Protection Agency controls smokestack pollutants at generating stations, the Federal Power Commission controls wholesale prices on interstate sales of electricity to other utilities, the Equal Employment Opportunity Commission wants to know about the utility's minority-group employees... the list goes on.

"SWOLLEN SHUT"

1:25 P.M.—Nancy sits in the family room talking to a visitor about the Environmental Protection Agency's ban on the insecticide DDT, which she blames for a plague of mosquitoes at their rented vacation home for the past few summers. "They don't spray at the beach anymore," she says.

The bites particularly bother her daughter. "Jennifer's eyes have been swollen shut."

8:30 P.M.—Friends begin to arrive for a small holiday gathering. The children watch a Christmas special on television, the ads for which would be screened for misleading statements under proposed Federal Trade Commission regulations. Tom pours drinks. The alcohol is measured and taxed by the Treasury Department.

Throughout this day and every day the Ruddells, like any other family in America, are affected by federal regulations when they sleep, eat, work, drive, shop or play.

Notes on the Sociology of Privacy

by Eric Josephson

This symposium is evidence, if any were needed, of mounting concern about threats to privacy in modern society. Further evidence is provided by an increasing number of newspaper editorials, articles, books, congressional hearings, and government reports devoted to the subject and in the sober deliberations of lawyers, social scientists, and even computer specialists. As for the public, while most Americans are no doubt preoccupied with such matters as the state of the economy, computerized data from opinion surveys (both of which are regarded by some people as invasions of privacy) show that a sizeable minority feel threatened by the machines that process the data. Safeguarding privacy has joined the long list of social problems which confront us.

In response, recent United States presidents, including President Nixon, have vowed that they will protect our "right" to privacy and proposals have been made for legislation or even a constitutional amendment that would presumably guarantee that right (at least three state constitutions already specify just such a right). The U.S. is by no means the only country in which this has become an issue and the United Nations has recently recommended that all governments establish minimum standards to protect the privacy of individuals by law.

Contributing to concern about threats to privacy are new-fangled electronic techniques of surveillance, the tremendous growth in the amount of information about individuals which is collected by the modern state and by other institutions, and above all the increasing "sophistication" of methods of storing and retrieving that information. The proliferation of computerized data banks (the very phrase suggesting an equivalence of information and money) is of course the development that has most aroused public as well as expert opinion. Thus, at latest count, U.S. government agencies maintained 858 such depositories and, with the technology at hand for linking them, not surprisingly it has been proposed that a national data bank be established. So too it has been proposed that one of those agencies, the Federal Bureau of Investigation, establish a national data bank to facilitate the exchange of "computerized criminal history" information between state and local police departments. The underlying assumption of most commentators on the problem is that computerized data banking and equally new-fangled techniques of influencing individual moods, attitudes, and desires threaten freedom itself and that the Orwellian nightmare is already upon us.

But Orwell could not forsee Watergate. Big Brother is not only keeping an eye and ear on individual citizens but on himself as well, the crowning—or, more properly, the dethroning—irony of Watergate. Of course, Watergate represents considerably more than the end of Nixon's career. The articles of impeachment reported by the Judiciary Committee of the U.S. House of Representatives—particularly the article dealing with Nixon's abuse of presidential powers—were based largely on evidence regarding various invasions of privacy.

One piece of evidence cited by the Judiciary Committee had to do with the establishment of a secret investigative unit in the White House which engaged in unlawful electronic surveillance of political opponents and not only attempted to "bug" the headquarters of the

Reprinted with permission from *Humanitas,* Vol. 11, No. 1, February 1975, pp. 15-25.
Dr. Eric Josephson is Associate Professor of public health at the Columbia University School of Public Health and Director of the Center for Socio-cultural Research on Drug Use at Columbia.

Democratic National Committee but also broke into the office of Daniel Ellsberg's psychiatrist (thereby violating the presumably sacrosanct "confidentiality" of the doctor-patient relationship). Another piece of evidence had to do with the abuse of "privileged" information collected by the Internal Revenue Service (perhaps most shocking to the tax payers on the Judiciary Committee). Still another dealt with the unjustifiable authorization of F.B.I. wiretaps on government employees and newspapermen. Finally, evidence was presented to the Judiciary Committee regarding the concealment of the truth about presidential misconduct by inappropriate claims of "executive privilege."

Neither the extraordinary ineptness of the 'plumbers,' nor the brilliant investigative reporting of newspapermen, nor the stalwart behavior of a few judges, nor the probing of congressional committees, nor even the fact that Nixon was forced from office provides grounds for complacency about the invasions of privacy as well as the abuse of power which Watergate represents. Perhaps the plumbers will be more careful next time.

Meanwhile, to understand as well as to cope with what is at issue, we need a working definition, which is simply another way of saying that my idea of privacy is not necessarily yours. However, perhaps to most people the word suggests the "right" to be let alone. The difficulty here, which has complicated the search for legal protection, is that neither in culture nor in law has any such right ever been clearly established. If not a right, then what is it?

Another and more helpful approach to the problem of defining privacy is offered by Westin. "Privacy," he writes, "is the claim of individuals, groups, or institutions to determine for themselves when, how, and to what extent information about them is communicated to others." And further, "Each individual is continually engaged in a personal adjustment process in which he balances the desire for privacy with the desire for disclosure and communication of himself to others, in light of the environmental conditions and social norms set by the society in which he lives. The individual does so in the face of pressures from the curiosity of others and from the processes of surveillance that every society sets in order to enforce its social norms."[1]

How much privacy people claim and how much they get varies widely within as well as between cultures. In some societies people are more "reserved" about themselves than in others, where custom may sanction the revelation of personal matters to strangers or to confidants such as priests or psychiatrists. But in no culture do people keep everything to themselves. Moreover, man, far more than the cat, is a curious as well as a gossipy animal, although it is not just out of curiosity that man observes his fellow creatures. Indeed, observing how others behave is fundamental to social control—i.e., ensuring that most conform to the norms of their culture; without it there can be no social order. This observation takes many forms—watching and listening—and it occurs within the family, at work, at play, in the streets—anywhere people are not physically alone. To be sure, some are observed more than others—e.g., infants and children more than adults—but few escape altogether. Here we have the greatest single constraint on individual privacy and the basis for the more formal, institutional kinds of surveillance which have aroused so much concern.

But if observation is necessary for social order, it has its limits—which is what we mean when we speak of the "need" for privacy or to keep some part of ourselves to ourselves. The idea of a society maintaining total, incessant surveillance (Orwell's fantasy) is not only unbearable; it is just as unthinkable as a society whose members altogether escape surveillance.[2] How to achieve a reasonable balance between society's "need to know" and the individual's need to have at least some part of him unknown is the central problem in the effort to defend privacy, especially as any society often wants to know more than the individual wants to reveal and since the observers usually have more power than the observed.

[1] Alan F. Westin, *Privacy and Freedom*. New York: Atheneum, 1967, p. 7.
[2] Robert K. Merton, *Social Theory and Social Structure*. Glencoe: The Free Press, 1957, p. 375.

Cultures also vary widely in the ways in which they define private space. Not all tend to organize family and work space "privately" as our society does. This is again partly due to cultural traditions, but perhaps largely to the resources available; if most families on earth huddle together when sleeping, this is because they simply cannot afford more space. Such "togetherness" facilitates observation within the group; but the very closeness of the group may tend to limit surveillance by outsiders and therefore may increase group, if not individual, privacy. In small village life there is relatively little privacy for individuals but much for the village.

A significant trend in the use of space is the worldwide movement of populations to cities. As regards privacy, this has been interpreted in different ways. Some commentators have suggested that the very anonymity of big city life offers more privacy to inhabitants than do small communities and some villagers move to the cities with this in mind (most of course are looking for work), perhaps getting more privacy than they bargained for. However, based on animal experiments and on ecological studies of human behavior, other investigators have claimed that overcrowding in cities and the presumed lack of privacy which this represents may have pathological consequences; thus violence and crime are concentrated in the most densely populated quarters of our cities (an alternative explanation is that this has nothing to do with the lack of privacy and is due to the greater opportunities for criminal activities which any city presents). On the other hand, there is no evidence that overcrowding "causes" mental illness, which is apparently more prevalent among people living alone than among those living with others, since many suffering from mental illness "drift" into solitary living arrangements.

Whether urbanized or not, in countries such as the U.S., the trend is unmistakably toward greater spatial privacy for families and for individuals within those families. To be sure, the private home is relatively new historically and the private bedroom as well as the private bath newer still and still rare. The model here is provided by the rich, who amass living space in part for conspicuous display but also for protection. The inequitable distribution of property, means of course, that some enjoy more spatial privacy than others; hence our tendency to speak of it as a "luxury." For most it is just that. (The fact that it was also the rich who first made use of the "private" telephone, the opening wedge for modern techniques of electronic surveillance, is just one of the many ironies in the sociology of privacy.)

Nevertheless, despite the inequities which prevail, with the decline of the extended family household, increasingly large numbers of people live in single family houses or alone. In the U.S. some 12 million persons, or approximately five percent of the total population, live quite alone, many of them elderly. Presumably, some of them "enjoy" more privacy than they need or want.

Many also live in fear of crime. To safeguard them against crime, engineers and architects have devised ingenious barriers and surveillance techniques for transforming middle class urban houses and apartments into veritable fortresses, again emulating the rich. In this respect privacy is sought to ensure that there is no sharing of our wealth with burglars or with traveling salesmen, or our opinions with public opinion survey interviewers. The fact that any individual in our society is in greater danger of homicidal assault from "loved ones" or friends than from strangers on the street has had little influence on the movement to make homes burglar-proof. Forgotten is the old adage that there is safety in numbers. In time many streets become empty and, by a self-fulfilling prophecy, more dangerous. Whether the result is an increasingly alienated society is, of course, a matter of interpretation; if, among many other things, alienation means separation or isolation from others, then the more spatial privacy we have, the greater our alienation.

As for work space, comparative international studies show that Americans are also apparently unique in the degree to which they work alone, even on blue-collar jobs. In white-collar work, the "private" office and the "private" secretary, like the private home, are major and therefore eagerly sought symbols of social status and power. But again this may be attributed largely to the resources available and to the belief, for which there is some substantiation, that we work more efficiently when we have privacy and are not under constant surveillance.

It is one of the ironies of our age that as people have gained more spatial privacy for family life and for work, institutional surveillance has become more widespread. But perhaps more such surveillance is required precisely because people have been able to erect greater spatial barriers between themselves and their observers. In other words, there may be an inverse relationship between the amount of physical privacy which people claim for themselves and the "need" of the state and other institutions systematically to collect and store information about them; in smaller and "simpler" societies formal surveillance is unnecessary.

In principle there is nothing new about the idea of collecting dossiers on individuals; census-takers, tax-collectors, policemen and spies have been doing it for thousands of years. But only recently have they had computers to aid them. Here it is worth recalling that the U.S. Constitution itself (which, according to some jurists, guarantees the right to privacy) mandates a decennial census of households—originally for purposes of enumeration but now of course far more wide-ranging in its purposes. With the expanding role of the federal government in the collection of taxes, the regulation of commerce, the defense of half the globe, and as provider of social security and health care, its record-keeping has grown enormously; hence the 858 data banks. To this we may add the data collected and stored by local school systems, health departments and hospitals, police forces, state registrations of automobile drivers, credit bureaus, employers, insurance companies; the list is endless. Not even the blind escape surveillance; more than a dozen states maintain "registers" of their blind inhabitants in order to monitor trends in the prevalence and incidence of this impairment. Nor must we forget the innumerable surveys of opinions and behavior which are conducted by governmental and non-governmental agencies. In most such cases, the information collected is relatively innocuous.

In other cases, however, the information collected is not innocuous. Of the 858 U.S. government data banks, 29 of them are primarily involved in storing derogatory information—or misinformation. Derogatory information is also collected and stored by school systems. police forces, employers and credit bureaus. Illustrative here are the psychological tests administered by employers to probe for personality "defects," loyalty oaths, surveys conducted to help us "understand" deviant behavior, "registers" of narcotics users, the surveillance of welfare applicants and recipients to determine whether they have violated eligibility requirements, as well as the domestic political surveillance of "radical" groups which has been conducted on a large scale by such agencies as the F.B.I. and even the U.S. Army.

The response to increased surveillance and computerized record-keeping has taken various forms. Most people are cooperative, some no doubt because they are intimidated by the data collectors, but most because they feel they have nothing to hide or consider that in order to get essential social services they must provide the information requested of them. This, it has often been said, is part of the "price" we pay for such services. Indeed, the willingness and sometimes the eagerness of many people voluntarily to provide information about themselves, even when no tangible reward is offered them—as in the case of the U.S. Census or public opinion surveys—is a far greater asset to the data collectors than their computers. The fact that Census enumerators and household interviewers are almost always strangers to their respondents is still another asset to the data collectors, perhaps particularly when it comes to "sensitive" areas of questioning.

Another reason for cooperation is that most people trust the data collectors. That trust is not always misplaced. Thus, the U.S. Census Bureau is justifiably proud of its modern record in protecting the confidentiality of its files, as are most survey research organizations.

But other agencies have been less successful—e.g., the Internal Revenue Service bowing to pressure from the White House to yield information on Nixon's political opponents, or the F.B.I. passing on information about "subversives" to Senator McCarthy.

To be sure, there are some who object to or even refuse to cooperate with the data collectors and record keepers. Thus a few people escape census enumeration (because they are hard to find or don't want to be found), a few fail to file income tax returns (the very rich and the very poor), others avoid contributing to Social Security as long as possible (although this may become increasingly difficult if, as has been proposed, infants are assigned Social Security numbers at birth) and some—not many—refuse to answer the questions of interviewers. Still others provide false information.[3]

All of this may change in the future, but as yet in the U.S. (in contrast with smaller and more efficiently policed European countries) it is still possible for some people to hide from the snoopers—an old frontier tradition and a strong motive for frontier settlement, one step ahead of the sheriff. Today, however, the frontier is likely to be deep inside our big cities. This can be illustrated by the problem of drug "abuse," particularly heroin use, which, presumably concentrated in big city ghetto communities and because of the fear of drug-related crime, has aroused considerable public concern. But despite this concern and the very considerable amount of surveillance which has resulted from it—hundreds of thousands arrested, treated, or interviewed about their use of drugs—we still know relatively little about the dimensions of the problem, i.e. how many people are abusing drugs, let alone what leads to such behavior or what to do about it. Like deviants of other kinds, many drug abusers remain hidden from sight—and with good reason.

Whether the information collected is innocuous or derogatory and provided voluntarily or involuntarily, what provides grounds for legitimate concern is the apparent insatiability of the data collectors for information about individuals and, as noted earlier, the capability now at hand for linking their data files.[4] Why the tremendous demand for personal information? The bureaucratic response is that in an increasingly complex society people cannot be governed or served efficiently unless the bureaucrats have access to that information. But how much is "enough" when, in typical bureaucratic fashion, means become ends and data collection and storage have become industries?

The question that presents itself is how individuals about whom data are being collected and stored can be informed about the purposes of such surveillance, control access to the information and, perhaps most important, correct that information when correction is justifiable or when it turns out to be misinformation. The case of the criminal who has "gone straight" yet is stigmatized and discriminated against because of his earlier delinquency is the most obvious example of this type. Records, like Javert pursuing Jean Valjean, have a way of following and hounding people.

Still another response to modern techniques of surveillance and data storage has been to search for or establish a right to privacy under the law. Like Talmudic scholars, some American jurists and lawyers have searched in the U.S. Constitution and particularly in the Bill of Rights for such protection. This effort was led by Brandeis, who originally became concerned about invasions of privacy because of a newspaper story about the "private" wedding of a friend's daughter. Indignant about the invasion of their privacy, Brandeis and his friend made its defense a cause.

---

[3]There has also been collective resistance to surveillance, such as efforts to smash the computers, raiding and exposing F.B.I. files, and burning draft cards; but these have been more in the nature of political acts than defenses of individual privacy.

[4]James B. Rule, *Private Lives and Public Surveillance.* New York: Schocken Books, 1974.

Since the time of Brandeis, a number of Supreme Court decisions, perhaps most notably Griswold vs Connecticut (in which the Court invalidated a Connecticut law forbidding the dissemination of birth-control information) have been based on the notion that the Constitution guarantees a right to privacy.[5]

However, it is worth noting that not all civil libertarians on the Court, such as Justice Black, have agreed that the Constitution can be interpreted in this way. In fact, Black denied that there was any such right. This issue remains unresolved.

This is not to say that the law and its interpretation afford no protection against invasions or privacy. Noteworthy here is the recent and apparently unprecedented ruling of a federal judge who ordered the F.B.I. to destroy its file on a girl of 17 who, as part of a classroom assignment, had requested information about a radical political group.

This ruling gets to the heart of the issue—i.e., the right of individuals to control access to information about themselves and, equally important, to correct or even destroy that information. It is in this context that proposals have been made to establish a Privacy Protection Commission, to amend the Constitution to guarantee the right to privacy, or to have the federal government issue regulations limiting access to data about individual citizens. All of which is very well, but *quis custodiet ipsos custodes?*

What then are the prospects? The collection and storage of information about individuals do not represent the only threats to privacy in the modern age. Perhaps far more threatening are the evolving techniques of psychologists and pharmacologists to modify individual behavior and mood—the real Orwellian nightmare. So too, some physicians have become increasingly concerned about the computerization and dissemination of presumably "confidential" information about their patients.

Some trends point towards greater personal privacy for individuals—e.g., the ways in which we organize space for living and for work, or "permissiveness" regarding certain forms of "deviant" behavior, such as homosexuality or the use of marijuana. However, without question other trends lead toward increased surveillance by the warfare/welfare state and by other institutions.

An optimistic view is that the data collection and storage systems will become over-loaded and break down, which has sometimes happened—thereby confirming the notion that excessive observation or surveillance can become dysfunctional. A pessimistic and prevailing view is that the computer specialists will get most of the "bugs" out of their systems and that there will be no escaping the modern techniques of surveillance and data processing. Still another view, rarely expressed, is that in our society those who defend privacy are actually defending privilege. According to this conception, in a truly egalitarian and fraternal society there would be little need for privacy as we define it. Many will respond that in such a society the individual "self" would be destroyed. But perhaps this response in turn merely reflects the ways in which we have been socialized about privacy.

Meanwhile, in order to govern and serve us the institutions of our society demand ever more information about individuals. But this exchange is not between equals and the relative powerlessness of the individual citizen as against the data collecting and storing agencies of the modern age is perhaps the most disturbing problem of all. Whether the law can provide the protection that some desire remains to be determined; the many ambiguities in our privacy norms—the "need" to know versus the "need" to withhold information—cannot be resolved by law, only reflected in it.

But it must also be recognized that it is not only individual privacy which is at issue, but the power of the institutions which govern and serve us to claim their own privacy—i.e., to work in secret ways. Getting information about individuals is not very difficult; but getting

[5]Westin, op. cit., Ch. 13.

information from and about bureaucracies is far more difficult. In both cases of course the aim is to make them accountable for their actions. If individuals are losing much of the privacy they claim, the institutions responsible are gaining privacy for themselves. This is the real problem for those who would try to achieve a reasonable balance between society's need to know and individuals' need to keep part of themselves to themselves. The law may help here, but in the final analysis the solution of the privacy problem, if any, will be political.

3B FAMILY IN THE SOCIAL SYSTEM

The Concept of Fallout

The word fallout is used here in a specific and special way. It refers to persons—persons who have "fallen out" of the development process by which the majority of persons in our society move from infancy to self-sufficiency and attainment of their wants at an acceptable level. This paper defines fallout as it is used here, and it describes the development process in broad terms.

Economic fallout is the lack of individual economic self-sufficiency and the absence of a relationship with a source of willing support. Fallout is a much smaller class than dependents. There are many persons who cannot support themselves and are dependent upon someone else—wives, children, college students, grandparents. They are not fallout. There are today many who are temporarily or permanently unable to work or earn who are not dependent on any person but are very dependent upon an impersonal fund—insurance, sick leave, workmen's compensation, an annuity, etc. They are not fallout. Thus, only some non-earning persons are economic fallout. Only those are fallout who are unable to earn an income and who have no person or fund to provide for them.

There are three broad intertwined explanations for fallout: (1) the underdevelopment or misdevelopment of human individuals; (2) limitations in opportunities afforded by the market and economy; (3) special or specific adverse circumstances.

THE HUMAN DEVELOPMENT PROCESS

There is today greatly increased awareness and understanding by social scientists and lay people of the elements producing physical health, intellectual development, emotional growth, and social behavior for both the child and adult. It is as though survival alone were not accepted. "Becoming full" man or reaching human potential is sought. Although we are capable of reaching higher levels of human accomplishment than ever before, there are millions of disadvantaged people who are so underdeveloped as to be less than self-sufficient in today's society.

The four areas or dimensions of human development—physical, intellectual, emotional, and social—represent the focus of the rapidly expanding social and behavioral sciences. Information is not complete and never will be. Certain differences and uniqueness of individual human behavior cannot be fully explained, or changed or controlled by the variables that we understand at this time. Nevertheless, if some strategic elements of the environments can be altered, if new investments in underdeveloped children and adults can be made, if educational tech-

Reprinted with permission from Dimensions of Iowa Welfare, a public affairs education program of Iowa State University, Ames, the University of Iowa, Iowa City, and the University of Northern Iowa, Cedar Falls.

niques can be found and used, and if we do these things, the level of human development for most members of disadvantaged groups is sure to increase.

The process of human development is an important concern. An understanding of it is necessary before evaluating and planning health, education, and welfare services which are society's interventions in the human development process. If we are to have more people self-sufficient, attention must be given to the explanations of fallout, disadvantaged, or "culturally deprived" populations. Often in the explanation of a problem, the keys to its solution are exposed.

Concept of Development

Development was originally a biological concept. It is used to describe the process by which living systems progress toward their innate potential. The ability of the individual is limited at the peak of development either by genetic potential if the environment has been extremely favorable or more likely limited at a lower level by a deprived environment. From this biological conceptual base, human development is portrayed as a continuous dynamic process involving the total human individual who becomes more perceptive, responsive, self-controlled, and productive. Development encompasses the social, emotional, intellectual, and physical components as separate sub-systems. The human personality emerges as the sum total of development and is the result of the unique combination of individual heredity and environment.

Principles of Development

A few principles or generalizations about human development have gained wide acceptance.

1. Development proceeds in a more or less orderly fashion; there is a sequence of stages or development that are rather regular and predictable. Each step is an outgrowth of the one preceding it; and provides a base for further development. Poor development of one stage makes the next more difficult.

2. Development is multi-dimensional and the development of all dimensions need not be balanced, equal or proceed at a constant rate. The uneven level and rate of growth among dimensions is most pronounced in disadvantaged children. They may be large in size but small in intellect and misshapen emotionally. To some extent this variation in growth rate among dimensions of development is explained by the individual concentrating on one and pushing the other into the background. The variation is also due to the environment providing the inputs for normal development on one dimension and not on another. Severely arrested development on one dimension is enough to cause fallout and is most often due to the individual environment not supplying a necessary ingredient at the crucial time.

3. The impulse to grow is strong. The individual grows on what the environment offers. Environmental conditions must meet to some degree the fundamental needs for the individual or he cannot develop sufficiently to be self-sufficient and socially acceptable.

Issues in Human Development

The following three issues are crucial in understanding development and planning programs to intervene to speed up human growth and development.

Heredity-Environment Interaction

There is evidence and widespread conviction today that attainment is not predetermined, and seldom limited by inherited capacity. The capacity for development is much greater for most humans than their realized or actual skills. It is now considered accurate by social scientists to view the genetic base as providing a relatively high ceiling and the environment as influencing the extent of realized development.

Yet, great variations among individuals can be observed in intellectual, social and emotional development even in the same school and neighborhood. Most casual observers ascribe a large role to heredity. To assume or grant a strong determinant in human development need not be pessimistic. First, relying rather heavily on heredity implies that even a deprived environment cannot fully eliminate the fundamental qualities and capacities of curiosity, understanding, gregariousness, and love.

Early Experience and Stimulation

Freud and many others emphasize the crucial importance of early experience in development. The young child is impressionable. The treatment he receives emotionally, intellectually, and socially from his mother, father, and other security figures strongly affects his ultimate personality. The young child is also very pliable and takes more from the environment in early years than later.

There are several critical inputs to personality development that need to be provided early and at fairly specific times. 1) Constant or continuous warm permissive interaction with a single parenting figure is considered necessary to develop a capacity to relate to people and accept social rules. 2) A variety of early "sensory or feeling" stimuli are crucial in development of intellect and responsiveness. 3) Love expressed through bodily contact seems to be needed in the last half of the first year of life. From research with institutional children there is evidence that if this stimulation is not presented at this time, the children may have great difficulty developing a capacity to relate to other people.

The relative significance of early years on development is difficult to measure. The opportunity to "make up" for earlier years' deprivations decreases with time, but we don't know how fast.

Motivation for Learning and Socially Acceptable Behavior

Low intellectual development among the disadvantaged is thought to stem from the early environment a) not providing stimulating experiences, b) providing actual negative rewards for trying to learn, c) providing little reinforcement or encouragement for learning. Sequential patterns exist in learning. Disadvantaged people may gain less from a later experience because they did not have a necessary previous mental concept, word, or data.

Achievement motivated behavior is directed toward the attainment of approval or the avoidance of disapproval by good performance in situations where standards are set. This kind of behavior evolves (or fails to develop) from the experience of pleasant (or unpleasant) feelings about meeting (or failing to meet) set standards.

Some disadvantaged or dependent people are thought to be low achievers who refuse to try when standards are set. Thus, it is suggested that children, especially children from culturally deprived families, need achievable standards set for them. They should be protected from frequent impossible tasks posed by the immediate environment. They need appropriate rewards and new experiences for trying hard and achieving.

Motivations are learned or conditioned. Intellectual development results from learning and motivation. How to motivate, stimulate, reward, and punish to produce high achievers with socially acceptable behavior is a big issue.

Stages in the Cycle of Development

The foregoing may be summed up by an illustration. An analytical scheme of personality development assumes a central problem or need for each stage of development. The developmental need exists throughout life, but the stages represent the most crucial and appropriate times for meeting it.

This sketch of life stages and personality traits to be developed during each stage assumes that the various "senses" once developed will persist. Each personality is, thus, a unique combination of the traits as developed and under-developed. The stages and traits are, of course, over-simplified.

LIFE STAGE	CAPACITY TO BE DEVELOPED
Infancy	- a basic sense of trust of people (vs. mistrust). The trait develops by having needs met in a consistent fashion and from being loved for one's own self and receiving healthy, consistent response to behavior, i.e., stimulation and reinforcement.
Early Childhood	- a sense of autonomy, self-confidence (vs. shame and doubt) a feeling of being independent with freedom to make some choices and assume responsibility.
Preschool age	- a sense of initiative, self-direction, self-starting (vs. hesitancy) a pleasure of doing, of expression, the internal push to explore and investigate.
School age	- a sense of work and competence (vs. inferiority) a drive to acquire skills and accept and complete tasks. Work habits are formed at this time and support is needed from teachers and parents.
Adolescence	- a sense of identity or wholeness (vs. diffusion). The need to discover and clarify who one is, what roles are to be played, and what response one should make and expect from others.
Young adult	- a sense of intimacy (vs. isolation) an ability to completely share oneself with others, to be able to relate to different kinds of people in changing situations.
Adult	- a sense of generativity of group service (vs. self-absorption) a motivation for behavior derived from concern for others, the ability to postpone one's own gratification to gratify another.
Maturity	- a sense of integrity and completeness (vs. despair) the ability to accept one's life history and future as having meaning and purpose, and accept this for others also.

Implications for Intervention and/or Investment in Human Development

Heredity is an important factor or force in human development but heredity is seldom limiting on human development.

Environment is important. This implies that parts of the environment are candidates for adaptation to increase the level of human development. There is virtual consensus that the earlier years have a persistent effect on later behavior, personality, and development. Therefore, for some young children, if a deprived or barren environment could be improved, the human development of these children could be increased. The effect would continue—in school, in marriage, in work, in society. Economic fallout would be reduced in the next generation. Physical underdevelopment is seldom the cause of dependency and disadvantage. Emotional, intellectual, and social underdevelopment are often the cause of economic fallout and dependency. The very early years before school are almost dominant and determinant of eventual social, intellectual, and emotional development. The significant environmental factors in these early years are in the home and especially in the relationships and activities between the parents and the children. In this critical intimate early family environment, society is reluctant, inexperienced and not very capable at intervention. Research evidence, however, is piling up to show that if development of children in deprived families is to improve, the family needs help from society at this stage. The family needs help to do the job it wants to do but is having difficulty doing. Much more effect at much less effort could be accomplished in the early years before school than if intervention is postponed until school, adolescence, or adulthood. Much can be done to improve the school environment. But priority for intervention seems to lie in improving the environment of the early preschool years if social, intellectual and emotional development is to be enhanced.

Some neighborhoods and social economic classes exhibit a higher proportion of low achievers and deviant behavior. This is human underdevelopment or misdevelopment. The cause is a widespread weakness in the environment; it lacks or is unable to provide some of the ingredients needed for human development. The implication for intervention is that these concentrations need group methods, massive changes in the environment both inside the home and in the schools, on the streets. There is a fear and a possibility that large concentrations of deviant behavior and underdeveloped human populations might persist over generations because of internalization of values and motivations, child rearing patterns, etc. The implication is that they cannot "pull themselves up by their bootstraps" but require a massive outside "investment" which would intervene to improve the environment and raise the level of human development.

FALLOUT NOT DUE TO HUMAN UNDERDEVELOPMENT

Even if a person has been able to develop his physical, intellectual, and social qualities to the fullest, he may still be prevented from utilizing and benefiting from these attributes. Circumstances in the economic setting may not afford job opportunities to enable him and his family to live comfortably. And special setbacks may cause severe income or family living hardship.

The Economic Environment

The particular state of the overall economy when a person enters the employment stream, has a lot to do with the extent to which he is able to utilize his developed capacities and secure a decent living level. Recall the bright, well-educated college graduates of the Depression days, who felt lucky to earn $15 a week selling shoes or clerking in small offices. Even the most efficient of Iowa farmers have a hard time getting along at the bottom of the hog price cycle.

A booming U.S. economy and a low overall rate of unemployment doesn't necessarily mean well-being for all. The kinds and amounts of human services demanded are continually shifting from one industry to another and one place to another as a result of changes in population locations, consumer preference, technological advances, and transportation facilities. Here in Iowa we find many people confronted with such problems at some stage of life: young couples who are struggling on farms that are too small in counties where there are few opportunities for employment off the farm; shopkeepers in outlying rural towns whose customers are driving over new highways to do their buying in larger cities; the workers of a town left unemployed when the local packing plant is closed down. Over the long pull, we would expect people to prepare themselves for new kinds of occupations or to move elsewhere, but these shifts are not always easy for a person to make, especially if he is beyond his 20's and 30's.

There are some groups who—no matter how prosperous their locality, how well-prepared they are to fill job needs, and how much they desire to find productive roles—have difficulty in finding means of supporting themselves and their families adequately. Women, non-whites, and persons with police records may find themselves discriminated against when seeking jobs, offering professional services, or attempting to establish businesses. Many have to take work at lower incomes than others doing the same thing, or they may have to go into occupations that do not make full use of their capacities.

Older people are a special and increasingly important group among the "discriminated" whom economic prosperity frequently passes by and who often find themselves in situations of economic hardship. Medical breakthroughs are resulting in more people living much longer; yet at the same time, the tendency is for employers to insist on workers retiring at an earlier age. Even with the expansion of Social Security and various private retirement plans, many occupational groups do not have adequate provision for all old age support. The plight of many old people is worsened by the fact that they are having to live on fixed annuities or investment incomes in the midst of rising living costs. Hand in hand with their economic problems are the psychological problems of the elderly—the feelings of uselessness associated with the longer years outside the employment stream, the isolation brought about by tendencies for friends and relatives to disperse to other places, increasing reluctance to become dependent on children for support, etc.

Special Adverse Circumstances

Even in a society where all young people can develop to their full potentials and all have adequate income-earning opportunity, there will still be some temporary or permanent fallout as a result of special unfortunate circumstances.

Illness, injury, or death of the family wage earner, can place a family in dire straits. Many occupations are still not covered by adequate insurance, compensation, or medical plans, and the plans which are available are usually geared more to the status of the wage earner than to the needs of family members dependent upon him were there to be an emergency. People are prone to hope for the best, rather than to set money aside for a "rainy day," either directly or through private insurance arrangements. And, whereas 100 years ago families and neighbors took it upon themselves to buffer one another against such setbacks, there is probably less feeling of mutual responsibility today.

There may be special setbacks caused by external events beyond the control of any one individual. It is difficult for most families to hedge themselves against all the kinds of calamities that might happen—fire, tornadoes, floods, disease epidemics, riots, losses from crime or fraud, etc. The odds of one or more of these events confronting an Iowa family are low, but being the victim can shift one rapidly from a well-off situation to dire circumstances.

IMPLICATIONS OF ECONOMIC FALLOUT

The consequences of human fallout go far beyond the loss of economic well-being to the individuals directly affected. Family poverty disorder sets off a spiral effect (poorer human development influences, living in less desirable neighborhoods, less opportunity for good schooling, etc.) which makes it difficult for children of such families to develop to full genetic potential. Secondly, there are the multiplied effects on other people in the community, state and nation: (a) the loss of national production resulting from persons who have not been able to develop and utilize their inherent capabilities, (b) pain, fear and embarrassment (fear of being crime victims, discomfort of encountering poverty and disadvantages), and (c) the social costs of measures to help disadvantaged people or to prevent others from becoming disadvantaged.

The three interrelated sources of fallout that we have discussed—poor human development, lack of economic opportunity, and special setbacks—cannot all be alleviated entirely by individual families alone. The family is the key element at the early stages of a person's lifetime in developing his physical, emotional, intellectual, and social qualities. The schools continue the development of the growing young person. He also needs to be steered into an occupation that has a future and to be equipped with the vocational and human qualities needed for his productive, orderly life. A community can help to create local job opportunities, good schools. The general economic climate that an individual finds himself in is very much a reflection of success at the national government level in stimulating investment, stabilizing price and employment cycles, and buffering declines in certain regions or industries. And, no matter how prosperous the state or nation is as a whole, there will always be "disasters" beyond the power of a family or community to solve without the help of outside resources.

Are the most serious bottlenecks in the area of human resource development, or in providing additional and more equitable economic opportunities, or in buffering the consequences of special adverse circumstances?

The issues leaders and professional welfare workers must help solve center around four questions:

1. Who is disadvantaged?
2. How much help should they receive?
3. Which kind of help is best?
4. Who should pay?

Proposal for a New Institution:
The Family as a Corporate Entity

by Sol Tax

For decades we have watched what many have thought was the disintegration of the family, as its traditional functions have been pre-empted by other social institutions in the industrializing world; as mobility has increased; and with increasingly single-standard sex freedom. Alarms that "the family" is becoming extinct are countered by data showing that in many of the populations of our most industrialized nations nuclear families continue strong, and in others, that large extended families maintain functional cooperation even when their members are geographically dispersed.

I recently attended a conference at the University of Chicago on "Social Policy, Social Ethics, and the Aging Society." The advance notice indicated as the first two of the *Illustrative Issues to be Addressed*:

1. Questions of intergenerational allocations: what proportion of the society's resources should go to the young, to the adult, and to the aged? What proportion of the GNP should go into private and public pension systems? Or, with regard to health services, where some thirty per cent now go to the ten per cent of the population who are over sixty-five, is this a "just" distribution? In answering such questions, shall we follow a cost-benefit analysis, where benefits are weighed in terms of economic productivity? Or should we look to the rights older persons possess because they are members of the society, whereby their claims rest not upon their potential or past productivity but upon their humanity? How do we balance questions of the individual's rights against the good of society?

2. Can a society whose goal is the improvement of the material standard of living fulfill the more profound needs of the human spirit, whether the person is young or old? What does it mean to grow old in a society oriented toward productivity? As societies have historically become less bound by biological and economic constraints and have developed higher forms of culture, should the presence of large numbers of the old be itself regarded as a measure of human achievement? Should we cherish the aged because their presence symbolizes man's most humane values?

Excellent papers were prepared; the participants were good; the discussion was lively and serious. I learned a great deal. What struck me was that throughout the conference there was a complete by-passing of "the family" as a unit of the larger society. Institutions like Retirement, Hospitals, Social Security, Health Insurance were much in discussion; so were individuals as recipients of services; and classes of individuals, especially age-cohorts. This was best illustrated by discussion of the political dilemma raised by the fact that growing segments of the "unproductive" population—those under eighteen and those over sixty-five—must be supported from public funds provided by a shrinking "productive" segment which would sooner or later rebel. I wondered if the middle-aged taxpayers would not realize better than we that we were talking about their own children in school, on the one hand, and their own parents on the other; and whether they would think it better or worse if the financial responsibility for their education and care were to revert entirely to them. And it occurred to me that whatever the answer, we were discussing policy as though family units had ceased to exist, and that nothing except special interest groups now stands between the whole society on one side and our individual identification number on the other.

Reprinted from the *Center Report*, a publication of the Center for the Study of Democratic Institutions, Santa Barbara, California.

Dr. Sol Tax is Professor of Anthropology at the University of Chicago and is Director of the Center for the Study of Man at the Smithsonian Institute.

Yet at least some families exist and join in old-fashioned church congregations and community mutual help organizations. The problem might be, I thought, that though we value families in political oratory, and in commercial celebrations of holidays, we are effectively by-passing and neglecting them — and perhaps not for any better reason than that we are all equally caught up in the system. Might we — public officials and scholars — sitting in this conference hall, only by counting them out, be encouraging the atrophy of the family and other local institutions?

In the days that followed, thought and inquiry suggested that with rare exceptions, government indeed does not recognize the existence of the family. The household as a census and income-tax unit, yes; the marriage relationship and legal disabilities of children, yes. There are other exceptions to emphasize the rule that the family is not part of our political thought. In 17th and 18th century Europe no great geographical mobility moved households away from their kin, and most were doubtless located in extended families. But the political philosophers seem to have seen only nuclear families of parents and young children, each ending as soon as the children could survive independently. In developing theories of the state, they could therefore ignore kinship units. In "the war of each against all," the "each" referred to a man who was protecting his wife and children as well as property.* A reason why English, French, and American government policy deals rather with individuals (and fictive individuals) than with families may lie in such perceptions. The families which were empirically important in those times may also have been neglected by social theorists because scholars early distinguished the political economy from the domestic (family or household) economy — as in the opening pages of Rousseau's *Discourse on Political Economy* — and developed theory concerning the first alone. Indeed, studies by Europeans of family systems did not crystallize until the second half of the 19th century, after they had learned of such non-European kinship oddities as matrilineal systems. It is therefore possible that accidents of intellectual histories, rather than social realities, lie behind a current disjunction between national policies and the fulfillment of particular goals that are in fact desired.

The question of what to do about something is always somewhat independent of analysis of the cause. Thus the cause of a fire in the attic might be some oily rags in a corner, or a short circuit in the wiring; but it is still put out with water, and one normally goes for water first. So in the present case I wondered at once what one could do to make use of an institution that may be weakened from disuse, but persists strongly in sentiment and more strongly than we are aware in our population. My suggested answer: *Give the family legal status as an entity.* I outlined it in a letter to several colleagues, as follows:

> *I have an idea of how public policy might be enlisted to slow down and even turn around the continuing tendency toward weakening the family. The 'idea,' most badly stated, is to give legal status to extended families who want it, and making this advantageous. A new variant of corporate-form, e.g., partnerships, cooperatives, or small (non profit?) corporations would be chartered for families which find it advantageous (under such a charter) to pool resources over some generations, perhaps including health and life insurance, pensions, social security, etc. 'The family' as a voluntary corporate group might begin with the three generations but extend indefinitely horizontally and vertically, with new members enlisted by marriage (involving choice of family) and subsequent births. The law would of course provide means for individuals to leave the corporate group, and for the corporate group to be dissolved.*

*A negative proposition is difficult to document; but I have looked again at relevant parts of Locke's *Concerning Civil Government*, Hobbes' *Leviathan*, Montesquieu's *The Spirit of Laws*, Rousseau's *A Discourse on Political Economy* and *The Social Contract*, and Adam Smith's *The Wealth of Nations;* and see no hint that a nation might be thought of as a multitude of families as it has been, for example, in China.

The incorporation of the family would be functional to the degree that it could take advantage of other institutions in the private and public sectors of our society that provide advantages to groups and which limit liability in cooperative endeavors. But the value of such a new institution would be greatly enhanced if the administration of social services now going to individuals would alternatively and advantageously be offered them to encourage the growth and spread of the new institution as a matter of public policy. This contrasts with a situation in which most social services tend to replace rather than to utilize family ties. What I am suggesting is not simply better use of the three or four generations who now remain in contact, but the possibility of continuing groups also horizontally. Recent work on black extended families is suggestive here.

The above was a bare-bones statement of the proposal. I now have other "first thoughts," some of which I mention only to provoke dialogue about the possibility of developing a reliable model of the legalized Family.

A child born into the family is a member (shareholder) to begin with, the share coming from some common pot into which those of deceased members also go. But otherwise being a member (shareholder) is voluntary, and a newly married couple retain their individual memberships, or together choose one or the other family, or none (or possibly half-shares in each, if multiple memberships become part of the model).

It is everybody's inalienable right to "join" one or another of his/her families which have already been chartered or which he/she might help to organize and charter.

Kinship includes adoption; and a chartered family as a whole can adopt a person. (If multiple memberships become part of the model, there might be a distinction between adoptive and other kin).

Geographic propinquity is not a condition of membership.

A single household of husband-wife-children is not chartered as a family at least until one or more of the children marry. At some point, they can get a charter to be a new family, or can stay where they were.

After legislation is passed by Congress, Federal charters are available as freely as possible, within the law established and entirely on a voluntary basis. An individual can remain unattached forever (except those born into families, who will at some point be free to opt out or to change families).

Once families are chartered they may be treated in law as fictive individuals for many purposes, some spelled out in the original legislation, others from time to time as governments and the private sector offer new services and benefits. Income tax liability, and such contracted benefits as for retirement and social security might be pooled for chartered families.

In its subsequent evolution, a family might join larger family-type groups, so that members of an endogamous religious sect, or a community of American Indians, might make themselves legally a single family.

It is clear that to go further in establishing models of the new institution will require further analysis by people with as wide a variety of relevant knowledge as possible. For instance, the part of the model most interesting and difficult to develop might be the functional equivalents of management and of corporate directors and officers. Depending on what the family "does," these may be unnecessary; and in any case, they are likely to be very different; to imagine alternatives requires a great deal of recent knowledge of the operation of non-hierarchical groups.

Public Social Policy and Families in the 1970s

by Catherine S. Chilman

Partial, inexpensive programs addressed primarily to changing people rather than systems can not meet the problems created by a supertechnological society

In the 1960s, official concern about public social policies rose to new heights. There was less public concern about families as families during this period, although much attention was given to individuals and families who were victims of racism and poverty.

Today, the United States appears to have become almost a different country. Official interest in public social policy, in terms of positive development of a high quality of life for all people, has dwindled to a small flicker, and concern for the poor, the non-white, and the Spanish-speaking has been all but extinguished under the deluge of cries for law and order and lower taxes. It is even claimed that families no longer have a function. Attempts to defuse the population bomb plus other contemporary forces of social change have undermined long-cherished beliefs about the values of family life.

The high hopes of the early 1960s that the country was again mobilizing itself to reduce its numerous social problems through enlightened rational action have been all but destroyed by the tragic events of the last ten years. And many American families, lacerated by these tragedies and the stresses of a supertechnological society, have found their marriages faltering under the impact of contemporary conditions. Many parents who earnestly strove in the past several decades to create healthy, happy children are stricken by troubled youngsters who have been battered by the pressures of a society grown increasingly hostile and uncaring of its young.

Along with the current disillusionment with public social policy, with the potential contributions of the family, with the legitimate rights of the poor and excluded goes another dangerous trend: a disbelief in the importance and power of rational planning to deal with the problems of our society. We can not afford these disillusionments and disbeliefs. We can not permit our nation to drift on a tide of disengagement, fear, weariness, and pessimism. Despite the agonies of the past decade, it is imperative to try again.

Public social policy can and must be developed in a far more knowledgeable and effective way than in the past. Although it may take many different forms in the coming years, the family does have a future. People will continue to need to belong to small, intimate groups based on love, commitment, interdependence, and shared activities. The need for close, supporting human relationships is probably more crucial than at earlier times in our history because the larger society has become so impersonal and complex. Although most families in the future will be smaller, the majority will probably have children—and children will always need parents to whom they uniquely belong, even though child care centers may increasingly share the task of child-rearing.

To a considerable extent, the well-being of society is intertwined with the well-being of its families, and the reverse is also true. Although families at all socioeconomic levels are suffering from contemporary stresses, the poor and excluded suffer the most. If we do not improve

Catherine S. Chilman, Ph.D., *Social Casework,* Vol. 54, No. 10, December 1973, pp. 575-585. Published by Family Service Association of America. Reprinted with permission.

Dr. Catherine S. Chilman is Professor and Coordinator of Research, School of Social Welfare, University of Wisconsin, Milwaukee, Wisconsin.

on the efforts of the recent past to bring them into full, secure membership in our communities, we will have neither the right nor the power to continue as a modern, industrialized, largely urban nation.

The problems that confront us are enormous. We should take heart from the knowledge that some of them have been partially reduced by public policies evolved over the years. However, progress has been slow and partial; at almost no time have these policies been purposefully addressed to the well-being of families, even though families have often benefited from them. It is time to press for more rapid and extensive development of public social policies that take into account both individual and family welfare.

By family welfare, the writer does not mean that family unity should take precedence over all considerations of individual welfare. In fact, we have often sacrificed the needs of individuals to the value of family stability. We have often asked the well members of the family to sacrifice themselves for the sick ones and, quite typically, have expected that wives and mothers should put aside their own needs and interests for those of children and husbands. Policies and programs that support family well-being should support the developmental needs of all family members and, simultaneously, take into account the importance and sensitivities of family relationships. These policies and programs need to be related to broad public social policies.

RISING INTEREST IN PUBLIC SOCIAL POLICY

Social policy is frequently written and talked about, but much less frequently defined. An often encountered view is that social policy consists of statements of principles emanating from some vague place in Washington, such as "Every child shall have free access to high quality education," "The family is America's most sacred institution and we shall move in all ways to protect and strengthen it," or "No family shall know hunger." Much can lie between such stated principles and their development and implementation; if policy is to mean anything, it must be translated into action.

Many social scientists with a special interest in the family emphasize a national family policy as distinct from an overall national social policy. Some call for a bureau or department of family development operating at federal and state levels. They take their lead from such countries as France and Belgium, where strong family organization movements push for national policy devoted primarily to the economic well-being of the family.

A variety of family assistance programs tied to a national family policy has developed in these countries over the past forty years. However, in most of the Scandinavian countries and in England and Holland, there is considerable confusion as to whether family policy is a distinct entity that might be clearly differentiated from social policy. Alva Myrdal makes a strong case for national social policies, implemented by rational social planning, which support the total needs of individuals and families—health, housing, employment, education, economics and recreation. She describes the Swedish system to illustrate her arguments.[1]

This writer agrees with Myrdal's position. There is much to be lost and little to be gained by arguing that public policy in the United States should be subdivided into various segments, with one of the segments being family policy. Since virtually all public policies affect families, it is more realistic to promote sound social, economic, and political policies that offer promise of aiding the people of the country, nearly all of whom belong to families, in one way or another. As these policies are developed, the needs and characteristics of a diversity of families and family members should be taken into account.

---

[1]Alva Myrdal, *Nation and Family* (Cambridge: The M.I.T. Press, 1968).

In the past, it has proven virtually impossible to build sufficient support for comprehensive government family policies in this country.2 Persistent American values are involved: The American tradition of individualism, rather than familialism, affords little basis for this support. The historical division of church and state in the United States appears to have the same effect, concern with the family being traditionally allocated to church rather than to state. Political power groups are generally organized along occupational, rather than family-oriented lines; strongly held cultural values regard the family as being uniquely private—the last refuge of the individual against overpowering and huge public and private bureaucracies.

A MORE COMPREHENSIVE APPROACH

Public social policy should be based on an understanding that social problems and their solutions are intricately related to each other and to the much larger system of which society is a part—the economic, political, and social subsystems of the societal universe. The concepts of physical ecology are becoming increasingly clear to policy-makers, planners, and at least part of the citizenry; a greater conceptual clarity about what might be termed social ecology is also needed. The concept of social ecology means that all the subsystems of society are intricately interrelated. A change in the economy, for instance, affects both governmental and social operations; changes in the government affect economic, as well as social, functioning.

For this reason, public social policy needs to be linked to economic and political policies in knowledgeable and planful ways. This concept might well call for a highly centralized, authoritarian superstate, although the experience of nations that have taken this route warn of the many dangers and problems involved. Can we not somehow muster the enlightened good sense and popular commitment to a common cause that seeks to accomplish a sophisticated, comprehensive planning approach within a democratic framework?

It is appropriate for those who decry increases in governmental powers to consider the presence of enormous private corporate power in the United States today. The capacity of the business-industrial-communications complex to control and manipulate our lives is only dimly recognized. Many of our apparent freedoms are illusory; many of our opportunities for individual decision-making are sharply restricted. Partly because families have no special lobby, they are particularly weak in the face of organized corporate interests. The average citizen can have almost no impact on private power, but, through his vote and other forms of political activity, he has a far greater chance to affect the operations of public power.

If a family is to enjoy a state of well-being in today's society, it must have sufficient income; adequate housing; opportunities for health care, education, employment, and recreation; ready access to transportation; effective community services; and a chance to participate in decision-making in both the private and public sectors of the society. When only some of these factors are present, families and their members are likely to be in trouble.

In general, we have tended to try to resolve "people problems" by partial methods aimed at changing individuals rather than the larger society. We have pushed the schools—and the children and their parents— to educate all youngsters so that they could eventually become self-supporting, well-behaved, knowledgeable citizens. When this operation fails to produce such paragons in great numbers, the schools —or the parents—are blamed. But education, alone, can not solve the problems of human growth and development and adaption to a complex, frequently inhumane society. Nor can the families who send their children to school.

2The only specific national, public family policies that we have at present come close to being anti-family policies. They include family planning programs addressed primarily to reductions in the birth rate and AFDC programs that, in over twenty states, exclude families when an able-bodied male is in the home, provide miserly public assistance, and particularly emphasize getting mothers off welfare and into the work force.

All systems of society must operate effectively together to make it possible for children to develop adequately and to have a chance to use their developed talents as youths and adults. All systems of society must operate together effectively if families are to establish and maintain a climate that supports the continuing growth and development of both children and adults. But this kind of operation alone is not sufficient.

These systems of society need to take into account the dynamics of the family which is a small ecological system interacting with the rest of society. Society's systems tend to make strenuous and frequently conflicting demands on the family. For example, the school may ask working parents without a car to participate in a conference with the teacher about one of their children; these same parents may have another child with a serious physical ailment requiring distant and expensive medical services; the mother may need to work overtime to avoid endangering her job; the children may belong to youth organizations that complain because neither of the parents contributes leadership or extra donations; money may be a constant problem to this family, partly because housing is expensive in the "good" neighborhood where they want their children to grow up. Such parents feel overwhelmed with the demands and inadequacies of the many systems with which they must interact; they rightfully feel that the family has little power to counteract the situation.

Pressures reverberate throughout a family, affecting the marriage and parent-child relationships and the resultant hostilities and anxieties affect the behavior of both children and parents in their interactions with society. Insensitive feedback from the various social systems then affects each family member and intensifies internal disturbances. And society is apt to proclaim that the family has "failed"; socialized in today's culture, the members may well accept this diagnosis, which makes their problems worse.

What is needed is better policy-making that includes awareness of the needs of families as dynamic interaction units linked to all the social systems. These more powerful systems need to protect and support the family as a complex unit, rather than demanding that families be strained and fragmented in an attempt to cope with an inadequately organized and only partially adequate society. These systems, moreover, as suggested above, need to be updated, modified, and coordinated through enlightened public policies, planning, and programs if society and its families are to weather the stresses of the years ahead. Thus, staffs and advisory councils of government agencies engaged in social policy and planning should include specialists in family functioning. And persons concerned about the well-being of society and its families need to add to their skills some knowledge of the public social policy processes so that they can affect the political and other governmental processes that both create public policy and put it into operation.

PUBLIC SOCIAL POLICY AND ITS PROCESSES

Social policy is a process, rather than a mere statement of principles. Public policy is constantly in flux and, therefore, is most appropriately studied and discussed within the framework of the policy-making process. This process is a species of decision-making activities involving large numbers of individuals and groups.

Public policy might be seen as consisting of three related parts: the development of a set of guiding principles; ongoing decision-making through legislative, judicial, and administrative processes; and policy implementation through governmental arrangements.

FACTORS AFFECTING PUBLIC POLICY-MAKING

Although rational public social policy processes directed toward comprehensive planning for the well-being of society and its people are both desirable and necessary, the question remains as to whether they are likely to occur. There are a number of constraints that are apt to inhibit the rational, overall approaches that are needed. These constraints include the nature and structure of federal, state, and local governments; the operation of special interest or power groups; the processes by which legislation is developed and adopted, budgets are constructed, appropriations passed, and programs are administered; the inadequate development and input of scientific knowledge; the impact of group attitudes and values; and the resources and situation of the nation.

Operation of the Federal Government

One might call the government of the United States a nongovernment government. It is no wonder that our symbol is Uncle Sam—an uncle with only indirect and vague powers over his nephews and nieces, the states. Domestic policy, as distinct from foreign policy, is only partially developed at national levels. With a few exceptions, Washington proposes but the states make the actual decision as to whether they will or will not accept the proposals. The federal government has had at its disposal federal aid for various social purposes such as public housing, community mental health centers, welfare services, family planning programs, and to acquire these benefits the states are asked to contribute some of their own funds and live up to certain standards. To varying degrees, states have cooperated with Washington, but the resulting alliances have been generally fraught with continual bickering and nagging incompatibilities. At present, action by the president to impound much of the funding for these constitutes a grave threat both to the programs and to the democratic process.

Another problem—or perhaps salvation—resides in the so-called balance of powers at the federal level. No one person or group of persons has final power in the development and passage of legislation, the formation and passage of appropriations, the development and implementation of policy, or even settling the question of whether or not legislation is constitutional. The miracle is that legislation passed by Congress ever becomes operative at state and local levels. That it does so is a tribute to the vitality, intelligence, and awareness of citizen groups at all levels of government. Here, again, there is current concern for the erosion of Congressional powers most vividly seen in the frequent use of the presidential veto, as well as impoundment of appropriations.

The Power of Special Interest Groups

It is well known that the federal government is strongly influenced by special interest groups: business and industry, the military, labor, organized medicine, and education. These interest groups are mostly occupational and a central interest is the economic well-being of their memberships. Such lobbies, by their very nature, are not particularly interested in supporting public social policies directed toward the well-being of people in general or families in particular. Their focus is largely on the economic security and advancement of the individuals who belong to these groups, making it difficult to mobilize support for social policy that includes family needs.

Social policy, in fact, differs from other types of policy, and these differences are of a character to make the discovery of who formulates it most difficult. Policies in such fields as agriculture, business regulation, and the like, are pointed to a specific, easily defined group. Social policy, in contrast, is more like urban policy. The clients are diffuse, normally unorganized, and, even more significant, the policies are designed for people primarily in their consuming roles, rather than their producing roles. Yet, society to the extent that it is organized into interest groups tends to organize around production roles rather than consumption roles. Consumer groups (including, importantly, the family), those for whom most social policy is designed, tend to be the most unorganized, and therefore, politically the weakest. . . .

> *The great periods of economic reform in American life were from 1870 to 1914 and the New Deal years. . . . It seems unlikely that a politically powerful majority coalition made up of a number of minority groups pressing for social change is possible today. It is somehow difficult to imagine that a working political coalition of civil rights groups, college students, clergymen and the poor can replace the familiar triad of organized farmers, organized labor and small businessmen.*[3]

The fact that a national social policy is far less specific, readily amenable to quantitative measurements, and less clearly concerned with nationwide problems than a national economic policy makes it more difficult to mobilize public support for it. It took the severe economic depression of the 1930s to convince the people of this nation that a national economic policy was needed. The current social depression should, however, provide impetus for support of a national social policy, although it may be difficult to achieve. Among other things, in support of such a policy, we need further development of social indicators and a social advisory council to the president and Congress.

Process of Developing Legislation

Although legislation may be proposed by the executive branch of government, it is disposed through the actions of the House of Representatives and the Senate and their various committees; adoption obviously depends on political factors. Public policy, as shaped through the legislative process, can be significantly affected by an extremely small group of senators or representatives, many of whom have gained powerful committee positions by mere seniority. Attempts to reform this system have been notably feeble; greater public pressure on this score is surely called for. A closely related problem is that congressmen are immensely and necessarily concerned with gaining widespread recognition for their political leadership in relation to specific problems of intense concern to the electorate—not only the electorate of their own state or district but of the nation as a whole.

An appeal to congressmen to press for a broader, more comprehensive approach to social legislation is apt to have little acceptance, because such an approach cuts across committee structures, diffuses lobby supports, and detracts from the congressman's special significance. Therefore, problem-specific leadership in such a field as mental illness, mental retardation, family-planning, public assistance, or drug addiction has a far greater appeal to a legislator than leadership in such a field as comprehensive social planning; social planning is a concept that is difficult for voters to grasp, involves an approach that is extremely expensive, and gives little or no recognition to special interest groups.

Once legislation has been passed and its administration delegated, programs spread across the states and tend to become institutionalized. New weaknesses are added to old ones. Thus, a plethora of projects and programs ensue at various stages of infancy, maturity, and senility.

Increased public understanding of the necessity for reordering our policies and programs and for taking a broader approach to problem solution together with support of congressmen and presidents who take such a stance should help bring about the kinds of more comprehensive legislative programs that are needed. The task is huge, partly because the United States, itself, is so vast, so complicated, and so heterogeneous. Yet these very factors have their assets. This is also a nation with vast resources of all kinds and a tradition of creative problem-solving.

Unfortunately the vast majority of citizens are naive in governmental matters. Many apparently believe that once legislation is passed, they can relax their concerned vigilance. Legisla-

[3]Alan K. Campbell, Who Makes Social Policy. Speech given at National Conference of Social Welfare, June 3, 1970 (Mimeographed), Maxwell Graduate School of Citizenship, Syracuse University, Syracuse, New York.

tion means little unless money is appropriated for its implementation and unless it is competently administered.

The Funding of Programs

The appropriation process has a number of complex components, including the budget estimates made by the department which is to implement the policy, the recommendations of the office of budget and management, the actions of the Congress and of the president. Whether an adequate appropriation is made depends on the political pressures brought to bear on the Congress and the president, the state of the national economy, tax revenues, other federal budgetary commitments, and the like. As noted earlier, the office of the president has powers to release, reduce, or withhold actual expenditures. Concerned citizens need to be alert to developments and make themselves heard on the matter of program financing.

The sharing of federal revenue with the states has become a policy of the Nixon administration, the plan being to reduce the cumbersome grant-in-aid mechanisms that became impossibly complicated with the numerous programs of the 1960s. While the time has certainly come to simplify and coordinate these many programs, a simple return of federal income to the states, with almost no standards set, threatens existing and future social programs.

For instance, many problems need national or regional, rather than state or local, approaches; numerous state and local governments see federal revenue-sharing as a way to reduce taxes through cutting back on social programs formerly required by the grant-in-aid systems; there is apt to be a more narrowly political approach to program development and administration when federal standards are reduced; and the actual amount of money currently being returned to the states is minuscule in relation to the social needs of the people. However, one positive aspect of revenue-sharing is that this freer system gives the more progressive states a larger opportunity to forge ahead in their social programs, relatively independent of today's generally backward-looking domestic policies at federal executive levels.

A word is in order here regarding the way in which taxation policy affects social policy, over and above the total amount of revenue produced by taxes. One of the fundamental functions of taxation, besides the raising of revenue, is to redistribute the wealth of the country in an effort to promote a higher level of social and economic justice. Thus taxation policy is closely related to overall social policy goals. Taxation policy is also related to the well-being of families both because it heavily affects family income and because it provides the funding resources for public programs essential to family well-being.

At the present time, many serious inequities exist in the tax system, among them the antiquated taxing methods of localities (relying heavily on regressive property and sales taxes), tax loopholes and shelters available mostly to the affluent, and the recent easing of business and corporation taxes. As public expenses mount, far more equitable, simplified, and planful ways of taxation need to be found—not an easy task, considering the complexity of the problem and the many politically powerful special interest groups involved. Increased public understanding is seriously needed, together with a far greater recognition that tax dollars are not gifts to governments but payments for public services that would otherwise be inaccessible to the vast majority of people.

Administration Resources and Methods

In order to implement public policy, an effective administrative staff is needed, a fact frequently not appreciated by the public. One of the weaknesses in the implementation of the vast amount of social legislation passed during the Johnson administration was that very little provision was made for an administrative staff to carry it out. It was not uncommon to find one staff member with half of a small office and a half-time secretary attempting to administer a whole national program, if not two or three national programs at once. This responsibility included not only mastering the related legislation, its implementing guidelines, and its attendant appropriations but also a great deal about the subject itself. It also meant establishing cordial relationships with administrative and professional personnel throughout the country and learning as much as possible about the attitudes, resources, and situations of various localities. The "race to implement" grew more and more frantic during the mid-1960s as more and more innovative social legislation was passed, some of which called for new approaches.

Attempts are currently being made to further cut the staffs in the federal executive branch. In addition, the major thrust has been to politicize the system, to reduce the number of people on civil service appointments, to subject the whole operation to business management techniques, and to make the entire bureaucracy responsive to presidential decision-making. This situation is particularly true of the Department of Health, Education, and Welfare. Although the size of its staff seems large, it is small compared to the size of the nation and the number and importance of programs involved. Further staff reductions will probably further reduce the ability of staff personnel to implement the vast array of programs so important to the well-being of the nation and its people. The work of this department calls for a high caliber of professional personnel, motivated largely by conviction about the worth of the programs, rather than by political opportunism. The attempt to administer the Department of Health, Education, and Welfare as if it were a business corporation represents a serious misunderstanding of the complex professional and scientific nature of its programs—and of the public, rather than the profit-making, nature of its missions.

The concept of making federal departments totally responsive to presidential decision-making strongly suggests both a repudiation of democratic values and a miscomprehension about the inherent nature of administration of large complex organizations. One central administrator, or even a group of central administrators, can not possibly have the requisite knowledge and informed judgment to make all the important decisions about an enterprise so vast as a federal department.

General policy-making should be the joint prerogative of the president and the Congress, with frequent inputs from the Supreme Court. Policy administration is a series of decision-making processes, both overt and covert, making their way down from top levels into numerous federal bureaus and branches and, thence, to regional, state, and local administrative units. The practices and views of the current administration seem likely to further undermine the public's belief in, and respect for, the federal government, a condition that is apt to have severe consequences throughout our society.

Impact of Knowledge and Research on Social Policy

The push during the 1960s for new directions in social policy was occasioned, in part, by the rapid increase in knowledge generated by the biological, social, and behavioral sciences and by the great fact-gathering and research operations of the government. Although social and economic problems within the country were becoming aggravated, knowledge about these problems and information about how they might be prevented or mitigated raised the popular level of awareness about the need for appropriate programs. To know what problems exist, to know that they might be reduced or prevented, and to know that many of the needed resources are at hand or can be developed to reduce the load of human misery virtually requires men of goodwill to act. Knowledge available in the biological, social, and behavioral sciences that offers promise for a "better society for all" is still rather primitive. Some believe that much more research is needed before direct action can be taken. Yet the imperatives of the times seem to demand that the nation push ahead with what knowledge is available and that simultaneous provision be made to continue to gather more knowledge.

Such an action-now approach has numerous difficulties, many of which have been demonstrated in the past decade. A large number of programs were launched more on the basis of speculative social science theory than of firm knowledge. Examples included the 1961-1965 programs of the Office of Juvenile Delinquency, chiefly based on theories that delinquency is primarily caused by the denial to poor youths of access to the opportunity system of good jobs, high quality education, social status, and the like.[4] Many of the so-called antipoverty programs were also based on the same theory. The crux of the matter is that a single plausible theory among the many available was applied to large national programs before there were sufficient time and funds to test its applicability in pilot projects. It could also be remarked that the theory, itself, was never given much of a chance. The various social systems were never importantly modified. The major thrust was, and still is, to change people rather than the systems that so unfairly and so adversely affect them. Then, too, the crucial factor—lack of adequate income for individuals and families—remained untouched.

Unrealistic promises were made about the presumed effectiveness of many action programs, resulting in the current disillusionment that most programs did not live up to their claims. These exaggerated claims, however, should not be attributed to the social scientists who provided many of the concepts for them but, rather, to those who had the job of selling the programs to the president, the Congress, and the people.

Although there is currently a widespread disenchantment regarding the contributions that research and scientific knowledge can make to public social policy, our greatest hope for more effectively tackling social problems is to develop programs that derive their fundamental rationale from the available, related research and from survey data such as those supplied from such sources as the Census, and from the Bureau of Vital Statistics and the Bureau of Labor Statistics. Simultaneously, it is essential that there continue to be both public and private support for social and behavioral research, both basic and applied. Although there are many promising leads from this research at present, we are a long way from learning what we might about how public social policies could best contribute to the healthy development and functioning of people, their families, and society. There is a particular need for additional sophisticated program research to test the impact and effectiveness of various intervention strategies.[5]

VALUES, ATTITUDES, AND TRADITIONS

Much in our culture is against national public social policies and comprehensive, rational social planning addressed to the well-being of individuals and families. Much in our culture is against costly, comprehensive programs as a substitute for relatively cheap, fragmented, problem-specific services.

Pervasive cultural changes are called for, including a shift from the highly individualistic values cherished by so many—values holding that each person should be able to "make it on his own." If a person needs help from the community, his image as an adequate person is somehow undermined. Conversely, it is held that the community should give as little help to its citizens as possible for fear that such help might make them weak and dependent.

Such concepts derive from a now-fading small farm agricultural society and from earlier stages of industrial development in which entrepreneurship and a strong bent toward productive activity was needed and frequently rewarded. The economy, the expanding frontier, and the relatively open opportunity system fostered strong values of competitiveness. Although the conditions that fostered them have changed, the values have survived. "Healthy competition in a free enterprise society" is a phrase so frequently used that it has almost taken on an aura

[4]Richard Cloward and Lloyd Ohlin, *Delinquency and Opportunity* (New York: The Free Press, 1960).
[5]Donald Campbell, Reforms as Experiments, *American Psychologist,* 24:409-29 (April 1969): see also, Donald Campbell, *Methods for the Experimenting Society.* Paper presented at the 1971 meeting of the American Psychological Association, Washington, D.C.

of religiously sanctified natural law, despite the fact that the competition is often spurious, and individual enterprise has lost its freedom to big corporations that evade the puny efforts of government to restrain them.

If the United States is to adapt effectively to the crises that are crowding upon it, new values and attitudes must emerge that are favorable to public social planning: a sense of national and international community; an acceptance of government activity as being of equal integrity and importance to that of activity in the private sector; an appreciation of complexity in problem-solution; and a readiness to change social, political, and economic institutions which are no longer adaptive to the present situation.

There is hope that these values and attitudes will emerge. Typically, neither individuals nor nations face up to their problems until the crises are upon them. The crucial factor then becomes whether the individuals or nations have the strength to face up to the problem and the resources to handle it. The key word here is *handle,* not *solve.* If we ask that our problems be solved, we are asking the impossible. Human problems are not solved. The very essence of being human involves conflict with one's self and others as well as fulfillment through one's self and with others, failure as well as success, deprivation as well as enrichment, suffering as well as pleasure, and conformity to others as well as individual expression. We should look for ways of coping with our problems better, not for abolishing them. Part of the problems of the 1970s lies in the oversimplifications of the 1960s. There will be a longer and more difficult haul than many were led to anticipate.

DO WE HAVE THE ECONOMIC RESOURCES?

The needed social policies and programs are expensive. Unless we cut back military commitments radically, current domestic needs can not be met without raising taxes. Economies in government may be sought, but they will not be sufficient. Tax loopholes may be plugged, but even this step would not yield sufficient revenue. It is said that the people of this country can not, and will not, stand for higher taxes. Yet our people have higher average earnings and retain a substantially larger proportion of their personal incomes than do the peoples of most modern nations. Many citizens, especially those in the upper income brackets, could readily afford to pay higher taxes. The question is not so much "can they?" as "will they?"

The quest for economic security drives individuals and families to acquire larger and larger incomes so that they can be ready to meet such expenses as those of health care, higher education, unemployment, and transportation. If costs of health care and higher education were more adequately met through public funds, if unemployment benefits were sufficiently high and long-lasting, if low-cost and efficient public transportation were available, then individual and familial anxiety for a high personal income would be sharply reduced. Better public transportation, better paths for bicycles and walking, and better community planning would drastically lower the need for car ownership.

The quest for the good life drives individuals and families to seek higher and higher incomes so that they will have a margin for attractive and adequate housing in a pleasant community, enjoyable recreation, and a chance to attend cultural events. If adequate and attractive housing and related public community services were reduced in price through better government planning and support, the push for large sums of money for homes in well-organized communities would be far less. If public recreation facilities were expanded and if the arts were further subsidized from public funds, it would become far less necessary to create the good life out of personal earnings.

During the 1960s, the nation slowly moved in the directions sketched here. There is need for all to renew the concern for a high quality of life for all the people and the commitment to more public programs planned for public purposes. The concept of social insurance, spreading the risks of unemployment and old age through wide participation in a taxation program, needs to be expanded to sharing the risks of poor health, educational deficits, poor housing, transportation crises, community disorganization, and recreational and cultural deprivation.

The people of this nation have the resources to provide a good life for themselves and others if they are ready to understand and accept that the good life can be more nearly achieved by a greater pooling of resources to meet many of the physical, social, and psychological needs of all its people and of all its families. Our society already has a mixed public-private economy; we need to go further in the public direction.

SUMMARY

Public social policy, to be effective, should be seen as a process, rather than a mere statement of principles. It is a process that develops and implements public social programs. This implementation requires administrative action at all levels of government and the financing of these actions and programs. It also requires popular understanding and support.

It seems essential that the people of this nation move toward the adoption of social policies based on comprehensive, rational social planning because all aspects of the political, social, and economic systems are intricately interrelated and pervasively affect the well-being of all individuals and their families. Partial, inexpensive programs, especially those addressed to primarily changing people rather than systems, can not possibly meet the human problems—or positive human potentialities—created by a supertechnological society.

If we are to move in the directions indicated and retain democratic values and methods, it seems likely that needed social programs will be developed rather slowly and piecemeal. The disadvantages inherent in a piecemeal approach will be reduced if the overall requirements and basic comprehensive pattern can be understood and kept in mind by policy-makers and the general citizenry. An alternative approach, movement toward an authoritarian state and central decision-making by a small group, runs counter to our most fundamental values and experience, while another alternative, a return to the principles of official laissez faire, would probably plunge our entire society into chaos.

Public social policy should include, but not be separate from, public family policy. Just as it should recognize the complexity and interactional dynamics of social, economic, and political systems, so it should recognize the complex interactional dynamics of that much smaller and weaker system—the family.

There are at least six major factors that constitute potential obstacles to the making and implementation of rational, comprehensive, public social policies on a nationwide basis. These are: the antiquated nature and structure of government at all levels; pressures induced by selfish special interest or power groups; the complicated processes by which legislation is developed, funded, and administered; limitations in the formation and input of scientific knowledge; the impact of outworn cultural attitudes and values; and the poor uses of national resources. Although there are important obstacles inherent in these six factors, we should be able to reduce their effects by a positive, knowledgeable approach to their origins and nature.

At the present time, there is a tendency to pessimism, disengagement, and distrust of knowledgeable attacks on human and social problems. The enormous societal changes, over-expectations, and tragedies of the decade of the 1960s have created a mood of retreat and dispair. The problems that press upon us, that threaten all our families, are more intricate and difficult of solution than many of us thought. Since they are largely human problems, they can not be solved, but they probably can be modified through a reinvestment of popular intelligence, money, and concerned effort.

A Family Services Model for Value Integration and Human Needs

by Rosalie H. Norem

While the optimum level of assessing the policy decisions affecting families in our society might be at the national level, the present functioning of service delivery networks is more readily identified at the state or community level. The mills of the policy makers grind exceedingly slow and not always very fine. Perhaps some of the wheels can be oiled at a less complex stage in the heirarchy of policy making. For this reason, this paper will discuss some possibilities for communities to assess their provision of services to families and individuals and develop a model for doing such an assessment.

In his book, *Studies in Social Policy and Planning,* Kahn discusses the following difficulties which now exist in quantity, quality and delivery of services available to families:

1. *There are not enough services.*
2. *Many social services carry a stigma in their use.*
3. *Access to services is difficult, especially for the uneducated and poor.*
4. *There is inadequate provision for case integration and case accountability.*
5. *Specialization, bureaucratization, and historical accident have created some service boundaries which are inherently dysfunctional.*
6. *The balance between resources and facilities, on one hand, and diagnostically-rendered case services, on the other, may be inappropriate, given current social status.*
7. *Manpower shortages in the relevant professional fields are serious.*
8. *There are major gaps between the case service model and the service as actually rendered.*
9. *Processes are already underway that affect the service-delivery system with reference to many of the elements here in focus. There is need to consider seriously the implications and interrelations of the several trends. (Such as HEW separating public assistance administration from public social services operations.) (pp. 245-252).*

Kahn goes on to say:

There are here then, concern and opportunity. How is the subject to be approached? What are the options for local service delivery? Some suggestions are implicit in the recent experience of family and child welfare in the United States . . . that a social service system or network in the full sense is essential, that separate, occasionally interrelated islands of service will no longer serve (p. 252).

Although this was written in 1969 during the midst of activity within the human services arena resulting from the War on Poverty and the Office of Economic Opportunity programs, the difficulties still exist in many communities. The "separate, occasionally interrelated islands of service" result at least in part from the lack of systematic assessment of

This article was prepared especially for this book.
Rosalie H. Norem, Assistant Professor in the Department of Family Environment, Iowa State University, is a doctoral student in the Department of Family Social Science, University of Minnesota, St. Paul, Minnesota.

existing services, policies and needs within a community. Fahs Beck and Jones emphasize the necessity of such assessment in their report of a nationwide survey study of family service agencies by pointing out "In fact, every agency program or policy decision influences who will or will not be served. Clarity in regard to agency goals is therefore essential" (1973, p. 5).

THE ROLE OF THE FAMILY PROFESSIONAL

In an address to the Foundation for Child Development, Senator Mondale (Dem.-Minn.) asked the question, "How strong has our commitment to families and children been in the past . . . what challenges do we face today . . . and what must we do in the future?" In terms of a human service network, this question has special meaning for professionals in the family field. The role of the family professional in relating the impact on families of public policy needs to be examined.

In discussing the role of the helping professional in planning change, Combs says, "To be effective as an agent of change in the world he lives in, the helper must begin with a feeling that it is truly important to exert himself. . . . It is easy for helpers to become preoccupied with their tasks" (1971, p. 304). As a helping professional in the family field, I might paraphrase this as a question to myself and other family professionals. How important do we feel it is to influence policy decisions which affect the family, or are we too preoccupied with our tasks to be involved?

By virtue of our professional preparation and experience, including the contact with families in a variety of settings dealing with a complexity of values and a variety of needs we have the opportunity to add to the awareness of policy making bodies regarding possible impact on families of policy decisions.

As a professional group, we have the potential and the responsibility to be involved in assessing the "complex interactional dynamics of that much smaller and weaker system—the family" (Chilman, 1973, p. 585) which are affected by public social policy. Hopefully a family professional by definition will be consistently exploring and learning about these dynamics. The problem at present is that such awareness is seldom focused in a systematic manner on problems relating to policy decisions. Helpers basically work with families and individuals at a micro-social level in a community setting, through some type of agency structure. The helper as a person is also vitally involved as an interacting element in such a system of service delivery.

HUMAN VALUES

Values are an elusive influence on every part of human functioning in our society. Because of bureaucratic complexities and the myth of objective professionalism, this influence has been relatively ignored in the policy making processes at every level.

In assessing policy decisions at the community or any level, important consideration needs to be given to the values involved in such policy. Values are the deeply ingrained beliefs we hold about people, including ourselves, about the purposes of society and about the meaning of life. The decisions made individually and collectively draw on the values we hold. Some of our values are very personal while some are shared with other members of a group such as our family, our social or professional peers or the community in general. Societal values shape our public policy but little attention is given to how this influence is felt. In his book *Unravelling Social Policy,* David G. Gil discusses these influences.

A society's dominant beliefs, values, and ideologies appear thus to constitute crucial constraining variables which limit the malleability of its processes of resource development, status allocation, and rights distribution, and of the

social policies derived from these processes.
. . . public discussion of social policies in the United States tends to neglect
these crucial variables (pp. 27-28).

The values involved in any policy decision at the community or any level needs to be given specific consideration. Because these beliefs or values are so deeply a part of each of us, conflicts which arise because of value differences become very difficult to resolve. If an awareness of the values operating among various elements in a community or the larger society were heightened perhaps value conflicts which arise in implementing policy could be minimized.

HUMAN NEEDS

Human needs are supposedly the focus of any human service provision which develops from public policy making. The questions which are not given adequate consideration are "whose needs?" and "which needs?" in relation to whose values and which values. Human services are designed haphazardly in most communities in response to a hodge-podge of identified needs, based on unidentified value constructs. The implications for the delivery of these services which could be drawn from a systematic look at values and needs are lost in the shuffle more often than not.

Wright and Burmeister define human needs as "those ideas within men which they feel they must act on in order to provide for survival of the individual, his family, his community" (1973, p. 1). This kind of definition puts the idea of a needs assessment into the realm of social interaction within a community. In doing an assessment of needs related to the provision and delivery of human services we may then focus on the basic and acquired needs of individuals within that community, as well as on the needs of the family, the agency, the community and also the human services professional. As Wright and Burmeister go on to say, "For many persons now, survival includes health and well-being, not simply existence. In either case, the focus is on the ideas concerning survival that man holds at a particular point in time. This definition of human need is appropriate for our consideration in today's world" (1973, p. 1).

A COMMUNITY BASED FAMILY IMPACT MODEL

I am suggesting a model for focusing awareness on needs, values, and resulting implications for the provision of helping services. This awareness would then allow a policy making body to take into consideration this input as part of a policy making process.

This model will define the elements operating within the community system for the delivery of human services as the individual client, the client's family, the agency being contacted for services, the individual helping professional and the community at large. The actual delivery of services operates as an interface within this system, affected by the values and needs of each of the interacting elements. The following figure illustrates this model and may facilitate awareness and assessment of those values and needs which influence the functioning of the system for the design and delivery of services.

If each of the circles can be viewed as an element within the system of helping services at the community level, it becomes possible to assess the needs of each of these elements relating to a specific policy matter and to become more aware of the values operating for each of these elements. Interaction of the needs and values of each element within the system contributes to the philosophy about helping services which is developed by that element. Ultimately those needs, values and philosophies operate within the interface influencing the type of services to be provided and the manner in which they will be made available.

To illustrate this model, we can look at a hypothetical community in terms of services provided for physically disabled adults. Each of the elements identified has values relating to

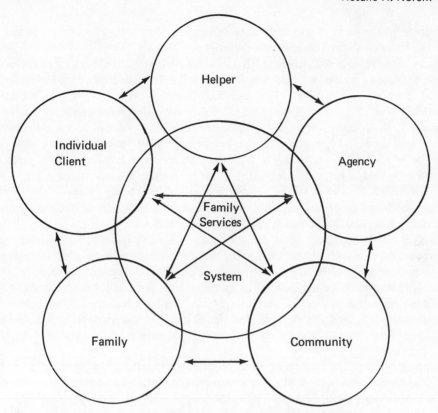

Figure 1. Community Based Family Impact Model.

physical disability. The client (the disabled adult) may value self-sufficiency, self-reliance and independence. Because of other value inputs from our society, this value of self-sufficiency may be wrapped up in the ability to have a job which permits financial independence, especially if the client is a male head of a family. Beliefs about work for pay relate to feeling worthwhile as a person for many adults in our culture.

The family of the client may value economic security and maintenance of the family unit. The spouse and children of a disabled adult family member may experience very real fears about losing a level of living which has become very important to them. This again also reflects value inputs from the larger society which places a high priority on "upward mobility."

The rehabilitation agency being contacted may value serving as many clients as possible. This could be because of strings attached to funding or struggles about eligibility requirements or any number of similar red-tape hassles. The resulting beliefs of the agency administration present a value orientation which sets a high priority on serving large numbers of people.

The community may value conformity to existing norms as most communities do. They may be uncomfortable at being asked to provide special facilities which allow disabled persons access to public places. They may be ill at ease about dealing with a disabled businessman or professional. It is easier not to have to confront such exceptions to our normative images of health and well-being, unrealistic though these images may be.

The individual helper working with the disabled adult may value the worth of each person as a unique individual, wanting to confirm the client's individuality and self-esteem. Such values about the importance of a positive self-concept are a part of a helping professional's educational background as well as a personal orientation of most persons working in this area. These examples are illustrative and not exhaustive.

Several possible value conflicts exist. If a disabled adult seeks to uphold his or her value of independence by seeking whatever employment is feasible regardless of level of income, the value of economic security held by the family may be in conflict in some situations because of disability benefits being jeopardized. If the family value of economic security is given priority and full disability benefits are secured, the community value of normative behavior may be threatened in a community which is non-accepting of a "public assistance lifestyle." The values of a rehabilitation agency to serve numbers may be in conflict with the personal values of an individual helper to use whatever time is necessary to confirm the worth of an individual client. To design a service delivery network without being aware of these possible conflicts builds in frustration and complications which ultimately cost each of the elements in the system a great deal, economically, politically and socially.

If policy making bodies can include an awareness of existing values as part of their decision making process, changes might be made in the process which would facilitate minimizing such costs. One example relating to the situation being discussed here of provision of services to disabled adults might be the inclusion of an educational program for the community about the abilities and talents of disabled persons. A similar kind of educational effort has been made through public media by the "Hire the Handicapped" messages on television. Without recognition of existing values which could cause conflict, such provisions often get left out of policy formulations.

As previously stated, the values operating in a specific situation are only one part of this model. The needs of each element also are extremely important and can be more systematically assessed than typically is done. To use the same example as above regarding the provision of services to a physically disabled adult, the following needs are examples which might be considered.

The client has a need for special transportation facilities; the family has a need for affordable housing; the agency has a need for a central location; the community has a need for a balanced budget; the individual helper has a need for identifying existing resources and coordinating them to function as an effective helper for the client. Perhaps a small community which cannot afford public transportation but is a source of inexpensive adequate housing is served by a rehabilitation agency in a nearby city.

Through an assessment of needs of the various elements of the model several examples of a conflict of needs operating in the delivery of services interface are identified. If such a needs assessment were done as part of a policy planning process in the design of a human services system perhaps a more realistic system would develop. Obviously just being aware of values and assessing needs will not resolve arising conflicts. However, it would seem that the family professional could make an important contribution to the emerging focus on family impact by systematically applying such awareness and assessment to the planning process as it relates to the delivery of services.

REFERENCES

Chilman, Catherine. "Public Social Policy and Families in the 1970's" *Social Casework,*
    Vol. 54, No. 10, Dec., 1973, pp. 575-585.
Combs, Arthur, et. al. *Helping Relationships.* Boston: Allyn and Bacon, Inc., 1971.
Fahs Beck, Dorothy, and Mary Ann Jones. *Progress on Family Problems.* New York: Family
    Service Association of America, 1973.
Gill, David G. *Unravelling Social Policy.* Cambridge, Mass.: Schenkman Publishing Company,
    1973.

Kahn, Alfred J. *Studies in Social Policy and Planning.* New York: Russel Sage Foundation, 1969.
Wright, Joan and William Burmeister. *Introduction to Human Services.* Columbus, Ohio: Grid, Inc., 1973.

3C POLICY DIRECTION AND OUR VALUE SYSTEM

Child Care Policy

An article in *The Washington Post*, "Trouble Seen in Shrinking U.S. Families," reported on the decline in members per family and the effect this would have on various aspects of family life. In general, the predictions were negative, with the increase in single-person households, families headed by single women, and families with both parents in the workforce cited as major problems. However, Virginia Satir, family therapist and author, was quoted as saying of the census report, "I think those are kind of nice statistics myself. The positive part is that if families are getting smaller, this means we really are beginning to look at, in a more human way, the fact that it takes a lot to develop people. . . . Human institutions—marriage, the family—are changing in the direction of becoming more human . . . and will present a lot of people with new ways of making choices. It's not always going to be easy . . . A lot of people will feel very uncomfortable. But I think it's a healthy sign."[1]

If fewer numbers of children will mean that each child will benefit from more responsible parenting and from those programs aimed at helping families with children, then we may be entering a golden age for childhood. It is at the macro level of national policy making that the micro needs of families must be incorporated. The parameters of child care policy are confusing because it is first necessary to decide what we wish to support before we can decide how we are going to implement a program. What, indeed, does becoming "more human" mean? If this is a value we prize, does it mean seeing that each child is a wanted child? Does it include guaranteeing the right to be born free of birth defects? Does it include the right to health for every child? Is it the prerogative of every person to receive the optimum level of education? Does it mean provision of child care facilities so that both parents can share in the workforce?

These decisions are compounded by the boundary maintenance of various helping programs. Population, health, education, welfare, and child care policy are all interrelated. Duplicity of direction and intent occur even though most programs are under one umbrella, the Department of Health, Education and Welfare. As a result, agencies that deal with child care find it necessary to outguess policy-makers in anticipation of which "cause" will receive funding for a particular year. Legislation is often problem-specific as the result of emotional involvement with an issue that has popular appeal. There are fewer political rewards for the kind of steady, total view that might result in a comprehensive policy for children everywhere.

---

[1]Warren Brown, "Trouble Seen in Shrinking U.S. Families," *The Washington Post*, Sunday, March 21, 1976.

Although caring for all the nation's children would be the ideal, the focus is usually on those programs that are created to help needy children. Aid to Families with Dependent Children, or AFDC, is somewhat infamous for the effect it had in its early years of forcing fathers from the home since aid was not given to families where an able-bodied man was present. Some states have still not changed their procedure to conform with the federal ruling that this is no longer valid. Head Start Programs during Johnson's War on Poverty have had varying degrees of success depending on what was expected of them. Keniston elaborates on these in one of the following articles.

Currently, the focus is on support for day care, and it is here that the fear that the government is taking over family life is most apparent. In 1971, President Nixon vetoed the Comprehensive Child Development Act because it would undermine the authority of the American family. The Child and Family Services Bill, co-sponsored in 1976 by Walter F. Mondale (Dem., Minn.) and John Brademas (Dem., Ind.), was attacked for the same reason. Both bills had provisions for day care funding and regulation as well as other measures for child care. The double bind in which day care centers now find themselves is that federal standards set in 1968 and updated in 1974 must be met by July 1, 1976. Because he favored block grants to the states, President Ford vetoed a suspension of the standards and a $125 million subsidy to states to help the centers improve their facilities and staffing. Congress failed to override the veto, and the new standards will be in effect with no money to meet them. Since the federal aid is confined to centers that care for children whose families qualify for public assistance, it will be the poorest children, most often black, who will suffer most.

While the regulation and funding for day care centers continues to be a political football, there are community efforts of total child care that might serve as models for combining the best features of day care with primary health care. Bruce Mallory describes such a program in New Hampshire in the article "The Child Care Provider as Change Agent."[2] Promoted by the Greater Manchester Child Care Association and in cooperation with Harvard University's logitudinal studies of human development, the plan involves nineteen family day care homes with one center-based agency providing a continuum of child care services from birth to school age.

With this administrative support, GMCCA is able to apply its own standards as well as state and federal regulations. Seminars held weekly with a staff development team cover such topics as health care, working with parents, normal child growth and development and meal planning. The goal is to end the contractual relationship after twelve months so the family day care home can assume an independent basis for providing quality care.

Each family day care home contracts with GMCCA to provide comprehensive care from birth to three years for each child, with reimbursement made at a contracted rate based on actual cost of care. Administrative leadership, a twelve-week intensive training program for the mothers in charge of the homes, consultation services for each home and a complete well-child health services program are provided by GMCCA.

The health services program is primarily preventive with a fulltime nurse practitioner and a licensed practical nurse visiting the homes to provide such screening examinations as vision and hearing, blood tests and measurements. This primary health care is the most neglected of our national health needs. That it is being successfully combined with child care needs in this community-based program is a tribute to their total view of child care.

The articles included in this section will raise more questions than they will answer, but they may help focus on what is really going on in a nation that considers itself child-centered.

Commentary—Evelyn Eldridge, ed.

[2]Bruce Mallory, "The Child Care Provider as Change Agent," *Voice,* Vol. 9, No. 2, March, 1976.

Do Americans *Really* Like Children?

by Kenneth Keniston

Two and a half years ago, the Carnegie Council on Children was established by the New York foundation of the same name. We are a small private commission, a group of 12 women and men chosen not to represent particular constituencies, professions, or groups, but because we share a common concern with the needs of American children and their families. We are not a blue ribbon group, but simply a dozen individuals from diverse backgrounds, fields, and perspectives, most of us in our thirties and forties, most of us parents. Assisted by an able young staff, we have not been doing original scientific research, but rather attempting to learn from the experience, action, and studies of others where children fit today in America, what are the unmet needs and problems of American children and families, and which of these problems most urgently deserve our response. Our work is not yet complete, so that what I say here, although a kind of introduction to some of the perspectives of the Council, must be understood as my own view, often stolen from other Council and staff members, but not necessarily reflecting their opinions. In the course of the next year and a half, we will be issuing a series of reports and other communications, and these will present the conclusions of the Council more adequately.

Let me start from the questions with which we began our work: Do Americans really like children? Are we the child-centered, child-loving people we claim to be? We began with these questions because of facts with which all of you are so familiar that I need not recite them in detail.

Recall that while we promise health and physical vitality to all our children, our infant mortality rates place us fifteenth among the forty-two nations ranked by the United Nations, just below East Germany and just above Hong Kong. Infant mortality rates for American non-whites are much higher, and among groups like American Indians, they approach the rates in the most underdeveloped countries. While surgeons perform an estimated 500,000 unnecessary tonsillectomies on children each year, we are among the few modern nations that do not guarantee minimum health care to all mothers and children. Or consider the nutrition of American children. Although overeating has become the nation's most vexing nutritional problem, a United States Department of Agriculture survey showed that between 1955 and 1965, a decade of rising affluence and agricultural productivity, the percentage of diets deficient in one or more essential nutrients actually increased. And today, for all of the programs that try to provide adequate nutrition to American children, millions remain hungry and malnourished.

We say that children have a right to the basic material necessities of life. Yet of all age groups in America, children are the most likely to live in abject poverty. One-sixth of all American children live below the officially defined poverty line, while one-third live below that level defined by the government as "minimum but adequate." And we are the only industrial democracy that does not have a system of income supports for families with children.

We say that we are a nation that believes fervently in families as the best way of raising children. Yet, our families are becoming increasingly depopulated. Divorce rates have risen more than 700% in the last half century, and today at least a million children are affected by

A version of this article was originally delivered as a speech to the American Orthopsychiatric Association. Dr. Kenneth Keniston is Chairman and Executive Director of the Carnegie Council on Children.

divorce each year. The proportion of our children raised in single-parent families has increased astronomically in the last two decades. And we are virtually alone among industrialized nations in that we have no national child or family policy, no comprehensive system of family services and supports, no way of helping children and families navigate the crises of family life.

We say we believe all children are entitled to loving, responsive care. But a third of mothers of pre-school children are in the labor force, and a half of mothers of school age children work outside the home. And we have yet to provide any system to assure that these children receive adequate care when their parents must be away from home. Here, again, we are backward by the standards of other nations of the world.

We say that we value children and acknowledge that value tangibly through the children's deduction in our tax system. Yet that deduction gives the greatest tax credit to families that need financial help the least. To a very rich family, two children are worth the equivalent of $750 or more in a direct grant from the government; to a middle income family, two children are worth only $300; a family too poor to pay any taxes receives nothing at all.

We say we have created a school system that equalizes opportunity and the chance to succeed for all children. Yet 12 years of public schooling actually increases the gap between rich and poor students. Far from equalizing opportunity, our school system exaggerates the inequalities with which children enter the schools. We have yet to devise ways to fulfill the promise that schooling would provide all children with equal opportunity.

Our middle-class children are awash in skateboards and stereos, but they fall prey to alcohol, drugs, aimlessness and boredom. At all economic levels, couples debate whether to have children at all.

All of you could cite other statistics that make the same point. The conclusion is simple: we are a rich, prosperous nation, endowed not only with material goods but with knowledge and with human talent. We pride ourselves on our devotion to children. Yet if we search for programs that support the development of children and help meet the needs of their families, we are a backward society, an underdeveloped nation. Other countries of the world may look to us for technological advances and material achievements, but we must look to every other industrial nation in the world for more advanced and adequate supports for children and families.

Why is this? Why are we an underdeveloped nation in our policies toward children and families? Is it because at some level, we secretly hate and despise our children, because our lip-service to the next generation is insincere? Or are there other reasons?

To answer these questions requires us to look at some of the most pressing problems that face American children and their parents. Here I will discuss three of the problems that deserve attention, so as to indicate the general nature of our answer. These problems are what I will call the depopulation of the family, the intellectualization of the child, and the perpetuation of exclusion.

THE DEPOPULATION OF THE FAMILY

In 1974, a crucial watershed was crossed in the history of the American family. For the first time, more than one-half of all school-aged children in two-parent families had mothers who worked outside the home, mostly full-time. For children under six in two-parent families the proportion of working mothers has reached one-third, and continues to grow rapidly. In single-parent families, mothers are even more likely to work for wages. For the first time in our national history, *most children now have mothers who work outside the home*, and most of these mothers work full-time. The speed with which women have entered the labor force is staggering; in every category, there has been a doubling or trebling of labor force participation by women with young children since the end of the second World War. The modal American family today is a two-parent family where the mother works outside the home. Work is abetted as a depopulating force by divorce.

A particularly depopulated set of families are those with one parent. In 1948, only one out of 14 children under six were brought up in a single-parent family. In 1973, that proportion had doubled to one out of seven children. Behind this increase is the extraordinary rise in the number of divorced, separated, or unwed parents, almost all mothers. Between 1960 and 1972, the proportion of children living in such families increased from one in 20 to one in eight. Largely for this reason, it is estimated that two out of every five children born in the 1970's will live in a single-parent family for at least part of their childhoods.

Another related trend is the disappearance of non-parental relatives from families, and especially from single-parent families. In 1949, about half of children under six in single-parent families lived with another relative who was the head of the family. By 1973, this proportion had dropped to one in five. In less than a quarter of a century, the presence of other relatives, usually grandparents, aunts and uncles, in the single-parent family has dropped from 50% to 20%. Kinship networks have been dispersed as parents relocate to follow jobs and promotions.

Other children are also increasingly scarce in our families. At the peak of the post-war baby boom, the median completed family size was almost four. Today, completed family size is below the zero population growth rate, about 1.9. Sixteen years ago, the average child had three siblings; today, the average child has one or less.

Let me cite one final statistic, the increasing proportion of births that are illegitimate. In 1960, about one out of every 20 live births was illegitimate; by 1972, this figure had increased to one out of every eight live births.

Taken together, these statistics—mostly culled from Urie Bronfenbrenner's work, which he will present at this meeting—mean that the family is increasingly emptied of people of all kinds, and in particular of kin. More mothers in the labor force, astronomical increases in the proportion of single-parent families, the disappearance of other relatives from the family, the sharp decline in the number of siblings, rapid rises in rates of divorce, separation, and illegitimacy—all these factors interact to mean that more and more children's lives are spent in homes empty of people for longer and longer stretches of time. With a speed that has few precedents in our history, the nature of family life in this country has changed, and in ways that we have yet to appreciate, much less respond to.

What has replaced the people in the family? For one, television has become a peculiar kind of flickering blue parent for many children, a technological babysitter, an electronic wonder that occupies more of the waking hours of American children than any other single force, including both parents and schools.

A second replacement is, of course, the peer group. With parents, older relatives, and siblings increasingly absent from the family, other unrelated children play a larger and larger role in socializing the young.

The third institution that has replaced the child's family members are schools, pre-schools, and the various child care arrangements that must be made by working parents. The average age of entry into some form of schooling or pre-schooling has decreased rapidly during the last decades, while more and more children are involved in some form of out-of-family child care, be it a neighbor lady, a licensed or unlicensed family day care center, a babysitter, a play group, or far more rarely a day care center. Whether we like it or not, millions of American children are today being raised for larger and larger portions of time by non-relatives, often completely outside of their family.

Finally, there are growing numbers of children who are simply not cared for at all for increasing periods of time—latch-key children who stay alone in empty houses; children locked at home while their parents work; children who play unattended in the streets. For them, there is simply no replacement at all for the family members who are not there.

The depopulation of the family and the replacement of family members by television, peer groups, non-familial caretakers—or no one—contradicts a central American value to which we all pay lip-service, and which most of us sincerely believe. This is the conviction that, other things equal, families provide the best possible environment for rearing the young. Since the first European settlements on these shores, the importance and sanctity of the family has been constantly reasserted. Even today, that majority of American mothers who work outside the home tend to feel guilty, inadequate, and remiss for fear they are neglecting their children. We persist in considering ourselves a family-centered, family-oriented nation. Perhaps as a result, we are so blind to the staggering changes that are overtaking our families.

But why have these changes occurred? Are they the result of the negligence or the hostility of individual parents? Do they reflect the growing indifference of American mothers and fathers to the fate of their children? Or are they the result of other forces in our society? Are we witnessing a "flight from the family" that springs primarily from the individual psychology of American parents? Or are parents themselves pushed out of the family by social and economic forces over which they have little control?

My answer is that the explanation does not lie with the individual motivations of American parents, but rather with the social and economic pressures of our larger society. Part of the Council's work has consisted in an effort to trace the changes in the experience of parents and children throughout our history. Many factors have helped transform American families from largely self-sufficient farm families of colonial days to the rapidly emptying dormitories that they are becoming today. But of all the forces that have changed family life, changes in our economic system are most fundamental. To summarize a long story in a few words, the disappearance of the agricultural family, where mother, father, and children worked together at the tasks of farming was stimulated above all by the development of national agricultural markets, by the specialization of farm production, and by the growth of industry and commerce in the 19th century. The family was gradually redefined not as a productive unit, but as a retreat from the harsh work-a-day world; woman's role was transformed from that of co-worker in the family economy to pure guardian of the hearth and aethereal socializer of the young; children were redefined not as economic assets to the family, but as future producers who, as adults, should aspire to rise above their parents through hard work to economic success.

In the 19th century, we developed the first universal public school system in history, thus replacing many of the family's traditional functions. But from the start, that public school system was explicitly justified by its early advocates like Horace Mann in economic terms—as a means of providing trained manpower for the economy, while socializing all children into American values so that social discontent would be reduced.

If today we ask what single factor contributes most to the entry of women with small children into the labor force, the answer is clear: economic pressures. The highest rates of female labor force participation, for example, occur in families of average and below average income. In these families, women work not primarily or only for purposes of fulfillment and dignity, much less in pursuit of exciting and challenging professional careers. They work because their income is needed to provide their families with a decent standard of living. And most mothers without husbands work because their income is the only source of sustenance to themselves and their children. Women's work is concentrated in the most underpaid, boring, and menial occupations. Even when women do the same jobs as men, they were traditionally, and still are, paid less.

Today, as before, the needs of our economy play a central role in transforming the families of American children. For it is useful to our economy to have available a large reservoir of employable females who are willing to accept dead-end jobs, to do without fringe benefits, to perform boring, menial, and even degrading work—all at low wages. The availability of such workers keeps profits up, keeps prices down, permits services to be performed for low rates, and provides, as we are witnessing today, a pool of workers without job guarantees who are among the first to be laid off in times of economic recession.

The entry of women, including mothers, into the occupational system seems to me irreversible and in many cases desirable. Women are simply gaining a right that men have always had—the right to seek productive, rewarding, and remunerative employment. And there is no evidence that maternal employment harms children, unless women feel pressured or coerced to work. But approximately 50% of all women who work say that they would not do so if they did not need the money. To my knowledge, no one on our Council believes that women should not have the same opportunities for productive work that men have. Nor do we believe that we should pressure women to stay at home. Our effort is not to condemn but to try to understand.

Even rising divorce rates are indirectly related to economic forces. Our technological economy has virtually destroyed the family farms and corner stores that once made husbands, wives and children partners in productive economic units. Today, the main glue that holds families together is the husband's and wife's capacity to satisfy each other's emotional needs.

When no shared economic tasks remain, interpersonal dissatisfactions more often lead to divorce. Perhaps one result is fewer chronically unhappy marriages. But another result is millions of children raised by a single parent who also must work full time to support his or her children.

In seeking this understanding, we have been led again and again to the nature and values of our economic system. It is an economic system that defines "work" only as paid participation in the labor force, but does not consider what women and men do at home, in particular the rearing of children, as an economically productive or rewardable activity. The growing depopulation of our families is largely attributable to the changes, assumptions, and needs of our economy. It is not the "fault" of individual parents, nor does it reflect any sudden decline in the devotion of Americans as individuals to their own children. Rather the draining of the family reflects the fact that we are all pressured by newly generated demands for consumption, and assumptions about what does and does not constitute valuable work. If families in America become little more than dormitories, quick service restaurants, recreation centers and consumption units, we must look not to the vices of American parents but to the pressures of the economy for the main explanation.

THE INTELLECTUALIZATION OF THE CHILD

I noted that one major substitute for family members is out-of-family child care, preschooling, and formal schooling. As the importance of family members in the rearing of children has declined, ever since the mid-19th century the role of non-family members and formal institutions has increased. The average age of entry into some form of non-familial care and/or pre-schooling is today dropping rapidly, while at the other end of the educational scale, the average age of school leaving has increased by one year a decade throughout this century.

Schools or preschools, and the values which they covertly or overtly transmit, are thus becoming increasingly important in the child's life. They are, next to families and possibly television, the major socializing influence on our children. It therefore behooves us to examine carefully what values and human qualities are stressed in child care programs, pre-schools, and schools, and to ask whether these values accord with our own aspirations for the next generation.

To state the conclusion in a few words, I believe that we are witnessing a growing emphasis upon the child as a brain, upon the cultivation of narrowly defined cognitive skills and abilities, and above all upon the creation, through our pre-schools and schools, of a breed of children whose value and progress is judged almost exclusively by their capacity to do well on tests of IQ, reading readiness, or school achievement. Although children are, like adults, whole people, full of fantasies, imagination, artistic capacities, physical grace, social relationships, cooperation, initiative, industry, love, and joy, the overt and above all the covert structure of our system of pre-schooling and schooling largely ignores these other human potentials to concentrate upon the cultivation of a narrow form of intellect.

Recall the educational response to the launching of Sputnik. It was to attempt to create, through schooling, a generation of Americans who would be capable of beating the Russians in the race to the moon, the planets, and the stars. This objective was translated into a heavy emphasis on mathematics, basic science, and those other technical skills thought to be important in this peculiar quest for international prestige. Studies of cognitive development burgeoned throughout this period, and school after school adopted a no-nonsense, test-performance and IQ-score based system of promotions and rewards, all sanctioned by the fear that we were falling behind the Russians. In this push for measurable cognitive achievement, other qualities were quietly discarded: the valuable ideas of progressive education were forgotten in a one-sided critique of its excesses; the notion of children as whole people, while often mentioned and occasionally implemented, was largely subordinated to the rush for cognitive development.

With the coming of the 1960's, and with the sudden rediscovery of poverty and racism in America, new initiatives were made to improve the quality of schooling and pre-schooling, especially for poor and non-white children. The original architects of the War on Poverty had in mind a many-leveled battle, including the creation of jobs, income supplementation, and the provision of services to all families and children who needed them. But characteristically in our national experience, the jobs and income components of this war were either forgotten or implemented at best in a half-hearted way. One of the human service programs that was implemented was the Head Start program. Its architect, Dr. Julius Richmond, will testify that this program as originally conceived had many objectives, among which the raising of IQ scores and the development of reading readiness was secondary. These other objectives included the empowerment of parents, the provision of services like health and dental care to children, and so on.

But when the time came to evaluate Head Start programs, evaluation consisted almost entirely in assessing whether they succeeded in irreversibly increasing the IQ scores of the children involved. The notion of most evaluators has been that "success" for Head Start meant a program that, in a few hours each day for a few months or a year, could overcome the overwhelming disadvantages of life for children born into poverty, into the segregation of a race-divided society, or into the squalor that characterizes the communities of millions of American children. It is a tribute to our optimism, if to nothing else, that we ever thought we could do so much for so many for so little.

Underlying much Head Start work was a theory of cultural deprivation. Essentially, this theory said that certain children—largely non-white and poor—were deprived of the cultural stimulation which middle class white children receive. Allegedly, their homes were without books, their parents did not interact with them verbally, and so on. To overcome these "deficits," it was argued, programs of cultural enrichment and intellectual stimulation were required. Thus, Head Start programs in general attempted to compensate for the alleged deficiencies of the child's family.

What is noteworthy is that so few asked at the time what was causing "cultural deprivation," who or what was doing the depriving, and whether the basic deprivation was really cultural at all. The term "culturally deprived" became, in short order, a euphemism for poor and black. For many Americans, it was another stigmatizing label, a polite way of pointing to the alleged "inadequacies" of families condemned to the cellar of our economy. There are of course two sides to deprivation: the deprived and the depriving. But little attention was paid to the factors in our society that might prevent some families from providing their children with cultural riches, intellectual stimulation, and rich verbal interaction. Most important, the concept of cultural deprivation, though benign in origin, neglected the basic question as to whether the deprivations of most families and children were primarily cultural at all. It seems an odd way of defining the problems of economically destitute families in inner-city ghettos, migrant camps, impoverished Appalachian villages or tenant farmer shacks to call their primary deprivation "cultural." On the face of it, it would make more sense to describe these "deprivations" as economic and political. And there were a few voices that noted these problems. But by and large, they went unheard.

As a result, few Americans ever asked whether a program aimed at attacking a symptom could possibly hope to succeed in its extraordinarily ambitious goals without also attacking the causes of that symptom. As has generally happened in our history, this reform program often ended by stigmatizing those whom it was intended to benefit, while it drew attention away from the root causes of the problem that it tried to solve.

In my own view, Head Start programs have been extraordinarily successful, even given the inadequacy of the theory on which they were evaluated. They showed that it was indeed possible to increase the ability of children in the bottom of our society to do well on tests. As long as children remain in most Head Start programs their gains, even measured in the narrow terms of test performance, are significant and marked. Head Start programs did succeed in empowering parents, and they have provided desperately needed health, dental and other services to a few children. But, a few hours a day in a cultural enrichment program for a few months or a year cannot hope forever to reverse the toll upon families and children of the economic and racial structure of our society.

Thus, Head Start, originally defined as only one component of a broader attack on poverty, and not conceived as primarily cognitive in its objectives, was quickly redefined as a program whose outcome and success was measured in terms of gains in the ability to do well on standardized tests. Head Start illustrates a broader tendency in our society, the tendency to rank and rate children, to reward and stigmatize them, according to their ability to do well in the narrow tasks that schools (or we psychologists) believe we can measure quantitatively. At every level of our pre-school and school system, this same ability to do well on tests is a primary determinant of the child's progress and position in the world of school and, to a large degree, in the later world of adults. Access to the "high" tracks, "superior" ability groupings, and even to good schools themselves is primarily determined by ability to do well on tests. We talk a great deal about the other human qualities of children, but when the push comes to shove—when it is a matter of promotion, receiving credentials, being praised or punished—it is the child who has learned to master test-taking who gets the goodies.

This one-sided emphasis on test-taking ability extends throughout our entire educational system. It persists despite the lack of evidence that the ability to do well on tests predicts much of anything about the ability to do well in life. But try getting into the college or preparatory track in most American high schools without the ability to do well on IQ forms, achievement measures, and classroom tests. And try getting into a college whose B.A. provides a passport to a rewarding, prestigious, and remunerative job without demonstrating the same ability at the end of high school. Or try getting into a law school or medical school without first getting high scores on their tests. Our schools are so structured that without the ability to get good "objective test scores" or high "grade point averages," a child is condemned to almost certain failure.

We could live more easily with this fact were it not for our professed devotion to a large number of human qualities that we say we value above the ability to do well on tests. We say that we want our children to be physically vital, caring, imaginative, resourceful, cooperative and morally committed. We talk a great deal about all of the qualities that we value in children, all of the virtues that we wish our schools to instill into them, all of the kinds of human merit that we value. In fact, on our lists of our hopes for the next generation, the ability to do well on tests does not appear at all. But in our educational system, whose power over the lives of our children increases annually, it is test-taking ability, and the narrow and learned form of intelligence that test scores reflect, that calls the shots.

Why is this? Is it because American parents and teachers are hypocritical in the lip-service they pay to human values other than narrowly-defined cognitive ability? Or is it, perhaps, because we are all responding to similar pressures in our society, pressures over which we have little control?

Once again, our answer is not to blame teachers or parents, but rather to point to the pressures of a modern technological society, and ultimately to the forces of our economy as embodied in the tracking and selection procedures for our occupational system.

Ours is a highly developed technological economy. Our society has also adopted, usually without knowing it, the implicit ideology of technism, an ideology that among other things places central value on what can be measured with numbers, assigns numbers to what cannot be measured, and redefines everything else as a recreation, self-expression, or entertainment. The development of so-called objective measures—in fact not at all objective—of IQ and performance is another expression of our propensity to label, grade, and rank individuals by numerical standards. We speak of a $50,000 a year man, of a $100,000 house, and of a child of an IQ of 95. We measure the effectiveness of education by whether or not it produces measurable income increments, not by whether it improves the quality of life of those who are educated. And we measure the success of individual schools not in terms of the kinds of human beings that they promote, but in terms of the increases in reading scores which they produce. Asked to endorse this narrow standard of measurement, most of us would rebel, asserting other values as more important. But in practice, we have allowed this standard, so central to our economic system and our way of thinking about it, to become the central yardstick for our definition of children's worth.

A related characteristic of our highly developed technological economy is its need for some mechanism to sort individuals into various occupational slots. In principle, there might be a variety of ways of doing this. The intellectualization of children by testing and tracking in schools assists in classifying and sorting them for the labor force. The tracking that usually begins in first grade feeds ultimately into the many tracks of our adult occupational system. And we all know that by the time a poor, black, handicapped or uncared-for child reaches third or fourth or fifth grade, a consistent position in the bottom track of the grade has become an almost inescapable adult destiny. Thus, the intellectualization of the child reflects the school's role in classifying and sorting the labor force.

Were there time, it would be important to discuss the origins of the testing movement. Given what we today know about the racial, economic, and cultural biases inherent in so-called objective tests, it is not surprising to learn that many of the early advocates of intelligence testing were explicit racists, who believed that their results showed the constitutional degeneracy of Blacks, Mediterraneans, Slavs, and Jews. By way of summary, it seems fair to say that intelligence testing has overall served to perpetuate the status quo, assuring that most of the children who begin at the bottom will end at the bottom, while most of those who start with what we call "advantages" will end up retaining them.

In tracing the origins and causes of the intellectualization of the child, we are led step by step back to the nature of our economic system, to the reflection in our schools of our economically-derived lust to quantify and measure, to the utilization of schooling as a means of providing a suitably tracked and channeled labor force, to the use of schools and tests as a means of perpetuating the relative social positions of existing groups in American society. It is not that teachers or parents are to blame, or that the values that we proclaim for our schools and for our children are hypocritical. It is, rather, that we are the unwitting accomplices and victims of structures in our society related to the ideology and workings of our economic system.

THE PERPETUATION OF EXCLUSION

The two problems I have so far mentioned affect all American children, rich and poor, black and white, male and female. The problem to which I now turn is the problem of the excluded quarter, of children born in the cellar of our society and systematically brought up to remain there. This is a problem that also affects and involves us all, although some of us are unwittingly the short-term beneficiaries of this exclusion, while others are its undeniable victims.

We estimate that one-quarter of all American children today are being brought up to fail. This figure is an estimate, but we believe it to be on the conservative side. The children about whom I am talking are children who are being actively harmed today, deprived of the opportunity to realize a significant portion of their human potential, injured, hurt, deprived at times even of the right to live. Four factors cooperate in this process of their exclusion. The first is race; the second is poverty; the third is handicap; and the fourth is being born of parents too overwhelmed by life to be able to care responsively and lovingly for the child.

Let me once again regale you with statistics. One out of every five children in America is non-white, and these children must somehow cope with the persistent institutional and psychological racism of our society that the rest of us are seldom aware of because we do not experience it. One out of every three children lives below the minimum adequate budget established by the Department of Labor, and each of these children must face the multiple scars of poverty. One out of every 12 children is born with a major or minor handicap, and all of these children face the possible stigmas and social disabilities that accompany any handicap. One out of every 10 children has a learning disability, and given our school system this disability will normally undermine that child's sense of herself or himself as a competent human being. Approximately one-quarter of all American children do not receive anything approaching adequate health care, nor did their mothers before they were born. It is these children whose unnecessary deaths at birth or in early childhood make our national infant mortality rates an international disgrace. Million upon millions of children live in sub-standard housing. Millions of children attend schools that are ill-equipped, run-down, inadequately financed, poorly staffed and chaotic—schools where teachers are overwhelmed by their powerlessness, relegated against their wishes to the role of keepers of order and babysitters. One out of every eight children born today is born illegitimate. We have no estimates of the number of parents who are themselves so overwhelmed by their pasts or, more important, by the pressures of their present lives that they are unable to provide responsive care for their children. But clearly there are millions of such parents, rich and poor.

All of these facts are well-known to any one concerned with the state of children in America. What makes their impact upon children so devastating is the frequency with which they occur together. For both white and non-white children, extreme poverty and growing up in a single-parent family go together. Poverty is irrevocably linked to inadequate medical care and inadequate prenatal care. Bad schools are most common for those children who most desperately need good schools, with facilities to deal with the fears and disabilities with which many children enter them. Hunger among children is especially concentrated among the poor, and a hungry child can rarely do as well in school as a child who is well-fed. The list could go on and on.

The process by which children are disabled in our society is no mystery to its victims. It is a daily process whereby physical vitality, emotional caring, resourcefulness, and moral commitment in the child are undercut. It is also a cumulative process, in which inadequate prenatal care of mothers increases the chances that children will be born dead, defective or sickly, in which early malnutrition decreases the hope for robust physical vigor, in which inadequate health care increases the chances of illness or makes minor illness escalate into permanent handicaps. If a child is born poor, or non-white, or handicapped, or of emotionally drained parents, even the chances of physical survival to adulthood are decreased.

But the most powerful forms of exclusions are not physical but social and psychological. In a land of plenty, a child of poverty grows up in want and hardship, denied those needs that most Americans consider fundamental. One reason children who are poor are greatly less likely to survive into adulthood is because they live in a world that is more dangerous than that of the prosperous—an urban world of broken stair-railings, of busy streets as playgrounds, of lead paint, rats and rat poisons—or a rural world, hidden from the view of most of us, where families cannot maintain the minimal levels of public health considered necessary a century ago. This is a world of aching teeth without dentists to fill them, of untreated colds that result in permanent deafness, a world where even a small child learns to be ashamed of the way he or she lives. And it is often a world of intense social danger, a world where adults, driven by poverty and desperation, are untrustworthy and unpredictable. Thus it can be a world where a child learns early to suppress any natural impulse to explore the world, substituting for curiosity a defensive guardedness toward novelty, a refusal to reach out for fear of being hurt. Living in a world that is indifferent or systematically hostile, the child turns off initiative and the eagerness that other children bring to learning the basic skills of our culture.

Such children are systematically trained for failure. The covert lessons their environment teaches them about themselves and about the world are astonishingly consistent. As people they are defined as no good, inadequate, dirty, incompetent, ugly, dumb, and clumsy. The world in which they grow up is a dangerous, hostile place, where the best strategy for coping is never to venture out, to take no risks, and to stay on guard. It is this sense of self and this view of the world—constantly reenforced, rarely mitigated, in fact an accurate perception of the messages our society gives these children—that condemns them to lives of failure in social if not in human terms.

By the time a child of desperately poor parents in Appalachia reaches school age, that child is often so turned off by the world and its dangers that even the most benign forms of help and sympathy avail but little. To the inner-city black child, brought up in a dangerous, chaotic and unpredictable environment from which the most loving parents cannot protect a child, the lesson that the world is a hostile place has been learned by the age of three. A child whose parents are so drained by hardships that they cannot respond to him or her in terms of his or her own needs learns in the first four years a virtually indelible lesson about the untrustworthiness and unresponsiveness of human relationships. The messages a child receives about self and world tend to be consistent and mutually reenforcing. They invoke in the child a kind of withdrawal or aggression that elicits still further messages as to the child's inadequacy and the hostility of the mainstream world.

Confronted with such facts, we commonly reassure ourselves by recounting success stories: the poor boys who made it, the blacks who became a tribute to their race, the handicapped who made contributions to our society, and the neglected children who grew up into strong, resourceful adults. But these success stories are the exceptions; they are systematically misleading. A quarter of our children are being actively harmed today, many of them in ways that no later good fortune or help can surely repair. It takes an extraordinary parent or parents to raise an open, lively, resilient, and caring child in the slums of Harlem, in the backwaters of Appalachia, or in the migrant camps of Colorado. That as many parents succeed as do is a tribute to their miraculous tenacity, love and inspiration. But miracles occur rarely.

Were we a society politically committed to the perpetuation of a caste system, dedicated to the continuation of gross inequality, eager to waste human potential, or happy with the exclusion of a large minority of the next generation, these facts would cause us no concern. But in fact, they violate our most central values as Americans.

If any single theme dominates the social and political history of our nation, it is the continuing (though never fully successful) effort to include all those who live in this land as full citizens. Each generation, and each individual in each generation, we have promised, would have an equal chance in life. Our society, we have believed, should impose upon the child no special burdens that will limit him or her in the exercise of freedom, in the pursuit of fulfillment. Nothing in our constellation of basic value even hints that our society should impose special burdens upon special children. The promise we made to the 35 million immigrants who came to this land, like the promise we made to the native Americans who inhabited our continent long before white settlers arrived, was that they, too, would be included as full members of our society.

Even the most superficial reading of our history will show how far we have departed from this high ideal in the past. Exclusion is in no sense new. Slaves and their descendants, native Americans, other non-whites, immigrants, women, and a host of others have been effectively disenfranchised. But to each generation we have repeated, and we continue to repeat, the same promise: your children will be included; all of you who live here will become full members of the community of Americans. And much of our history has been an effort to confirm that promise, although in a painfully slow, erratic and incomplete way.

How, then, can we understand the perpetuation of exclusion? One answer, for almost two centuries in America, is that those who live in the cellars of our society are there because they belong there, because they lack human virtue, merit, industriousness, or talent. They are morally culpable, idle, dependent, welfare chislers, profligate, intemperate, licentious, and dangerous to the social order. They are to blame for and they deserve their own exclusion. Or they are said to inherit from their unfortunate parents a genetic propensity toward "low I.Q." or "concrete thinking."

But there is another possibility as well. It is that the exclusion from the mainstreams of our society of a large minority of each generation is a product not of the individual viciousness, inadequacy, or immorality of those who are excluded, nor is it a result of the conscious and deliberate exploitation of the majority, but rather that it is a product of the way our society works and has worked for more than a century.

Again it is necessary to summarize a long argument into a few sentences. The promise that we have made to each successive generation that all would be included in the mainstreams has remained persistently unfulfilled for over a century and a half. The distribution of wealth and income in this nation has not changed materially in 150 years. While many people have moved ahead of their parents economically, groups ahead of them have moved up also, leaving little net change. The distribution has not been changed. All of our promises of equal opportunity, all of our efforts at schooling, all of the general increases in our national prosperity, all of our efforts to reform and change and uplift those at the bottom of our society—none of these has succeeded in including those who are kept out. The core social problem behind exclusion is the problem of a society that permits and perpetuates gross economic and racial inequality.

The key explanation of exclusion lies, I believe, in the nature of our economic system, and in our passive acceptance of how that system works and of the ideology that buttresses it. It has proved economically useful (and perhaps even necessary) to our society as it industrialized to have available a relatively large minority of individuals and families driven by economic need to accept menial, dead-end, low-paying, insecure, hazardous, and boring work. In every society there are menial and boring jobs to be done. There are bed pans to be emptied in hospitals, there are grapes to be picked in California and there is cotton to be picked in Mississippi, there are shirts to be ironed, garbage to be collected, suitcases to be carried, furniture to be moved, and dishes to be washed. There are even assembly-line jobs so boring and stultifying that many workers refuse to accept them. Today, most of these jobs could be mechanized. But mechanization requires money. And when there are workers who will accept low wages, no job guarantees or fringe benefits, in seasonal, repetitive, boring work—all because they are driven by the economic urgencies of the need to subsist—then it costs most of us less to buy the goods and services they produce. It has been this way for a long time in America and in other Western industrialized nations. It is still that way.

Exclusion persists, of course, not because of the plots or evil motives of individual entrepreneurs or average citizens. We all live in an economic system which decrees that profit, growth, and innovation are the criteria for economic survival. We did not make that system, and we must live within it until we decide to change it. Nor do those of us who benefit through cheaper services and lower prices from the existence of a large minority of economically and racially excluded Americans and their children consciously or deliberately approve that exclusion. On the contrary, most of us deplore it, and a great many of us contribute generously to the United Fund to help its victims. But in the short run we benefit—unintentionally, unknowingly—but nonetheless we benefit.

In the long run, it is another matter. In the long run we all lose. The problem of exclusion is not merely a problem for those who are excluded, but for all of the rest of us. In the long run, we lose a significant portion of the potentials for good, for contribution to our society, which excluded children could offer. In the long run, we and our children will pay a tangible price in remedial services, in social unrest and discontent, in prisons and mental hospitals. In the long run, we, and the children of the modestly well-off and the prosperous in America, will also pay a human and moral price because we have tolerated a system in which our advantage and privilege depends, unnecessarily, upon their being people who are clearly beneath us and who do our dirty work. For children this neglected price includes the pressures that are emptying families and cudgeling children to be narrow thinking machines. The short term benefits we derive from exclusion will be more than outweighed, even in narrow economic terms, by the price we who are within the mainstreams, and our children, will pay for the perpetuation of this exclusion.

INDIVIDUAL UPLIFT AND SOCIAL CHANGE

I have outlined three problems affecting children and their families in contemporary America: the depopulation of the family, the intellectualization of the child, and the perpetuation of exclusion. In each case, I have suggested that an understanding of the causes of these problems leads us not to blame the moral turpitude and failings of individuals, but to examine our entire society, and in particular the assumptions and workings of our economic system.

I will conclude by underlining this contrast between the theme of individual blame and uplift on the one hand, and the need for social and economic change on the other.

We Americans have always prided ourselves upon our individualism. There is much to be proud of in our emphasis upon individual responsibility, upon the cultivation of individuality, and upon our hope that we could, in this nation, create a community out of varied individuals, each of whom possessed equal freedom to live out her or his life. That same individualism has, however, systematically blinded us to the power of social, political and above all economic forces in our lives.

In the age of Jackson, between 1820 and 1840, with the break up of the old Colonial social order, we devised a way of viewing our society and of trying to change it that embodies that individualism and has dominated our tradition as a nation ever since. In brief, we adopted the two related doctrines of equal opportunity and schooling for mobility. Our national creed came to rest upon the initial conviction that every American child has an equal chance to make his or her way to the top, and on the second assumption that the development of a universal system of schooling would provide all children, no matter what their origins, with equal access to the skills, tools, and disciplines necessary for success.

As it happens, we know today that opportunity is not equal in America, nor has it ever been; we know that the initial inequality of condition of children largely determines the opportunities that will be open to them. We also know today that schooling, despite our success stories to the contrary, has not provided a significant avenue for upward mobility for young Americans: as I noted earlier, schooling actually tends to increase the gap between poor and rich. Nor do we have any solid evidence that success in school has much to do with success in the wider world, however we measure it. Nonetheless, these two articles of faith, the doctrines of equal opportunity and schooling for success, continue to dominate our national consciousness.

A corollary of these beliefs is our persistent American illusion that each individual's place in society is the exclusive result of his or her own efforts. Those who ended up at the bottom have thus been deemed inferior to those at the top—inferior in industriousness, in hard work, in diligence and, today, it is also assumed, inferior in IQ, intelligence, talent, or what have you. In the end, we have assumed that those who end in the basement of our society are inferior morally, that they suffer from that grand American trio of vices, namely, first, idleness, laziness, lack of enterprise, etc.; second, dependency, pauperism, willingness to live off of the hard work of others; and thirdly, a cluster of vices that have to do with sensuality and licentiousness—intemperance, promiscuity, degeneracy, and various other forms of sensual immorality. Though few of us would publicly voice these sentiments in precisely these terms today, they persist as deep assumptions about those who are condemned to failure in our society. Conversely, we continue to assume that most of those who succeed are especially virtuous, that they possess the qualities of hard work, self-sufficiency, and an absence of sensual indulgence.

A further consequence of this ideology is that if individuals alone are responsible for their position in society, and thus the sum of individual efforts explains the organization of our society, reform must be directed primarily at reforming and uplifting individuals. We have traditionally paid much lip service to what we call the "environment." But that environment has been defined in an extraordinarily narrow and circumscribed way. When, today, we speak of a child coming from a "good environment," we are almost always talking about his or her parents. And when we attempt to deal with the problems confronting children or parents, we habitually fall back upon the reflex response of reforming individuals one by one. Today, the moralism in these efforts at reform is disguised behind scientific language, and most of those involved in efforts at reform honestly feel little sense of moral superiority over those whom they attempt to help. Yet the moralistic and individualistic context remains. Thus our social policies, insofar as we have had any intended to improve the lot of parents and children, have been directed not at changing the social and economic conditions that create their problems, but at uplifting the victims.

I have here pointed again and again to the nature and ideology of our economic system because, of all the forces that one might single out, this one appears to be the most powerful in defining the kinds of lives we lead as parents, the kinds of futures we can offer our children, the kinds of forces that are brought to bear upon us as parents and them as the next generation. But we have been and remain largely blind to the pervasive power of that system. Head Start is a case in point; faced with a problem that is essentially an economic and racial problem—the problem of poverty and caste lines—we redefined it as a problem of cultural deprivation, rarely asked even who was doing the depriving, and targeted our efforts at providing "cultural enrichment" to the victims of the process of exclusion. The rest of the abortive War on Poverty was largely forgotten—the jobs, the income supports, the other services needed by all American families. We ended up by attempting to reform the victims.

You may ask what are the implications for policy of this kind of analysis. Does it mean that our efforts to help individuals are misguided and must be abandoned? And does it mean that there is no way of improving the condition of American children and families short of a total revolution?

I believe it means neither of these things. Our individualism and our focus on reforming the victims of our society have led us to an understanding unmatched in any other nation of the world of individual psychodynamics, of the complexities of individual development, and of the intricacies of parent-child relationships. We should not throw this out. Nor should we abandon, for one minute, those programs that attempt to undo the harms that are done to families and children. We need more, not less, Head Start, more and much better education, more not less services to communities and individuals. And even if the basic structures of our society were radically transformed, we would still need all of these things.

But we also need to understand that we are applying much-needed bandaids, attempting to salvage the victims, not dealing with basic causes. And we need to move beyond understanding—toward changing the undesirable features of our economic structure, even while we challenge some of the ideological assumptions by which it justifies itself. It will get us nowhere to blame evil capitalists or exploitative employers; there are evil and exploitative people in every stratum of society. The challenge is to stop blaming people and begin removing the causes of the problems facing families and children. Along with compensatory programs, we need the elimination of the entrenched barriers, the job ceilings, and the caste lines that prevent minority group members from full citizenship in our society. Along with programs to educate the poor, we need active programs of income supplementation, so that no child or family in America is deprived of the basic physical necessities of life. Along with job training programs (not so far notably successful) we need job creation programs, all in the context of a long-term effort to learn how to eliminate that secondary labor market whose continuation condemns so many of our parents and children to exclusion. And, we need to begin now to develop comprehensive and universally accessible services to support, not to replace, families in the rearing of their children. These services must be available to all families as a matter of right, and not because they demonstrate some particular inadequacy or some special need.

Some of what we need to do, like income support, could be easily done, had we the national commitment and will to do it. Other things, like job creation, will be more difficult; they will take decades; they will require constant experimentation and a persistent determination to accomplish our objectives. But the point is that we can and must begin, and we must begin not merely by helping the victims, but by identifying and then changing the forces and structures of our society that undermine the vitality, the passionate care, the resourcefulness, and the moral commitment of the next generation.

In unguarded moments, we Americans are fond of confessing to our children that we have made a mess of the world or a mess of our lives, and encouraging them to do better. This is a cop out. It is almost impossible for children to create a society that is much better than the one they grow up in. Instead of expecting our children to undo our individual failures and correct our social injustices, we the parental generation must do that now for their sake. We must not only try to create through our individual efforts as parents and carers for children a better generation of children, but to create a better society for them to grow up in.

Can Children Have Quality Life in Day Care?

by Bettye M. Caldwell

A few years ago it would have been impossible to try to approximate an answer or series of answers to the question, "Does day care mean a quality life for young children?" for the simple reason that for many years nobody bothered to try to find the answers. Another reason is that we do not really know what we mean by a "quality life" for children. Day care in America has grown in spite of social planning rather than because of it. It is as though we tacitly assumed for many years that if we didn't pay any attention to it, it would simply go away. Strong forces of public opinion actively resisted the growth of day care, asserting that more available day care would mean that more mothers would go out of the home to seek additional employment, thereby neglecting their children and increasing juvenile delinquency and all sorts of other social ills. Finally social planners began to realize that failure to provide good day care did not keep mothers at home. Furthermore, day care was a mandatory, not an optional, service for the large number of mothers left with full responsibility for child rearing, whose children might not have subsisted without the income that the mother could provide. Rather, the alternative to not providing good day care was to force mothers to settle for substandard day care. And the assumption was made that if the child was kept at home, he automatically experienced a quality life.

But suddenly day care, as a means of trying to offer a quality life, is very much in our consciousness. Where did it come from? With many people, the experience is like learning a new word. Before you learned that word, you never heard it before; now suddenly you hear it three times a day and wonder why people are suddenly using it so often! Day care, or simply child care, as most of us prefer to call it, has suddenly emerged as a force in American life, and it will not disappear again. It is with us to stay. There are a number of reasons for that emergence, at least one of which is that we have reached a new level of community orientation in our personal lives. One by one, the major areas of life that have throughout history been taken care of predominately within the family (except for a few people within each social group)—child bearing, routine health care, basic education, food preparation—have begun to be shared with others in the social group. Such sharing comes about in any field whenever specialization of function takes place and some members of the community are recognized as more skilled than others at a particular task. As techniques of child rearing have become a subject of scientific study, and as growth-inducing and growth-retarding practices have been identified, it has become inevitable that child care be gradually ever more professionalized. Whenever either self-proclaimed or consensually acclaimed "experts" appear who supposedly can do a better job at a given task, someone is sure to speak up quickly and say, "Then do it for me, or at least help me do it." It is useful to view day care in this context of social evolution as a manifestation of the professionalization of child care and not simply as an ad hoc procedure created to perform desired social services.

Day care in America took a quantum step during and after World War II. This increase in service did not include machinery that would provide objective feedback data on the effects

An earlier version of this paper was originally delivered as an S. and H. Foundation Lecture at Pacific Oaks College, Pasadena, Calif., February 9, 1972. The author's work is supported by Grant No. SF-500 Office of Child Development, Dept. of Health, Education, and Welfare.

Reprinted from *Young Children,* Vol. XXVIII, No. 4, April, 1973. Copyright © 1973, National Association for the Education of Young Children, 1834 Connecticut Ave., N.W., Washington, D.C. 20009.

Bettye M. Caldwell, Ph.D., is Professor in the College of Education at the University of Arkansas and is Director of the Center for Early Development and Education in Little Rock.

of the service, for early day care programs grew up almost outside the boundary of planned scientific inquiry. Simultaneously with the increase in day care in America, there occurred a build-up in the area generally called nursery education or preschool education. But certainly the leaders in that field did not talk to the people in day care, and vice versa! Indeed not. For, after all, was not day care a service designed to provide care and protection for unfortunate children whose mothers were forced to work? And did not use of day care automatically identify a family as one in which there was social pathology? After all, if there were not such pathology, the family theoretically would not have sought day care. Nursery education, on the other hand, was for children from storybook America, for the Dicks and Janes who would later appear in our readers, all blond and blue-eyed and fair-skinned, happily chasing their dog Spot in the grassy yard of their Cape Cod house surrounded by its picket fence. All of these children had two parents who went to PTA meetings. The father had a steady job (preferably as a physician or lawyer or a university professor), and the mother stayed home and baked cookies and lovingly applied bandaids when someone fell down. These children were exhaustively researched to the extent that we knew how they grew, what their conceptions of causality and deity were, how many words they knew at each age level, whether they played parallel or as isolates (heaven forbid), what their average IQs were, whether they responded better to autocratic or democratic leadership—and on and on and on!

But there were other children out there. It was just, as Michael Harrington (1962) charged, that they were invisible to us. And many of them were in day care—often of an improvised type, not in beautiful lab schools furnished with elegant equipment and futuristic jungle gyms. No, many of those of nursery school age were left with six- or seven-year-olds at 5:30 in the morning when mother had to leave the housing project to catch a train across town to arrive by 7:00 A.M. at the hospital where she worked. At 7:30 they went to an aunt's apartment three floors down, and she gave them breakfast and then took them, along with her two, to a decrepit day care center, following which she left for work. At 4:00 their mother picked them up, along with the two that belonged to the aunt, and took them home with her, where all the children stayed until the aunt came home—and so on. Certainly few people were interested in the child development of "those children." For how could we possibly generalize to the population as a whole if we used such a group for our research sample? That those children were probably far more representative than the small group being exhaustively studied never seemed to make an impression on anyone's consciousness until the early 1960s.

(This description obviously reeks of hyperbole and minimizes the contributions of pioneer workers in nursery school education and day care. However, as a description of the attitudes held by leaders in the broader field of early childhood, it appears accurate—as accurate, at least, as one can ever be when characterizing one time period from the vantage point of a different time period.)

But then things changed abruptly, and day care was given the impetus it needed to come into its own—into its own with full trappings of social respectability and that fraternity handshake of the intellectual crowd—data, facts, information. For it was in the early 1960s that early childhood as an important developmental period was discovered. Furthermore, with early childhood's discovery came the notion that it was not only there but that it might be critical for setting developmental limits for the child for the rest of his life. Intervention during the early years became the battly cry, and, for the first time, the primary target group was "those children" who previously had been totally neglected. Scientific ideas can never flourish, of course, unless they are compatible with the Zeitgeist. More and better nursery education of the two to three hour a day variety would not have filled a major social need. But more and better day care would indeed fill such a need. And so day care came out of the kitchen and, for the first time, began to eat in the dining room. It was no longer a pariah; it was really the prodigal son who had been misunderstood all along. And so, for the last six or seven years, we have been seriously trying to observe day care programs, to try to evaluate the extent to which they formulate objectives for the children and families and then meet those objectives, to conduct research on samples of children in day care and thus to understand them better and to broaden our understanding of all children. And, on the basis of the pool of knowledge now emerging, we can begin to determine whether day care can provide a quality life for children.

1. *A full range of experiences will be encountered by children in day care: one can no more speak of day care in the singular than one can of "school."* This has been documented more completely by Prescott and Jones (1967) than by anyone else. They observed for four 20-minute periods, daily for 10 days in 50 randomly selected day care centers in the Los Angeles area and noted such things as teaching style (use of restriction or encouragement), amount of training, program formats, spatial arrangements and staff attitudes. As would be expected if one paused to reflect on it, they found a wide variety on all their variables in the different centers they observed. Among their findings were such things as, in general, amount of training was a predictor of whether the program would be adult-centered or child-centered. More training was associated with a child-centered approach, although there were some very well-trained directors who were adult-centered and vice versa. Size of the facility and arrangement of equipment within the available space was an important determinant of teacher performance. They found that day care was most effective (as determined by the extent of the children's interest and involvement in the program) in those centers in which the staff was flexible and where children's needs were met. Positive behavior tended to be forthcoming in response to encouragement, to lessons in consideration, creativity, pleasure, awe and wonder, and to emphasis on verbal skills. Negative behaviors tended to be associated with restriction and to lessons in control and restraint and rules of social living. In short, in this important observational study, it was possible to place the programs of different centers along a variety of continua, both in terms of program input and child response. Neither in California nor in any other location can one refer to "day care" en masse and be doing anything other than obscuring important information.

2. *Children in day care develop motivationally and in terms of skills considered adaptive in today's world.* A few years ago, when a number of people began to do serious research on the effects of day care, critics of the field took the position that the task for the researchers was to prove that the experience did not harm the children. This was especially true if the day care population included children younger than three. This somewhat phobic reaction was generated by the fallacious assumption that group day care was the equivalent of institutional care, in which children experienced extremely depriving sensory cirsumstances and in which the problem of self-identity was difficult if not impossible to solve. Now we fortunately have an accumulation of data which demonstrates that quite the reverse can be true in well-planned and well-run programs. That is, children enrolled in day care on the average show significant gains on standard intelligence and achievement tests. One program from which data in support of this position can be cited is the Children's Center in Syracuse, N.Y. (Caldwell & Richmond, 1964, 1968). The underlying hypothesis guiding the Syracuse program was that the optimal time to begin enriching the experiential environment of a child was during early infancy—that is, after such time as he would have formed an attachment to his primary caregiver (his mother) and before such time as restrictive modes of communication and thinking had been established that would limit his future adaptivity. From 1966 to 1969, this program had a yearly enrollment of approximately 75 children, ranging in age from six months to five years and divided into five approximately equal subgroups. Age separations in the groups were not rigid, and during part of each day the children were in planned contacts with older and younger groups. Most of the children attended for a full six-to-nine hour day, with a teacher-pupil ratio being approximately 1:4 for all groups. The classroom activities offered

a balance between teacher-initiated and child-initiated activities. That is, in each day's schedule there were some activities that were carefully planned by the teaching staff and others that involved completely free selection of activity and expression of interest by the children. All groups were racially balanced, and an attempt was made to have approximately equal numbers of boys and girls in each group.

At this time data are available from some 86 children who had entered day care prior to age three, 22 who had entered after age three and 49 controls from comparable socioeconomic backgrounds (Caldwell, 1971). Each child used in the analysis had remained in the program for at least six months; many had remained for two to three years. Each child was assessed shortly after enrollment on a standardized test of early development and again immediately prior to this data analysis. The difference between the initial score and the subsequent score was statistically significant for both subgroups of children, with neither group gaining more than the other. For both the early and the late entries, the difference between the amount of change shown by the day care and the control children was substantial and statistically reliable.

It has been suggested that such gains are spurious and merely reflect greater familiarity with the test situation and greater ease and relaxation during the assessment period. This may well be the case. However, it is significant to note that in the Syracuse study, controls were themselves tested in circumstances which corresponded very closely to those under which the day care children were tested. That is, a one-week "nursery school" was established and no child was tested until he had achieved familiarity with the situation and the examiners. But even if the gains in the day care children are motivational rather than intrinsic cognitive gains, this in itself is important. Whether such gains hold up with time is quite another matter, and one to which a great deal more research attention needs to be directed in the future.

Findings from other carefully evaluated day care programs have shown either similar gains (Robinson & Robinson, 1971), or else no difference between day care and control children (Keister, 1970). Probably the most accurate generalization that can be drawn is that the greater the proportion of children in a program from environments which differ from the middle-class norm, the greater the likelihood that results will indicate an increase in cognitive functioning associated with day care; the greater the proportion of children from backgrounds already geared to the acquisition of skills represented in the developmental tests, the less the likelihood that there will be a statistically significant difference between day care and control children. But above both of these conclusions can be placed the superordinate generalization that intellectual development need not be adversely affected by participation in day care, as many people seemed to fear might be the case if children were separated from their families for large segments of the time during their early years.

3. *Children in day care can be kept healthy.* Certainly one aspect of a quality life is good health, and the question of the effects of day care on the health of children is a major one. Because of the potential health hazards, it would have been folly until just a few years ago to advocate bringing large numbers of young children, especially infants, together in groups—epidemics of measles or polio would have had disastrous consequences. Now, however, such illnesses can be controlled by immunization and, provided a family receives good medical care, they no longer need to pose a serious threat to the presence of young children in groups.

But what about the array of less serious, but still troublesome, illnesses that beset young children in groups? Specifically, what effect will day care have on the incidence and severity of colds and other respiratory illnesses? Will children in groups have perpetual runny noses and will one infant in a group so spread his illness that no one will be safe? These questions are especially relevant for infant day care.

Several infant centers are currently collecting data on this subject, but to date only the Chapel Hill, N.C., group has published results. Over a five-year period, this group studied respiratory illnesses in approximately 100 children who had participated for some length of time in the Frank Porter Graham Child Development Center. Most of the children entered day care before one year of age. The average incidence of respiratory illness by the group was 8.9 illnesses per child per year. The highest incidence rate of 10 per year was in the children under one year, with the figure dropping below eight per year in the three-year-olds. The Chapel Hill data were compared to data from a large metropolitan community which recorded an average of 8.3 illnesses per year for one-year-old children and 7.4 per year thereafter through age five. Glezen, et al (1971) concluded that infant day care might be associated with a slight excess of respiratory illnesses in children under one year of age, but that after that time the incidence figures were very similar to those reported for home-reared children.

Data from this study should be very reassuring to those who are interested in operating infant day care programs. In the Chapel Hill Center, no attempt was made to isolate the ill children unless this appeared necessary for the ill child's own well being. Of course, high standards of cleanliness were maintained by the staff. Also, all children received excellent medical care through the program and, by 1967, a fulltime nurse and parttime pediatrician were part of the staff. Thus, one should not, from the results of this one study, rush to the conclusion that infant day care will never be associated with increased incidence of illness. Obviously the data at hand are from a high quality program which strove for optimal conditions for the maintenance of health. But these data are important in identifying a standard of excellence in the area of health to which all day care programs can strive.

4. *Children in day care do not lose their attachment to their mothers.* The Syracuse group (Caldwell, Wright, Honig & Tannenbaum, 1970) investigated another extremely important aspect of social and emotional development of children in day care—the attachment of children to their own mothers, and the reciprocal attachment of the mothers to their children. Primary maternal attachment is considered an essential foundation to all other social attachments that a child forms in later life (Ainsworth, 1969). In order to obtain some information on how early day care affects this basic attachment, the Syracuse staff compared two groups of mother-child pairs. Children in one group of 18 mother-child pairs had been involved in the day care program from the time they were approximately one year old. Children in the other group of 23 mother-child pairs had remained in the exclusive care of their mothers during that same period. All assessments were made when the children were approximately 30 months of age. Based on observations of interaction between the mothers and the children in a three-hour session, interviews about the child's behavior at home and discussions of the mother's own child-rearing patterns, a cluster of ratings pertaining to attachment behavior was made for each mother and child.

In terms of the attachment of the children for their own mothers, there were no significant differences between the day care and the home-reared infants. That is, the children who had been enrolled in day care and had been exposed to several adults daily since before their first birthday were just as attached to their own mothers as were the children who had remained at home during this same period.

The children were also rated on *breadth* of attachment, i.e., in terms of their attachment of people other than their mothers. Their day care infants enjoyed interaction with other people more than the home-reared infants. This finding is compatible with data from a study by Schaffer and Emerson in Scotland (1964), which showed that infants who had had extensive contacts with other people tended to develop attachment to more people than infants who had been isolated.

In regard to strength of attachment of their *mothers* for their *children,* there were again no major differences between the groups. One important factor in this study was that all infants were at least six months old when they were enrolled in day care. This policy was adopted to permit the primary child-mother attachment to develop *before* the child was placed in a situation that might conceivably weaken it.

Other findings in this Syracuse study which, while not directly answering our question about the effects of day care upon attachment behavior, demonstrate the informational by-products that can generally be expected from broadbased research. For example, when the day care and home-reared samples were combined, we found that strength of attachment of a child for his mother was correlated with developmental level. That is, children whose development was *most advanced* usually were rated as the most attached to their mothers. Similarly, there was some evidence that the most advanced babies tended to have the most attached mothers. Both of these findings corroborate the generalization that one cannot effectively separate early manifestations of behavioral competence from other aspects of development.

Several other projects are continually monitoring the social and emotional development of infants whose early experience has included day care. Within the next five years a great deal of information on this topic should be available to us to help ascertain more definitively if this aspect of a quality life can be guaranteed children in day care.

5. *Young children in day care do not necessarily become emotionally disturbed.* This conclusion is also stated negatively, as there were valid theoretical reasons to remain alert lest this occur. Again data from the Syracuse project can be offered to substantiate the point. In 1968, Dr. Samuel Braun, a child psychiatrist, was asked to do what is generally called a "blind" study on all the children in the group of three-four-year-olds (Braun & Caldwell, in press). For many people, the only acceptable cutting point for enrolling children in day care was age three—any children put in such a situation at an earlier age were expected to become emotionally disturbed. Those who operated the Syracuse program were eager for reassurance that the procedure developed there to offer cognitive and social enrichment was not producing emotional damage. Accordingly, Dr. Braun spent a week with the children in the two oldest groups—helping in the classrooms, eating with them, going to the bathroom with them, riding to and from school with them, talking with their teachers, just observing them, etc. At the end of that time he rated each child on a scale of 1-5, with "1" indicating good adjustment and "5" indicating poor adjustment. Of the total group, only one child received a rating of "5" and only four received a rating of "4", indicating that, in general, the 30 children were relatively well adjusted. Then the data were examined to see whether the distribution of ratings differed for the children who had enrolled at or after age three. The distributions of ratings for the two groups were virtually identical, indicating that early enrollment (prior to age three) need not be associated with a high incidence of emotional disturbance.

6. *Children in day care develop a feeling of community.* For some time we have thought that our early day care children "cared for" one another more than one usually finds in groups of children of similar age. They are often deeply concerned about another child's rights, about whether Mary has had her turn or whether the teacher dealt adequately with Eric when he pushed Gerald off the tricycle. A hint that this might be the situation can be found in published reports (see Freud & Dann, 1951) of the social behavior of parentless children who were released from concentration camps in eastern Europe after World War II. These children seemed to find their strength in each other and to resist for some time the establishment of close ties with new adults and with other children. Currently, Lay and Meyer are collecting some observational data on 20 kindergarten children who are "graduates" of the Syracuse Children's Center, most of whom have been together in day care from early infancy. These

children are now enrolled in a school with 20 additional children who were not part of the original day care sample. Using a time sample observational technique, Lay and Meyer found that although the "new" children distributed their social encounters rather equally over the entire group of 40 children, the social interactions of the former day care children were largely among themselves. That is, they tended to stick with the children who had "graduated" to the new environment together, although over the course of the year (as new friendship patterns developed) this tendency weakened somewhat. This suggests that these little children from diverse family backgrounds moved to a new social setting as a small community—sticking together, helping one another, offering a familiar base until the new environment could be more readily apprehended. Several of the children were from unstable and disturbed families, and most were from families burdened in economic difficulties; yet their "togetherness" had helped them adjust to a new situation and had strengthened in them the feeling of community that we need to encourage in all children.

7. *Children in day care have a better chance of being Americanized.* This now almost archaic-sounding term — Americanize — is used for this point to highlight the absurdity of some of the charges leveled against the Comprehensive Child Care bill at the time of the presidential veto in December of 1971. In his message accompanying the veto, the President condemned the child care provision of the act for its "fiscal irresponsibility, administrative unworkability, and family-weakening implications of the system it envisions." The President was justifiably concerned about this veto, as, shortly after taking office, he had by Executive Order created the Office of Child Development and had committed his office to do everything possible to strengthen programs for children during the first five years of life. Although participation in the programs was to be voluntary, and although local parent councils would guide all programs that became operational, the President claimed to fear that the child development programs would eventually become mandatory and thus serve to destroy the family. He said: "For the Federal government to plunge headlong financially into supporting child development would commit the vast moral authority of the National Government to the side of communal approaches to child rearing over against the family-centered approach."

An illustration of this position can be found in the following quote from the Congressional Record, the remarks made by a California legislator who shall remain nameless:

> *Of course, Mr. Speaker, they do not yet ask for power to take children by force. That never comes first. But, Mr. Speaker, as surely as twilight follows sunset and darkness follows twilight, it comes last. It is the end to which all such programs logically tend. The family is the backbone of any healthy society. Destroy the family and we destroy America. This "child development" legislation aims at providing a substitute for the family in the form of committees of psychiatrists, psychologists, sociologists and social workers. But there is no substitute for the family. A Nation of orphanages cannot endure, a d should not. It is an offense to God and Man.*

This bit of impassioned rhetoric was followed by the *piece de resistance:*

> *Walk into the halls of the Department of Health, Education and Welfare and think of having it in place of a mother.*

This charge has come to be labeled the "Sovietization" issue — such programs mean that we are changing our basic socialization pattern to conform to that used in collective societies. This is, of course, a spurious issue, deliberately employed to confuse and mislead. A few careful substitutions in part of the above quotation will perhaps help to strengthen my point:

This "education" legislation aims at providing a substitute for the family in the form of committees of superintendents, principals, and teachers.

For is that not what we do in our public schools? Do we not now let teachers help our children learn how to read and cipher instead of their parents as used to be the pattern? And has not vocational education broken up the pattern of family apprenticeship? To assert that an experience which can help children achieve the goals for which this country stands will "Sovietize" them indicates just how far we have strayed from those original goals. Did we not develop a system of public education in this country precisely because our forefathers recognized that no set of parents could help to do all that was needed to educate (i.e., socialize) their children?

Thus, to counter some of the irresponsible charges as to possible consequences of progressive child development legislation, this author would suggest that early child development programs can help to provide a quality life by helping to Americanize American children. The following poignant anecdote will illustrate the point.

This occurred in the kindergarten of our extended day school, a comprehensive educational day care facility for children ranging in age from under one year up through sixth grade. One of the most popular children was a little White child whose two best friends, one a boy and one a girl, happened to be Black. In the middle of the school year, the girl's parents indicated their intention to withdraw her from the school, as the racial composition had shifted from about 50:50 to 75:25 Black-White. "It seems that she never talks about anybody but the Black children," complained the parents. One of our social workers talked to the parents about the matter, trying to accept their feelings without remonstrance while reiterating our policy of admitting children without regard to race and urging that the child be permitted to remain in what was obviously a highly rewarding and enjoyable environment for her. The parents thought the matter over and kept the child in school. The morning after the conference, the little girl bounced into the room, and, in her customary didactic style, pointed individually to each child in turn and announced, "I can play with you, and you, and I can't play with you, or you, or you. . . ." It took no great categorizing skill to perceive that skin color was the basis of the classification. With the honesty of a child she freely verbalized the agreement that had allowed her to remain in school: "If I do, my momma's going to whip me and my brother's going to beat me up." The earlier favorite friends of the child were crushed and the child herself had obvious difficulty remembering the new rules as she fell into her school routine. Fortunately, with the help of a sensitive teacher who gently interpreted that homes had rules and school had rules and that they were not always identical, the admonition was quickly forgotten and old friendships were restored.

To whom did the teachers in our day care school have an obligation? To those parents, whose love and devotion to their child expressed itself in a very un-American concept and type of behavior? Or to the child who deserved a better chance to learn how to adapt in a pluralistic society in which representatives of all ethnic and cultural groups have equal rights and privileges? Was the child, who was being encouraged to behave in the context of a set of values that obviously contradicted those of the home, being Sovietized? Communized? Not at all, but she was being Americanized. One of the nicer things that can happen to children in day care is that it gives them an opportunity to acquire the breadth of vision necessary to realize the full meaning of that now seemingly anachronistic phrase, the American dream.

SUMMARY

In this paper an attempt has been made to marshal evidence that day care can help provide a quality life for young children. In the few programs in which systematic evaluations have been conducted, quality day care has been found to be associated with intellectual gains, with the acquisition of adaptive social skills, and with healthy physical and emotional development. A response to such data might be a rejoinder that such experiences can obviously be good for children, but that they are seldom found in day care. What is the proportion of such programs among the array of centers and day care homes scattered all over the country? In how many do you find happy children, and in how many do you find children eating lunch off the lid of the garbage pail (to cite one recently published horror story). And in what proportion is there a sensitive program, geared to children's developmental needs in contrast to a steady diet of TV throughout the day? Unfortunately, we do not know the answers to those questions, but one of the more encouraging trends of the past five years is that we are beginning to bring all categories of day care under public scrutiny. All states now have some kind of licensing procedure for day care, albeit the standards vary widely from state to state. And, although licensing can in some respects be seen as encouraging premature crystallization of operational patterns without ample opportunity to explore and try different forms of service, in general, it offers one of the best protective mechanisms that we have. If consumers are to get good day care, they must realize their obligation to find out about the situation, visit centers and keep in contact with state and national legislation programs.

A commendable step in this direction has been taken by Mary Dublin Keyserling who chose *Windows on Day Care* as the apt title for her study of the variety of available operating programs and of the need for additional facilities.

We definitely need to open all possible windows on day care in order to know and to influence what is happening in the field. As citizens—not just as professionals or as day care consumers—we must all demand systematic monitoring of day care programs to ensure experiences for our children that are conducive to wholesale development. Today one hears cries from potential consumers for more and better day care, and sometimes these demands appear to show little concern for the welfare of the children involved. "We need more day care centers so their mothers can go to work and get off the welfare rolls." And, "We want more child care centers so that women can realize their potential." These are legitimate concerns of our society, for we do want our citizens to be able to function independently, and we do want our women to have an opportunity to realize their own destiny. But sometimes it is hard to shake the fear that those who make these demands are minimally concerned about what happens to the children. If day care does weaken family life, we need to know this, for as of this time we do not know of a successful way to rear children (in terms of how our society has traditionally defined success) apart from families. We must, in short, keep constantly attuned to generate continuing answers to the question asked in this paper. We can have cheaper day care by not bothering to monitor, by not bothering to care. But in the long run it will cost us more.

REFERENCES

Ainsworth, M. D. S. Object relations, dependency, and attachment: A theoretical review of the infant-mother relationship. *Child Develpm.*, 1969, 40, 969-1025.

Braun, S. J. & Caldwell, B. M. Social adjustment of children in day care who enrolled prior to or after the age of three. *Early Child Develpm. & Care,* 1972.

Caldwell, B. M. Impact of interest in early cognitive stimulation. In Herbert Rie (Ed.), *Perspectives in Psychopathology.* Chicago: Aldine-Atherton, 1971. Pp. 293-334.

Caldwell, B. M. & Richmond, J. B. The children's center—a microcosmic health, education, and welfare unit. In L. Dittmann (Ed.), *Early Child Care: The New Perspectives.* New York: Atherton Press, 1968. Pp. 326-358, 373-377.

Caldwell, B. M., Wright, C. M., Honig, A. S. & Tannenbaum, J. Infant day care and attachment. *Am. J. Orthopsychiat.*, 1970, 40, 397-412.

Freud, A. & Dann, S. An experiment in group upbringing. *Psychoanalytic Study of the Child,* 1951, 6, 127-168.

Glezen, W. P., Loda, F. A., Clyde, W. A., Jr., Senior, R. J., Schaeffer, C. I., Conley, W. G. & Denny, F. W. Epidemiologic patterns of acute lower respiratory diseases of children in a pediatric group practice. *J. Pediatrics,* Mar. 1971.

Harrington, M. *The Other America.* New York: Macmillan Co., 1962.

Keister, M. E. *The "Good Life" for Infants and Toddlers.* Washington: National Association for the Education of Young Children, 1970.

Keyserling, M. D. *Windows on Day Care.* New York: National Council of Jewish Women, 1972.

Lay, M. Z. & Meyer, W. J. Effects of early day care experience on subsequent observed program behaviors. Final report. U.S. Office of Education, Subcontract No. 70-007, Syracuse University, 1971.

Prescott, E., Jones, E. & Kritchevsky, S. Group day care as a child-rearing environment: An observational study of day care programs. Pasadena, Calif.: Pacific Oaks College, 1967.

————————. *Day Care as a Child-Rearing Environment.* Vol. II. Washington: National Association for the Education of Young Children, 1972.

Robinson, H. B. & Robinson, N. M. Longitudinal development of very young children in a comprehensive day care program: The first two years. *Child Develpm.,* 1971, 42, (no. 6): 1673-1683.

Schaffer, H. R. & Emerson, P. E. The development of social attachments in infancy. *Monogr. Soc. Res. Child Develpm.,* 1964, 29, 3, 1-77 (Whole No. 94).

Housing Policy

It is not the objective of this section to inform the reader of the vast housing policy network that has developed over the years. Rather, the intent is to reinforce the need for the consideration of human values in the decision process of providing housing for individuals and families.

Dorothy Lee, cultural anthropologist and lecturer, stated her views on values in a Penney's *Forum* interview. "There is basic to all existence the value of being me, of being unique, of what has been referred to as human dignity. But along with the value of being human is the value of community. By community I mean the other person or persons around me. For a number of groups (the ones we have called 'primitive'), community also included the air, water, rocks and trees. This is why they didn't pollute or destroy because they loved their community and were responsive to it. . . . The value of human dignity cannot exist without community. For instance, I don't believe I can actualize my dignity unless my community recognizes and honors it. I can feel proud that I am—not arrogant, but proud—when you recognize my existence."[1]

The two articles that follow are specifically chosen to contrast differing regard for the pride and dignity of the individual held by the planners of the two housing projects Pruitt-Igoe and Sursum Corda. It does little good to hold post-mortems unless something is learned in the process. The exhumed body of Pruitt-Igoe was given a hopeful rebirth as described in the article by George McCue. However, at the present time, even this attempt falters, and the infamous project that was once lauded as an architectural model of high-rise apartment complexes stands as a monument to designers who did not consider the needs of individuals, families or communities. By contrast, the planners of the housing project Sursum Corda have considered the fact that people will react favorably to their environment if they feel that their wishes have been heard and if they know that they have some input in decisions. They can then feel proud because someone "recognized their existence."

Commentary—Evelyn Eldridge, ed.

[1]Grace Richardson, "Are There Universal Values?" Penney's *Forum*, Spring/Summer, 1972, p. 22.

$57,000,000 Later: An Interdisciplinary Effort Is Being Made to Put Pruitt-Igoe Together Again

by George McCue

"Pruitt-Igoe, an internationally recognized public housing project—first for its unique application of planning economies; and second, for its failure as a social institution, has received more comment and written words than any other project of its kind in America. Its failure as a public housing project cannot be attributed alone to the architecture, to the community or to the tenants, but must be recognized as the object lesson of a series of social events and social conflicts."

This is from one of a series of reports by a task force commissioned to analyze what had happened to Pruitt-Igoe, and to see what could be retrieved from the ruins, just 16 years old at the time.

When the Wendell Oliver Pruitt Homes and the William L. Igoe Apartments were opened in 1954 and 1955, they were acclaimed as new prototypes of mass housing for poor people. St. Louis had wiped out 57½ acres of slums in a North Side high-crime district, just a few blocks from the downtown core, and had put up an apartment project that towered like a monument to civic pride and budget ingenuity above the crumbling houses and flats along its borders.

The two developments, completed a year apart, were named for a black St. Louis hero and a progressive former Congressman, and they were the biggest and most visible of a succession of slum clearance projects dating back to the 1930s and extending, off and on, for some 20 blocks between Broadway and Jefferson Avenue.

Pruitt, with 20 buildings, was designated as housing for blacks; Igoe, 13 buildings, was the city's first public housing to be nonsegregated. Together, they were praised for having provided "decent, safe" homes for 10,000 men, women and children in approximately 2700 units of one to five bedrooms as replacement for about 400 slum dwellings. All 33 of the new buildings had 11 stories, which advanced the density from about seven to about 45 units per acre.

A 1947 city plan for this area had proposed walk-up apartments, but additional stories were demanded by the federal formula for adjusting density to land value. So the architects, Hellmuth, Yamasaki and Leinweber, responded with elevator buildings.

Federal objections to what were considered needless amenities caused other revisions of both concept and physical disposition of the housing units. There were small economies, such as the elimination of wall paint in general circulation areas, and there was a large economy in lining up the buildings in six rows that followed the east-west patterns of vacated streets, so as to plug into existing utilities.

This eliminated cloistered private space, which was a little understood idea at that time, but the architects worked out a composition of their long, narrow structures that countered the effect of slab corridors by offsetting adjacent buildings to break up the ranks.

Although several playgrounds were provided, the ground area between and around buildings ended up empty, and a no-man's land. This was conceived of as public space, as much accessible to nonresidents as to tenants, and the long rows of buildings with their long walks

Ekistics, November 1973, Vol. 36, No. 216, pp. 42-45. Reprinted with permission.
George McCue was art and architecture critic for the St. Louis *Post-Dispatch,* now retired.

along phantom streets provided no separation of space where a group of tenants could establish even semiprivate territoriality.

There was one more major breakthrough in economy—the innovation of skip-stop elevators. The first three floors of all buildings were treated as a layer of walk-up apartments, and elevator stops were provided on the fourth, seventh and tenth floors where laundry rooms were spaced out along a broad corridor, planned as a children's play gallery. From the floors with elevator stops, tenants walked up or down one flight to residence floors. For a final touch of built-in disaster, first-floor toilets were scratched off the plans.

The apartment interiors were made light and airy by bands of windows, and kitchen equipment was included. But the kitchen-living-dining area of a four-bedroom apartment, housing up to ten people, was made the same size as that for a two-bedroom unit, and families that needed five bedrooms rarely had more than one bathroom.

So there stood Pruitt-Igoe, as the two developments soon became identified, under merged management. The bricks-and-mortar answer to slums. The award-winning design that pulled advantage out of adversity. The gleaming towers standing tall and apart from their shudderingly dilapidated surroundings. The project with the imbedded social time bombs ticking away.

The first signs of trouble showed up in units in the isolated southeast corner of the project site. These were hazardous to approach across the open wasteland, mentioned earlier, which had been created by building high to meet density requirements. The trouble quickly spread throughout the area—not only physical danger.

The fact that this 57½-acre tract is referred to as a "project," rather than as a neighborhood, speaks volumes, not only of its appearance but of its character as an isolated demoralizing *social* element.

The ravages of Pruitt-Igoe's sickness can be traced through their symptoms. Mothers on upper floors had no way of keeping surveillance over the playgrounds, and often kept their children inside. Children at play, with an impatient need for one of those non-existent ground-floor toilets, resorted to an elevator as a substitute. Elevator access was around a corner or two, with convenient lurking places. The pattern of rape began with capture on an elevator and completion in a hallway or vacant apartment.

There came a time when mailmen would not deliver packages, but would leave a note for the resident to present at the post office. Western Union refused to deliver telegrams. Retail stores stopped sending delivery trucks. Moving companies had trouble hiring men who would enter the grounds. Cab drivers refused to take passengers within the area at night. Firemen wouldn't answer alarms except with a police escort.

Once, when a playground was installed, workmen built a chain link fence around the building and play equipment to protect their materials. Tenants asked that the fence remain and the crime rate of that one building dropped a spectacular 80 percent. Eventually similar fences surrounded large portions of the area, but these were to keep people away from buildings that had been vacated—23 of them so badly vandalized that they were unusable.

The dismal arithmetic of Pruitt-Igoe's planning and construction economies was laid on the table. Original cost: $36,127,000. Interest on bonds to January, 1971, $12,403,900. Federal modernization funds, $5 million, with interest on that debt of $500,000. Operating subsidies, $1,092,286. Cost of closing down 23 apartment buildings and three others, $284,700. Operating deficits paid from other developments' surpluses, $1,765,848. Total cost, at that time: $56,973,734. The bonds, with 25 years still to run, would cost the federal government another $42,500,000 for normal retirement.

Thomas Costello, Executive Director of the Housing Authority, proposed that the Department of Housing and Urban Development recall the bonds and rebuild Pruitt-Igoe. "That's not too costly a mistake in comparison to the space program's and the Defense Department's billion-dollar cost overruns," he urged.

HUD's problem was similar financial difficulties in some 20 other cities, and the risky precedent of bailing one out. It authorized $60,000 for a study of private redevelopment of Pruitt-Igoe, and a blue ribbon consultant task force moved in.

This group set up shop in the Pruitt-Igoe Community Building from October, 1971, to June, 1972. George Romney, HUD's director at the time, visited the enterprise enough to know some tenants by sight. This all-out, highly dedicated effort, of financial advantage to no one, produced a plan that promises once again to make Pruitt-Igoe a prototype.

This plan found it would be unfeasible (because of floor plan and lack of a market) to convert the buildings to commercial, industrial or institutional use. In fact, it found most of them unusable for anything. The alternative? Make 1,009 dwelling units in remodeled existing buildings; 223 in new walk-up buildings, with an evenly divided mix of low-income and moderate-income households; convert the whole enterprise to nonpublic ownership and management; and create an urban living center for training in consumer lore, maintenance and use of apartment facilities.

To remedy one of the grievous defects of the original scheme—not even a place to buy an ice cream cone—it suggested shops within the apartment areas, a small shopping center on the north side and a large one on additional land to the south, both tied to Pruitt-Igoe with pleasant walks and streets. The buildings would be clustered in six "villages," still using the street-aligned utilities but not following the street patterns.

It also calls for considerable demolition. Only two of the 11-story slabs would be retained, but the corner elements of others would be converted to twin towers with connecting elevator shafts—stops on every floor. Families with children would be in walk-ups, with the elderly and childless higher up, but not marooned there. ("I met one eleventh-floor family in which the older members hadn't been out of the house in years because they couldn't walk down stairs," Sharpe said.)

The new scheme, prepared from painstaking and well-aimed research in both design and social implications, shows promise of making Pruitt-Igoe a neighborhood instead of a project.

Lower Income Housing
Sheds the High-Rise Stigma

A Maryland architect shows how human comforts can find room in central city shelter design

Lower income families have feelings, too.

Their own needs and wants in new rental housing should be considered as carefully as the details involved in financing their dwellings.

The advice comes from Arnold M. Kronstadt, an architect who should know, having proved that thoughtfully planned housing with abundant amenities need not be the sole province of affluent suburbia.

A partner in the architectural, planning and engineering firm of Collins and Kronstadt, Leahy, Hogan, Collins, of Silver Spring, Md., Kronstadt has stated his case well in a 199-unit housing development designed and built for low- and moderate- income families in Washington, D.C.

Aptly named Sursum Corda, the Latin for "lift up your hearts," the development expresses a new spirit in inner-city housing design—a spirit that aims at sparking a measure of community pride where human despair has become all too pervasive.

THE HUMAN ELEMENT

Standing in stark contrast to the dull and depressing structural designs so often standard in new low-income housing, Sursum Corda features such architectural counterpoints as:

Clustered townhouses, "designed to give each family a sense of individuality and identity."

Private access to individual living quarters.

Central air conditioning and large appliances, including washers and dryers in most cases.

Open courts, off-street parking and recreational amenities, including a community center.

These design features, of course, are not new nor iconclastic. They've been incorporated for years in higher cost housing.

What is unusual is that these and other elements were made possible at reasonable cost in such an unlikely location.

The location consists of five and one-half acres in the heart of Washington's Northwest No. 1 Project Area, itself a 95-acre urban renewal site that begins only three blocks from the nation's Capitol.

Upon the completion of its redevelopment, the overall area will provide approximately 1,100 units of new low- and moderate- income housing and 466 units of low-rent public housing. In addition, plans call for the rehabilitation of 241 units of existing housing plus new neighborhood shopping facilities, expanded schools, and new parks, playgrounds and pedestrian walkways.

The entire site plan "represents what we believe to be one of the best illustrations in our region of the utilization of relevant HUD programs to provide low- and moderate- income housing through urban renewal," comments Harry I. Sharrott, assistant Regional II administrator for renewal assistance of the Department of Housing and Urban Development.

Reprinted with permission from *Savings and Loan News,* June 1970, pp. 29-33.

Added to this, "over and above the physical aspects of renewal," he says, "is the emphasis on the human side of renewal. . . the full participation of the residents" in the renewal process within the project area.

Such was no less the case for Sursum Corda. In Kronstadt's words, the project required "careful, meticulous attention to detail" along with close analyses of the "inter-relationships of the various elements on costs and performance."

But what's more, he says, Sursum Corda could not have evolved as it did had it not been for detailed research aimed at "finding out what the prospective tenants really needed" and hoped for in housing.

"I asked myself," Kronstadt says, " 'What do I know about slum conditions and ways of life?' This bothered me, for I knew very little."

"Most architects," he says, "don't have the specific research and information needed today to design the type of housing most suited for lower income families."

Existing tabulated data weren't good enough, Kronstadt adds. "I felt, as should other architects facing a similar situation, that I should get out and see with my own eyes precisely what problems would be faced and what needs should be met."

A COMMUNITY RESPONDS

Kronstadt did just that. His firm having been commissioned by the D.C. Redevelopment Land Agency to plan and design Sursum Corda, Kronstadt went directly into the community whose residents would be affected by the development.

His way was cleared in 1967 by a community leader, Father Horace McKenna of St. Aloysius Catholic Church—one of five nonprofit interests, including two neighborhood schools and two social units of Georgetown University, which joined in sponsoring Sursum Corda under FHA 221 (d) (3) financing authority. This assured that the Federal National Mortgage Association would take out the permanent mortgage on the development under the special housing assistance authority it then held.

Father McKenna, Kronstadt recalls, had "amazingly close contacts with the community" where Sursum Corda was to be located. He knew its people and wanted his church to remain a force in their lives.

With the priest's help, Kronstadt was able to make at least 20 personal calls on families then living in mostly substandard housing set to be razed for Sursum Corda and the other developments planned for the Northwest No. 1 Project Area.

NO HOLDING BACK

The families were receptive. From personal interviews and observations of their living conditions, Kronstadt received the type of guidance he knew he would need in planning Sursum Corda.

There was the challenge, he says, that "the requirements to produce low-cost housing are more demanding, performance lapses more significant and failures more tragic." Thus, being "responsive to the needs of the community" was a must.

At the outset, Kronstadt learned that the development would have to accommodate families with six to 11 children in many cases.

He observed that some of the units then housing these families had two or three undersized refrigerators, bicycles stored in living rooms and bunk beds in bedrooms.

He also saw "lots of clothes" hanging from heat pipes, washing machines located in kitchens and generally inadequate lavatory facilities.

Kronstadt recalls that these units, mostly rowhouses, were "clean inside but had debris stacked outside." Exterior environments, he adds, also suffered from lack of play areas, crowded streets and other problems symptomatic of most urban ghettos.

Kronstadt considered all of these elements carefully, weighing their importance in the final design decisions which were yet to be made. He also asked a few leading questions about structural design preferences.

From his questions he learned, for example, that wood floors weren't desired. Instead, composition floors would be far better because they are easier to keep clean.

He also learned that ample closet space, though a must, need not be fragmented into many separate compartments. There was no objection to large common closets.

Further, Kronstadt was told that exposed block construction for interior walls would be perfectly acceptable. Families interviewed had friends in public housing who had such walls and found them acceptable.

These three and other elements would have a significant effect on Kronstadt's design decisions. Each offered substantial cost savings and would open the way for amenities that would not otherwise be possible within the project's $3.7 million budget limitations.

The interviews were followed by 10 monthly meetings with a special citizens committee, established to represent the interests of the community. Its members included block leaders and others who, Kronstadt says, "contributed significantly" to the design process.

Planning and design for low-income shelter should be this way, "a continuous process," he says. It should involve not only the people through all its stages but also "the full range of disciplines involved—the architect, planner, builder, lender, market analyst and property manager."

Consider the market analyst, for instance. His views, says Kronstadt, "may change when he sees some of the early proposed building designs or site studies."

Or take the builder or general contractor. Either "may not be as upset about the cost of, say, a large floor area when he views the low-cost mechanical and structural system," according to Kronstadt.

He adds that even the architect "may be shocked to learn from a property manager that large glass areas may be a problem in low-cost housing because of the high cost of window drapes and the problems of placing furniture in rooms of generally small size."

All of these considerations found their place in the development of Sursum Corda. According to Kronstadt, they were the outgrowth of "the cost-value relationship as viewed in its total concept: that is, what would the project cost to build, operate and maintain as well as what would be the immediate and long-range values produced?

THE REWARDS OF THOUGHTFUL PLANNING

What evolved bears witness that "there are no major broad brush strokes to achieving low-cost housing," as Kronstadt states. Designing such shelter takes much more than following the formula of high-rise conformity or simply blueprinting cheap imitations of higher cost housing.

The development, which welcomed its first families in June of last year, provides a mix of 44 one-bedroom units and 155 units containing from two to six bedrooms at a density approximating 37 units per acre. Of the larger units, 30 have two bedrooms; 39, three; 46, four; 20, five; and 20, six.

"The mix of units obviously has to be controlled by the market," Kronstadt says. "However, when building under a 221 (d) (3) program, for example, though you may find plenty of demand for efficiencies and one-bedroom units, few people qualify because their incomes are too high.

"Thus," he says, "the mix must be controlled by the qualified demand. This also holds true for conventionally financed projects."

He adds that "Mix should also control density of people—not dwelling units per acre."

GAUGING THE LAY OF THE LAND

The development houses most three-bedroom and all larger units in three-story town houses built on mostly uneven grading. All other units, also townhouses, are arranged in two-story "piggyback" fashion on a relatively steep sloping grade on one side of the development.

On the high side of this grading, residents of the two- and three-bedroom upper units are able to enter their dwellings by walking up a short flight of stairs. On the opposite side of the same buildings, where the grading is lower, residents of the lower one-bedroom units have access to their quarters at ground level through fenced patios.

This arrangement is in keeping with Kronstadt's finding that "If steeply sloping sites can allow us to design a multistory building at various levels without elevators, more units under the same roof and on the same foundation will result in good economies and an interesting site plan."

He also has found that "tighter densities between buildings can be used and higher densities achieved with sloping sites than with flat sites, thus reducing costs."

Cost savings, though, should not result from scrimping on land. Kronstadt would much rather "find ways of squeezing savings out of a building."

In multifamily housing projects, he notes, "land may represent only 10% of the total cost of the units and the property combined." What this means is that a 10% savings in land would equal a 1% savings in overall project costs.

"On the other hand," he says, "a 10% saving in building costs would equal a 9% saving for the same project."

By taking the construction cost-cutting approach, Kronstadt's firm achieved the goals envisioned for Sursum Corda. Some representative cost-cutting features:

- Textured "corduroy" block for exterior walls. This saved as much as $500 per unit over the cost of brick.
- Shallow-pitched roofs with asphalt shingles. Saving: $350 per unit over slate.
- Careful attention to framing and use of stock length lumber. Saving: $50 per unit.
- Close coordination between framing and ductwork. Saving: $50 per unit.
- Built-in concrete canopies over doorways. Saving: $150 per unit over conventional forms of entranceway shelter.
- Exterior stairways with open concrete steps. Saving: $300 per unit over cost of building interior public stairways and $30 per year per unit in maintenance costs.
- Vinyl asbestos tile floors. Saving: 25¢ per square foot or $125 for each townhouse story over the cost of wood floors.
- Ceiling heights lowered to 7'6". Saving: $50 per unit.
- Exposed block interior walls. Saving: $75 per unit.
- Waterproof materials other than ceramic tile, except around tubs. Saving: $150 per unit.
- One common, walk-in closet per two children's bedrooms. Saving: $50 per closet.
- Elimination of separate entrance foyers in favor of tenant screens or special furniture arrangements to achieve the same purpose. Saving: $125 per unit.
- Elimination of separate bathroom hallways in one-bedroom units. Saving: $250 per unit.
- Elimination of heat registers for inside, windowless bathrooms. Saving: $25 per unit.
- Central metering of utilities. Saving: 20% on the cost of electricity alone.

MONEY FOR AMENITIES

By achieving these and other cost savings, Kronstadt's firm opened the way for such amenities as garbage disposals, ranges, large refrigerators and central air conditioning in all units of Sursum Corda—amenities not usually provided in lower income housing.

The garbage disposals were installed "to cut down on vermin, insects and odors," according to Kronstadt. At the same time, "we felt that air conditioning was a necessity, considering the humid weather in Washington."

The air conditioning, he notes, was approved by the local regional office of the Federal Housing Administration at a time when some other regional offices were disallowing this amenity for other lower income projects backed by FHA.

Still other amenities attributable in large part to construction cost savings include washers and dryers in individual units with two bedrooms or more. These were included "because it was found that the housewife in lower income brackets has three or four loads of wash every other day and should not be away from home for long periods of time in order to do the laundry."

These appliances, incidentally, are conveniently located in kitchens, just where Kronstadt saw the old washing machines in the units he visited while gathering project design information.

The same visits also prompted bedrooms designed for bunk-bed arrangements and the provision of private storage sheds outside each larger unit for the safekeeping of bicycles Kronstadt had seen parked in living rooms.

Despite the substantial costs of these amenities—$385 for each washer and dryer combination alone—rents in the development have been held to a range of $93 to $175 per month. In the case of 110 families, these payments are partially covered by federal rent subsidies.

For families who stay long enough, the development offers the prospect of home ownership by applying rent payments to build equity in individual units.

'ABSOLUTELY BEAUTIFUL'

Sursum Corda, comments Wolf Von Eckardt, the noted architectural critic of the Washington Post, is "a really good project, absolutely beautiful." He particularly likes its "grouping, arrangement and sense of community," as well as its environmental amenities.

These amenities, which were provided at an average cost of $500 per unit, include a community center; open courts designed, as Kronstadt says, "to promote community interaction"; and separate enclosed yards or balconies "to accommodate the need for privacy."

Kronstadt, whose firm employs eight black staff architects and has designed more than 10,000 housing units nationally for lower income families, holds hope for the future of low-cost housing. But, he says, the rate of progress depends in large share on the easing of restrictive building codes.

Such codes "produce the greatest single roadblock to low-cost housing, particularly in multifamily structures," he says. For example, "Where we fight to cut the cost of an item by $2 or $3 and perhaps study and restudy framing systems that may finally save $10 per unit, building codes can throw away $500 per dwelling.

"Zoning ordinances that insist on linear arrangement of townhouses, each with its own street frontage of 18 feet, make for similar waste," he adds. "The clustering of townhouses into courts and commons is not permitted in many jurisdictions," even though clustering "can help to avoid bad ground areas or difficult slopes and still achieve the desired overall density at low cost."

WHAT ASSOCIATIONS CAN DO

Kronstadt adds that just as it is "our mutual responsibility to plan and design, so we all have the responsibility to support changes in codes and ordinances which result in waste." This includes savings association executives.

"The savings and loan man," he says, "must get more involved than ever" in these problems. As a lender, it is also his responsibility to support research aimed at determining "the true housing needs of people" and "know more about the product" he is called on to finance.

In short, says Kronstadt, the association official "should look with real sophistication" at such factors as appearance, landscaping, environmental elements and "what low-cost housing will cost to operate and maintain."

Health Care Policy

The rapidity of change brought about by scientific technology has affected no other industry as much, perhaps, as it has the medical machinery of keeping people well. In only three decades, medical technology has become the Pied Piper of our hopes and dreams that something can be done for all of our human ills. Through that technology, the nation has been able to manage acute, intensive care for people that is as good as any in the world. But few public policy issues have the potential for being as emotionally charged as do those involving life and death decisions. Few are as vulnerable to special lobby interests at the political level and few are as costly to the public. Let us look at this human need in the framework of economic, political and ethical considerations.

THE HIGH COST OF STAYING WELL

The rising cost of medical care is a fact of life. Health expenditures comprise about $100 billion annually, or about 8 percent of the gross national product. The outlay for each person in the United States is well over $500 per year and climbing. How did it get that way? Where are the highest costs?

Inflation is a factor in rising medical costs, but the total rise in the last decade is 300% for total cost of health care, a bit above the general inflation rate. At the present time, operating-room charges are rising fastest with hospital-room charges a close second. It is a problem of supply and demand, but the logistics are muddled by the middle-man in the form of health insurance.

Relationship of Cost and Insurance

Nine out of ten persons in the United States carry some form of health insurance, either private or public. Seldom does either provide for ambulatory care for patients. Even though a patient might better be cared for in a clinic, a doctor may hospitalize simply to obtain some compensation for his treatment. From the patient's viewpoint, this may be the only way to have aid in making payments. Patients relying on insurance premiums demand better service, more amenities, and as long a hospital stay as is covered by their policy.

Another way in which this almost universal insurance coverage has affected costs is in the fact that an insurance company is impersonal. That at least part of the cost of care will be paid by some corporation may contribute to reducing incentives for hospitals and doctors to be cost conscious. The Medicaid and Medicare programs for the elderly and indigent are examples of this. "Billions in Medicaid ripoffs," "Medicare computer errors cost millions," "Medicare increases hospital stay"—these and countless other news headlines echo the mounting concern over the lack of cost control in the use of tax dollars.

Whatever the future of national health insurance legislation, there is the built-in potential for cost increases by virtue of increased demands from a greater number of people. Without a corresponding regulatory mechanism, the individual consumer will pay more for the care he needs, at least in the short run.

Physicians' Fees

A second reason for the high cost of health care is insurance-related, but from the doctor's side of the issue. The rise in malpractice suits has made insurance against such a risk a necessity. This cost is passed along to the consumer in higher physicians' fees, as is the cost of added precautions the physician takes to practice "defensive" medicine in the form of added tests and x-rays to insure an accurate diagnosis. The reasons for the malpractice suits in the first place may be the fault of a few inept physicians performing unnecessary or inexpert surgery, or making wrong diagnoses, but the public may find the medical profession an expensive whipping boy for what may be a spillover from an eroded lack of confidence in other areas of our society.

Drugs and Competitive Pricing

To higher hospitalization costs and physicians' fees is added the increase in the cost of drugs as a third factor in the health-cost analysis. Substitution by a pharmacist of lower cost "generic" drugs for brand-name products if the doctor and consumer do not object is one possibility for lowering the costs. This is prohibited by law in some states. Efforts to change this may have some impact on bringing prices down on all drugs.

The Political Base of the Health Care System

If, as stated previously, rapid technological change has affected the medical field more than any other, then it may also be said that the lumbering gait of the political bureaucracy has impeded the distribution of that shiny new technology to the people. Again, more evident than in many other social policy concerns, health care delivery systems seem to be taking a long time to grow up. This inefficiency is a fourth factor contributing to the high cost of staying well. The distribution of health care is spotty, both in the concentration of physicians and nurses and in the provision of clinical and hospital facilities. Although over half of a physician's education is subsidized by government, and hospitals and equipment are partially funded from the tax dollar, the citizens who pay do not share their purchases equitably. Doctors have a tendency to prefer cities, especially those near large medical centers. How to woo them to the rural areas and smaller towns is a concern now before the national planning commissions.

THE HEALTH PLANNING AND RESOURCES DEVELOPMENT ACT OF 1974

A new effort at the federal level to combine and redirect efforts of various federally supported state and local agencies that have been active in community health planning has been enacted with the signing of the Health Planning and Resources Development Act of 1974. Under the Department of Health, Education and Welfare, it has authorization for a $1 billion three-year program of health planning and resource development. The design appears to sensibly designate broad geographic health service areas, with a local Health Systems Agency given authority in each area to develop a health systems plan with goals, an annual implementation plan, and decision power to approve or disapprove the use of Federal funds. A State Health Planning and Development Agency is to integrate state plans with the plans of the regional Health Systems Agencies of which it is a part. The process will undoubtedly be a long one. Time will tell if the proposed agency is more duplicatory of existing agencies than it is helpful. It is hoped that the proliferation of agencies that now occurs at various governmental levels can be fitted into this master plan so there will be less of the competition for funds and manpower than is now the case.

A Community-based Plan for Health Care

Some communities, regions and states have been successful in working together to make plans for their own health care needs. In the state of Iowa, for example, a proposed organizational structure for providing health services and medical care in the state was the result of a cooperative effort by the Health Manpower Committee of the Iowa Comprehensive Health Planning Council.[1] Plagued by the same shortages of doctors, particularly young doctors,

[1]John C. MacQueen, M.D., and Eber Eldridge, Ph.D., "A Proposed Organizational Structure for Providing Health Services and Medical Care in the State of Iowa," August, 1972.

in rural areas as exists throughout most of the nation, this committee recognized the need to conceptualize an organizational structure within which new methods for delivering care can be developed. It was clear to the committee that this structure could not be created by legislative action, but must be developed by those immediately involved with the provision of health services and by those who are the recipients. Based on the realization that attracting young physicians and other health providers is dependent on creating groups or clusters of these health professionals and relating their work to a state plan for continuing education, the first step for the committee was to survey the existing distribution of health manpower and facilities, county by county. Second, they identified the basic principles that should be used in designing a health care system. These were:

- A health care system should be based on the concept that "health is a right."
- A health care system should insure that health services are accessible.
- A health care system should provide comprehensive health services.
- A health care system should be designed to provide profitable and attractive working conditions for health providers.
- A health care system must be designed to function in cooperation with the existing social, economic, and governmental systems of the community.
- A health care system must include a subsystem concerned with the payment for services that make health care available.

The third step was to describe and propose the location of the organizational units required to provide a stratified health care system. It was felt that groups of health providers—nurses, physicians, and dentists—could function most efficiently if they were working under an organizational umbrella, if not in the same organizational setting. It was proposed that this basic organizational unit for providing medical care and health services be called an area health care center. These centers would function best if their areas coincided with established economic trade areas and if they worked with existing Area-wide Health Planning Councils or other accepted community planning organizations and cooperated with health providers and consumers in creating arrangements best for the particular area.

Provision of personal health services was felt in this plan to call for a stratified health care system of cooperating primary, secondary, and tertiary health care units, allowing a patient to enter the system in a primary care unit and move by referral to any other part. Specifically, the area health center, a primary care center, would most often function in a central town with a population of 5,000 or more, with the greatest distance from a patient to the area health care center being 18 miles, coinciding with the retail trade area commonly used. For those communities not large enough to support an area health center, the community health center would function as a satellite and would be staffed by non-medical personnel for primary health care. A regional health center for primary and secondary care would be located in a central city of a multiple-county region, serving in excess of 150,000 people, and no more than one hour's driving distance from any site in the region. A Medical-Health Center or University Medical-Health Center for tertiary care would combine specialized care with a teaching program, with emphasis placed on training physicians in sub-specialties.

The model outlined on page 273 indicates the kinds of care that would be provided in each of the proposed stratifications.

The cooperative planning described in this example may be adaptable, with minimal effort, to the plan proposed in the Health Planning and Resources Development Act of 1974, but the question remains as to the direction of the mandate—would a policy be more satisfactory and efficient if local plans are made to fit a master plan or is a grass roots effort viable? In either case, little can be done without sufficient funding, and the political wind blows

**The Health Services and Medical Care
Provided in a Stratified Health System[2]**

Tertiary Medical Care and Health Services -- *For a State or*
Multiple County Region

(Provided in a Medical Center or University Teaching Center)

Quality specialty care in a personalized fashion:
1. Specialized medical, diagnostic and therapeutic services for unusual and complicated cases.
2. Specialized surgical care for unusual and complicated cases (neurosurgery, organ
transplants, etc.)
3. Specialized dental care for unusual and complicated oral disease and surgery.
4. Emergency medical care.
5. Part of a comprehensive health care system.

Secondary Medical Care and Health Services -- *For a Region*
(Provided in a Regional Health Center)

Quality secondary and referral care in an available and personalized fashion:
1. Medical and surgical diagnostic services for complicated problems.
2. Surgical care and medical care for complicated problems.
3. Services for major surgical and medical emergency problems.
4. Specialty dental care—orthodontics, endodontics, peridontics.
5. Emergency medical care.
6. Part of a comprehensive health care system.

Primary Medical Care and Health Services -- *For an Area*
(Provided in an Area Health Center)

Quality primary care and health services in an available, personalized, and continuous
fashion:
1. Preventive services, case-finding services, and diagnosis and treatment for usual
and uncomplicated illness and disease.
2. Minor surgery and medical care for uncomplicated problems.
3. Home care programs—nursing services.
4. Preventive, diagnostic and restorative dental services.
5. Part of a comprehensive health care system.
6. (In large Area Health Centers, services for surgical and medical problems not requiring specialized personnel and equipment.)

(Provided in a Community Health Center, related to an Area Health center)

Quality primary medical care and health services in an available, personalized, and
continuous fashion:
1. Preventive services, case-finding services, and diagnosis and treatment for usual and
uncomplicated illness and disease.
2. Supervision of home care health services.
3. Part of a comprehensive health care system.

[2]Ibid. p. 18.

hot and cold on issues related to health needs. Implementation of such a complicated and costly machine as the health care system will in any event require continued legislative action at the federal and state levels.

Role of the Paraprofessional

Whatever structure is used in the delivery of health care, one aspect is becoming evident. There is room for the paraprofessional in both the physical and mental health fields. As previously stated, the United States is ahead in acute, intensive care. However, we are not outstanding in the area of preventive medicine. The erosion of doctor-patient relationships may be partly at fault as specialization and computerization have created an impersonal climate. Preventive medicine is not the physician's favorite target nor is it readily funded. It includes such areas as education in nutrition, prenatal care, immunization needs, and contraceptive choices. The paraprofessional can be a valuable arm of the health service system in these programs. In another way, personnel trained in human behavior and counseling can be providers of what Dr. Lewis Thomas in a subsequent article calls the third level of medical technology, or nontechnology—the time-consuming task of providing reassurance, explaining to patients and family what is going on, doing follow-up supervision for doctor-prescribed therapy and serving as family advocate.

IMPACT OF A FEDERAL RULING ON THE HEALTH CARE SYSTEM

Community Mental Health Centers

The federal government is not without precedent in establishing health care systems. The Community Mental Health Centers established in 1963 in President Kennedy's regime were hailed as a big step forward in the mental health field. By 1974, 591 centers had been funded under the CMHC Act, although not all are actually operating. The centers vary in character from being arms of university medical centers to combinations of pre-existing services in small rural towns. Varied also are the quality of leadership, style of treatment and quality and kind of professional training. Evaluations of program effectiveness through follow-up review of clients are not possible because funds are not available. The CMHC program has been continued and amplified by the vote of congressional members who find voting against the idea of mental health as difficult as voting against motherhood. The alternatives to community mental health centers are few. The system has its faults, but there is a great deal that is positive in that in many situations client therapy is available when it can be the most helpful.

A Court Decision and CMCH

The recent Supreme Court decision that every mental patient being held involuntarily in a treatment center has the right to be either treated or released has had an impact on the families of those persons, the communities to which they return and the community mental health centers where they may go for continued therapy. Outpatient services of all kinds are now increasing, so the mandate to empty the mental institutions is not the only reason for an increase of clients in the community based centers. For whatever reason, the emotional and social strains may have serious consequences for the community mental health concept. In an Ohio study of 125 patients released from three state hospitals and accepted back by their families, sociologist William Doll found that most families cared for the former patients, often with little shame or embarrassment, and usually didn't try to re-hospitalize them. But feelings of resentment and bitterness, of being trapped and hopelessly burdened, were evident in many of the families studied. Even though the patient is accepted physically, an ambivalent emotional attitude in the home may be catastrophic for the patient, the family and the community. The question may become to what extent over-crowding, underfinancing and other evils of the state institutions will be transferred to the centers and halfway houses. Communities are not unanimous in their approval of the release of what some consider to be potentially problem people. Indeed, even though the patient's problem may eventually cease to be mental, the social costs of vocational training, counseling, and housing may become community problems. From the patient's point of view, the return to community and family may be a return to a stressful environment from which escape is no longer possible. Families faced with the problem of what to do with a disturbed member now have the added guilt of re-institutionalization in state facilities. Since no one is certain how those institutions will survive the funding battles of social services, families are left to cope as well as possible. But cope they must, because the cost of private hospitalization is easily $50,000 yearly. It is virtually impossible to obtain medical insurance for the mentally ill. Since only the rich can afford private hospitalization, this, then becomes a form of economic discrimination.

ETHICAL CONSIDERATIONS AND HEALTH

Returning the mental patient to the community is only one of the instances where value conflicts in decision making between government and governed are evident. It is political, economic and ethical in its impact. Other vulnerable issues are abortion, the legal definition of death, the decision to grant organ transplants, the awarding of grants for medical research, and the entire area of genetic manipulation.

Dr. Lewis Thomas, former dean of the Yale University School of Medicine, points out in the following article that much of what has been called medical progress has happened without any cost-benefit analysis or even moral analysis of what it is we are about. We can prolong life with sustaining machines, substitute artificial organs for real, or do whatever is needed because we feel an obligation to do something. Dr. Thomas enlarges on this theme very adequately in "Guessing and Knowing—Reflections on the Science and Technology of Medicine."

In the second article Dr. Amitai Etzioni issues a citizen's alert to the ethical component of medical breakthroughs. Amniocentesis is only one of these, but it is an emotionally charged issue. If we proceed in an ad-hoc manner, as has been the case with most medical policies, we will be again concentrating on corrective measures after the damage is done.

Commentary—Evelyn Eldridge, ed.

Guessing and Knowing—Reflections on the Science and Technology of Medicine

by Lewis Thomas

Reflections on the science and technology of medicine

The technology of medicine has certain peculiar features that differentiate this field from all the rest. One difference has to do with the economics that seems to govern all other technological advances but has no discernible influence on the kinds of things we do, or think we do, in medicine. For example, engineers do not build new bridges at great cost without knowing in advance, quite precisely, what the transport requirements will be in the future and having some kind of assurance that the bridges will bear the traffic, meet all foreseeable demands, and stand up to all foreseeable stresses. But we will undertake the development of an artificial heart, at the cost of many bridges, without going through any sort of cost-benefit, logistic, or even moral analysis of what it is that we are making. Indeed, in medicine it is characteristic of our technology that we never count the cost, even when the bills begin coming in.

This is plainly a defect in our system—if we can be said to have a system. It is in part explainable by our history, by the brand-newness of any kind of technology at all in this field, and by our consequent unfamiliarity with any methods, or, indeed, any incentive in the first place, for technology assessment in medicine. We have had almost no genuine science to tap into for our technology until just the past three decades. As a profession, we go back a very much longer stretch of time, probably thousands of years. During most of our history, therefore, we have been accustomed to no technology at all or to pseudotechnologies without science. We acquired the habit long since of improvising, of trying whatever came to hand, and in this way we have gone through our cyclical fads and fashions, generation after generation, ranging from bleeding, cupping, and purging, through incantations and the reading of omens, to prefrontal lobotomy and Metrazol convulsions, and we have all gotten quite used to this kind of thing, whether we will admit it or not. Early on we became accustomed to the demand that a doctor must do something; doctors who didn't do something, no matter what, were not real doctors, just as shamans were not real shamans until they turned on the good spirits and turned off the bad ones. During the long period when we knew of nothing to do about typhoid fever except to stand by and wait for the patient to struggle through while we kept an eye out for the hemorrhages and perforations that might kill him at any time, the highest level of technology was the turpentine stupe—an elaborate kind of fomentation applied to the belly, very difficult to make without ending up with a messy shambles and capable, I believe, of doing absolutely no good whatever beyong making everyone feel that the doctor was doing something. This, by the way, is not a baroque item from our distant history. I learned to make a turpentine stupe at the Peter Bent Brigham Hospital in 1937; it is, in my view, a relatively recent, almost modern example of the way we develop technology, and it is not yet all behind us, as we shall see. We still have our equivalents of bleeding and cupping and turpentine stupes, and they are all around us.

The trouble with this kind of pseudotechnology is that it has become unbelievably expensive in its more modern forms, and at times it is dangerous. It is particularly dangerous and

Reprinted with permission from *Saturday Review,* Vol. 55, Dec. 23 1972, pp. 52-57.
Dr. Lewis Thomas is Director of Memorial Sloan-Kettering Cancer Center, New York, New York.

expensive when it takes the form of strong drugs or bizarre diets or surgery, which it sometimes does.

We may be in danger of forgetting the real reason why we have always done such things in the first place. Why, when we do not understand even faintly the underlying nature of a fatal disease and can do nothing about it to change its course, do we feel an obligation to do something—and why does society expect us to try? The answer, of course, is that we must; it is in our nature to try. The best definition ever given of a physician's occupation is the old one: "to cure sometimes, to relieve often, to comfort always." It is that word "always" that is operative. And one of the best ways to comfort is to keep trying, no matter what.

But now that science has entered medicine in full force, we must begin to sort out our affairs. From now on we will need, as never before, to keep these central enterprises—"to cure, to relieve, to comfort"—clearly separated from each other in our minds. They do not really overlap, but we tend to view them—and the public, of course, takes the same view—as though they were all of a piece, all the same body of technology, all derived from science, all modern. I think perhaps one reason we do this is because of an unconscious conviction that dollar values must be placed on all human enterprises; we do not like to confess to ourselves that so many of the things that we do are provided simply for comfort and reassurance. Somehow, these have come to seem less significant products than a cure; so we try, consciously or unconsciously, to pretend that there is more continuity than is really there, that everything we do is directed toward the same end.

In fact, in real life we are engaged in three, maybe four, entirely different kinds of technology in medicine. I have an idea that if we could conduct a sort of technology assessment on ourselves and come to some sort of general agreement about which technology belongs in which category, we might be in a better position to make intelligent plans and forecasts for the future, and we would almost surely be clearer in our minds about how to set priorities for the investment of scientific resources for the future.

Before beginning my own version of a classification, I would like to make a general declaration of faith and a general confession of optimism. My dogmas are as follows: I do not believe, first of all, in the inevitability of disease; I concede the inevitability of the risk of disease, but I cannot imagine any category of human disease that we are precluded by nature from thinking our way around. Moreover, I do not believe that when we succeed in controlling or curing one kind of disease, we will necessarily, automatically, find that it has been replaced by another.

Even if I am wrong about this and it should turn out that there is some law of nature that mandates the doling out of new diseases up to some optimal number whenever old ones disappear (which strikes me as a piece of illogic as well as high improbability), I still cannot imagine remaining helpless before all the new ones. Nature is inventive, I grant, but not so inventive as to continue elaborating endless successions of brand-new, impenetrable disease mechanisms. After we have learned enough to be able to penetrate and control the mechanisms of today's diseases, I believe we will automatically be well equipped to deal with whatever new ones turn up. I do not say this in any arrogance; it just seems to me reasonable.

I have no more difficulty in imagining a disease-free human society, or at least a society in which major diseases are held under control, than I do with the idea that valuable stocks of animals or varieties of plants can be maintained relatively free of disease.

I believe that disease is fundamentally unnatural. It is not, in my view, a normal or natural part of the human condition for aging human beings to become paralyzed and idiotic for long years before they finally die any more than it is normal for young people to develop acute leukemia. I believe that disease generally results from biological mistakes, misinterpretations of signals on the part of cells and tissues, and misuse of information. I believe that there is a general tendency, amounting to a kind of universal natural force, for living things to attempt to join together, to pool resources, to establish symbiotic relationships. Parasitism is what happens when this fundamental drive forces partnerships upon inappropriate, wildly asymmetric partners. In order to protect against such collisions, we are all provided with chemical signals of identity, by which the life of the earth is regulated and kept balanced. Certain major varieties of disease are due to the panic produced by such signals; for example, most mammals, and even certain invertebrates, such as limulus, read the signal of the lipopolysaccharide endotoxin extracted from Gram-negative bacteria as the news of absolute doom, and so violent an inflammatory reaction is set up inside the whole vascular compartment that the circulation of the blood is brought to a standstill. This happens, not because of any intrinsic, poisonous properties of endotoxin, but because of the way the information contained in its molecule happens to be read by an animal host. In my view, much of human disease works in this way, and the mechanisms involved are, I believe, quite open to intelligent intervention and reversal whenever we learn more about how they operate.

To say it another way, I do not consider that the ambition to control or eliminate disease, which is an ambition shared by everyone in biomedical science, is either unthinkable or any distance beyong imagining. What makes it seem to many people like an outlandish, even outrageous way to be talking is that it becomes assumed that we are talking about human happiness, which is really quite another matter, or about human mortality, which is also quite another matter. As for the first, it is, of course, true that disease has long been a major cause of human despair and wretchedness, but this is no reason to believe that we will all become happy, well-adjusted people by being rid of it. We will still be left with an abundance of worrisome problems, and we will still have ample reasons for despair, and no medical science—not even psychiatry—has any foreseeable contribution to make in these matters. War and bombs, failure and anomie, clouding of the sun by particles of our own waste, the shutting off of oxygen, the loss of room to move around in—these are problems that will still be with us, healthy or ailing, for some time to come, and I hope that no one will suggest that these are in any sense problems for medicine—or we will never get any of them solved. But perhaps human society will be better equipped to think its way through these imponderables if, at least, we no longer have today's roster of diseases to worry us at the same time.

As for mortality, I have a hunch that we will discover someday that disease and death are not as inextricably interrelated as we tend to view them today. All the rest of nature undergoes, in its variable cycles, the physiological process of death by the clock; all creatures, all plants, age finally, and at the end they all die. Diploid cells in tissue culture have finite life spans, which are different for different lines of cells and characteristic of particular cell stocks. Some live for forty generations and then die, others for seventy. They do not develop fatal diseases. It is not a catastrophe; they simply reach the end of a life-span programed for them in their own genomes, and at the end of that span they die.

I believe that we are also like this. If we are not struck down prematurely by one or another of today's diseases, we live a certain length of time and then we die, and I doubt that medicine will ever gain a capacity to do anything much to modify this. I can see no reason for trying and no hope of success anyway. At a certain age it is in our nature to wear out, to come unhinged, and to die, and that is that. My point here is that I very much doubt that the age at which this happens will be very drastically changed for most of us when we have learned more about how to control disease. The main difference will be that many of us will die in relatively good health, in a manner of speaking—rather after the fashion of Bertrand Russell—or we may simply dry up and blow away.

And even if our technology were to become so dazzlingly effective as to rid us of all the major diseases that now kill many of us off before our time of wearing out, I doubt that the increase in population caused by this would make more than a marginal difference to the general problem of world overpopulation. Indeed, it might help some, since there would be smaller numbers of us in hospitals or living out our lives in various degrees of incapacitation and suffering. Overpopulation is bad enough, as social problems go, but to be overpopulated with so many of us disabled by disease, especially by the chronic diseases of the elderly, let alone schizophrenia, presents an unthinkable prospect for the approaching century.

In any case, we do not really owe much of today's population problem to the technology of medicine. Over-population has been coming on for several centuries, and the alarming upward slope began long before we had developed a genuine capacity to change the outcome of disease. Modern medical science arrived only recently, when the world population had already been set on what seems to be its irreversible course by the civilizing technologies of agriculture, engineering, and sanitation—most especially the latter. From here on, the potential benefits of medicine greatly outweigh any conceivable hazard; we will perhaps change slightly the numbers of us living at any moment in time, but it lies within our capacity to change very greatly the quality of life.

Well, where do we stand today as a science? This is not the same question, of course, as the one concerning the state of our technology. Our science is the science of the biological revolution, and we have scarcely begun to apply any of it. We do not yet, in fact, know where to begin. In contrast with today's genuinely high technologies of biology or neurobiology or cellular biology, with the immense power of their instruments for exploring the most fundamental questions about the processes of life, the condition of our knowledge of disease mechanisms has a primitive, nineteenth-century look, and our capacity to intervene in disease is not much better. This is the general shape of things today, but tomorrow will be very different indeed. I simply cannot imagine any long persistence of our ignorance about disease mechanisms in the face of all that is being learned about normal cells and tissues. Our time for the application of science on a major scale is approaching rapidly, and medicine will be totally transformed when it happens. The hard problem just ahead will be for us to set priorities and make choices between options. We will be obliged, as never before in our history, to select between alternative possibilities in technology; we will be compelled to make long-range predictions as to the outcome of this course or that; in short, we will be thrust into the business of technology assessment, just like all the other great national enterprises.

It is a curious position that we are in today, poised as we are between the old world of trial-and-error empiricism, superstition, hunch, and resignation to defeat and the new world just ahead of hard information and applied science. We seem to work, as of now, with three different levels of technology.

First, and necessarily foremost, is what might be termed the high technology of medicine, equivalent in its sophistication and effectiveness to the high technologies of the physical sciences. It is a curious fact that although the accomplishments here represent the major triumphs of medicine to date, most of us tend to take them for granted, and we often forget what they mean for the quality of life in modern society. This is the genuinely decisive technology of modern medicine, exemplified best by methods for immunization against diphtheria, pertussis, and various virus diseases and the contemporary use of antibiotics and chemotherapy for bacterial infections. The capacity to deal effectively with syphilis and tuberculosis represents a milestone in human endeavor, even though full use of this potential has not yet been made. And there are, of course, other examples: the treatment of endocrinologic disorders with appropriate hormones, the prevention of hemolytic disease of the newborn, the treatment and prevention of various nutritional disorders, and perhaps just around the corner the management of Parkinsonism and sickle-cell anemia. There are other examples, and everyone will have his favorite candidates for the list, but the truth is that there are not nearly as many as the public has been led to believe.

The point to be made about this kind of technology — the real high technology of medicine— is that it comes as the result of a genuine understanding of disease mechanisms, and when it becomes available, it is relatively inexpensive, relatively simple, and relatively easy to deliver.

Offhand I cannot think of any important human disease that medicine possesses the capacity to prevent or cure outright in which the cost of the technology is itself a major problem. The price is never as high as the cost of managing the same disease was during the earlier stages of ineffective technology. If a case of typhoid fever had to be managed today by the best methods of 1935, it would run to a staggering expense. After, say, about fifty days of hospitalization, requiring the most demanding kind of nursing care, with the obsessive concern for details of diet that characterized the therapy of the time, with daily laboratory monitoring and, on occasion, surgical intervention for abdominal catastrophe, I should think $10,000 would be a conservative estimate for the illness, as contrasted with today's cost of a bottle of Chloramphenicol and a day or two of fever. The kind of technology that was evolving for poliomyelitis in the early 1950s, just before the emergence of the basic research that made the vaccine possible, provides another illustration of the point. It is the cost of those kinds of technology and their relative effectiveness that must be compared with the cost and effectiveness of the vaccine.

Pulmonary tuberculosis had similar episodes in its history. There was a sudden enthusiasm for the surgical removal of infected lung tissue in the early 1950s, and elaborate plans were being made for new and expensive installations for major pulmonary surgery in tuberculosis hospitals. Then the drug Isoniazid and the antibiotic streptomycin came along and the hospitals themselves were closed up.

It is when physicians are bogged down by their incomplete technologies, by the innumerable things they are obliged to do in medicine when they lack a clear understanding of disease mechanisms, that the deficiencies of the health-care system are most conspicuous.

This brings me to the second level of technology in this classification, which I have termed the "halfway technology" of medicine. This represents the kinds of things that must be done after the fact, in an effort to compensate for the incapacitating effects of certain diseases whose courses we are unable to do very much about. It is a technology designed to make up for disease or to postpone death.

The outstanding examples in recent years are the transplantations of hearts, kidneys, livers, and other organs and the equally spectacular inventions of artificial organs. In the public mind this kind of technology has come to seem like the equivalent of the high technologies of the physical sciences. The media tend to present each new procedure as a breakthrough and a therapeutic triumph, instead of the makeshift procedure that it really is.

In fact, this level of technology is by its nature highly sophisticated and at the same time profoundly primitive. It is the kind of thing that we must continue to do until there is a genuine understanding of the mechanisms involved in disease. In chronic glomerulonephritis, for example, a much clearer insight will be needed into the events leading to the destruction of capillaries in the kidney. There is solid evidence that abnormal immunologic reactions are the basis for this destruction. If more information can be obtained, it should become possible to intervene intelligently, to prevent the process or turn it around. When this level of understanding has been reached, the technology of kidney replacement will not be much needed and should no longer pose the huge problems of logistics, cost, and ethics that it poses today.

An extremely complex and costly technology for the management of coronary heart disease has evolved, involving specialized ambulances and hospital units, all kinds of electronic gadgetry, and whole platoons of new professional personnel to deal with the end results of coronary thrombosis. Almost everything offered today for the treatment of heart disease is at the level of technology, with the transplanted and artificial hearts as ultimate examples. When enough has been learned for us to know what really goes wrong in heart disease, we ought to be in a position to figure out ways to prevent or reverse the process; and when this happens, the current elaborate technology will be set to one side.

The impending development of an artificial heart illustrates the kind of dilemma we are placed in by today's emphasis on halfway technology. Let us assume that heart disease, for all its manifold origins and its complexity, does represent an approachable scientific problem—that if we study the matter with sufficient imagination and energy, making use of all the new information about muscle structure and function and blood coagulation and lipid metabolism and making capital use of new information along other lines as yet unguessed at by any of us, we will eventually solve this problem, and we will then learn how to intervene before the onset of irreversible muscle or valve disease, to prevent the process or to turn it around. As a non-cardiologist, an outsider, I have total confidence that this can be done, that sooner or later it will be done, and my colleagues who know a lot about heart disease have, I sense, this same kind of confidence for the long term. This, then, is one option and an altogether wise one to adopt. But the artificial heart represents a completely different, opposing attitude. To be willing to invest the hundreds of millions of dollars that will probably be necessary for this one piece of new technology almost demands of its proponents the conviction that heart disease represents an unapproachable, insoluble biological problem. It tends, as I see it, to write off scientific research. It assumes that the best we will be able to do, within the next few decades anyway, is to wait until the underlying mechanisms of heart disease have had their free run, until the organ has been demolished, and then to put into the chest this nuclear-powered, plastic-and-metal, essentially hideous engine. I am convinced that this is the wrong way to go. Even if it works—which, I am afraid, is not at all unlikely—I cannot imagine how society will solve the problems of cost, distribution, and priority. Who will be entitled to buy and have installed these engines: those with enough wealth to pay for them? Those who strike the rest of us, or our committees, as potentially useful citizens? Once we have started on this endless line of insoluble problems, there may be no turning back. If there ever was an urgent, overwhelming important problem in biomedical science, it is with us now: someone simply must provide us quickly with a solution to the problem of coronary arteriosclerosis. If this can be done, the artificial heart will become overnight an interesting and ingenious contraption, something clever and decorative, with some of the charm of a Tiffany lamp—a sort of instant antique—but no longer a practical thing, and we will all be better off for this transformation. Otherwise, we are in for real trouble just ahead, and I'm not sure we have the collective intelligence in medicine to deal with it.

Much of what is done in the treatment of cancer, by surgery, irradiation, and chemotherapy, represents halfway technology in the sense that these measures are directed at the existence of already established cancer cells, not at the mechanisms by which cells become neoplastic. The policy problems that confront us now, with the nation's declared commitment to conquer cancer, are somewhat like those involved in the artificial-heart question. There will be, for a while anyway, a running argument between two opposing forces. There will be on one side those who believe that cancer is a still unsolved but eminently approachable scientific puzzle, requiring only enough good research by imaginative investigators on a broad enough biological base, and that, provided with enough financial support and enough time, we will, in one way or another, find ourselves home and dry. On the other side there will be those who believe themselves to be more practical men of the real world, who feel that we have already come about as great a distance toward understanding cancer as we are likely to come for some time and that we should give the highest priority to applying on a much larger scale what we know today about this disease—that with surgery, chemotherapy, and radiation we can now cure or palliate a considerable number of patients and that what we need at this time is more and better technology of essentially today's model. I do not know how this argument will come out, but I believe it to be an issue of crucial symbolic significance; whichever way it goes may possibly indicate the drift of biomedical science for the next decade. I only wish that we could find a more comfortable zone of middle ground between those who believe that we already know enough to cope with it by today's approaches. Personally, I would prefer a middle ground, for I generally like a comfortable position, but I am afraid that I belong with the first group of extremists in this one—for, to be honest, I regard cancer as an entirely unsolved problem, wide open to research and soluble; and I regard the technology of today's forms of therapy as paradigms of halfway technology, directed at the end-results of the disease rather than at underlying mechanisms.

It is characteristic of this kind of technology that it costs an enormous amount of money and requires a continuing expansion of hospital facilities. There is no end to the need for new, highly trained people to run the enterprise. And there is really no way out of this at the present state of knowledge. If the installation of specialized coronary-care units results in the extension of life for even a few patients with coronary disease (and there is no question that this technology is effective in a few cases), it seems to me an inevitable fact of life that as many of them as can be built will be put together and as much money as can be found will be spent. I do not see that anyone has much choice in this. We are obliged by the very nature of our professional responsibility to adopt any new technology that will benefit patients with otherwise untreatable diseases, even when only a very small percentage will be benefited and even when the costs are very high. Neither we nor any other sector of society controls this aspect of our economy. We cannot, like other industries, withhold a technology from the market place because it costs too much money or benefits too small a percentage of patients; the only thing that can move medicine away from this level of technology is new information, and the only imaginable source of this information is research.

The best we can do when the economic or logistic problems associated with our technology verge on the insupportable or when the odds are too high against the success of our procedures is to try to improve the technology or to discover an altogether new technology as quickly as possible. Meanwhile, however, we must continue to employ the less-than-satisfactory ones.

The near-miraculous achievements of the antibiotic drugs in controlling or eliminating our most serious bacterial infections — such as typhoid or lobar pneumonia or epidemic meningitis — are useful indicators of the future direction of technology in medicine. They are, in fact, pieces of solid evidence that technology does work. But they should not be mistaken for symbols of the whole of medicine.

And this brings me to the third level of technology. This is the large body of what is best termed "nontechnology." It is, in effect, the substitute for technology that medicine has always been compelled to use when we are unable to alter either the natural course of disease or its eventual outcome. A great deal of money is spent on this. It is valued highly by the professionals as well as by the patients. It consists of what is sometimes called "supportive therapy." It tides patients over through diseases that are not, by and large, understood. It is absolutely indispensable. It is not, however, a technology in any real sense.

It includes the large part of any good doctor's time that is taken up with simply providing reassurance, explaining to patients who fear that they have contracted one or another lethal disease that they are, in fact, quite healthy.

It is what physicians used to be engaged in at the bedside of patients with diphtheria, meningitis, poliomyelitis, lobar penumonia, and all the rest of the infectious diseases that have since come under control.

It is what physicians must now do for patients with intractable cancer, severe rheumatoid arthritis, multiple sclerosis, stroke, and advanced cirrhosis. One can think of at least twenty major diseases that require this kind of supportive medical care because of the absence of an effective technology. I would include in this category a large amount of what is called mental disease and most varieties of cancer.

The cost of this nontechnology is very high and getting higher all the time. It requires not only a great deal of time but also very hard effort and skill on the part of physicians; only the very best of doctors are good at coping with this kind of defeat. It also involves long periods of hospitalization, lots of nursing, lots of involvement of nonmedical professionals in and out of the hospital. It represents, in short, a substantial segment of today's expenditures for health. It is not as great a financial problem for the future as halfway technology, but between them nontechnology and half-way technology will sooner or later drive into bankruptcy any system of health care that we may devise.

If I were a policymaker, interested in saving money for health care over the long haul, I would regard it as an act of prudence to give high priority to a lot more basic research in biological science. This is the only way to get the full mileage that biology has to offer the science of medicine, even though it seems, as used to be said in the days when the phrase still had some meaning, like asking for the moon.

Public Policy Issues Raised
by a Medical Breakthrough

by Amitai Etzioni

Amniocentesis, which detects mongolism and other serious abnormalities in a fetus in utero, will prevent the birth of thousands of afflicted children yearly once current research on its safety justifies its wide use. But this genetic intervention raises crucial questions of public policy, and lest we risk doing to our bodies what we have done to the environment, we must face them now. For example: Who shall be tested—all women who want to be or only those in high-risk categories? What shall the test be used for—diagnosis of debilitating diseases only, or also of the XYY ("criminal") chromosomes, or even for "breeding purposes"? And whatever the question, who shall decide the answer?

According to two recently published studies, about half of all children born afflicted with mongolism need not be. Dr. Sarah Bundey, reporting in the September 3, 1973 issue of *Modern Medicine,* writes: "If all mothers 35 years of age and older were screened during pregnancy and therapeutic abortion done in every instance of trisong-21 [the technical indication of Mongolism], the incidence of Mongolism would be halved." While this finding is based on data from Great Britain, a report by Drs. Zena Stein, Mervyn Susser, and Andrea Guterman in the February 10, 1973 issue of *Lancet,* using American data, reaches a similar conclusion. Yet over the next twelve months roughly 14,000 mongoloid children will be born in the United States alone.

Dr. Aubrey Milunsky of Harvard has estimated that each year over 20,000 infants in the U.S., and over 700,000 worldwide, will be born with either mongolism or one of the other serious chromosomal abnormalities that can now be detected and averted.[1] Many of these children will die before they reach the age of seven, heart troubles and leukemia being the most common causes of death. The rest will suffer from varying degrees of mental retardation as well as from complications due to the malformation of one or more of their vital organs. Many, ignored by their parents and removed from society's view, will end up in public institutions which are often the contemporary equivalent of the notorious nineteenth-century "snake pits." The estimated cost to the American public of this primarily custodial and ameliorative, not curative, care is reaching $1.7 billion a year.

The medical procedure which, if more widely utilized, could alleviate much of this suffering and cost is amniocentesis. The technique entails withdrawal of a sample of the fluid in which the fetus floats, somewhere between the fourteenth and eighteenth weeks of pregnancy. The fetal cells found in the fluid are then cultured and studied for chromosomal abnormalities. Illnesses other than mongolism can also be detected: these include serious sexual abnormalities (Turner and Klinefelter syndromes) and galactosemia (which can cause cataracts, cirrhosis of the liver, and mental retardation). If the test is "positive" and intervention is desired, abortion is necessary. Because of the "lateness" of the abortion, often toward the end of the fourth month of pregnancy or beyond, the use of hypertonic saline is considered the safest way to terminate the pregnancy.

[1]Aubrey Milunsky, *The Prenatal Diagnosis of Hereditary Disorders* (Springfield, Ill.: Charles C. Thomas, 1973).

© 1975 by the Regents of the University of California. Reprinted from *Policy Analysis,* Vol. 1, No. 1, pp. 69-76, by permission of The Regents.

Dr. Amitai Etzioni is Director for the Center for Policy Research, Inc., New York, New York.

While any woman who desires amniocentesis can approach a qualified physician and ask for the test to be performed, at present the procedure is not widely used; many women are unaware of it and many physicians will not recommend it. In a survey just completed by sociologist Nancy Castleman at the Center for Policy Research,[2] gynecologists chosen via a national random sample were asked whether or not they would recommend the procedure. A mere 4.7 percent answered in the affirmative; 90.2 percent in the negative. Asked whether they would recommend it for women over 40, the age at which the risk of mongolism rises sharply (from 1 in 600 for all women to 1 in 100 for those above 40), 59 percent indicated that they would, while 31 percent indicated that they would not.

The reasons why some physicians will not recommend amniocentesis even for older women are many, ranging from religious opposition, to the abortion entailed if the test finds are to be acted upon, to simple resistance to a new procedure. The most important reason, though, is caution. Thus far, amniocentesis has been used in only several hundred cases, and the risks it poses to mother and fetus are still being evaluated. In some instances it may cause miscarriage, and infection in the mother, or—in very rare cases—damage to the fetus.

In order to assess the safety and effectiveness of this new medical procedure, an unusually intensive research effort is being undertaken: nine medical centers—among them Yale in New Haven, Mount Sinai in New York, and the UCLA and San Diego Medical Schools—are collaborating in a study comparing a thousand amniocentesis test subjects to a matched control group of 1,000 pregnant women not given the test. The study is being coordinated by Dr. Charles Lowe, the scientific director of the National Institute for Child Health Development, Bethesda, Md. While I was allowed to sit in on a recent day-long meeting of the study directors, I am committed, like all of them, not to comment on the partial findings of the study until it is completed. Final results summarizing the effects of the test on the mothers will be available in about a year, and data on its effects on the infants, somewhat later.

However, public debate and policymaking on several of the critical issues raised by amniocentesis must not be delayed until after the findings of the super-study are compiled. Fortunately, such an assessment is possible now. In the first place, the results of studies using smaller numbers of patients than in the super-study are available. Second, unlike drugs which are not permitted on the market until after they have been tested, new medical procedures remain on the market until they are found unsound. While amniocentesis is being evaluated, doctors are continuing to provide it to patients other than those included in the study population. Third, the issues the public and public authorities will have to face once the procedure is fully evaluated are highly complex; we would be wise to reflect upon them now and thus be armed with some forethought when the time for decision arrives. Most important, as we shall see below, the main policy questions raised by amniocentesis are predominantly normative, dependent only in part on medical considerations. They need not await the results of the medical study.

THE ISSUES

There are four complex normative issues of concern: who shall be tested, what shall the test be used for, what are the costs and benefits of the test, and how can patients in need of the service best be reached?

Who Shall Be Tested?

Because the procedure itself entails a measure of risk, the most elementary question to ask is whether we should test every pregnant woman or only those who have a high risk of bearing an afflicted child. Because there is a clear association between incidence of mongolism

[2]Nancy Castleman and Amitai Etzioni, "Amniocentesis: A Forerunner of the Genetic Fix," *Connecticut State Medical Journal* 38 (September 1974).

and age of mother, as we reported above, few doctors favor testing every pregnant woman. The majority favor limiting the test to older women, 40 being the most agreed-upon age at which to start. On the face of it, this appears to be a strictly medical issue: given the fact that the test itself entails a small, but not trivial, risk, it should be given only to those who have a high likelihood of benefiting from it. Actually, the issue is highly charged with personal and moral values. The question each woman, her husband, and their physician must ponder is how strongly the couple feels about the possibility of having a mongoloid child—some parents feel that this would be a catastrophic event, while others feel that they could learn to accept it— compared to how undesirable a test-induced miscarriage (or other complication) might be. Similarly, the same test-associated risks would probably seem quite different to a woman who had already borne several children, and was considering an abortion anyway, than to an older woman pregnant for the first time. The answer which suggests itself is that the decision should be made by each woman (or couple) after they have been thoroughly informed about the risks involved in the test—and in not testing.

What Shall the Test Be Used For?

Aside from revealing some severe illnesses, as already indicated, the test also detects milder illnesses as well as genetic attributes which may be asocial but not a danger to health (e.g., the so-called "criminal chromosomes" XYY). Finally, it indicates sheer physical attributes (the sex of the fetus).

Writing in the August 1973 issue of *Prism,* Dr. Albert Dorfman, Director of the Joseph P. Kennedy Jr. Mental Retardation Research Center, draws a distinction between severely debilitating diseases entailing limited life expectancy and less serious illnesses, such as Farby's, with which the child suffers severe physical problems but as a rule survives and grows up without mental retardation. Dr. Dorfman goes on to voice his concern, shared by other doctors, over whether it is reasonable to carry out prenatal diagnosis and abortion of fetuses afflicted with other, even milder and treatable, illnesses (such as diabetes) which may soon be detectable via amniocentesis. In the quest for ever more "perfect" babies, there must be a place where the risks and costs of testing and abortion outweigh the gains. But where should the line be drawn, and by whom?

If that question is a tough one, ponder the next: What should be done about a fetus which has XYY chromosomes? True, available data on the effects of the XYY chromosomes are inconclusive and highly controversial. Nevertheless, there is some evidence that persons with XYY have a somewhat higher chance to end up criminally insane. Should parents be told when the test shows the fetus to have an XYY profile? If they are told, will not thousands of otherwise normal fetuses be aborted, including a high percentage of those with XYY who would not have become criminally insane? If the parents are not to be told, on what grounds can such withholding of information be justified? Should the public interest enter the picture? In view of our great concern with crime, is it in our interest to promote such a screening?

As for the determination of desirable physical traits, there are instances on record where the test has been used by parents as a basis for deciding to abort a male (or female) fetus because they wanted a child of the other sex. In a survey just completed by Dr. James Sorenson of Princeton,[3] 96 percent of the genetic counselors questioned opposed such a use of amniocentesis, the main reason being that it entails taking a medical risk for a non-health purpose. Still, if parents have the patience to shop around long enough, they can find a doctor who will administer the test for sex choice. Should amniocentesis be outlawed for such "breeding" purposes? And if so, on what grounds, now that abortion is legal "on demand"? Or from the

---

[3]James Sorenson, *Social Aspects of Applied Human Genetics* (New York: Russell Sage Foundation, 1971).

viewpoint of the public interest, should laboratories be limited to illness tests until enough testing capacity is available for illness-determination and only then be allowed to test for sex?

Cost-Benefit Analysis

We have learned to worry about the costs of new interventions lest they exceed the benefits. After all, hundreds of women must be tested before one afflicted fetus will be found. Dr. Aubrey Milunsky[4] has estimated that it would cost about $60 million a year to test all pregnant women aged 35 or older (each test costs about $150). Assuming that all women told they were carrying genetically afflicted fetuses were to seek abortions, the added costs would be $3,250,400. But the cost of institutional care for these children, if born, is conservatively estimated at $460 million a year—and at about $2 billion over their lifetimes. This burden must often be shouldered by the taxpayers. Is it "worth it," then, for society to encourage the use of amniocentesis? Is it in the public interest to make the test cheaper? Free? At least for persons who cannot afford it?

Public Education Campaigns

The Nixon administration (and the Ford, it seems), I am told by civil servants who refuse to be cited, had a strong desire not to be associated with any programs which entailed or implied abortion (or, for that matter, even birth control). A brochure entitled "Mongolism, Hope through Research," published by the Department of Health, Education, and Welfare, carefully plays down amniocentesis and does not mention at all that it may involve abortion. And a new brochure about amniocentesis, recently issued by HEW, avoids discussion of abortion. Should we not begin designing a major and detailed educational campaign now, so that when the super-study findings are available the public can be properly alerted to their implications?

WHO SHALL DECIDE?

The foregoing policy issues and others surrounding amniocentesis are not unique to this particular medical procedure. They are also raised by other recent developments in the area where genetics and medicine meet, such as mass screening for sickle cell anemia and premarital gene testing. Overarching all the specific issues relating to specific medical techniques is the question of who should make these complex and literally vital decisions. The more personal decisions—whether or not to have the testing done, whether or not to proceed with abortion—can be left to pregnant women and their husbands, in consultation with their physicians. But who shall decide whether the government should subsidize the costs of the amniocentesis test, or whether a crash program to expand lab facilities should be launched, or whether a major public education campaign should be undertaken? Should Congress make some decisions, passing a law forbidding the use of amniocentesis for sex choice, or forbidding its use without the husband's consent?

The technical questions could be dealt with easily enough by appropriate agencies; for example, issues of public education could be decided by the Surgeon General, and those of lab development by, say, the Public Health Service (prodded into action—I hope—by the respective congressional committees). But the main public policy issues require a higher-level, more encompassing and coordinated review than the crazy quilt of federal agencies and congressional committees can provide. Senator Walter Mondale's bio-ethics bill seems to me to provide the needed mechanism for such a comprehensive overview. Senator Mondale suggests that a congressional bio-ethics commission be set up to deliberate on these matters and to formulate appropriate guidelines. Such a commission would be composed of fifteen pro-

[4]Milunsky, *Prenatal Diagnosis of Hereditary Disorders.*

fessionals in fields ranging from law to medicine, theology to technology. It would be granted a research staff and an annual budget of one million dollars.

Some might argue that such a commission is no longer needed, as Congress has recently passed Senator Edward Kennedy's bill providing for a commission to regulate experiments with human subjects. However, little if any duplication is involved. The Kennedy Commission is regulatory in intent and sharply focuses on one significant but narrow issue: the regulation of research lest scientists abuse those mental patients, prison inmates, or fetuses who serve as experimental subjects. The Mondale Commission would be reflective in nature and much broader in scope, covering not only those issues raised by amniocentesis (which concern every pregnant woman, husband, *and* tax payer) but also the myriad questions raised by other recent breakthroughs in medicine, from organ transplants to the right to die with dignity, from mass genetic screening programs to test-tube babies. Whether these deliberations would take place in a congressional commission, as Mondale suggests, or in a presidential one, or via some other societal-guidance mechanism, their purpose would be to answer our need for a systematic and comprehensive perspective on new genetic interventions. Of these, amniocentesis is but a forerunner; there are many more to come.

A GENETIC "STEAM ENGINE"

We are like the citizens of Britain when they first saw the steam engine. Few perceived, and even fewer acted upon, the notion that this technological innovation, in conjunction with others soon to follow, would promote very far-reaching societal changes—changes whose political, economic, and cultural consequences would amount to what is now known as the Industrial Revolution. Amniocentesis and mass genetic screening are but the path-breakers of ever more far-reaching genetic interventions which even now are being readied. Down the road are artificial wombs, cloning (making genetic copies of persons via asexual reproduction), and genetic surgery. More and more genetic procedures are turning issues heretofore settled by nature into matters which we must decide, both as individuals and as members of society. We must pay greater attention to the normative and policy questions that these new tools pose for us, so that we can channel their consequences more effectively than we did those of the Industrial Revolution, when we allowed technology to adapt society to its logic and needs. Our tardy treatment of the issues raised by the new breakthroughs suggests that we have learned little from our past. Once again we are proceeding in an ad-hoc manner. Will we delay in our examination of where bio-medical technology is leading, thus doing to our bodies what we have already done to our environment? Will we again limit our policy to corrective measures, after the damage is done? Or this time will we reflect upon the kind of future we want, anticipate alternative courses of action, and choose among them—before the genetic Pandora's box is fully opened?